ROMANTIC CARTOGRAPHIES

Romantic Cartographies is the first collection to explore the reach and significance of cartographic practice in Romantic-period culture. Revealing the diverse ways in which the period sought to map and spatialize itself, the volume also considers the engagement of our own digital cultures with Romanticism's 'mapmindedness'. Original, exploratory essays engage with a wide range of cartographic projects, objects, and experiences in Britain and globally. Subjects range from William Wordsworth, John Clare, and Sir Walter Scott to Romantic-era board games and geographical primers, revealing the pervasiveness of the cartographic imagination in private and public spheres. Bringing together literary analysis, creative practice, geography, cartography, history, politics, and contemporary technologies – just as the cartographic enterprise did in the Romantic period itself – *Romantic Cartographies* enriches our understanding of what it means to 'map' literature and culture.

SALLY BUSHELL is Professor of Romantic and Victorian Literature and co-director of The Wordsworth Centre in the Department of English Literature and Creative Writing, Lancaster University. Her research seeks to open up new modes of interpretation by shifting the focus of literary criticism from interpretation of semantic content to comparative understanding of other aspects of the work that illuminate traditional means of interpretation but also potentially redetermine those means.

JULIA S. CARLSON is Associate Professor of English at the University of Cincinnati. She is the author of *Romantic Marks and Measures: Wordsworth's Poetry in Fields of Print* (University of Pennsylvania Press, 2016), winner of the British Association for Romantic Studies First Book Prize 2017. She researches the cartographic, prosodic, and inscriptional contexts of eighteenth- and nineteenth-century poetry.

DAMIAN WALFORD DAVIES is Pro Vice-Chancellor and Head of the College of Arts, Humanities and Social Sciences at Cardiff University. His research works to reframe and defamiliarize cultural texts in new interdisciplinary and geographical contexts, often drawing on the affordances of creative-critical methods.

T0372721

ROMANTIC CARTOGRAPHIES

Mapping, Literature, Culture, 1789–1832

EDITED BY

SALLY BUSHELL

Lancaster University

JULIA S. CARLSON

University of Cincinnati

DAMIAN WALFORD DAVIES

Cardiff University

CAMBRIDGE
UNIVERSITY PRESS

CAMBRIDGE
UNIVERSITY PRESS

Shaftesbury Road, Cambridge CB2 8EA, United Kingdom

One Liberty Plaza, 20th Floor, New York, NY 10006, USA

477 Williamstown Road, Port Melbourne, VIC 3207, Australia

314–321, 3rd Floor, Plot 3, Splendor Forum, Jasola District Centre, New Delhi – 110025, India

103 Penang Road, #05–06/07, Visioncrest Commercial, Singapore 238467

Cambridge University Press is part of Cambridge University Press & Assessment, a department of the University of Cambridge.

We share the University's mission to contribute to society through the pursuit of education, learning and research at the highest international levels of excellence.

www.cambridge.org
Information on this title: www.cambridge.org/9781108459419

DOI: 10.1017/9781108635936

First published 2020
First paperback edition 2023

A catalogue record for this publication is available from the British Library

ISBN   978-1-108-47238-8   Hardback
ISBN   978-1-108-45941-9   Paperback

Contents

Illustrations

Notes on Contributors

ALAN BEWELL is Professor of English at the University of Toronto. His primary field is British Romanticism, with additional interests in literature and colonialism; postcolonial theory; ecopoetics and environmental history; and science, medicine, and literature. His recent work has focused on the ways in which the ecological impact of British colonialism is registered in eighteenth- and nineteenth-century literature. Bewell's first book, *Wordsworth and the Enlightenment: Nature, Man, and Society in the Experimental Poetry* (Yale University Press, 1989), examined how Wordsworth's poetry engages with eighteenth-century anthropological thought on human origins. He has also written *Romanticism and Colonial Disease* (Johns Hopkins University Press, 1999) and edited Medicine and the West Indian Slave Trade (Pickering and Chatto, 1999). His most recent monograph, *Natures in Translation: Romanticism and Colonial Natural History* (Johns Hopkins University Press, 2017), discusses the manner in which the global transport and exchange of plants, animals, and natural commodities shaped how the British came to understand themselves, English nature, and the natural world. He is currently working on a book entitled Romanticism and Mobility, which studies how Romantics reacted to a world of moving people, things, and ideas.

SALLY BUSHELL is Professor of Romantic and Victorian Literature and co-director of The Wordsworth Centre in the Department of English Literature and Creative Writing, Lancaster University. Her research seeks to open up new modes of interpretation by shifting the focus of literary criticism from interpretation of semantic content to comparative understanding of other aspects of the work that illuminate traditional means of interpretation but also potentially redetermine those means. Her last book, *Text as Process: Creative Composition in Wordsworth,*

Tennyson and Dickinson (University of Virginia Press, 2009), explored the margins of textuality by developing a method for interpreting works in a state of process. Her forthcoming monograph, *Reading and Mapping Fiction: Spatialising the Literary Text* (Cambridge University Press, 2020), is centred on paratextual relationships between maps and texts and the question of how the reader spatializes literature. She is also interested in digital projects for literary mapping and is principal investigator on the Arts and Humanities Research Council (AHRC)–funded project 'Chronotopic Cartographies', as well as leading an educational project using Minecraft to map literary worlds (LITCRAFT).

JULIA S. CARLSON is Associate Professor of English at the University of Cincinnati. She is the author of *Romantic Marks and Measures: Wordsworth's Poetry in Fields of Print* (University of Pennsylvania Press, 2016), winner of the British Association for Romantic Studies First Book Prize 2017. She researches the cartographic, prosodic, and diagrammatic contexts of eighteenth- and nineteenth-century poetry and is currently writing a second monograph on inscriptional practices, transcriptional technologies, and 'digital interactivity'. She is a co-editor of *Romanticism on the Net* and has co-edited a special issue of *Essays in Romanticism* entitled *Romanticizing Historical Poetics* (2018). With the Multigraph Collective, she co-wrote *Interacting with Print: Elements of Reading in an Era of Print Saturation* (University of Chicago Press, 2018).

SIOBHAN CARROLL is Associate Professor of English at the University of Delaware, where she specializes in nineteenth-century literature and the history of exploration. Her book *An Empire of Air and Water: Uncolonizable Space in the British Imagination, 1750–1850* (University of Pennsylvania Press, 2015), which was shortlisted for the British Association for Romantic Studies (BARS) Prize in 2016, turns to artefacts such as board games in order to describe the relevance of "uncolonizable" geographies, such as the North Pole and the atmosphere, to British imperialism. Her current book project examines the relationship between human agency and nature in the long nineteenth century.

DAVID COOPER is Senior Lecturer in English at Manchester Metropolitan University, UK, where he co-directs (with Rachel Lichtenstein) the Centre for Place Writing. A founding co-editor of the international journal *Literary Geographies*, he has published widely on contemporary

British place writing, and he is increasingly exploring the relationship between critical and creative approaches to space, place, and landscape. His research on digital literary cartography includes the development (with Ian N. Gregory) of literary Geographic Information Systems (GIS) and the publication of the co-edited collection *Literary Mapping in the Digital Age* (Routledge, 2016). He is currently a co-investigator on 'Chronotopic Cartographies' (AHRC funded 2017–20), led by Sally Bushell.

STEPHEN DANIELS is Emeritus Professor of Cultural Geography at the University of Nottingham and a Fellow of the British Academy. From 2005 to 2012 he directed the AHRC Landscape and Environment programme and since then has undertaken research funded by the Leverhulme Trust and the Paul Mellon Centre. He is the author and co-author of a series of volumes on landscape history, art and design, including *The Iconography of Landscape* (Cambridge University Press, 1988), *Fields of Vision* (Polity Press, 1993), *Humphry Repton: Landscape Gardening and the Geography of Georgian England* (Paul Mellon Centre for Studies in British Art, 1999), and *Landscapes of the National Trust* (Pavillion Books, 2016), as well as curator of the exhibitions *Art of the Garden* (Tate 2004–5), *Paul Sandby: Picturing Britain* (Royal Academy, 2009–10), and *Repton Revealed* (Garden Museum, 2018–19). He is currently completing a book on the nineteenth-century topographer John Britton.

CHRISTOPHER DONALDSON is Lecturer in Cultural History at Lancaster University and Research Coordinator at The Ruskin Library, Museum and Research Centre. His research is principally concerned with changing perceptions of the value of landscape and the environment during the eighteenth and nineteenth centuries. He is editor of the *Ruskin Review* and co-editor of the Digital Forum for the *Journal of Victorian Culture*.

RACHEL HEWITT is Lecturer in Creative Writing at Newcastle University and deputy director of the Newcastle Centre for Literary Arts. She is a writer of creative non-fiction, and her interests include nature and landscape writing, biography, feminism, and emotion. She is author of *Map of a Nation: A Biography of the Ordnance Survey* (Granta, 2010), which won the Royal Society of Literature Jerwood Award for non-fiction. She is also author of *A Revolution of Feeling: The Decade that Forged the Modern Mind* (Granta, 2017), which won a Gladstone's

Library Political Writing residency. She is currently working on *In Her Nature* (Chatto & Windus, 2022), about women's myriad encounters with the natural. She has published academic and general-interest articles in the national press (e.g. *The Guardian*, *The Telegraph*, and the *Financial Times*). Hewitt is a Fellow of the Royal Society of Literature and was one of the first cohort of New Generation Thinkers elected by the AHRC and BBC Radio 3.

CARL THOMPSON is Reader in Romantic Literature at the University of Surrey. His authored or edited publications include *The Suffering Traveller and the Romantic Imagination* (Oxford University Press, 2007); *Travel Writing*, in Routledge's New Critical Idiom series (Routledge, 2011); *Romantic-Era Shipwreck Narratives: An Anthology* (Trent Editions, 2007), and *The Routledge Companion to Travel Writing* (Routledge, 2016). More recently he has edited a special issue of the journal *Women's Writing* entitled *Journeys to Authority: Reassessing Women's Travel Writing, 1763–1863* (2017) and is currently working on a monograph on the career of the early-nineteenth-century travel writer and intellectual Maria Graham (1785–1842).

DAMIAN WALFORD DAVIES is Pro Vice-Chancellor and Head of the College of Arts, Humanities and Social Sciences at Cardiff University. His most recent publications include articles on Keats and Coleridge from a medical humanities perspective and articles on the work of Ronald Lockley and island writing, together with the edited volumes *Counterfactual Romanticism* (Manchester University Press, 2019) and *Roald Dahl: Wales of the Unexpected* (2016). His monograph *Cartographies of Culture: New Geographies of Welsh Writing in English* (University of Wales Press, 2012) develops new theories and practices of cartographic reading. He has a particular interest in the locatedness of writing and in 'critical-creative' modes of analysis. His creative work includes the poetry collections *Docklands* (Seren, 2019), *Judas* (Seren, 2015), *Alabaster Girls* (Rack Press, 2015), and *Witch* (Seren, 2012).

JOSHUA WILNER is Professor of English and Comparative Literature at the City College and The Graduate Centre of The City University of New York, as well as the former president of the International

Conference on Romanticism. He is the author of *Feeding on Infinity: Readings in the Romantic Rhetoric of Internalization* (Johns Hopkins, 2000).

PAUL YOUNGQUIST teaches English at the University of Colorado, Boulder. He writes on Romanticism, black resistance in the Caribbean, Jamaican Maroons, and contemporary music. His most recent book is *A Pure Solar World: Sun Ra and the Birth of Afrofuturism* (University of Texas Press, 2016).

Preface

Romantic Cartographies is the first collection to reveal the full reach and significance of cartography in Romantic-period culture. It aims to define and exemplify the forms of cartographic criticism emerging from various 'spatial turns' that have energized the humanities since the 1980s. Thus, the volume calibrates the significance of the carto-graphic imagination for the Romantic period itself, as well as the various cartographic frames through which Romanticism has been recognized and de-familiarized.

The volume interrogates fully the concept of Romantic cartography in historicized terms as well as from the perspective of our own highly spatialized culture. It seeks to diversify the ways in which critical Romantic cartographies are written by approaching them through a wide range of forms: textual, visual, tactile, and digital. It argues for the emer-gence of a cartographic imagination in the period and for the importance of literary cartography as a practice in our own time. As such it engages, on the one hand, with acts of mapping in the Romantic period, asking: In what ways did Romantic-period culture seek to map itself? What is specifically *Romantic* about the cartographic projects that dominate the period as we understand them? On the other, it explores the way in which the period has been mapped and re-mapped critically over time, posing such questions as: To what extent are the ways in which we map the world or understand maps underpinned by Romantic preconceptions? To what kind of imaginative paradigm did practices of mapping give rise (and vice versa)?

This book therefore moves beyond a purely metaphoric use of the term 'mapping' to engage with the concept in more meaningful interdisciplin-ary ways. Until now, this more specific sub-discipline has not been defined or explored in any coherent or sustained way – despite major cartographic advances during the historical period and despite there now being a range of theorized approaches, all of which are developed in the present collection by key figures in the field (e.g. Bewell; Bushell; Carlson; Cooper; Hewitt; Walford Davies). Opening up a dialogue between literature, science, geography, and the social sciences, *Romantic Cartographies* aims to disclose the 'map-mindedness' of Romantic-period culture as a whole.

Acknowledgements

The editors would like to thank Kate Ingle for her patience and dedication as editorial assistant for this volume and Andrew Lacey for his meticulous work on the index. They also thank the external readers for their insightful comments and suggestions; the contributors; and Cambridge University Press, particularly Bethany Thomas as commissioning editor, for exemplary support in preparing the volume for publication.

Romantic Cartographies

The three-part structure of this introduction reflects the larger organization of the volume as a whole into three linked and overlapping sections that each represent a wide range of approaches to the cartographic culture of the Romantic period but also reflect on and contribute to each other. Anticipating the structure of the main volume then, Part I of the Introduction is written by Damian Walford Davies; Part II by Julia S. Carlson; and Part III by Sally Bushell.

I Romantic Maps, Romantic Mapping

Two material fold-out maps – deeply embedded and embodied in the literary texts that carry them, and crucially interrelated within a culture of Romantic sociability and disciplinary exchange – offer a way, at the outset of this volume, of triangulating the affordances and effects of Romantic-period cartographic work and Romantic Studies' own interpretative lenses. A relational reading of these maps helps us to measure the angles, as it were, between mapping theories and practices, modes of envisioning space and place, and the sociocultural field of the Romantic period that are the composite subject of this book.

Both maps are productions of amateurs, published at a moment when the technologies of survey (still fundamentally aligned with seventeenth- and eighteenth-century modes of mensuration) and the professional credentials of the cartographer (which had not fully exorcised aesthetic modes of seeing) were achieving ever-increasing visibility in the form of the national work of the 'Trigonometrical Survey of England and Wales' – soon to be known as the Ordnance Survey.[1] The first map, by the art collector and poet George Cumberland, likely engraved by William Blake, is included in Cumberland's slim volume *An Attempt to Describe Hafod* (1796).[2] Sketch-like and annotated with the dotted lines of three walks described in the book, the map delineates part of the estate of Thomas

Johnes, whose aesthetic, agricultural, and economic improvements had, since 1783, created a scintillating, if often sodden, Xanadu in the Cardiganshire uplands of Wales. Designed to 'unveil [Johnes's] Elysium', the text – from the title itself and the gatefold map to the clotted, allusive writing that seeks to chaperone and direct the reader on walks around the estate – testifies to a fundamental anxiety concerning one's ability to know, articulate, and navigate a place. It is an anxiety explored further in a number of chapters in *Romantic Cartographies*.

No graphic material is reproduced in Cumberland's book beyond the map (Figure 0.1). Seeking to 'describe as faithfully as [he] wish[es] to draw', Cumberland refers to having previously 'meditated the design of composing a description' of the area to accompany his drawings. His formulae betray a struggle between a variety of potential modes of representation. It is his map – unprepossessing, sketchy, almost childlike – that becomes preeminent. Anterior to the verbal text, it arrogates all the representational modes between which Cumberland cannot decide. Indeed, his succeeding verbal chorography becomes a merely second-hand and second-order articulation of Hafod's time-space – an ekphrastic negotiation of the verbal-graphic object of the map itself: 'The first ramble I should chuse for a stranger would be, to take him down, through the lawn before the house ... to the river Ystwith; where, instead of passing over the long Alpine bridge, one turns short to the left' (13). Poets and painters are mentioned during the course of the book, as mediators of Johnes's supercharged estate, but not the cartographer. Yet it is cartography – amateur, non-trigonometrical, not-to-scale, and no less powerful for that – that commands the reader's view and step. It is only in the account of the third walk that verbal description asserts itself more robustly than at any other point hitherto – and only at the very moment when the author announces 'Here we leave the map' (37). As the chapters in *Romantic Cartographies* show, the generic interrelations and (unstable) hierarchies between ground, map, and language traceable in Cumberland's work are at the heart of Romanticism's cartographic cultures.

The second map, also engraved by William Blake, is by a child – a child who had recently died (see Figure 0.2). Appearing a decade after Cumberland's book, Benjamin Heath Malkin's *A Father's Memoirs of his Child* (featuring a frontispiece designed by Blake and engraved by Robert Cromek, in which the dead child ascends to heaven, leaving behind a pair of compass dividers) is dedicated to Thomas Johnes and is thus an uncanny co-text of Cumberland's attempt to parse Hafod. Malkin recalls how Johnes had urged him to publish his recollections of young Thomas

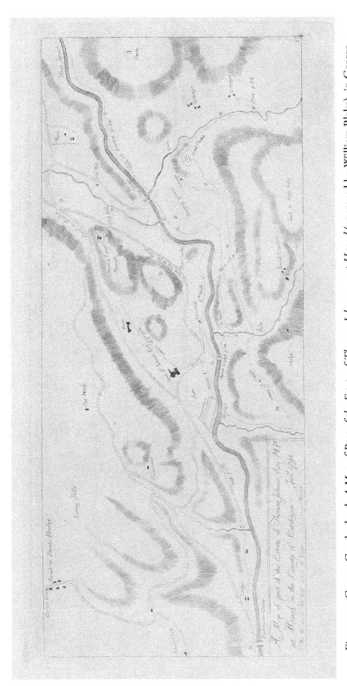

Figure 0.1 George Cumberland, *A Map of Part of the Estate of Thomas Johnes … at Havod* (engraved by William Blake), in George Cumberland, *An Attempt to Describe Hafod* (1796).

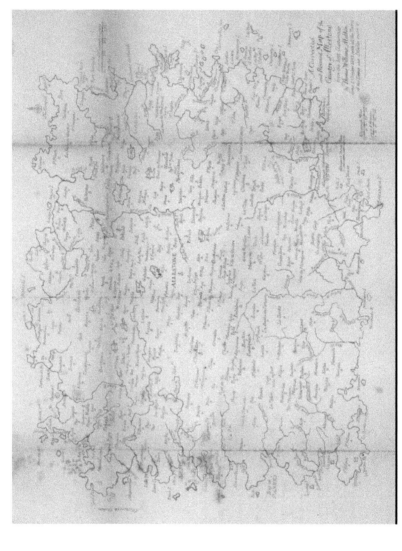

Figure 0.2 *A Corrected and Revised Map of the Country of Allestone* by Thomas Williams Malkin. Engraved by William Blake. Cambridge University Library. Keynes. U.4.10.

Williams Malkin (1795–1802) during conversations the two men had on the very walks at Hafod that had been mapped by Cumberland.

Thomas's letters to his relations are liberally quoted in what is more an evidentiary anthology delineating the 'early progress of a mind, too lately come into the world' than a memoir.[3] What emerges is a portrait of a boy learning about geography and about the materiality and rhetoricity of maps, by (dis)assembling 'dissected' – that is, jigsaw – cartography: 'I have a new map. Thomas can put it together – and when Mama takes some counties out, Tom can tell what they all are' (11). Malkin notes that the child 'had acquired a most happy art in copying maps': 'Were one of his performances . . . put into the hands of an engraver', he goes on, 'it would contract a stiffness, destructive of its identity' (31). As we shall see, Romantic-period authors were alive to cartography's own flattening stiffness, the violence it does to the dimensionality of space and the experience of dwelling in it. However, it is precisely to an engraver that Malkin gave an example of his son's cartographic cloning, commissioning Blake to engrave Thomas's *A Corrected and Revised Map of the Country of Allestone from the Best Authorities*, reproduced as a fold-out sheet in the book.

Allestone is an invented island (a type of Hafod), which the child further populated in various literary pieces. For the map, Thomas drew a vaguely rectangular body of land with an island-studded coastline of headlands and bays; topographical features are sidelined in favour of busy toponymic play as Thomas riffs fractally on single names: 'Allastone', 'Allastone I', 'St Alles la Stone'. As Malkin emphasizes:

> The map is . . . not so much to be looked at for the neatness of its appearance, and the symmetry of its proportions; but as an exercise of the mind comparing the propriety of its own nascent ideas and inventions, with the performances of adult artists, founded on observation and authority. (95)

Captured here are some of the characteristic frissons – and tensions – of literary-cartographic culture in the Romantic period. Maps are always made in relation to other 'texts' (of which topography is one). The father's comment both contrasts and reconciles 'invention' with 'observation and authority', imagination with scientism. On the subject of the boy's map, Malkin goes on to quote Blake – no friend (or so we have come to believe) of the *esprit géometrique* and the mensurative parcelling out of space on which geodesy depends. For Blake, it has the 'character of the firm and determinate', bespeaking 'a strong imagination, a clear idea, and a determinate vision of things in [the child's] own mind' (34). Though Thomas's map is of course of an imagined kingdom and more picture than map, Blake's assessment hints at an awareness of the ways in which even the increasingly institution-alized science of cartography (the word had to wait until the 1820s to be coined) was a creative as well as a critical act. Further, Malkin's use of the word 'symmetry' uncannily links the child's cartography with Blake's 'The Tyger', which is reproduced in full in the book's prefatory section, dedicated to Thomas Johnes (xxxix–xl). The geometric principles of the boy's pseudo-scale map enter into a complex relation with the sublime inscape of Blake's creature, Blake's graphic-verbal texts and his infernal method of relief etching, together with the landscape symmetries (and cultivated irregular-ities) sought by Thomas Johnes at Hafod. Thomas's map of Allestone is also available to be read as cartographic parody (other place names include 'Mapp', 'Shite' and the obviously windblown 'Horte fart') – an ontology in which cartography itself is implicated in view of its distorting burlesque of landscape. Scrutinizing such multi-genre and multimodal forms of Romantic-period cartography is one of the principal aims of Parts I and II of the present volume.

What makes the imbrication of literature and cartography in the Romantic period such a layered field is the transitional and contingent nature of cartography itself at this time. While the late eighteenth and early nineteenth centuries saw the further professionalization and institutional-ization of cartography as a national project in a European context (enabled by technological advances and the expectations of an increasingly carto-graphically literate audience for whose technical needs maps were pro-duced), Romantic-period mapping remained porously situated alongside established traditions of topographical representation. The implied carto-graphic positivism of the uniform scale map remained in creative dialogue not only with pictorial traditions of landscape painting, bird's-eye views, picturesque prospects, estate plans, and the city views of county histories but also with debates concerning ways of 'envisioning' and inscribing landscape, practical projects of landscape 'improvement' and possession, and phenomenologies of local attachment and national identity. John Barrell, Denis Cosgrove and Stephen Daniels, among others, have enabled us to recognize the sociopolitical meanings of these traditions.[4]

The spatial turn in the humanities that began in earnest in the 1980s and 1990s, which marked the interpenetration of cultural geography and social theory, and which is still in the process of being theorized within new technological paradigms, prompted the deconstruction of the map as a valuative cultural actor. That post-structuralist recalibration of cartog-raphy was coterminous with the forging of various modalities of Romantic

New Historicism whose materialist commitments embedded the Romantic literary text in wider cultural practices and geographies, and whose specifically deconstructionist bent defamiliarized texts, allowing us to see them as contingent and occlusive performances. The hierarchical and rhetorical distinctions between maps and texts now levelled, the Romantic-period map entered into a new relation to the Romantic-period literary text, whose mapmindedness – its adjacency to cartographic texts and its performance of cartographic 'work' – could now be explored within a conceptualized frame.[5]

The past two decades have witnessed the rise of an increasingly stringently theorized 'literary geography' or 'geography of literature' committed to exploring the ways in which the literary text is produced by, processes, and in turn inflects geographical knowledge and 'forms of thinking and feeling about space'.[6] Its more nuanced forms remain sensitive to the distinctive contours of the literary text by focusing on the ways in which its form is conditioned by the author's (and reader's) emplaced position. Comparatively early on, the spatialization of the literary text in Romantic literary geography took a specifically cartographic turn, as New Historicism's catholic breadth of context was deployed to reveal the embeddedness of the literary work within wider networks. The national project of the Ordnance Survey – mapped anew by Rachel Hewitt in 2010 in the context of eighteenth- and nineteenth-century European cultures of science, technology, and national identity (and modes of seeing and feeling) – together with the poetry of William Wordsworth and John Clare featured prominently in this project. Crucially, this critical mapping went beyond the historicization of literature in the context of related disciplines and domains of print; beyond an analysis of cartography's intimate relation to topographical writing, the tour, aesthetic theory and the graphic arts; and beyond a focus on the place of maps in the political culture and imaginative literature of the age. It certainly sought to go beyond the fundamentally quantitative 'extension'-views and spatial abstractions of Franco Moretti's 'distance reading' model.[7] The project – a nascent critical Romantic Cartography – went further by seeking to articulate Romantic-period experiences of and with maps, revealing how literary activity deployed maps and mapping as a heuristic and how literary texts themselves performed recognizably cartographic moves. Crucially, Romantic Studies saw fit to announce the viability of 'cartographic readings' that re-encountered the literature and culture of the period.[8]

The four essays in Part I of *Romantic Cartographies* are concerned with the ways in which the Romantic period sought to understand itself cartographically and how it mapped itself conceptually as well as technologically. Specific examples of material cartography are considered in the context of the cultural networks and economies in which maps (as practical tools, commercial products, and agents of commemoration and political commentary) circulated. A portrait emerges of the interpenetration of cartography, literature, tourism, art, antiquarianism, historiography, science, sociological analysis, and quantitative data-gathering, with each element both reinforcing and critiquing the others. While Britain and British mapping projects are the primary focus of Part I – as in the volume as a whole – this is so always (necessarily) in relation to global mapping enterprises and coordinates. Indeed, the volume begins both outside and within the borders of 'Britain's' mapping.

It is the imbrication of cartography and the natural history of Canada that concerns Alan Bewell in the first chapter. Again, the human and cultural networks behind the material reality of a map are revealed. Also highlighted, with detailed attention to the design and paratextual embellishment of four specific maps, are the ways in which imperial cartography elides indigenous populations and registers the natural environment in ways that emphasize colonial possession of the land while servicing an appetite for multidisciplinary knowledge. Reading his chosen maps of the North American North-West in terms of the graphic separation of cartography and natural history and their 'imperial alliance', Bewell emphasizes the palimpsestic nature of each venture. He ends by reminding us of the need to recover – while we can – the distinctiveness of that which existed before maps rendered them invisible.

Developing her work on the history and cultural capital of the Ordnance Survey –formally established in June 1791, though indebted to decades of British and continental surveying practice and theory – in Chapter 2 Rachel Hewitt focuses on literary constructions of the figure of the Survey's director, William Mudge. Identifying the cultural, imaginative and organizational conditions that allowed cultural alidades to be focused on Mudge in the period 1798–1820, Hewitt – like Bewell, as well as Stephen Daniels in the succeeding chapter – reveals the networks of people, ideas and organizations on which cartographic ventures relied. As empirical observer, capable of reconciling diversity in unity by virtue of his oversight of the Survey's unified scale map of a '*united* kingdom', Mudge is seen to take on the role of ideal 'national commentator' in the literary imagination. Hewitt argues that, at this particular moment, literary representations of Mudge triangulate with changing public conceptions of professional knowledge, the proximity of military and civilian cultures, and discussions of national character and cohesiveness.

Stephen Daniels's Chapter 3 reveals complex ecologies of maps, texts, patrons, and publishers in a commercial context, focusing on the topographical-historical 'delineations' of counties of England and Wales begun in 1801 by John Britton and Edward Wedlake Brayley and on the cartographic sister-project *The British Atlas*. Daniels reveals the practical challenges of such a multi-author, interdisciplinary venture, offering a portrait of a sociable (and unsociable) effort involving the commissioning of artists and engravers, historical research, fieldwork, and networks of correspondence. Daniels brings out the problematic plenitude and uneasy currency (in all senses) of these projects, which were invested in conflicted ways in constructions of industrial modernity, the celebration of a pre-industrial past, the performance of civic virtue, the articulation of county and national identities, and the recording of personal debt.

Anticipating the concerns of Part II, Damian Walford Davies focuses in Chapter 4 on a 1798 example of cartographic commemoration by an otherwise unknown local land surveyor, Thomas Propert. Walford Davies offers a historicist-ekphrastic reading of this verbal-graphic text, which maps and narrativizes the *descente* by French troops on the coast of Pembrokeshire in February 1797 (the last invasion of mainland Britain). Again, on display are the paradoxes, anxieties, and generic miscibility of the cartographic project. Taking Propert's map as a test case in (the limits of) historicized literary-cartographic reading, Walford Davies argues that the map is equally committed to the values of scientific mensuration and those of distortion, caricature, and the grotesque. A text of multiple laminations and unresolved cultural conflations, the map is recursive, the tense traffic between caricature and cartography deepened by the range of ideological positions articulated by its graphic codes.

II   Cartographic Encounters

We have learned to read the official, state-supported maps and surveys of the eighteenth and nineteenth centuries as ideological inscriptions conveying attitudes about the place and populations being mapped; about the cartographic images themselves (that they are disinterested representations of spatial and ontological truth); and about their makers (that they possess epistemological, cultural, and political authority). Maps are the construct of 'a gaze', Matthew Edney argues in his history of the cartographic making of British India, 'a concerted observation, that is always appropriative, domineering, and empowered' – and had real effects in British engagement

with the subcontinent.[9] This gaze is an aspect of the 'autonomous individual ego' described by Jonathan Crary as a subject-effect of the epistemological paradigm of the camera obscura.[10] During the seventeenth and
eighteenth centuries, rationalist and empiricist philosophers construed the
camera as a model both of vision and of how visual observation 'leads to
truthful inferences about the world' (29). The model depended on
a structural analogy between the human visual apparatus and the camera,
with its eye-like aperture through which images are projected on the walls
of the mind-like inner chamber. The camera's modelling of observational
truth relied on its strict Cartesian spatial delimitation between interior and
exterior and its 'decorporealization' of vision; the device 'sunder[ed] the act
of seeing from the physical body of the observer', who understood the
objects of the external world only as they appeared as images to be
contemplated within the space of reason (39). In Crary's analysis,
Vermeer's portraits of *The Astronomer* (1688) and *The Geographer* (1668–9)
(Figure 0.3) situate maps within the 'optical regime' modelled by the
camera obscura (37). The one-windowed interiors in which the pictured

Figure 0.3 Jan Vermeer Van Delft, *The Geographer* (1688–9). Städel Museum,
© Städel Museum – ARTOTHEK.

astronomer and geographer work illustrate that the 'production of the camera is always a projection onto a two-dimensional surface – here maps, globes, charts, and images' (46).

After the critical interrogation of visual media's role in legitimizing the individual subject as a source of 'true' knowledge, it has not, J. B. Harley has argued,

> proved difficult to make a general case for the mediating role of maps in political thought and action nor to glimpse their power effects. Through both their content and their modes of representation, the making and using of maps has been pervaded by ideology. Yet these mechanisms can only be understood in specific historical situations

through analysis of the broader discursive contexts of particular maps.[11] The choice of projection and centering location, the selection and omission of features, and the mode and style of cartographic signs are symbols whose meanings are activated and refracted 'in the social world' and in relation to other cultural texts.

The chapters in Part II of this volume focus specific historical situations of map production and use in order to broaden our understanding of Romantic cartographic culture. They look beyond those eighteenth- and nineteenth-century projects of measuring and marking nation and empire that have occupied historical and critical attention – the Ordnance Survey of Great Britain (1791–1891), the Ordnance Survey of Ireland (1824–46), and the Great Trigonometrical Survey of India (1802–71) – in order to illuminate the range of uses that maps served in the Romantic period and the variety of ways in which people interacted with them. In the process, they challenge the epistemological model set out in Crary's account of maps as part of an 'optical regime'. What has been seen as an 'appropriative, domineering, and empowered' overview by a disembodied, rational eye was, in practice, inflected and deflected by use-contexts in which maps were materially changed and semiotically reconfigured, and in which they interacted with other media (verbal, visual, and tactile) and other discourses and genres (particularly poems, novels, primers, and portraiture). Romantic cartography was richly diversified and produced a range of social, subjective, environmental, and political effects.

Romantic-era guidebooks such as *Blacks' Picturesque Guide to the English Lakes* physically intermingled maps and large-scale charts with descriptive poems and prose, with picturesque views, with itineraries, and with outline views of mountains. Integrated in these material and ideological contexts, maps' modelling of physical space became subject to multiple interpretive possibilities, while they, in turn, unpredictably shaped the interpretation of the visual and literary passages among which they were embedded. For tourists, the maps became part of a complex set of readerly choices by which they could both organize knowledge of a visited place and develop sophistication as interpreters of representational media. This set of choices could be operated differently on different occasions: once home again, rereading the passages and re-perusing the maps in various sequences, travellers could not just revisit but also transform, from the multimodal page, encounters with previously visited places. Thus a variable temporalization of the map became possible; the reader did not gain or regain a unitary commanding view so much as experiment with constructing a variety of different perspectives, including many not experienced on the spot. The contextualized map becomes an agent of imagined (and even imaginary) vision and of escape from the tyranny of the singular, whether spatial (there or here) or temporal (then or now).

Examples of the contextualization of maps in diverse print formats are the star charts that appeared in Alexander Jamieson's 1822 pictorial star atlas, which was designed for amateurs and, as its title signals, interactive: *A Celestial Atlas Comprising a Systematic Display of the Heavens in a Series of Thirty Maps Illustrated by Scientific Descriptions of Their Contents, And accompanied by Catalogues of the Stars and Astronomical Exercises* (1822).[12] These charts were repurposed in *Urania's Mirror; or, A View of the Heavens* (1824), an 'elegant' boxed-set of thirty-two celestial cards, each 'beautifully coloured' and showing from one to twelve of Jamieson's constellations.[13] Advertised as an 'AN ACCEPTABLE PRESENT', and accompanied by *A Familiar Treatise on Astronomy* containing *Numerous Graphical Illustrations*, *Urania's Mirror* promised to reveal 'all the constellations visible' to the naked eye 'in the British empire' – no telescope required.[14] Punched with holes of varying circumference to let through varying magnitudes of star-mimicking candle-light, each eight-by-five-and-a-half-inch card put 'Infinity in the palm of your hand' – or at least a segment of the imperial sky (Figure 0.4).[15]

The star cards and guidebooks evince Romantic cartography's mingling of edification and pleasure. They also suggest, contra Crary, that cartoliteracy spread by means of mediating interactions with instructional and illustrative genres that disrupted the attainment of a centralized commanding view – not least by implicating the body. Many Romantic-era maps demanded physiological engagement. Some, like the celestial charts of *Urania's Mirror*, were discernable by hands as well as eyes. Legible to the fingers, they posited an observing subject unlike the imperial officer who

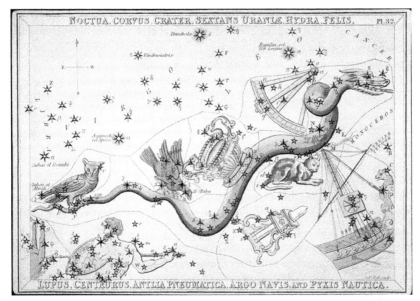

Figure 0.4 "Noctua, Corvus, Crater, Sextans Uraniæ, Hydra, Felis, Lupus, Centaurus, Antlia Pneumatica, Argo Navis, and Pyxis Nautica" (Plate 32). *Urania's Mirror; or, A View of the Heavens* (London: Printed for Samuel Leigh, 1825). Engraved by Sidney Hall. Courtesy of Library of Congress, LC- USZCA-10077 DLC.

The figure shows the pictorial realism of Romantic-era star charts and the material innovation of hole-punched stars. In the lower right appears the constellation Pyxis Nautica (1752), or mariner's compass, used for orientation and navigation; in the upper right, Sextans (1687), or astronomical sextant, used for measuring the angles between stars.

knows the world he governs by its visual projection on the rationally ordered surfaces of surveys and maps.

Reading maps as tactually, as well as visually, interpreted media – their 'view' of the world shaped by the physiological, material, and social contexts in which they were used – the chapters collected in this section emphasize Romantic cartography's lack of conformity with an overall 'optical regime'. In Chapters 5 and 6 Carl Thompson and Siobhan Carroll challenge the association between Romantic cartography and the inculcation of a '"territorialized national identity"' (Carroll) or 'proto-imperialist "geographical subjectivity"' (Thompson). '[W]ithout denying that some aspects of the modern, scientifically constructed map strongly encourage a dominating and acquisitive sensibility', Thompson argues that the multimodal, multi-sensory pedagogical contexts in which maps were embedded skewed these effects. Focusing on the geographical primers of Sarah Atkins Wilson, Thompson shows how the 'yoking of maps and narrative story-telling . . . produces subtly discordant moments' that 'highlight the limitations . . . of cartographic representation' and dramatize women's typical exclusion from the realm of geographical knowledge production. Thompson posits the formation of a critical mapmindedness by the very literature that trains children in map use and, ostensibly, imperial ideology.

Likewise, the generic and contextual relations between the board game, historical romance, and topographical poetry that are discussed in Carroll's chapter enable her to reframe maps not as reifications of stable order but as tools for navigating the tumultuous Romantic world. Examining the repurposing of previously published maps in geographical board games, Carroll shows how a new mode of using maps oriented around pleasure, entertainment, and play flourished between 1790 and 1840. While these cartographical games had an educational function, instilling knowledge of geography, history, and culture, they also mediated players' relations to a spatial, social, and political world in flux. The printed map remade as the surface of a chance-based game mobilizes the fixed image of the represented world: historical annotations in the game's rule-book inscribe geopolitical change and imply an undetermined future, structuring the player's relationship to the passage of time in ways comparable to the genres of the historical novel and newspaper. Unlike these genres, however, the chance-based nature of the cartographical game 'allows players to experience unpredictable, unmerited departures from order' and historical narratives 'with new winners and losers'. As they move their pieces along the superimposed racetracks, players immerse themselves in, rather than command, the world's extension.

'[M]aps are at least as much an image of the social order as they are a measurement of the phenomenal world of object', states Harley in 'Deconstructing the Map'.[16] That image may be critically refocused by its adjacent literature, as Thompson shows, or destabilized by the conversion of the map into a narrative genre activated temporally by players, as Carroll argues. It can also be displaced from primacy, as Julia S. Carlson shows in Chapter 7, in the case of maps that appeal less to the sight than to other senses. Carlson investigates the development of mapping for blind people in France and Britain, identifying Denis Diderot's description of tactile maps as a turning point in the philosophical representation of tactility and blindness – a point at which maps' participation in an 'optical regime' came into question. Diderot's arguments, she contends, led to the establishment of the world's first school for blind children, in which geography was taught by the tracing of fingers across maps' raised surfaces. The tactile map became a potent symbol not only of the epistemological and moral powers of tact but also of the blind as sympathetic and useful members of the public sphere. Tracking the translation of these ideas into Britain, Carlson considers blind Scottish poet Thomas Blacklock's influence on the establishment of educational institutions for the blind in Britain, as well as the impact of their foundation of literacy and social integration on cartoliteracy. Tactile maps confronted sighted people with powerful evidence that cartography was not solely a visual means of modelling the world; they were also powerful drivers of cartography's remodelling, providing haptic access rather than optical surveillance.

In Chapter 8 Joshua Wilner explores a further destabilization of the map, and of the order it seems to enforce, by reading against the grain a narrative genre that has often been thought to place the cartographic gazer in a position of command. Wilner exposes the formal and narrative fractures that subtend a paradigmatic scene of the unifying Romantic imagination – Wordsworth's Snowdon vision in *The Prelude*. In a close reading of the episode, Wilner argues that the fractal formal patterning that opens onto the poet's vision of eternity, as he stands, like a map-reader, looking down on 'the shore' of 'a huge sea of mist', uncannily anticipates the symbolic importance of the Western coast of Britain, in Benoit Mandelbrot's *Fractal Geometry of Nature*, as the epitome of an erratically curved, and thus infinite, coastline.[17] Challenging influential readings of the Snowdon vision as a culminating moment of retrospective self-totalization, Wilner shows how it emerges from the poem's recursive self-generation of figures of fracture at reduced levels of scale, in the very manner of fractal forms in nature. The Snowdon episode emerges as the formal instantiation of a non-Euclidean geometry of nature that troubles the modern cartographic project of measurement and holistic representation.

III   Beyond Romantic Cartographies

All three parts of this book clearly illustrate that if, on the one hand, the early nineteenth century represents a significant turning point in the official history of cartography, on the other, as mapping becomes more systemized and unified, alternative creative forms of representing or of moving through place and space spring up and find expression. Part III of the book addresses the polymorphic nature of Romantic cartographies from the perspective of our own time and in anticipation of future ways of mapping. One question we might pose, in relation to new forms of mapping and visualizing literature in the twenty-first century, including digital methods, is whether these are something new or merely a subset of something old – nothing more nor less than an adapted form of thematic mapping. We can consider this question briefly here, using it as an example of the ways in which highly innovative and creative modes of mapping from the past continue to vitally inform the present and future.

While thematic mapping in the Romantic period remains a 'scientific' form to some extent – an acceptable and authorized professional form for the mapping of data – the *nature* of the thematic map means that it also allows considerable scope for creativity within that model.[18] It is usually focused on a single spatial variable:

> A thematic map, as its name implies, presents a graphic theme about a subject. It must be remembered that a single theme is chosen for such a map: this is what distinguishes it from a reference map. A reference map is to a thematic map what a dictionary is to an essay.[19]

To achieve its goals, such a map needs 'something that is measurable, a method by which to measure it, and some way of visually exhibiting the results over a selected geographic region'.[20] Thematic maps rose to full prominence in the mid-nineteenth century with industrialization and resulting socioeconomic conditions (such as population density, crime, poverty, disease) that can best be represented in this form. However, they also existed much earlier (Edmond Halley was an early practitioner in the first half of the 1700s) and their creative potential is exemplified in the Romantic period by the remarkable maps of Alexander von Humboldt.

Humboldt's five-year expedition across the Americas (1799–1804) provided him with a wealth of information about the natural world from which he developed (almost literally) groundbreaking thematic maps representing data concerning volcanology, geology, botany, meteorology, and much more. One of the most famous of these, from his attempt to ascend Mount Chimborazo in Ecuador, is his representation of plant life in relation to altitude (Figure 0.5).

The map is remarkably creative in its combination of different kinds of data – objective and subjective. The left-hand scale provides the *toises* (measure of height) in metres as well as day- and night-time temperatures at each height. The bar on the right allows comparison of the effects of altitude in the ascent of this mountain with the results of other scientific experiments, including information such as 'Balloon of Mr. Lussac, 16 September 1804' (which references the trials in terms of the effects of

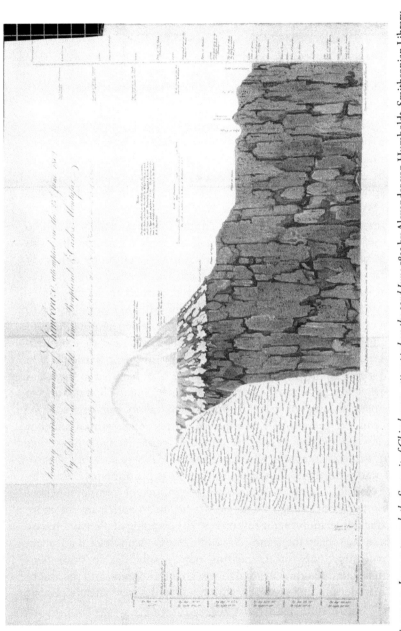

Figure 0.5 *Journey towards the Summit of Chimborazo, attempted on the 23rd June 1802 by Alexander von Humboldt. Smithsonian Library.*

altitude on the body and breathing by Joseph Louis Gay-Lussac in Paris). The three annotations positioned above the mountain just off the right-hand slope read (from the bottom up):

> The travellers began to bleed from the eyes, the lips & the gums
> Lecidea geogr: on the bare rocks of trachyte
> Cleft which prevented the travellers from reaching the summit –
>   Bar: 167.2 lines. Ther, 1°, 7c. (3016 Toises)

While the different kinds of data represented are for strictly scientific purposes (botanical, geological, medical), the *mode* of presentation opens up meaning creatively. This is felt in the higgledy-piggledy writing of plant names for vegetation growing at different altitudes on the left and in the combination of personal experience on the mountain with hard data about it.

By its nature then, a thematic map is strongly visual and might be said to 'tell a story' – in Humboldt's case to tell not only a scientific but also a human (bodily, psychological) one. Of course, the currently dominant critical-cartographic approach asserts that this is true of *all* maps, but the *particular* nature of the thematic map brings this aspect to the fore.

Maps such as Humboldt's and Charles Joseph Minard's (see Figure 0.6) display a characteristically creative response to more conventional uses of cartography in ways that feed directly into apparently 'new' digital cartographic forms in the twenty-first century. Recent advances, particularly in the field of geographic information systems, or GIS, have led to fresh and dramatically effective ways of mapping data (including the literary) and of 'telling stories' through powerful forms of visualization, but, here too, the past informs the present. An example of proportional symbol and dot distribution mapping by Minard (Figure 0.6) immediately demonstrates the point. Minard's map strongly resembles the GIS visualizations that we have become familiar with in the last 20 years or so but anticipates them by 150 years. Equally, Humboldt's combination of different forms of meaning in relation to the mapping of a single site begins to anticipate the more layered, qualitative multimedia response to the mapping of place offered by concepts such as 'deep mapping'. So, while recent technological advances undoubtedly open up for us exciting new possibilities in both two-dimensional and three-dimensional forms, core techniques, and the ability to display understanding creatively through graphics were already present from the mid-Romantic period onward.

These examples of *early* thematic mapping allow us to see that past and present are vitally connected and that the 'cartographic imagination'

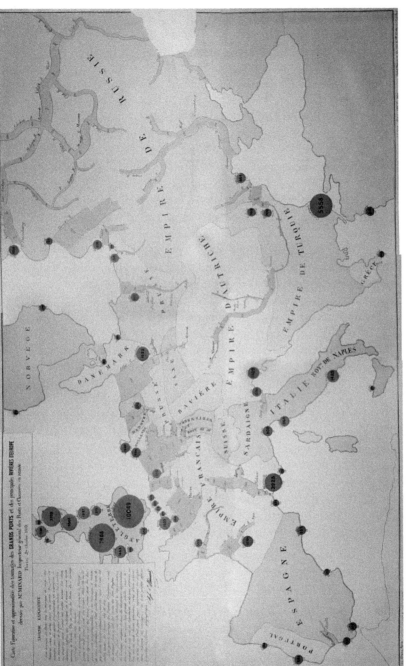

Figure 0.6 Charles Joseph Minard, *Carte Figurative des tonnage des GRANDS PORTS et des principales RIVIERES D'EUROPE. 27th Octobre 1859*. Reproduced by kind permission of Guillaime Saquet and Isabelle Gautheron from the Bibliothèque de l'École Nationale des Ponts et Chausées (ENPC). ENPC: Fol 10975, 3564/C184.

applies not just to writers but to scientists and even to literary critics. In our own day, the digital medium offers us new ways as academics of interpreting as well as expressing creativity through literary cartography. In the early part of the twenty-first century this took the form of trying to adapt a scientific model (GIS) to the humanities, with leading work in the field of qualitative GIS undertaken by David Cooper (working with Ian Gregory and Sally Bushell).[21] Comparable work, taking Moretti's codex model into the digital arena, was undertaken by Barbara Piatti and others on the Literary Atlas of Europe project, and a range of approaches are explored in the recent collection *Literary Mapping in the Digital Age,* co-edited by Cooper, Donaldson, and Murrieta-Flores.[22] In recent years, then, researchers working in a diverse range of disciplines – across the arts, humanities, and social sciences – have moved towards more qualitative forms of GIS.[23] An initial sense of seeking to adapt scientific models has started to be replaced by a need for approaches that recognize the particular needs of literary studies and other related humanities disciplines (e.g. history, classics). Such approaches feed directly into the emerging concept of 'deep mapping'.

This term seems to have been first used by American author William Least Heat-Moon in *PrairyErth: A Deep Map* (1991) to describe a composite work focused upon a particular place that uses a range of visual and verbal media to document and represent that place.[24] Least Heat-Moon combined different kinds of mapping, from the formal grid maps of Rand-McNally to maps of names and 'mental maps' created by residents as he wandered through Chase County, Kansas. This initial free-flowing artistic concept was concerned with trying to access and create a different kind of engagement with place that drew upon the lives and histories that welled up out of it. Taking such ideas forward into the digital environment, David Bodenhamer and others at the Virtual Centre for Spatial Humanities, Indiana University, have started to develop the concept specifically in relation to spatial narratives.[25] Bodenhamer gives a fuller definition of deep maps in his chapter in *Literary Mapping in the Digital Age*:

> A deep map is a finely detailed, multimedia depiction of a place and the people, animals and objects that exist within it and are thus inseparable from the contours and rhythms of everyday life.[26]

Bodenhamer's definition respects the origins of the concept in defining deep maps as living holistic entities that, as he puts it elsewhere, 'do not seek authority or objectivity, but involve negotiation between insiders and outsiders, experts and contributors, over what is represented and how.

Framed as a conversation and not a statement, deep maps are inherently unstable.'[27] This leads him to suggest that they are also constantly developing; 'A deep map is a platform, a process and a product . . . a new creative spaced that is visual, structurally open'.[28]

As this brief account of the power of visualization over time suggests, the chapters included in the final section of this book bring us up to the present moment but always do so in sympathetic connection with the past as well as with an eye to the future. Chapter 9, by Christopher Donaldson, reassesses Sir Walter Scott's historicity by exploring his quiet resistance to the explicit mapping of literary place and his preference for 'practical geography'. Donaldson shows how the writer's sense of place is strongly empirical and experiential, founded in sensory experience. For Scott, geography is bound up with history and memory. In a somewhat counter-intuitive way, then, his antiquarian approach (old-fashioned even in the Romantic period) can be seen to anticipate deep mapping – respecting the full temporality of a place and its peoples over time.

In Chapter 10, Sally Bushell traces a layered history of critical and creative re-mappings of the poet John Clare through key interventions: the anticipatory work of John Barrell in *The Idea of Landscape and the Sense of Place*; the adoption of Barrell's maps by Franco Moretti in *Graphs, Maps, Trees*; and the creative appropriation of Clare by Iain Sinclair. Clare is read in and through others in order to generate a multilayered response that highlights the range of spatial forms of interpretation embraced by literary studies. The second half of the chapter then 'unmaps' Clare by prioritizing time over space to offer an alternative conceptualization of the poet's spatiality.

Chapter 11, by David Cooper, considers the creative-critical status of cartographic practices in literary reimaginings of the much-trodden post-Wordsworthian landscape of the English Lake District. Through an engagement with the intersecting fields of critical cartography and creative geographies, the chapter explores ways in which recent writers (Alfred Wainwright, Sean Borodale, and Richard Skelton) have embedded maps and performative mapping practices in their attempts to reclaim the overdetermined topography of the Lakes.

Finally, the collection ends as it began, by considering loaded cultural acts beyond British shores – remapping as appropriation – in the Romantic period. In Chapter 12, Paul Youngquist takes up the challenge made at the end of Cooper's piece by moving towards a more creative-critical form of expression in his engagement with the subject. His writing shifts between past and present Jamaican history, recorded and experienced acts of mapping, in search of indigenous rights and ownership of space, not only intellectually and empirically but also on the ground, in the company of Chief Grizzle. Employing critical cartography to read the official maps against themselves, Youngquist traces a genealogy of hidden space in relation to the Maroon common to uncover the enduring tensions that continue to configure the struggle for indigenous territorial independence in Jamaica today.

Reading across the four chapters of Part III, shared themes emerge that also run across this entire collection: a focus on mapping time as well as space; the necessity of setting a diachronic sense of the cumulative mapping of place against a synchronic model; the importance of memory, personal or collective, and the way this works against or within more formal cartographies; a sense of play in relation to acts of mapping; the direct experience of place and of acts of mapping through the body and senses other than the visual; and last – but by no means least – the desire to find new and stimulating ways of engaging with Romantic cartographies, critically, digitally, creatively.

Notes

1. See Rachel Hewitt, 'Mapping and Romanticism', *Wordsworth Circle* 42:2 (2011): 157–65; and Hewitt, *Map of a Nation: A Biography of the Ordnance Survey* (London: Granta, 2010).
2. George Cumberland, *An Attempt to Describe Hafod, and the Neighbouring Scenes about the Bridge Over the Funack, Commonly Called the Devil's Bridge, in the County of Cardigan. An Ancient Seat Belonging to Thomas Johnes, Esq. Member for the County of Radnor* (London: W. Wilson, 1796), vii.
3. Benjamin Heath Malkin, *A Father's Memoirs of his Child* (London: Longman, Hurst, Rees, and Orme, 1806), xliii.
4. See John Barrell, *The Idea of Landscape and the Sense of Place, 1730–1840* (Cambridge: Cambridge University Press, 1972); *The Iconography of Landscape: Essays on the Symbolic Representation, Design and Use of Past Environments*, eds. Denis Cosgrove and Stephen Daniels (Cambridge: Cambridge University Press, 1989); *Envisioning Landscape, Making Worlds: Geography and the Humanities*, eds. Stephen Daniels, Dydia DeLyser, J. Nicholas Entrikin, and Douglas Richardson (Abingdon: Routledge, 2011).
5. 'Mapmindedness' is P. D. A Harvey's term (quoted in D. K. Smith), *The Cartographic Imagination in Early Modern England* (Aldershot: Ashgate, 2008), 8.
6. Wystan Curnow, 'Mapping and the Expanded Field of Contemporary Art', in *Mappings*, ed. Denis Cosgrove (London: Reaktion Books, 1999), 253–68, 256. See also Marc Brosseau, 'Geography's Literature', *Progress in Human Geography*

18:3 (1994): 333–53; Andrew Thacker, 'The Idea of A Critical Literary Geography', *New Formations: A Journal of Culture/Theory/Politics* 57 (2005–6): 56–72; Angharad Saunders, 'Literary Geography: Re-forging the Connections', *Progress in Human Geography* 34:4 (2019): 436–52; Sheila Hones, 'Literary Geography: The Novel as Spatial Event', in *Envisioning Landscape, Making Worlds*, eds. Daniels *et al.*, 247–55.

7. Franco Moretti, *Graphs, Maps, Trees: Abstract Models for a Literary Geography* (London: Verso, 2005); and Robert T. Tally's review, *Modern Language Quarterly* 68:1 (2007): 132–5.

8. See Julia S. Carlson, 'The Map at the Limits of His Paper: A Cartographic Reading of *The Prelude*, Book 6: "Cambridge and the Alps"', *Studies in Romanticism* 49:3 (2010): 375–404; Damian Walford Davies, *Cartographies of Culture: New Geographies of Welsh Writing in English* (Cardiff: University of Wales Press, 2012), 20–42.

9. Matthew Edney, *Mapping an Empire: The Cartographical Construction of British India, 1765–1843* (Chicago, IL: University of Chicago Press, 1990), 63.

10. Jonathan Crary, *Techniques of the Observer: On Vision and Modernity in the Nineteenth Century* (Boston: Massachusetts Institute of Technology Press, 1990), 29–39.

11. J. B. Harley, *The New Nature of Maps: Essays in the History of Cartography*, ed. Paul Laxton, introduction by J. H. Andrews (Baltimore, MD: Johns Hopkins University Press, 2002), 79.

12. Inspired, like his predecessors, by John Flamsteed's lushly produced *Atlas Coelestis* (1729), Jamieson followed the Frenchman Jean Nicholas Fortin, *Atlas Céleste de Flamsteed* (Paris: F. G. Deschamps, 1776) and the German Johann Bode's *Vorstellung der Gestirne . . . des Flamsteadschen Himmelsatlas* (Berlin: Gottlieb August Langer, 1782). Nick Kanas, *Star Maps: History, Artistry, Cartography* (Berlin: Springer Praxis, 2009), 176.

13. Quoted from an advertisement for *Urania's Mirror; or, A View of the Heavens*, in *Monthly Critical Gazette* (December 1824), 578. Ian Ridpath, 'Alexander Jamieson, Celestial Mapmaker', *Astronomy & Geophysics* 54 (February 2013): 1.22–1.23, 1.23.

14. *Urania's Mirror; or, A View of the Heavens* (London: G. & W. B. Whittaker, 1824).

15. P. D. Hingley, 'Urania's Mirror – A 170-Year-Old Mystery Solved', *Journal of the British Astronomical Association* 104:5 (1994), 238–40, 238. 'Auguries of Innocence', *The Pickering Manuscript: Electronic Edition*, ed. Morris Eaves, Robert N. Essick, and Joseph Viscomi, *The William Blake Archive*, object 16, www.blakearchive.org/images/bb126.1.13.ms.100.jpg.

16. J. B. Harley, 'Deconstructing the Map', in *The New Nature of Maps*, 149–68, 158.

17. William Wordsworth, *The Thirteen-Book Prelude*, ed. Mark L. Reed (Ithaca, NY: Cornell University Press, 1991), XIII, 42–3.

18. The main methods of visualization for thematic maps are: choropeth mapping; proportional symbol mapping; Isarithmic or Isoline mapping; and dot

distribution mapping. Choropeth mapping presents aggregated data across a region in varying hue to show regional differences.

19. Borden D. Dent, *Cartography: Thematic Map Design*, 2nd ed. (Georgia State University; Wm C. Brown Publishers, 1985), 8.

20. 'Qualitative Maps: An Introduction', Historic Map Collection: Princeton University Library, http://libweb5.princeton.edu/visual_materials/maps/web sites/thematic-maps/introduction/introduction.html (accessed 31 July 2018).

21. See David Cooper and Ian Gregory, 'Mapping the English Lake District: A Literary GIS', *Transactions of the Institute of British Geographers* 36:1 (2011): 89–109. The pilot project 'Mapping the Lakes' (Cooper with Gregory and Bushell) was the first to attempt a qualitative comparison using GIS. See www .lancaster.ac.uk/mappingthelakes/Interactive%20Maps%20Introduction .html.

22. David Cooper, Christopher Donaldson, and Patricia Murrieta-Flores, eds., *Literary Mapping in the Digital Age* (Abingdon: Routledge, 2016). For the Literary Atlas, see www.literatureatlas.eu/en/.

23. See, for example, Stanford's experimental crowd-sourced site 'Mapping Emotions in Victorian London', which uses textual extracts to explore the historical affective geography of the capital: http://blog.historypin.org/wp-content/uploads/2015/04/Main-map-1.png.

24. William Least Heat-Moon, *PrairyErth: A Deep Map* (Boston: Houghton Mifflin, 1991).

25. See also *Deep Maps and Spatial Narratives*, eds. David J. Bodenhamer, Trevor M. Harris, and John Corrigan (Bloomington: Indiana University Press, 2015); and Les Roberts, ed., special issue, Deep Mapping and Spatial Anthropology, 'Deep Mapping', *Humanities* 5:5 (2016): 1–7.

26. David J. Bodenhamer, 'Making the Invisible Visible: Place, Spatial Stories and Deep Maps', *Literary Mapping in the Digital Age*, eds. Cooper *et al.*, 207–20, 212.

27. David J. Bodenhamer, Trevor M. Harris, and John Corrigan, 'Deep Mapping and the Spatial Humanities', *International Journal of Humanities and Arts Computing* 7 (2013): 170–5, 174.

28. Bodenhamer, 'Making the Invisible Visible', *Literary Mapping*, 213.

PART I

Romantic Maps, Romantic Mapping

CHAPTER I

Cartography and Natural History in Late-Eighteenth-Century Canada

Alan Bewell

In 1750, seven months after the newly appointed governor of Nova Scotia, Edward Cornwallis, sailed into Chebucto harbour with a fleet of thirteen transports carrying soldiers and settlers to build the fortified town of Halifax and to take military control of the region, the *Gentleman's Magazine* announced (with some fanfare on its contents page) that its February issue would be of special interest:

> N.B. The Nova Scotia PLANTS, FRUITS and ANIMAL, represented on the Plates of this month, may be seen properly colour'd according to the original, at the print-shop [on] the corner of St Martin's Lane in the Strand; where also may be seen the real butterflies brought from new Halifax; and we have had some dozens colour'd in order to send one to each of our correspondents who shall desire it.[1]

It was not simply miles that separated eighteenth-century British readers from Canada but also knowledge of the place itself. Although fishermen had been plying its eastern coasts since early in the seventeenth century, it was only when Britain decided to extend its military control over Nova Scotia that there was a keen interest in knowing more about this place. The February issue of the *Gentleman's Magazine* included a botanical illustration of five plants 'drawn from life at Halifax' (73). More striking, however, was the appearance of an unusual map – *A Plan of the Harbour of Chebucto and Town of Halifax* – bordered with brightly coloured armorial escutcheons of some of the baronetcies of Nova Scotia, with more than one-quarter of its space devoted to the display of the single 'Animal' referred to on the contents page – a somewhat ratty-looking porcupine – and three Canadian insects: a white admiral butterfly (*Limenitis arthemis*), an orange underwing tyger (*Catocala antinympha*) and a longhorn beetle (Figure 1.1). Both the botanical plate and the map were drawn and engraved by Moses Harris, who would later become famous as a natural history illustrator and an authority on English butterflies and moths following the publication of

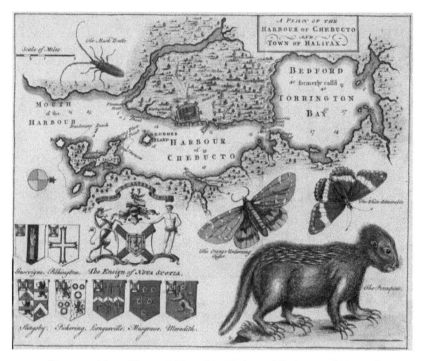

Figure 1.1 Moses Harris, *A Plan of the Harbour of Chebucto and Town of Halifax* (1750). Map Collection, Rare Books and Special Collections, McGill University Library.

The Aurelian; Or, Natural History of English Insects, Namely, Moths and Butterflies (1766). As a member in the 1760s of the Aurelian Society, Harris was part of a small nucleus of insect collectors, among whom were Dru Drury, James Lee, Henry Smeathman and Daniel Solander.[2] Although it is likely that Harris's main interest was in the insects shown on the plate, it appears that the editor of the *Gentleman's Magazine*, Edward Cave, must have thought that readers would want something more dramatic, so a porcupine was added and the plate was inserted between two pages providing a verbal description of the appearance and habits of this curious rodent, headed 'Of the North American Porcupine. See the Plate'. The *'Porcupine Map'* – as it is now called by historians of cartography – brought together natural history, mapping and the colonization of Canada. It is thus a useful place to begin a discussion of the relationship between these activities during the latter half of the eighteenth century.

Moses Harris was nineteen when in 1749 he abruptly terminated his apprenticeship with the London geographer Charles Price to sign up with his wife for passage on the transport *Winchelsea* to Chebucto. Although he is identified on the shipping list as a 'sawyer', this was probably a mistaken transcription of 'surveyor', since that is how Harris describes himself in the elaborate cartouche that graces the original hand-drawn version of *A Plan of the Harbour of Chebucto and Town of Halifax* that he drew during his short stay.[3] There can be little doubt, given Harris's avid interest in entomology, that his ulterior motive for travelling to Halifax was to collect Canadian insects and – as he hoped – to establish a reputation in the burgeoning new field of natural history. The settlement of the new colony in Nova Scotia thus provided him with an opportunity to travel to a part of the world whose nature had suddenly become of great interest to British naturalists. Shortly after arriving in late June 1749, Harris almost immediately began corresponding with the *Gentleman's Magazine*, contributing letters on the progress of the colony, dated 28 July, 17 August and 7 December.[4] He also drew three maps, the other two being *A Plan of the Town of Halifax*, which appeared in the October 1749 issue of the *Gentleman's Magazine*, and *A View of Halifax Drawn from ye Topmasthead*. By December, Harris must also have been in contact with the royal geographer, Thomas Jefferys, in London, because Jefferys published an advertisement in the magazine that month announcing that he was about to publish a composite map of the region from Harris's drawings. *A Map of the South Part of Nova Scotia and Its Fishing Banks* (printed in January 1750), incorporated the three maps produced by Harris, along with another originally published by the French royal geographer, Jean-Baptiste Bourguignon d'Anville (Figure 1.2). Dedicated to the Board of Trade and Foreign Plantations, the cartouche – decorated with images of builders and fishermen, and displaying a cannon, an ensign and the tools of the map-maker (a globe and an engraving stylus) – clearly indicates that the map was intended to promote the colonization of Nova Scotia.

Both Harris's and Jefferys's maps were produced at a time when Cornwallis, fresh from three years spent violently 'pacifying' the Highland Scots after Culloden, was busy doing the same thing to the indigenous Mi'kmaqs and the French Acadians. Both maps symbolically engage in erasing the Mi'kmaq presence from the region.[5] Historians have long been aware of the extent to which imperial mapping played a key role in erasing indigenous peoples and their knowledge from the

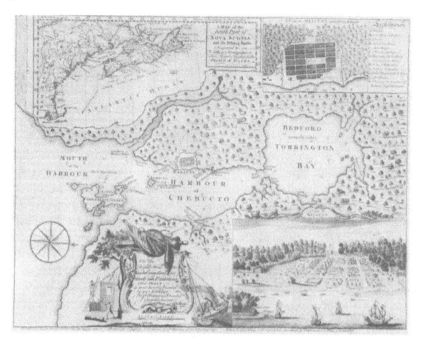

Figure 1.2 Thomas Jefferys, *A Map of the South Part of Nova Scotia and Its Fishing Banks* (1750). Morse Historical Map Collection, Special Collections, Killam Library, Dalhousie University.

territories European nations sought to acquire. With regard to the American West, historian Jared Farmer observes that 'inescapably, the making of the National Map brought about the unmaking of indigenous geographies'.[6] A key element of this practice lay in the naming and renaming of places. The only indication that the new settlement of Halifax is situated on Mi'kmaq land is the mention of 'Chebucto' harbour, which was the French pronunciation of the Mi'kmaq name *K'jipuktuk*, meaning 'great harbour'. Place names on maps, as Thomas F. Thornton suggests, 'tell us something not only about the structure and content of the physical environment itself but also how people perceive, conceptualize, classify, and utilize that environment'.[7] Whereas indigenous names are often descriptive, referring to an outstanding geographical feature of a place, a historical event that occurred there or the plants, animals or tribes found in a particular location, a large percentage of British colonial place names were symbolically possessive, either as place-name transfers (Nova Scotia and Halifax) or as commemorative eponyms, mostly of figures connected with the British aristocracy and colonial administrations involved in exploration. Harris's and Jefferys's maps do provide some information about the fauna of the region depicted, in the names 'Gull Point', 'Lobsters Hole', 'Hawks River' and 'Stags Point', but most of their place names assert that the importance of these localities lies in their connection to people and places existing somewhere else. With some poetic justice, we can also see that these erasures even extended to the British themselves. What was 'formerly' 'Torrington Bay' (named after the First Lord of the Admiralty) in Thomas Durrell's 1732 survey of Nova Scotia is renamed 'Bedford Bay', after the secretary of state, the Duke of Bedford. The place known as 'Rowses Island' on the first version of Harris's map is now called 'Cornwallis Island', while 'Hawks River' has become 'Sandwich River' (after the First Lord of the Admiralty). George II also has another island named after himself.

Shortly after returning to England, probably sometime in December 1749, Harris must have inquired into the possibility of publishing in the *Gentleman's Magazine* engraved plates of the specimens of Nova Scotia plants and insects that he had drawn and collected. Since natural history was becoming an increasingly popular topic in the magazine, Edward Cave as editor appears to have envisioned a more extensive project that would implicitly commemorate both the founding of the new colony and the increased opportunities for studying natural history that it would afford. An engraved plate of the five plants that Harris had drawn in Halifax was produced, and Harris supplied a prose commentary for each. As a further scientific flourish, Cave also arranged for 'a very eminent English Botanist' to identify them and add additional comments.[8] Something similar might have been done for the insects, but, instead, Harris brought natural history and map-making together by providing a new engraving of his map of the Harbour of Chebucto that included what were the first illustrations of insects from Canada in its margins. Although Harris would probably have been quite happy to associate Canada entirely with insects, Cave must have reasoned that his readers would want something a little more dramatic, so (as noted earlier) an image of Canada's second-largest rodent – the porcupine – was chosen to play a leading role on the plate. Harris had eaten porcupines in Nova Scotia but unfortunately had not collected any, so he copied the illustration and prose description of the animal from the first volume of George Edwards's *A Natural History of Uncommon Birds*.[9] (Even Edwards seems to have been taken by the rare attractions of this animal, given that he included it in a book on birds.) Unfortunately, the skin that Edwards used for his illustration was a particularly poor specimen in Hans Sloane's collection.

To emphasize British possession of this portion of the natural world, Harris blazoned the lower left-hand corner of the map with the Ensign of Halifax and the coats of arms of seven baronetcies of Nova Scotia. The idea for including these must also have come from Cave, since the *Gentleman's Magazine*, in its mid-January 1750 printing of its annual Supplement for the previous year, produced a blazon of the Scottish and Irish Peers' Arms. There were 249 baronetcies in Nova Scotia, but the *Gentleman's Magazine* appears to have decided – in view of the recent uprising in Scotland and Cornwallis's role in putting it down – to include only those baronetcies linked to England.[10] To promote the February issue, Cave also arranged for coloured copies of the map to be made available to correspondents, and the magazine encouraged readers to visit Thomas Jefferys's print shop, where they could see the insects originally collected by Harris and obtain a coloured version of *The Porcupine Map* (probably done by Harris) and a copy of Jefferys's composite map.

Harris's inclusion of these striking natural history illustrations has affinities with early colonial maps, which often sought to include illustrations of native flora and fauna. By the end of the seventeenth century, however, as Wilma George notes, if plants and animals 'occur on maps at all', they 'are used decoratively, in cartouches'.[11] One of the most unusual of these maps is Herman Moll's *A New and Exact Map of the Dominions of the King of Great Britain on ye Continent of North America* (1715), which includes a vignette of an industrious community of beavers building a dam below Niagara Falls (Figure 1.3). In what is essentially an allegory of colonial settlement, the beavers, who walk upright, are shown cutting down trees, carrying them on their shoulders and using their flat tails as a plasterer's hawk to carry the mortar they have mixed for the dam. Against this highly fanciful portrayal of Canada's best-known, fur-bearing animal, Harris's insects and porcupine display the same commitment to scientific accuracy that structures modern maps. Natural history has become just as scientific as mapping. Nevertheless, his decision to use a butterfly, a moth, a beetle and a porcupine to represent Canadian nature is eccentric. Whereas in the elaborate cartouche that he originally drew for his map Harris had included images of a prowling bear and crouching lynx, the natures portrayed on *The Porcupine Map* have been chosen for both aesthetic and scientific reasons, for their capacity as 'natural curiosities' to elicit admiration and wonder.

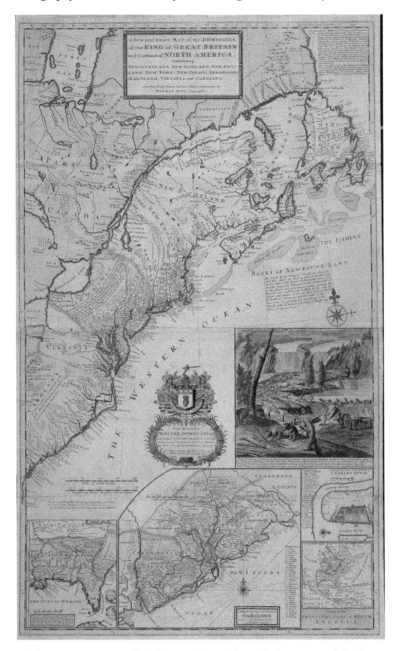

Figure 1.3 Herman Moll, *A New and Exact Map of the Dominions of the King of Great Britain on ye Continent of North America* (1715). Library and Archives Canada, R12999-0-2-E, H1/1000/1715.

The map is thus very much a reflection of the scientific interests of the virtuosi, for whom the primary purpose of science was to collect and put on display the rare and unusual. For Harris, the surface of the plate is a space that allows him to bring together and to display uncommon things. The goal here is not to show anything systematically but instead, like a curiosity cabinet, to provide, as Katie Whitaker remarks, the 'close juxtaposition of very different things crammed together in a confined space'.[12] In her discussion of the intimate connection between seventeenth-century Dutch art and map-making, Svetlana Alpers suggests that such maps were arts of description that sought 'to capture on a surface a great range of knowledge and information about the world'; rather than seeking to be 'a window on the world', they provided 'a surface on which is laid out an assemblage of the world'.[13] Harris uses the engraved plate in a similar manner as a surface to assemble different kinds of things, from different sources. In its incorporation of a map, armorial escutcheons, insects and a porcupine, his map is analogous to the 'magazine' or printed 'storehouse' in which it first appeared.

The appearance of *The Porcupine Map,* with its links to print culture, collecting, connoisseurship and consumption, registers the degree to which common British readers in the 1750s were primed for empire by graphic practices that promoted the pleasures of being curious about the natural world around them. It also powerfully emblematizes the manner in which places were being increasingly visualized through a combination of the skills of the cartographer and of the naturalist. In keeping with eighteenth-century mapping practice, Harris separates the insects and porcupine from the map proper. The combined need for both detailed maps and natural history illustrations rested on a division of labour that increasingly informs eighteenth-century geographical communication. With advances in the technologies of mapping, it was possible to see a map as a perfectly scaled-down version of the earth's skin, which meant that a blank space on a map was now seen as meaningful. Maps were emptied of native peoples, plants and animals, which were now relegated to the margins of the map or to cartouches, where indigenous people were often represented as being subservient to colonial authorities and only those plants and animals that were useful or curious to Europeans were displayed. Jeffers Lennox notes that Harris in his first map 'offered evidence that Halifax was in Mi'kma'ki, not Nova Scotia', by including an indigenous wigwam 'nestled among the trees' (*Homelands and Empires,* 142). The removal of indigenous people and animals from colonial spaces took place on maps before it took place on the ground. In this sense, eighteenth-century maps ignore inconvenient truths about the places they chart. This division of labour suited naturalists, too. Given the sheer number of new species of wildlife being discovered during the eighteenth century, and given the increasing importance of proper scientific description and illustration in the development of taxonomies and archives, it made sense for natural history to be accorded its own space in conjunction with imperial map-making. The representation of the natural history of a region was thus removed from maps, and the enormous task of visualizing global natures was taken up by the descriptive technologies of natural history – a discipline that now functioned alongside mapping as one of the primary means by which worlds were communicated across distances. In this regard, *The Porcupine Map* can thus be seen as one of the last examples of an Enlightenment colonial map in which indigenous animals are still displayed as belonging to a map.

On 26 August 1768, His Majesty's Bark *Endeavour*, under the command of Captain James Cook, departed Plymouth on a voyage that for the next eighty years would serve as a model of the ways in which cartography and natural history might work together in the collaborative production of geographical knowledge of the globe. From the beginning, the voyage was understood as both being scientific and state-authorized, having been initiated by the Royal Society of London and supported by the Admiralty, as part of an international effort to increase the utility of astronomical observations in the calculation of longitude (and thus the utility of global mapping) by observing the transit of Venus from different points on the earth. On 3 June 1769, in Tahiti, observations were duly taken – by Cook, by the British astronomer Charles Green, and by the two naturalists on board the *Endeavour*, Sir Joseph Banks and Daniel Solander. Having met the publicly stated goal of the expedition, Cook then turned to his other mission, which was to search for the Southern Continent and, were that to be found, to employ himself, as his instructions noted, 'diligently in exploring as great an Extent of the Coast as you can ... and also surveying and making Charts, and taking Views of such Bays, Harbours and Parts of the Coast as may be useful to Navigation'.[14] Cook returned to England having charted a significant portion of the eastern coast of Australia and the coastline of Tasmania. The impact of the voyage was enormous, and over the next decade, with two subsequent expeditions in 1772–5 and 1776–80, Cook would be lionized as embodying the character traits and technical skills that underpinned Britain's scientific hegemony as a global power, enshrined in global exploration and cartography. For late-eighteenth-century Britons, Cook expressed a new kind of national heroism: he was a figure whose leadership, courage and determination – but most of all his commitment to making scientifically accurate measurements in recording his travels – had made it possible to map new worlds.

Sir Nathaniel Dance-Holland's famous portrait of Cook (1776), which now hangs in the National Maritime Museum, was commissioned by Sir Joseph Banks and hung above his fireplace in his town house in Soho Square until his death in 1820. It was a fitting place for the painting, for, although it was Cook's navigational and mapping skills that laid the groundwork for British colonial territorial claims, it was natural history that captured the British public imagination and reinforced those claims. Much of the excitement produced by the three voyages arose from the manner in which cartography and natural history came together in an expanded idea of what a scientific geographical survey was, making it possible for Europeans to visualize the peoples, cultures, plants, animals and places that had previously been unknown to them. As multimedia productions, using detailed charts, coastline surveys, landscapes, narratives, and anthropological, botanical and zoological illustrations, artefacts and specimens, these voyages brought new worlds back to Europe, enabling many Europeans, as I have suggested elsewhere, to experience these worlds in translation and, by so doing, to believe and claim that they knew these places better than the people who inhabited them.[15] As Daniela Bleichmar has observed, 'eighteenth-century European natural history – both in the Spanish empire and elsewhere – was a dominantly visual discipline, with a methodology based on acts of expert viewing. Naturalists developed specialized ways of seeing by means of multimedia training that involved plants, texts and images.'[16] Cartography and natural history were pre-eminently verbal and graphic activities that, when brought together, provided a powerful medium for 'making the empire visible' while reinforcing the idea that empire was validated as much by the knowledge as by the new possibilities for trade and commerce that it produced.

It was Joseph Banks who first saw the possibility of an imperial alliance between cartography and natural history. The sheer amount of information that needed to be collected and displayed by the naturalists could not be achieved in the margins of a map, but the cartographer and the naturalist could combine their skills to produce a composite survey of the physical and cultural geography of a place. The idea probably had its inception two years earlier when Banks arranged his own personal natural history expedition to Newfoundland and Labrador. Whereas Moses Harris had found it necessary to sign up as a settler colonist to travel to Canada,

Banks, as an immensely wealthy, newly elected member of the Royal Society of London, was able to use his close friendship with Lieutenant Constantine John Phipps and his connections with John Montagu, fourth Earl of Sandwich, to obtain transport on HMS *Niger*. This was charged with carrying a party of mariners to Newfoundland and Labrador in order to build a fort at Chateau Bay and to do some coastal surveying, now that the area was almost completely under Britain's control as a result of the Treaty of Paris (1763). Banks's six-month stay was extraordinarily successful and catapulted him into the upper echelon of British natural history. Over the course of the expedition, he collected, described and identified approximately 302 species of plants, 86 species of birds, 8 mammals, and a small number of fish, crustaceans and insects.[17] Shortly after returning home, Banks arranged for the collection to be properly archived and illustrated. The bird skins were prepared for display, and he hired Sydney Parkinson, who would later serve as the natural history illustrator for the *Endeavour* voyage, to produce illustrations of them, along with some of the fish. For the plants, he brought in the famous botanical painter Georg Dionysius Ehret. The well-known naturalist Thomas Pennant, who was at the time working on what became the two-volume *Arctic Zoology* (1784), drew substantially on the notes, specimens and illustrations that Banks loaned him, and he arranged for additional drawings of the birds to be done by his assistant Peter Paillou. Johann Reinhold Forster and John Latham also made extensive use of these materials. The sheer number of people whom Banks employed in preparing, illustrating and archiving specimens indicates the degree to which he already understood natural history as a collaborative activity, indeed as a surveying activity, akin to mapping, that used specimens, images, and verbal descriptions and narratives in order to communicate information about these natures to others. Whereas a virtuoso, like Moses Harris, collected only those things that were rare, wonderful or intricate, Banks collected and communicated everything that he could find in Newfoundland, on the principle that the most important task of natural history was to produce complete inventories. As Linnaeus remarked in his 'Instructions for Naturalists on Voyages of Exploration' (1759), a naturalist, transported into a new world, should '*observe everything* ... so that nothing escapes his sharp eyesight and rapt attention'.[18] And he should write everything down.

It should not surprise us, given that the Treaty of Paris had made Canada an immediate focus of interest for colonial administrators and naturalists, that both Banks and Cook achieved individual distinction in their respective fields by engaging in surveys of Newfoundland. Cook was in Newfoundland when Banks arrived, and they may have briefly met just before Banks left for England. Having established a reputation as a meticulous surveyor for the charts that he drew of the St Lawrence River preparatory to the assault of Quebec in 1759, Cook was appointed in 1762 as the official surveyor of Newfoundland. He had already spent four years producing an extraordinary hydrographic survey and map of the island's coasts and harbours that covered 'six thousand miles of coastline'.[19] Cook had used the eclipse of the sun on 5 August 1766 to establish Newfoundland's longitude, which was communicated to the Royal Society through the physician and astronomer Dr John Bevis. Cook was, therefore, the obvious choice to lead an expedition to observe the Transit of Venus and to undertake a mapping expedition to the South Seas. When Banks got wind of the planned expedition, he once again drew on his membership in the Royal Society and his connections with the Admiralty to be invited to join the voyage. This time, however, Banks was not just seeking transportation. Instead, he made the case for an expanded role for natural history on the expedition, one that made it integral to advancing the economic interests of Britain. Reconceptualizing natural history in terms of its economic 'utility' rather than its capacity to satisfy 'curiosity', he persuaded the Admiralty that it was a 'science in the service of empire'.[20] The Admiralty's 'Instructions' duly reflected this new emphasis, for Cook was now required

> carefully to observe the Nature of the Soil, and the Products thereof; the Beasts and Fowls that inhabit or frequent it, the fishes that are found in the Rivers or upon the Coast and in what Plenty; and in case you find any Mines, Minerals or valuable stones you are to bring home Specimens of each, as also such Specimens of the Seeds of the Trees, Fruits and Grains as you may be able to collect, and Transmit them to our Secretary that We may cause proper Examination and Experiments to be made of them.[21]

As a meticulous hydrographer and skilful navigator, Cook did not need to be told that a naval vessel was an important tool for accurately mapping coastlines.[22] It was Joseph Banks, however, who first recognized that, when properly outfitted, it could also serve as an ideal laboratory for natural history research. First, it could transport the naturalist across great distances while also providing safe storage and transport for the specimens collected. It could also carry all the equipment necessary for collecting, identifying and preserving specimens. Once equipped with a good library, the ship could also host taxonomic and descriptive work; further, given the simultaneous mapping activities being undertaken on board, a naturalist always knew exactly where he was. On the *Endeavour*, Banks had all of these things. As John Ellis observes in a letter of 19 August 1768 to Linnaeus:

> No people ever went to sea better fitted out for the purpose of Natural History, nor more elegantly. They have got a fine library of Natural History; they have all sorts of machines for catching and preserving insects; all kinds of nets, trawls, drags, and hooks for coral fishing; they have even a curious contrivance of a telescope by which, put into the water, you can see the bottom to a great depth, where it is clear. They have many cases of bottles with ground stoppers, of several sizes, to preserve animals in spirits. They have the several sorts of salt to surround the seeds; and wax, both beeswax and that of the *Myrica*.[23]

Importantly, Banks was not alone; he brought with him trained scientific staff, so that the graphic and textual work of producing natural history – that is, illustrating, archiving, describing, and identifying specimens, as well as drawing landscapes and describing peoples – could be done during the voyage. There was Daniel Solander, one of the most knowledgeable Linnaean naturalists in Britain; two painters, Sydney Parkinson and Alexander Buchan; Herman Diedrich Spöring, as an assistant naturalist, secretary and additional draughtsman; together with four servants who were familiar with natural history. The voyage was extremely successful, with Banks collecting over 30,000 botanical and zoological specimens.

In the preparations for Cook's Second Voyage, Banks pushed hard to make HMS *Resolution* suitable for an even larger staff of naturalists by adding an additional deck. However, this affected the ship's manoeuvrability and seaworthiness, thus setting him at odds with Cook and the Admiralty, and Banks resigned any further role in the voyage. Nevertheless, he had established the model for subsequent scientific voyages. Kathleen Wilson remarks:

> The voyages were celebrated for marking new departures in empirical observation, discovery and collection of data. Their contribution to knowledge was widely hailed as prodigious: perfecting navigation, aiding astronomy, expanding botanical, geographical and cartographic knowledge, preserving seamen's health, and furnishing, through the vast quantities of 'first-hand' information acquired on different peoples and customs, the materials for a new 'science of Man'.[24]

Thus, natural history, by displaying and archiving the natures of other people and other places, *combined* with mapping to establish the hegemony of England as a scientific, navigational and colonial power. As it competed

with England to colonize the South Seas, France adopted the same model.
Nicholas Baudin's expedition to Australia (1800–4), for instance, included
five naturalists, two natural history painters, two mineralogists,
a cartographer and a geographer. For added emphasis, the two ships were
named *Le Géographe* and *Le Naturaliste*.

Both colonial mapping and natural history had in common the idea that
they were sciences of naming. Those who mapped *terra incognita* (i.e.,
places not yet known to Europeans) or those who first published scientifically correct descriptions of 'nondescripts' (i.e., animals or plants previously undescribed) had the right to name them, since naming, they
believed, was authorized by knowing. Natures that already had names
but had not been described scientifically were renamed. For Linnaeus,
the foundation of natural history as a science lay in systematic name-giving.
'The first step in wisdom', he writes, 'is to know the things themselves; this
notion consists in having a true idea of the objects; objects are distinguished and known by classifying them methodically and giving them
appropriate names. Therefore, classification and name-giving will be the
foundation of our science.'[25] As in mapping, knowing and naming were
inseparable. 'If you do not know the names of things', Linnaeus declared in
Philosophia Botanica (1751), 'the knowledge of them is lost too'.[26]
Consequently, for Linnaeus a species existed as a species only once it was
named. There is no question that Linnaean taxonomy made it possible to
order the natural world. Prior to his system, the same species could have
different names in different cultures, or different species could have the
same name. Linking naming to scientific knowledge prevented this confusion. However, it also took the authority for naming out of the hands of
indigenous peoples and put it into those of European naturalists, in the
same manner that cartographers claimed that by making a map they had
the right to name the places on it. Charles W. J. Withers has observed, in
relation to mapping, that 'attention to the name alone, either on the
ground or on an historical map, runs the risk of concerning itself with
ends and not with means; of ignoring, or, at best, underplaying the social
processes intrinsic to the authoritative act of naming'.[27] Since naturalists
associated naming with knowing, natural history could be used to promote
the view that Europeans knew the flora and fauna of places across the globe
better than their indigenous counterparts.

Inland expeditions in northern and north-western North America also
sought to combine map-making with a state-authorized commitment to
gathering information in natural history. In the famous Lewis and Clark
expedition (1804–6), Meriwether Lewis was responsible for most of the

natural history observations, while William Clark did the majority of the mapping. On John Franklin's first Coppermine expedition (1819–22), he did the surveying, while John Richardson served as the appointed natural-ist. Unlike maritime mapping expeditions, this kind of expedition depended on the knowledge, assistance and good will of First Nations people, who served as guides and often provided maps that were subse-quently incorporated into European maps, such as Turnor's large compos-ite *Map of Hudson's Bay and the Rivers and Lakes Between the Atlantick and Pacifick Oceans* (1794). As Richard I. Ruggles observes, during the period 1670 to 1870, 'the records refer to over fifty Indians and Inuit who drew original maps or provided sketches and information to the Europeans who used these as the basis for other maps'.[28] Inland mapping in the North American North-West during the eighteenth century, in other words, was accomplished by a wide range of intercultural collaborations, and the resulting maps, as David Bernstein observes, 'were hybrids of native and newcomer forms of knowledge'.[29] In striking contrast to the maps pro-duced by the great maritime expeditions, which conveyed the idea of indigenous lands as being empty and unmapped, and which allowed Europeans to claim that they were giving names to places that were being discovered for the first time, the maps of the north-west interior express a recognition – born from more than a century of cultural inter-action – that the places described on maps were *already* well known to First Nations people and that their place names were also perfectly suitable for the purposes of trade.

During the late 1760s, the Hudson's Bay Company was facing serious threats to its monopoly over trading in the vast inland area it controlled, called Rupert's Land. Efforts had been made during the 1740s, particularly by Arthur Dobbs, to revoke the Company's charter, based on arguments that opening up trade to others would immediately generate more trade and, with it, more economic benefit to Britain. The Hudson's Bay Company was also portrayed as an archaic institution, standing in the way of more scientific and progressive forms of knowledge that would lead to increased exploration of northern Canada and, it was hoped, to finding a North-West Passage.[30] To add to the difficulties of the Company, despite Britain's success in the Seven Years War, its coastal trading factories were now losing a substantial amount of the fur trade to more aggressive competition coming from new companies based in Montreal. As Andrew Graham, the chief trader at Severn House and the second at Fort York, remarked: 'Before the Conquest of Canada the French had houses for trade above us, and since the year 1765 have returned again, and now under the

English government seems [*sic*] to be carrying trade on with our Indians amongst the lakes &c with greater vigour than before, which will certainly oblige the Hudson's-bay Company to take some method to hinder the Canadian traders from running away with the prime furrs.'[31] Graham would eventually conclude that the best answer to this competition was for the Company to expand inland. Unfortunately, little was known about the geography of the north-west; the Company needed maps. At the same time, as part of a broader public relations campaign, it also needed to show that it was an enlightened, progressive entity, and what better way to demonstrate a commitment to science than by promoting natural history?

In 1772, Graham wrote the memorandum that authorized Samuel Hearne to establish the Company's first inland trading post, Cumberland House, on the Saskatchewan River in 1774. Also in 1771–2, Graham produced the first map of the intricate waterways west of Hudson Bay, basing it on information obtained from company employees and First Nations people. This map would be expanded and revised in *A Plan of Part of Hudson's-bay, and Rivers, Communicating with York Fort and Severn* (*c.* 1774) (Figure 1.4), which covers parts of what are now the provinces of Manitoba and Saskatchewan. There Graham indicated the First Nations lands through which these waters passed: the Keskachewan Nation (Plains Cree), who originally settled the Hudson Bay area from the coast to Frenchman's Lake (Lake Winnipeg) but had since moved south and west after the arrival of the English traders; the Western and Eastern Asinepoets (Assiniboine); the Ateemouspecky or Dog-rib Indians (Dene); and the Nekawawucks (Northern Ojibway), who began appearing in the region in the 1740s. In striking contrast to Harris's map, Graham's is filled with indigenous place names: for example, Manitouapau Lake and Hills, Athico Lake, Pemochicimo Lake, Auteatewan Lake, Kepehagan River, Shehonan Lake, Mistequonon Lake, Sakatakow Hills, Ascutimeg Lake and Nouchepan Mountains. Most of the English place names refer to trees or animals, suggesting that they are English translations of indigenous toponyms: Sturgeon River and Lake, Pine River, Deer Lake, Fox River, Moose Lake, Goose Lake and Eagle Hills. Graham also notes on his map the buffalo summer grounds, the location of Keskachewan tents near a buffalo pound in the Eagle Hills, and the region where the Cree and the Archithinue (Blackfeet) met to trade. He notes the vast prairie grasslands to the south, commenting: 'Barren ground. Buffalo plenty in winter.' What Graham's map represents is a region that is inhabited by many indigenous tribes and traders; it even registers the earlier French-Canadian fur trade in the name 'Frenchman's

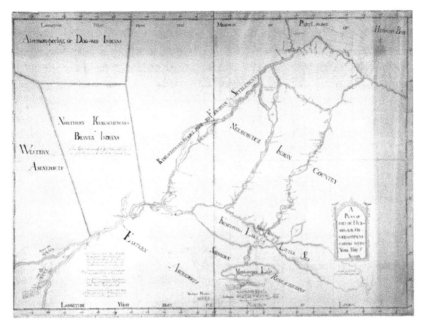

Figure 1.4 Andrew Graham, *A Plan of Part of Hudson's-bay, and Rivers, Communicating with York Fort and Severn* (c. 1774). Hudson's Bay Company Archives, Archives of Manitoba.

Lake'. Populated with First Nations and plant and animal names, the map points to the deep connection between indigenous people and a natural world that was being severely exploited by the fur trade.

Graham was also a devoted naturalist. Originally hired in 1749 as an 'Assistant Writer' at York Factory, he followed the example of its chief, James Isham, who in the 1740s supplied George Edwards with more than thirty species of bird, eight of them previously undescribed. In 1767, having gathered information about trading activity at the Hudson's Bay Company, First Nations people and the zoology of the region, and having also obtained through trade many 'skins stuffed and dried . . . from inland', Graham, who was by this time master at Severn House, began to put these materials together in a manuscript entitled 'Observations on Hudson's Bay'.[32] The result, as Glyndwr Williams comments, is 'an invaluable record of [a] man's experience in the human, wildlife and trading world of the Canadian North over a period of a quarter-century or more' ('Andrew Graham and Thomas Hutchings', 6). Graham completed the first draft of the section on mammals and birds in 1768–9, setting down all he knew or could learn about their life, habits and importance to First Nations people.[33] He lacked any natural history reference books, so animals were identified using whatever common names – either Cree or English – he knew. Thus he speaks of 'beavers', 'otters', 'wolves' and 'seals' without providing their indigenous names, while referring to others – 'musquashes', 'jackashes', 'wejacks', 'winusks' and 'waskesews' – without mentioning their respective English names ('muskrats', 'mink', 'fishers', 'woodchucks' and 'elk', respectively). The result is a culturally hybrid natural history whose multilingualism brings together the different kinds of knowledge that structured the understanding of the wildlife of Hudson Bay during the late eighteenth century.

During the winter of 1769–70, Graham was given leave in London. There he obtained a copy of the second edition of Thomas Pennant's *British Zoology* (1768–70), which he used to identify and name species and to adopt a more scientific model in his descriptions. Also, while in London, it seems likely that he met Pennant and (as Richard Glover argues) that they hatched a scheme 'to gather a collection of natural history specimens from Hudson Bay' (Williams, *Andrew Graham's Observations*, xxii). Daines Barrington, a friend of Pennant, then made an application to the Company on behalf of the Royal Society, and shortly thereafter the officers of Hudson's Bay Company trading posts were requested by the Committee to collect and send home 'Sundry Species' (Williams, 'Andrew Graham and Thomas Hutchings', 7). In 1771, Graham sent sixty-four skins of thirty-nine bird species, including type specimens of the great grey owl, boreal chickadee, blackpoll warbler and white-crowned sparrow. With the shipment, he also included a manuscript entitled 'Descriptive and Historical Remarks on the Several Articles sent from Severn River in Hudson's Bay', which has since been lost. However, before joining Cook on the Second Voyage, Johann Reinhold Forster used this manuscript to produce two articles that appeared in *Philosophical Transactions* in 1772. That year, there was also another shipment of seventy-two bird specimens along with a revised version of the mammal and bird section of Graham's *Observations on Hudson's Bay* manuscript, which now provided the indigenous names for most of the species, as well as offering additional information. Much of the new work on the manuscript was done by Thomas Hutchins, who had taken the post of surgeon at York Factory in 1766. Graham, who was acting chief at York that year, had asked him to provide more detailed scientific descriptions of 'the plumage of the Birds'.[34] Through the descriptive lists and the specimens sent by Graham, as Glover remarks, 'a whole generation knew better which birds inhabited the wild and remote Canadian north than which were to be found in the flourishing and well-settled eastern United States'.[35]

Although eighteenth-century naturalists emphasized their centrality within this knowledge-making activity (since they were the scientists who wielded the pens and had the power to classify and name natures), we should not forget that colonial natural history was an activity conducted in the context of a truly global, multi-disciplinary network, a massive archiving not only of the world's natures but also of different peoples' understanding of the natures around them. Unfortunately, in both maps and natural histories, the indigenous understanding of places and natures was often improperly acknowledged or underwent erasure. Map-making and natural history became a symbolic mode of possessing places and natures by renaming them. Nevertheless, the amount of natural knowledge that was gathered by colonial naturalists is little short of astonishing and clearly speaks to the enormous importance of natural history as a new information technology and to the energy with which this new science was pursued, both in the field and in collaborative interaction with indigenous peoples. Humphrey Marten, chief at Albany, who contributed a small number of birds to the 1772 shipment to the Royal Society, remarks on the challenges that faced Hudson's Bay Company employees as they sought to produce Canadian natural history:

> I hope those Gentlemen that inspect the aforewritten history of birds will observe, that I do not absolutely declare all I have set down to be truth, except in what regards the swallow and martin. As to those birds I was a constant eyewitness ... for more than two years. As to the others, as to number of eggs, food, and the difference between male and female, I was obliged to have the best Indian intelligence I could get. I trusted not the assertions of any single person, let his age or experience be what it would, therefore hope I am near the truth, if not quite so.[36]

The possibility of alternative ways of understanding nature thus remains embedded in early Canadian maps and natural histories, to the extent that they voice not only European conceptions of new and unfamiliar places and natures but also those of indigenous peoples from within their own distinctive cultures and ecologies.

During the 1780s, the manuscript of *Observations on Hudson's Bay* had an enormous impact on British metropolitan naturalists, including figures such as John Latham and Thomas Pennant. It was Pennant who requested that Graham supply the indigenous names of Canadian mammals and birds, and he included these names in his *Arctic Zoology*. John Richardson, publishing the natural history materials emerging from the two Franklin land expeditions in *Fauna Boreali-Americana* (1829–37), expanded this commitment. For example, after noting the scientific name and classification of the pine marten (*Mustela martes*) – citing Linnaeus, Johann Friedrich Gmelin, Pennant, Sir Edward Sabine and Richard Harlan – he indicates that the animal is called 'Wawpeestan' among the Cree and 'Wawbeechins' among Algonquins. Furthermore, American fur dealers knew it as a 'sable', while the lists of the Hudson's Bay Company refer to it as a 'martin'. Richardson clearly recognized that, to understand an animal, one needed to know as much about the history of its names and its place within different communities as about its place in a scientific taxonomy.[37] As the nineteenth century progressed, however, much of the hybrid world of natural history was erased. Just as the indigenous place names on maps began to disappear, so did the indigenous names of most of Canada's animals. Although one can still point to the 'moose' or 'moosu', very few Canadian animal names still express a direct connection to indigenous cultures. The 'musquash' – that creature whose head 'bobs above the water' – was soon translated into a 'musk-beaver' by metropolitan naturalists and now goes by the name 'muskrat'. The 'waskasew' is no longer translated as 'red deer' but instead is called an 'elk', which gives rise to the strange historical irony that the city of Red Deer, Alberta, and the river on which it is situated are named after an animal that is no longer known by that name in Canada.

In a country where natures and places were possessed in and through translation, it is perhaps not surprising to learn that even naturalists were not immune to being erased from the histories they wrote. Initially asked by Graham to amplify the scientific descriptions of the bird section of *Observations on Hudson's Bay*, Thomas Hutchins continued to expand Graham's work until, by the 1780s, he had convinced himself that he was its true author. He had developed a knack for natural history descriptions and probably thought that Graham could now be considered as a native informant whose role in the writing of the manuscript no longer needed to be acknowledged. Metropolitan naturalists apparently believed him. Richardson, who read the manuscript in the Hudson's Bay Company offices, also thought that Hutchins was the author, noting that 'in a few first sheets of this work Mr. Graham is through mistake quoted as the author of these manuscript notices'.[38] That is why, when it came to naming a subspecies of the Canada goose, Richardson honoured Hutchins: 'We have designated the *Apistiskeesh* [the indigenous name for the bird] by the name of *Hutchinsii*, in honour of a gentleman from whom Pennant and Latham derived most of their information respecting the Hudson's Bay birds'.[39] In this gesture, Graham's enormous impact, like that of indigenous people, went unacknowledged, until 1969, when *Andrew Graham's Observations on Hudson's Bay 1767–1791* was finally published under the auspices of the Hudson's Bay Record Society.

For colonial cartographers and naturalists, power lay in naming peoples, places and things. Because *knowing* was integrally bound up with *naming*, those who claimed the authority to describe and redescribe, to name and to rename, the geography of the earth and all its inhabitants, both human and non-human, were also through their maps and taxonomic lists staking claims across the globe. Map-making and natural history were inherently palimpsestic activities, forms of knowledge-making that possessed the earth by erasing or rewriting what was originally there. That is why the history of the production of colonial maps and natural histories is so important. It allows us to begin to do the historical work of recovering what the earth, its peoples and the non-human world were like before there were maps and natural histories.

Notes

1. 'Table of Contents', *Gentleman's Magazine* 20 (February 1750): 50.
2. See Starr Douglas, 'Dr John Fothergill: Significant Donor', in *William Hunter's World: The Art and Science of Eighteenth-Century Collecting*, eds. E. Geoffrey Hancock, Nick Pearce and Mungo Campbell (Dorchester: Ashgate, 2015), 165–75, 167.
3. For this version of the map and for detailed discussions of the relationship between the Thomas Jefferys map and those Harris produced, see Joan Dawson, *The Mapmaker's Eye: Nova Scotia Through Early Maps* (Halifax: Nimbus Publishing and the Nova Scotia Museum, 1988), 25–8, 112–15; and Jeffers Lennox, *Homelands and Empires: Indigenous Spaces, Imperial Fictions, and Competition* (Toronto, ON: University of Toronto Press, 2017), 140–6.
4. Published in the September and October 1749 issues (408–10, 472–3) and the February 1750 issue (72–3) of the *Gentleman's Magazine*, these letters were anonymous, but internal evidence indicates Harris as author.
5. For the role of maps in this conflict, see Lennox, *Homelands and Empires*.
6. Jared Farmer, *On Zion's Mount: Mormons, Indians, and the American Landscape* (New York: Cambridge University Press, 2002), 11.
7. Thomas F. Thornton, 'Anthropological Studies of Native American Place Naming', *American Indian Quarterly* 21:2 (1997): 209–28, 209.
8. *Gentleman's Magazine* 20 (February 1750): 73.

48 ALAN BEWELL

9. George Edwards, *A Natural History of Uncommon Birds . . . Containing the Figures of Sixty Birds and two Quadrupeds*, 4 vols. (London: Printed for the author, 1743–51), I, 52.

10. See Walter K. Morrison, 'The Porcupine Map', *ACML Bulletin* 62 (March 1987): 18.

11. Wilma George, *Animals and Maps* (Berkeley: University of California Press, 1969), 82.

12. Katie Whitaker, 'The Culture of Curiosity', in *Cultures of Natural History*, eds. N. Jardine, J. A. Secord, and E. C. Spary (Cambridge: Cambridge University Press, 1996), 75–90, 87. See also Barbara M. Benedict, *Curiosity: A Cultural History of Early Modern Inquiry* (Chicago, IL: University of Chicago Press, 2001); and Lorraine Daston and Katharine Park, *Wonders and the Order of Nature* (New York: Zone Books, 1998).

13. Svetlana Alpers, *The Art of Describing: Dutch Art in the Seventeenth Century* (London: John Murray, 1983), 124.

14. Commissioners for the Admiralty, 'Instructions', in *The Journals of Captain James Cook on His Voyages of Discovery*, 4 vols., ed. J. C. Beaglehole (Cambridge: For the Hakluyt Society at the University Press, 1968–74), I, cclxxxii.

15. See Alan Bewell, *Natures in Translation: Romanticism and Colonial Natural History* (Baltimore, MD: Johns Hopkins University Press, 2017), 33–52.

16. Daniela Bleichmar, *Visible Empire: Botanical Expeditions and Visual Culture in the Hispanic Enlightenment* (Chicago, IL: University of Chicago Press, 2012), 8, 9.

17. See A. M. Lysaght, *Joseph Banks in Newfoundland and Labrador, 1766: His Diary, Manuscripts and Collections* (Berkeley: University of California Press, 1971), 293, 397–421.

18. *The Linnaeus Apostles: Global Science and Adventure*, 8 vols., ed. Lars Hansen (London: I. K. Foundation, 2010), I, 204.

19. J. C. Beaglehole, *The Life of Captain James Cook* (Stanford, CA: Stanford University Press, 1974), 68.

20. See John Gascoigne, Science in the Service of Empire: Joseph Banks, the British State and the Uses of Science in the Age of Revolution (Cambridge: Cambridge University Press, 1998).

21. Beaglehole, ed., *Journals*, I, cclxxxii–cclxxxiii.

22. See Richard Sorrenson, 'The Ship as a Scientific Instrument in the Eighteenth Century', *Osiris* 11 (1996): 221–36.

23. James Edward Smith, ed., *A Selection of the Correspondence of Linnaeus and Other Naturalists*, 2 vols. (London: Longman, Hurst, Rees, Orme, and Brown, 1821), I, 231.

24. Kathleen Wilson, *The Island Race: Englishness, Empire and Gender in the Eighteenth Century* (London and New York: Routledge, 2003), 58.

25. Carl Linnaeus, *Systema Naturae, 1735. Facsimile of the First Edition*, ed. and trans. M. S. J. Engel-Ledeboer and H. Engle (Nieuwkoop: B. de Graaf, 1964), 19.

26. Carl Linnaeus, *Linnaeus' Philosophia Botanica*, trans. Stephen Freer (Oxford: Oxford University Press, 2003), 169.

27. Charles W. J. Withers, 'Authorizing Landscape: "Authority", Naming and the Ordnance Survey's Mapping of the Scottish Highlands in the Nineteenth Century', *Journal of Historical Geography* 26:4 (2000): 532–54, 533.

28. Richard I. Ruggles, *A Country So Interesting: The Hudson's Bay Company and Two Centuries of Mapping, 1670–1870* (Montreal, QC: McGill-Queen's University Press, 1991), 7.

29. David Bernstein, 'Negotiating Nation: Native Participation in the Cartographic Construction of the Trans-Mississippi West', *Environment and Planning A: Economy and Space* 48:3 (2016): 626–47, 627. See also Barbara Belyea, 'Amerindian Maps: The Explorer as Translator', *Journal of Historical Geography* 18:3 (1992): 267–77; and 'Mapping the Marias: The Interface of Native and Scientific Cartographies', *Great Plains Quarterly* 17:3/4 (1997): 165–84; Theodore Binnema, 'How Does a Map Mean? Old Swan's Map of 1801 and the Blackfoot World', in *From Rupert's Land to Canada: Essays in Honour of John E. Foster*, eds. Theodore Binnema, Gerhard Ens, and Roderick C. Macleod (Edmonton: University of Alberta Press, 2001), 201–24.

30. For an important study of the ways in which this economic and scientific debate shaped how Canadian weather was understood, see Morgan Vanek, 'The Politics of the Weather: The Hudson's Bay Company and the Dobbs Affair', *Journal for Eighteenth-Century Studies* 38:3 (2015): 395–411.

31. Glyndwr Williams, ed., *Andrew Graham's Observations on Hudson's Bay 1767–1791* (London: The Hudson's Bay Record Society, 1969), 260.

32. Glyndwr Williams, 'Andrew Graham and Thomas Hutchings: Collaboration and Plagiarism in 18th-Century Natural History', *The Beaver* 308:4 (1978): 4–14, 7.

33. This version is available as 'Andrew Graham's Bird Observations Written at Severn, 1768', Manuscript E.2/5, Hudson's Bay Company Archives, Provincial Archives of Manitoba, Supplementary Document #1 to C. Stuart Houston, Tim Ball and Mary Houston, eds., *Eighteenth-Century Naturalists of Hudson Bay* (Montreal, QC: McGill-Queen's University Press, 2003).

34. 'Thomas Hutchins' Manuscript Accompanying Bird and Mammal Specimens Submitted to England from York Factory, 28 August 1772', Property of the Royal Society of London, England, Supplementary Document #2 to Houston *et al.* (eds.), *Eighteenth-Century Naturalists of Hudson Bay*.

35. Williams, ed., *Andrew Graham's Observations*, xiii.

36. Williams, ed., *Andrew Graham's Observations*, 80–1, n. 5.

37. See John Richardson, *Fauna Boreali-Americana; Or, The Zoology of the Northern Parts of British America: Containing Descriptions of the Objects of Natural History Collected on the Late Northern Land Expeditions, under Command of Captain Sir John Franklin*, 4 vols. (London: John Murray, 1829–37), I, 51.

38. Richardson, *Fauna Boreali-Americana*, II, xxxix.

39. Richardson, *Fauna Boreali-Americana*, II, 470.

CHAPTER 2

'That Experienced Surveyor, Colonel Mudge'

Romantic Representations of the Ordnance Survey Map-Maker, 1791–1830

Rachel Hewitt

Surveying

In March 1798, Captain William Mudge was appointed 'Superintendant [sic] and Director of the Trigonometrical Survey', a body charged with conducting a nationwide triangulation that would underpin a new, pioneeringly accurate topographic map of the United Kingdom.[1] Triangulation, or 'trigonometrical surveying', was a relatively innovative surveying technique whereby the observation of angles between 'trigonometrical stations' or 'trig points' facilitated the creation of a lattice of accurate measurements between key landmarks across a large territory. The resulting matrix could be used for the numerical data it produced about the latitude and longitude of certain spatial positions. It could also provide the foundation for a detailed plotting or 'interior survey' of the topography of the landscape on which the triangulation was superimposed. Triangulation's efficacy was vastly improved in the mid-eighteenth century owing to the development of instruments and lenses capable of measuring angles between sightlines to a greater degree of minute accuracy than ever before.

In June 1791, the 'Trigonometrical Survey' was formally established as an endeavour overseen by the Board of Ordnance, a military body among whose responsibilities map-making was a minor, but significant, component. Enthusiasm for launching a comprehensive, up-to-date map of the nation had been building in military and scientific communities throughout the second half of the eighteenth century. In the early 1790s, following the outbreak of the French Revolution, the project was catalysed by a renewed eagerness for surveying and improving Britain's coastal fortifications against the threat of invasion. June 1791 marked eleven months since the death of the surveyor William Roy, who had played a crucial role in conducting a military survey of Scotland in the wake of the 1745 Jacobite rebellion. In the 1780s, Roy had become convinced that 'the honour of the nation' depended on creating 'a map of the British islands' that was 'greatly superior in point of accuracy to any that is now extant', and he had made inroads into fulfilling that ambition, overseeing a triangulation between the Greenwich and Paris observatories.[2]

In June 1791, the Master-General of the Board of Ordnance, Charles Lennox, third Duke of Richmond, built on Roy's work and secured George III's consent and funding to proceed 'with the Trigonometrical Operation begun by the late Major General Roy'.[3] Known in its early days as the 'Duke of Richmond's survey', the 'General Survey', the 'British Survey', and most often as the 'Trigonometrical Survey', its surveyors were initially concerned with conducting a triangulation across the counties of East and West Sussex, Kent, Essex, Hampshire, Surrey, Dorset, Devon, and Cornwall.[4] The trigonometrical survey would eventually extend across the nation, all the way from Land's End in Cornwall up to the Shetland Isles. In 1795, the project's scope became more extensive. Interior surveyors were employed to flesh out the evolving skeleton framework and produce detailed topographic maps of each county, and from 1809 to 1810 onward – once the paper maps themselves had begun to appear – the undertaking gradually acquired the name 'Ordnance Survey', after the Board of Ordnance under whose aegis it operated.[5] That designation persisted even after the military applications of the map-making project had, by the mid-nineteenth century, diminished in importance as a result of the increasingly civilian nature of the initiative. Today, the name 'Ordnance Survey' is retained despite the mapping project's status as a public corporation controlled by central government, rather than a military endeavour. The twenty-first-century Ordnance Survey is Britain's national mapping agency, the foremost provider of paper maps and digital geographical data to consumers including the military, the public sector (including councils, the NHS, and national parks), and private sector agencies and companies (e.g. energy, telecommunications, transport, land and property, and financial services) – as well as enthusiastic individual hikers, fell-runners, cyclists, and tourists. I will anachronistically employ the name 'Ordnance Survey' throughout this chapter to refer to an endeavour that originated in intertwined efforts to improve military engineering, geodesy, and mathematical instruments in the late Enlightenment but which swiftly became integral to the infrastructure of a newly united nation and to the day-to-day lives of many citizens across the industrializing nation.

During the first two to three decades of its activities, the Ordnance Survey attained a certain prominence in publications ranging from newspaper reports to travel writing, topography and natural history, poetry, philosophical reflections, assessments of the effect of taxation, and scientific appraisals of its methods and utility. That the Survey sparked general interest early on is indicated by the fact that it was evoked in seemingly incongruous settings. In *Elements of the Philosophy of the Human Mind* (1814), for example, the Scottish philosopher Dugald Stewart presented the Trigonometrical Survey as a material, real-world example of the perfect logic usually reserved for abstract geometry.[6] The rapidity with which the Ordnance Survey pervaded popular consciousness is partly explained by the decision taken by its principal surveyors, William Mudge and Edward Williams (who died in 1798, after which Mudge succeeded as its director), together with their assistant Isaac Dalby, to disseminate information about the triangulation project to the reading public in 'Accounts' published in the *Philosophical Transactions of the Royal Society* in 1795, 1797, 1800, and 1803.[7] In 1799, Mudge and Dalby collated the first two *Philosophical Transactions* articles, appended a lengthy preface, and published a stand-alone volume, *An Account of the Operations Carried on for Accomplishing a Trigonometrical Survey of England and Wales.*[8] Second and third volumes of the *Account* appeared in 1801 and 1811, and the 'first series' of the maps themselves began appearing on the 1-inch-to-1-mile scale between 1801 and 1873. The first maps were sold from the Board of Ordnance's headquarters in the Tower of London and from the engraver William Faden's premises at 6 Charing Cross; the price ranged from three guineas (£3 3s) per county survey (for the first map of Kent) up to six guineas (£6 6s) for the 1816 map of Devon. Civilian access to these first maps, which were printed on enormous rectangular sheets, each around thirty inches wide and twenty inches high (the Devon map extended over eight sheets), was primarily restricted to wealthy 'gentlemen' who sought 'to procure a map of the country surrounding their own habitations'.[9] Over the next half-century, the price of a county map diminished to 2s 6d, which was considered to be 'within the reach of all who may require such aid'.[10]

For the purposes of this chapter, I propose to concentrate on the presence of the Ordnance Survey's director William Mudge in a range of texts published between the mid-1790s and the 1820s. These textual representations of Mudge are notable, since they indicate a departure from depictions of the figure of the map-maker or surveyor in earlier eighteenth-century literature and since very few real-life Ordnance Survey map-makers or specifically named surveyors – as opposed to cartographers as a generic category – figure in literary texts in quite the same way. Depictions of Mudge variously deployed the figure of the map-maker as a route to exploring, among other things, late-eighteenth-century conceptions of the impartial spectator's role in politics and science or the significance of elevated observation of landscape. Writers' representations of Mudge were sometimes prompted by their interest in his personal background or by the emergence of the map-maker as a prominent civil or military servant rather than a private employee. The visibility to civilian onlookers of military activities, together with the relatively recent importance of accurate surveying to military strategy, also lay behind the cultural prominence of the military map-maker. The figure of Mudge was used to interrogate the significance of the trained observer in late-Enlightenment efforts to improve accuracy and as part of discussions surrounding appropriate means of representing and experiencing landscape – a defining feature of literary Romanticism. Mudge's cultural presence was the product of a certain historical moment in which all these strands coincided, coming to light in public discussion in the space of only a few decades. The disappearance of the Ordnance Survey map-maker from cultural view after the brief moment of Mudge's textual visibility can be traced, in part, to shifts that Lorraine Daston and Peter Galison track in conceptions of the role of the individual observer in the process of attaining 'objectivity'. Alterations in the Ordnance Survey's own organizational structure and its specific undertakings also, arguably, played a part in the disappearance of the OS map-maker from literary view.[11]

The fleeting appearance of the Ordnance Survey map-maker in literature has been literally relegated to a footnote in history: Mudge appears, albeit unnamed, in a note dictated by William Wordsworth to Isabella Fenwick in 1843, explicating an 'inscription', 'Written with a Slate-pencil on a Stone, on the Side of the Mountain of Black Comb', that he had composed thirty years earlier.[12] But the argument of *this* chapter is that the apparently ephemeral interest in Mudge's temporary cultural presence, followed by the disappearance of the named Ordnance Survey map-maker from literary representation, in fact illuminates far wider and more significant shifts in British science and the relationship between military and civilian cultures.

Mapping Mudge

Before exploring how Mudge was represented in Romantic-era texts, it is necessary to consider the familial context in which he was raised. Mudge's family connections situated him in close proximity to prominent figures and debates in mid-Enlightenment Britain; their influence undoubtedly shaped Mudge's conception of the Ordnance Survey's national role and prompted his own relative fame.

William Mudge was born in 1762 into a family with well-established cultural and mathematical connections. Mudge's uncle, Thomas Mudge, had been apprenticed as a teenager to a London watchmaker, after which he set up his own successful business and was commissioned to construct timepieces for King Ferdinand VI of Spain. Thomas entered into the long-running eighteenth-century 'longitude debate', during which mathematical instrument makers, navigators, and astronomers competed to ascertain the most accurate, reliable method of determining longitude at sea, for a prize of £20,000 offered by the Board of Longitude.[13] Like his predecessor John Harrison, Thomas Mudge defended the 'chronometer method' of calculating longitude on board ship, arguing that if a mariner could transport a clock set to the time of the home port, the time difference between that port and the precise time measured at the ship's position (determined through astronomical observations) would allow longitude to be accurately ascertained. But it was an almost insurmountably difficult task to construct instruments capable of keeping time despite the rolling of the ship and the dramatic changes in temperature and air pressure experienced during global voyages.

Harrison had constructed five such timekeepers. After his death in 1776, Thomas Mudge produced three more, which were tested and found to exceed Harrison's in accuracy over the long term. But, like Harrison, Thomas Mudge was acting in opposition to the Astronomer Royal, Nevil Maskelyne, who doubted whether – even if a single, sufficiently accurate and hardy timekeeper could be made – it could be duplicated cheaply enough to allow each and every mariner across the world to benefit from it. Maskelyne supported an alternative, potentially more accessible method of determining longitude: the 'lunar distance method', according to which time on board ship was measured by observing the moon's position and compared to the time in Greenwich by consulting a volume of 'lunar tables'. Calculation of the time difference between the two revealed the longitudinal difference. Maskelyne's resistance to Thomas Mudge's methodology led to the Board of Longitude's financial reward being withheld from the latter, and in 1793 Mudge's eldest son Thomas – William Mudge's cousin – brought his father's case before Parliament, seeking remuneration.[14] He was eventually presented with the sum of £2,500, but Maskelyne and Joseph Banks, president of the Royal Society, remained concerned that any reward given to the chronometer method would 'discourage the advancement of knowledge'.[15]

Thomas Mudge Sr's efforts linked the family name to Enlightenment advances in mathematical instrument-making, and William Mudge almost certainly derived his own early interest in horology from his uncle's enterprise. Much later, when Mudge took up the directorship of the Ordnance Survey, he was acutely sensitive to that project's indebtedness to an Enlightenment scientific tradition responsible for rapid mid-century progress in navigation, astronomy, and instrument-making, in which his own uncle played a role. However, the specific terms of the 'longitude debate' positioned Mudge's family in opposition to the scientific institutions of the Royal Society and the figureheads of its president and the Astronomer Royal. Seeking to publicize the Ordnance Survey's activities and establish for the Survey the authority of a national, scientifically rigorous institution, Mudge needed to cultivate the Royal Society's approval. Its journal, the *Philosophical Transactions*, offered a wide-reaching forum for dissemination of the Survey's aims, methods, and results. So, perhaps with an awareness of the family history of antagonism with Joseph Banks and Nevil Maskelyne, Mudge was chary of alienating such figures and institutions, and, although he later inserted a small note of support for his uncle's chronometers into the 1800 'Account of the Trigonometrical Survey', he was, in general, notably reticent about this aspect of his family history.[16]

Throughout this chapter, I challenge the dominant popular narrative concerning the Ordnance Survey's origin: that it lay chiefly in an acute military response, necessitated at the crisis point of the early 1790s by the outbreak of the Revolutionary War. I hope to show that, as a project, the Ordnance Survey emerged from ongoing, interlinked trajectories of progress in civilian geodesy and scientific instrumentation, alongside other cultural shifts such as the budding impetus towards data collection and survey methodology, exemplified, for example, by Sir John Sinclair's *Statistical Accounts of Scotland* (1791–9). It is also important to consider the historic associations of maps with state control and surveillance – an aspect of the Survey's identity that demanded consideration during its mapping of Ireland in the 1820s and 1830s. I argue that Mudge's far-sighted and daring innovation lay less in seeing the potential of accurate topographical surveying for military defence (although he was certainly aware of the French military's advances in this area) than in recognizing the potential for a national military institution to host and sponsor a trigonometrical surveying project whose principal importance lay in its scientific and instrumental advances. As I will show, a notable feature of the Ordnance Survey's early reception is the fact that very few people commented on its military utility; there is little evidence of military use of the published maps themselves on the ground.

Instead, the Ordnance Survey provides an example of the cross-fertilization of military and civilian cultures in the eighteenth century. Mudge himself – his background, expertise, decisions, social networks – embodies such fruitful interchange of ideas, ambitions, and methods across fields that include mathematical instrument-making, geodesy, art, astronomy, ordnance and surveying. Mudge's ambition for the Survey lay primarily in its potential to provide the civilian population with vastly more accurate and wide-ranging information about the national territory than currently existed. In a period whose literary and aesthetic endeavours were marked by explorations of the relationship between the individual, landscape and nation state, the Ordnance Survey possessed far-reaching cultural relevance alongside its scientific significance. That cultural relevance was not a coincidence: Mudge grew up on the periphery of one of the most important cultural networks of the mid-Enlightenment.

If William Mudge's uncle provided a direct familial link to the scientific advances of the age, other members of his family offered a route into one of the most prominent cultural circles of eighteenth-century London. Mudge's father, John Mudge, had grown up in a village north-east of Plymouth, Plympton St Maurice, where he became close friends with the son of the local headmaster Samuel Reynolds, a boy named Joshua. By the age of eight, the young Joshua Reynolds had taught himself the rudiments of perspective and was engaged in drawing 'the schoolhouse according to rule'.[17] He was particularly fond of William's grandfather, Zachariah Mudge, vicar of St Andrew's Church in Plymouth. Zachariah had published a well-received selection of politically conservative, monarchist sermons in 1739, stressing how there is 'something sacred in the Persons of Princes, a kind of Divine Cloud hovering over their Heads'.[18] It was subsequently said of Reynolds, once he had become founder and first president of the Royal Academy of Arts and a major European portraitist and painter, that he owed 'his first disposition to generalize, and to view things in the abstract, to old Mr Mudge'.[19]

After training at Plymouth Hospital, William's father, John Mudge, became a physician specializing in the treatment of smallpox and respiratory illnesses; 'Mudge's Inhalers' were advertised widely.[20] His friendship with Joshua Reynolds survived beyond childhood, and in 1752 the latter travelled to Devon to consult his physician friend about his poor health and painted his portrait. A few years later, when John Mudge's eldest son was too ill to travel from London to Devon to celebrate his sixteenth birthday with his father, Reynolds instead painted a portrait of the boy and dispatched it to his old friend, reportedly exclaiming, 'Never mind! I will send you to your father!' (Flint, *Mudge Memoirs*, 117). In 1762, Reynolds visited John Mudge in Plymouth, along with Samuel Johnson, and the pair resided with Mudge for nearly four weeks, attending Zachariah's sermons and visiting the newly built lighthouse on Eddystone Rocks, a recent construction of Mudge's friend, the civil engineer John Smeaton (Flint, *Mudge Memoirs*, 15; Leslie, *Sir Joshua Reynolds*, I, 116–17).[21] John Mudge's second wife, Jane, was heavily pregnant with William Mudge at the time, and during William's childhood, his father and grandfather were regular fixtures among a London-centred social circle that included Reynolds, Johnson, David Garrick, Oliver Goldsmith and Edmund Burke. In the early 1790s, Burke arranged for Zachariah Mudge's sermons to be republished in Britain as part of a counter-revolutionary effort to assert the need for monarchic hierarchy; he was said to 'esteem' Zachariah as 'an idol', 'a learned and venerable old man' (Flint, *Mudge Memoirs*, 20; Reynolds, *Works*, I, xxxiii–iv). It was likely that William Mudge was introduced to Burke: the latter was recorded reminiscing, 'I have lived in intimacy with two generations of Mudges, and have much pleasure in making the acquaintance of a third' (Flint, *Mudge Memoirs*, 20). Biographers of the Mudge family claim that Samuel Johnson was made godfather to William Mudge and that, when Mudge was accepted into the Royal Military Academy at Woolwich, aged fifteen, Johnson visited him, bestowing a gift of a guinea and a book.

In 1779, aged nineteen, William Mudge gained a commission in the Royal Regiment of Artillery, was sent to South Carolina to participate in the American War of Independence and returned in 1781 when, at the age of twenty-one, he was dispatched for training in the Drawing Room at the Tower of London among the Board of Ordnance's surveyors. In 1791, Mudge's old tutor, Charles Hutton, Professor of Mathematics at the Royal Military Academy, recommended him to Charles Lennox, third Duke of Richmond, as an ideal candidate to assist the newly founded trigonometrical survey, and in 1798, after the death of its first director, Edward Williams, Mudge acceded to the directorship.

Mudge's family circle therefore provided him with access to many of the most prominent cultural figures of Enlightenment Britain, which shaped his approach to his directorship of the Ordnance Survey. Certain comparable predecessors in Enlightenment military surveying – for example,

Hugh Debbeig, who was employed in the 1760s on 'a Secret Service to Survey the principle sea-ports of France & Spain & to make Sketches and Drawings and to take Plans thereof with a view to Discover and State the Strength and weakness of those places' – arguably engaged with military cartography in a way that was mostly restricted specifically to military intelligence and strategy.[22] But Mudge saw himself more in the tradition of the late-eighteenth-century military surveyor William Roy. Alongside conducting a Military Survey of Scotland in the 1740s, followed by maps of Minden and Dunkirk, descriptive and cartographic surveys of the British coast, barometric measurements of landmarks around London, and the geodetic measurement between the observatories of Paris and London, Roy was also a dedicated antiquarian. He was a prominent member of the Society of Antiquaries, who clearly perceived the opportunity presented by military surveying for recording historical and cultural aspects of landscape and topography. 'While the ranges of mountains, the long extended valleys, and remarkable rivers, continue the same, the reasons of war cannot essentially change', Roy wrote in *Military Antiquities of the Romans in North Britain*.[23] Landscape was the theatre in which a variety of human activities took place; in his view, surveyors enjoyed privileged opportunities to chart relics of human and geological activity – 'to compare present things with past' and 'converse with the people of those remote times' – that exceeded direct military relevance (*Military Antiquities*, i).

So although the Ordnance Survey was initially housed in the military context of the Board of Ordnance, staffed by military engineers, it owed its inception more to civilian traditions of Enlightenment advances in geodesy, navigation, and mathematical instrument-making, as well as to William Roy's creative, expansive conception of military cartography's applications, than to the immediate military requirement for a new survey of the British coastline that emerged in the early 1790s. Mudge's personal background was rooted more deeply in civilian aesthetic and scientific cultures than in military protocol. He continued in Roy's tradition, repeatedly asserting the public utility of the military map-making project under his jurisdiction. Mudge willingly contributed the data resulting from the Ordnance Survey's triangulation to a number of civilian projects, including the thirteenth edition of Daniel Paterson's *New and Accurate Description of the Roads in England and Wales, and Part of the Roads of Scotland*, which thanked 'the very ingenious Major Mudge' for the 'Measurements of the Heights of Mountains and other Eminences, so accurately taken in the grand trigonometrical survey of the kingdom'.[24]

Mudge knew that private estate surveyors and county map-makers would use the Ordnance Survey's data to underpin their own projects, and he appears to have been supportive of this appropriation of information.[25] He also donated free copies of the Ordnance Survey's maps to libraries, institutions and associations, through which those who could not afford to purchase them might still witness the new surveys.

Today, such devolved use of Ordnance Survey data does not appear remotely strange: the twenty-first-century OS provides data to private and public-sector organizations, across retail, energy, telecommunications, transport, financial services, and town, parish and community councils. But in 1803, this creative, expansive vision of the Ordnance Survey's potential applications was an innovative utilization of military information. Mudge was key to the decision to make the Ordnance Survey's maps accessible to the public, and he passionately, albeit unsuccessfully, defended his position in 1811. Then the new master-general of the Board of Ordnance, Henry Phipps, first Earl of Mulgrave, issued a command to 'withhold every map from the public' until well after the end of the Napoleonic Wars; his concern related to potential French access to detailed information about Britain's harbours, coasts and fortifications.[26] William Mudge's consistent assertion of the Ordnance Survey's wide-ranging relevance set the stage for the eventual transfer, in 1870 (well beyond Mudge's own lifetime), of the map-making project away from the military's Board of Ordnance to the government department known as the Office of Works, located within the Office of Woods, Forests, Land Revenues, Works and Buildings. Undoubtedly, Mudge's expansive vision of the Ordnance Survey's civilian application was also a key factor in the extent of cultural interest in the Ordnance Survey that coincided with the dates of Mudge's directorship (1798–1820).

Prospects and Stations

From the late 1790s, Mudge's hopes for the civilian applications of the Ordnance Survey were reciprocated in the form of public curiosity about his endeavour. More specifically, contemporary print culture shows evidence of numerous engagements with Mudge's own persona, as well as commentary on his role in shaping national identity. Newspapers frequently reported on the Trigonometrical Survey's progress. As the first maps began to emerge from the presses in 1801, journals and newspapers covered the interior survey's advance across the country and described the paper maps themselves. A few quotations among many give a flavour of the level of detail in the reporting. The *Weekly Register* for 21 August 1799 described the appointment of 'Mr. Woolcut, an eminent mathematician, from Devonshire ... under the grand Trigonometrical Survey of England, under Capt. Mudge', and recounted how

> Mr. Gardner, of the drawing-room in the Tower, follows Capt. Mudge with a portable theodolite, for determining the exact situation of every church and remarkable object, and to fill up the plans in a style of accuracy and elegance never hitherto attempted: and these maps the Board of Ordnance have very liberally determined to publish for the benefit of the public.[27]

The *Caledonian Mercury* explained the process of triangulation for a lay readership, calling on passers-by to help conserve the makeshift trig points set up by the surveyors at each trigonometrical station:

> In the course of this very important survey, the points from which the different angles are set off, are marked on the tops of the most prominent hills, by the erection of a pillar of loose stones, staves, or other objects, upon their summits, by which their position and distances from each other, and their height above the level of the sea, are ascertained with the greatest precision.
>
>   As these marks become *data* of the utmost importance to the land surveyors, either in the construction of county maps, or private estates, our object for noticing the subject at present is, to call the attention of the public to the obvious utility of preserving these marks.[28]

In the second half of the 1810s, after the maps had been returned to public sale following the five years of restricted access imposed by Phipps, newspaper reports of the Ordnance Survey's activities and publications appeared far more frequently. For example, *The Times* covered in detail a collaboration between 'Colonel MUDGE, and his able assistant, Captain COLBY' and the 'French Institute of the Academy of Sciences' to extend the meridian arc between the Paris and Greenwich Observatories, measured in the 1780s, up to the Orkney Islands.[29] The same newspaper notified its readers when each new sheet became available, listing their prices. It also reported on an exhibition at the Royal Military Academy of 'some most beautiful drawings ... (the landscapes were copies from the famous Paul Sandby)' at which 'the Lieutenant-Governor Colonel Mudge' was present.[30] (Sandby had been employed in his youth in colouring many of the sheets of the Military Survey of Scotland, under William Roy.) A recurrent presence in such newspaper stories, in which he was identified as a 'celebrated and scientific' map-maker, Mudge appeared more as a catalyst of geodetic advancement than as an enhancer of specifically military intelligence and defence.[31] In those contexts where Mudge was praised for maintaining the 'honour of the nation', like his predecessor William Roy, it was usually for his contribution to 'the finest piece of Topography in Europe' in the name of scientific progress, rather than for the predicted utility of the maps in defending against French invasion (Flint, *Mudge Memoirs*, 144).

Literary writers utilized the figure of Mudge and his family in a range of ways. Under the pseudonym Peter Pindar, the satirist John Wolcot composed *Peter's Prophecy ... Or, an Important Epistle to Sir J. Banks, On the Approaching Election of a President of the Royal Society*, in which the poet urges that 'Fame and glory' be given not to Banks but instead to 'Dr. Mudge of Plymouth' – William Mudge's father – 'whose head contains more nous / Than (trust me) ever lodg'd in Herschel's house'.[32] Perhaps to William Mudge's subsequent dismay, the satirical poem cemented the opposition between the Mudge family, including Mudge's horologer uncle Thomas, and the scientific establishment that was centred around the Royal Society and the Astronomer Royal. That John Mudge was connected in the public imagination to his son William is possibly suggested by a punning review in the *Morning Chronicle* in 1795 of a portrait of Dr Mudge by James Northcote, which explicitly deployed cartographical language: the painting is not 'a *mere map of a face*', the reviewer stresses, 'but a delineation of the mind'.[33]

A similarly glancing connection to Mudge occurs much later, in the latter half of the next century, in Jules Verne's *Around the World in Eighty Days* (1873) and *Adventures of Three Russians and Three Englishmen in South Africa* (1872; sometimes given the title *Meridiana* or *Measuring a Meridian*). Verne's close acquaintance with 'Geodetical operations' is revealed throughout the latter, which followed an expedition to measure a meridian arc. Verne describes in detail the process of triangulation: 'At each signal, a triangle comes out, whose angles are given by the aforementioned instruments with a mathematical exactitude. Indeed, any object whatever – a bell, the day, a reflector, the night – can be remarked with perfect accuracy by a capable observer, who discerns them by means of a telescope, the object-glass of which is half obscured by a threaded net.'[34] Verne extensively referenced the 1806–9 endeavour by Dominique François Jean Arago and Jean-Baptiste Biot to extend the Parisian meridian arc down to the Balearic Islands and he namechecked 'Colonel Everest' – George Everest, the surveyor, geographer and surveyor general of India. In the context of Verne's close familiarity with eighteenth- and nineteenth-

century geodesy, the presence of 'Mudge' as a 'confident' navigator in
Around the World in Eighty Days is a likely nod to the British surveyor.

These are peripheral literary depictions of the Ordnance Survey map-
maker and his family. The most direct and revealing appearances of
William Mudge explicitly in his guise as Ordnance Survey map-maker
occur in early-nineteenth-century landscape poetry. In a poem entitled
'The Vale of Ilkley' (*c.* 1820–8), the Airedale poet John Nicholson (1790–
1843) portrayed 'the crown of wide-spread Rom'lies' Moor' or 'Rombald's
Moor' – a stretch of moorland to the south of Ilkley, West Yorkshire:

> the vast scene is stretched to either shore.
> There we behold the hills of many a shire;
> The lofty mountains to the clouds aspire;
> Whernside uprears on high his snow-clad crest,
> While the blue Pendle trembles in the west;
> The hills of Derbyshire are southward seen,
> Though vales divide, and rivers roll between;
> Old Ingleborough lifts his time-worn head,
> And Yorkshire as one spacious map is spread
>   . . .
> A scene like this, within old England's coast,
> Nor Matlock, Buxton, nor proud Bath can boast.
> Grandeur and peace upon the Station dwell,
> and Health sits smiling at the mountain well . . . [35]

Nicholson appended a footnote to the description of the 'Station', revealing it to be an Ordnance Survey trig point: 'The Station is the highest point
on Romilies' Moor, from which place Captain Mudge took his observations nearly seventy years ago' (*Poems by John Nicholson*, 134). Nicholson's
positioning of the ghost of William Mudge at the highest point on the
moor, revelling in the 'vast scene' laid out before him, echoes the eighteenth-
century tradition of landscape or prospect poetry described extensively by
John Barrell in *The Idea of Landscape and the Sense of Place* (1972) and *English
Literature in History* (1983). Barrell locates the significance of the wide-
ranging prospect – the 'equal, wide survey' of British landscape that occurred
frequently in mid-eighteenth-century landscape poetry – in contemporan-
eous changes that were occurring to the concept of 'unity' in Britain. Ideas of
social coherence were transformed by geopolitical union between England
and Scotland (followed at the turn of the nineteenth century by the Anglo-
Irish Union) but were most dramatically impacted, Barrell argues, by 'the
increasing belief that British society was becoming highly differentiated in
terms, particularly, of occupation'.[36] In the context of the reading public's

emerging alertness to social divisions according to rank, occupation and income, Barrell argues that English literary culture became charged with inspecting 'the variety of elements that compose a society, by representing them in the form of occupational variety, and by understanding them therefore as no longer necessarily, or no longer simply, disruptive of social coherence, but capable also of confirming it' (*English Literature in History*, 25).

Poetic representations of the prospect – the far-ranging elevated view of landscape – became mechanisms not only for depicting national variety and difference but also for conjuring up a human figure uniquely capable of perceiving unity within diversity. In the modality of mid-eighteenth-century prospect poetry practised by James Thomson and John Dyer, the figure 'to whom the task of reconciling opposed interests is assigned' is the landed gentleman who possessed a stake in the successful accord and stability of his nation through his permanent ownership of land, while simultaneously enjoying a disinterested remove from, or elevation above, the mundane details of division of labour by dint of his 'freedom from engaging in any specific profession, trade, or occupation which might occlude his view of society as a whole' (*English Literature in History*, 32–3).

As Barrell's subtitle to *English Literature in History* – 'An Equal, Wide Survey' – indicates, cartographic discourse, including the phrases 'like a map' and 'as in a map', recurred in eighteenth-century prospect poetry to depict the wide-ranging, unified viewpoint available to the elevated, impartial gentleman. John Hughes's 'A Monumental Ode' (1714) urged the 'Muse' to behold how 'Nature's Hand ... / ... far around in beauteous Prospect spreads / Her Map of Plenty all below'.[37] Robert Dodsley's *Agriculture: A Poem* (1777) recounted how

> There sweet prospects rise
> Of meadows smiling in their flow'ry pride,
> Green hills and dales, and cottages embower'd,
> ...
>
> In those fair scenes of wonder and delight,
> Where, to the human eye, Omnipotence
> Unfolds the map of Nature, and displays
> The matchless beauty of created things.[38]

The 'equal, wide survey' of Barrell's subtitle is taken from James Thomson's *Seasons*. The phrase was deployed in that poem to describe how the gentleman's 'saving Virtues' – peace, love, charity, truth, dignity of mind, courage, temperance and so on, but especially 'That first paternal

virtue, *Public Zeal*' – throw 'o'er all an equal wide survey', thus discovering
the unifying 'great design' within the apparent disparity of the 'common
weal'.[39] The occurrence of cartographic metaphors in the context of mid-
eighteenth-century prospect poetry connotes the genre of the estate survey:
the elevated, disinterested gentleman pores over the extensive view in the
same way that landed male figures in literature were repeatedly imagined
leaning over privately commissioned surveys of their estates and the
surrounding territory.

By the close of the eighteenth century, the same figurative cartographic
language – used to profile an extensive view of landscape granted to an
elevated observer and compared to a map – was being used to trace the
emergence of very different types of individuals to whom the task of
finding unity in variety was assigned. In Erasmus Darwin's *Botanic
Garden* (1791), the lone figure who 'Journey[s] on high' was not a landed
gentleman but a 'calm Philosopher' who 'Views broader stars, and breathes
in purer gales; / Sees, like a map, in many a waving line / Round Earth's
blue plains her lucid waters shine'.[40] The elevated, detached observer in
Darwin's poem is a natural scientist and experimenter in the mould of
'great Mongolfier', the hot-air balloonist. For the poet Anna Seward, in
'Addressed to the Rev. Thomas Sedgewick Whalley, on Leaving His Seat,
Mendip Lodge, in Somersetshire' (1804), the disinterested observer stood
'High on thy mountain-eminence' and saw 'vales, and woods, and lesser
hills expand, / As in a map, the verdant steeps below'.[41] But the observer
was not the landed gentleman himself: Whalley's own eyes were 'seal[ed]'
by 'the grave's iron slumber' and 'must never view thy bright domain';
rather, the observer was the female poet, the 'Friend', who attained
a similar elevation and observational capability to the 'upraised' dead
male landowner through sympathy, reflection and poetic composition.
Throughout these examples, a shift is visible in which the idealized
national commentator is no longer being imagined in relation to his
inherited wealth and property ownership but instead is being celebrated
for empirical observation, dispassionate rationality, and familiarity with
key scientific institutions and personae. That shift in the understanding of
the qualities necessary for political commentary and judgement was
reflected in changing deployments of cartographical metaphors. It was
also paralleled in a shifting notion of the role and significance of the map-
maker, both as a literary device and as a public figure.

By the beginning of the nineteenth century, it was William Mudge
himself who was being cast in the figure of the elevated observer capable
not only of perceiving unity in multiplicity and disparity but also of

displaying that unity for everyone privileged enough to come into contact with the Ordnance Survey's maps. The maps were explicitly celebrated for providing a visualization of a *united* kingdom in material form: the *Daily News* described how 'the maps fit together at the edges without any overlapping or duplicate engraving, so that they form, not merely separate maps, but ... one map'.[42] Nicholson's 'The Vale of Ilkley' positions Mudge smiling above a view that encompasses Cumbria, Derbyshire and West Yorkshire and imaginatively brings into focus counties as distant as Somerset. Through Mudge's eyes, the poem offers a vision of a unified nation – one in which the distinctive regional identities of 'county commonwealths' persist, while centralized unity is emphasized above all.[43] The poem deliberately recalls the map metaphors of mid-eighteenth-century prospect poetry: 'Yorkshire as one spacious map is spread.' But whereas the cartographical language of the poem's mid-eighteenth-century predecessors invoked the estate map as the frame of reference for the gentleman observer, in Nicholson's poem the estate surveyor is replaced by the map-maker as public servant and military scientist, and the national 'Ordnance Survey' is evoked in place of the privately commissioned estate map.

The Quantifying Spirit: Range and Limits

Nicholson's ideal political commentator – the individual peculiarly suited to be an impartial, elevated spectator – was not the mid-eighteenth-century landed gentleman, detached from a specific state role, but William Mudge: an employee of the state, a military surveyor from a family background rooted in civilian literary, medical and scientific culture. On a simple level, this shift in conception of the impartial spectator was a product of the Ordnance Survey's prominence. Thanks to its fame, the Ordnance Survey map had achieved the same visibility in the literary imagination as the estate survey. The wide-ranging bird's-eye view of the prospect poem brought to mind a map, but, by the early nineteenth century, the map that most readily came to mind was as likely to be the OS map as the cartographic delineation of a private estate or county.

Nicholson's literal and figurative elevation of Mudge also marks a significant shift in conception of political power. The ideal commentator and legislator was no longer a member of the landed classes who warranted political responsibility through inheritance of land but a senior public servant whose distinction had been earned largely meritocratically through successful execution of his role. This mirrored the rising significance of the middle classes as a political force in Britain.[44] It also aligned the figure of the map-maker with public officials tasked with monitoring or measuring the population as part of democratic processes – the 'surveyors' of James Harrington's *Oceana* (1656), for example, who roamed across parishes 'teaching [the People] their first lesson, which was the Ballott', or statisticians like Sir John Sinclair, who saw his role in collecting detailed local information for the *Statistical Account of Scotland* (1791–9) as crucial to government's ability to promote citizens' welfare.[45] By the 1820s, Mudge's triangulation data was being used in comparable contexts; the economist Henry Beeke praised the 'very excellent trigono-metrical survey' for providing measurements that would enable him accurately to calculate counties' revenue from taxation on the basis of newly exact measurements of their areas.[46] Such figures as Mudge and Sinclair were granted a wide-ranging view of national territory through their public service, rather than from their private inheritance, and were charged with collating and comparing those data in order to discern concepts such as 'truth', 'accuracy' and the 'normal', in the name of improving national infrastructure, data and well-being.[47] Nicholson's representation of Mudge valorized and idealized bureaucratic measure-ment and rational democracy, in place of the hereditary aristocratic system celebrated by the mid-eighteenth-century prospect poem.

The appearance of Mudge in Nicholson's poem also points to the visibility of military research in civilian public life at the end of the eighteenth century and the extent of reciprocal influence between military and civilian cultural spheres in Enlightenment Britain. Neil Ramsey and Gillian Russell have recently shown how, in the period 1750–1850, military concerns achieved heightened visibility in Britain, particularly when the army, militia regiments and volunteer forces were rapidly expanding against the backdrop of the Revolutionary and Napoleonic wars. In the space of twenty years, the regular army increased from around 40,000 to over 250,000 troops; many British families contained at least one son who entered the military. The enlarged presence of military matters in civilian British life drove 'an early modern military revolution' in which dramatic military advancements played 'a pivotal role in fashioning the infrastruc-tures of modern industrial life'.[48] For example, practices of military drill and surveillance influenced the design of disciplinary institutions such as factories and prisons, and the demands of war catalysed the development of roads, shipping and postal networks. In the Romantic period in particular, the military became the subject of spectacle for civilians, through camps and parades in which drilled troops performed synchronized marches in elaborate uniforms to the accompaniment of martial music.[49]

The Ordnance Survey was a prime example of the civilian embrace of military science and engineering, just as it was – vice versa – of the rapid absorption of principles, methods and discoveries of Enlightenment quantification, geodesy, mathematics, geometry and astronomy into military theory and practice. Military surveying activity lent itself well to the civilian hunger for public military demonstrations. From mid-June to mid-September 1800 – shortly before the appearance of the Ordnance Survey's first map, and after the publication of many of Mudge's and Dalby's 'Accounts' of the survey's progress – the Establishment for Military Education in London's Knightsbridge hosted weekly public displays of 'Geometrical and Trigonometrical Operations upon the Ground' (Ramsey, 'Exhibiting Discipline', 122).[50] Even in the Ordnance Survey's early days, its triangulation methodology was adopted by educational manuals for 'the liberal instruction of boys', which encouraged students to replicate Mudge's trigonometrical measurements.[51]

Aside from the trigonometrical survey, the Ordnance Survey's interior survey and its pictorial representation of landscape provided a fruitful opportunity for the interfusion of military and civilian influences. Embryonic surveyors at the Royal Military Academy at Woolwich were tutored by illustrious landscape painters including Paul Sandby, and the Ordnance Survey interior surveyor Thomas Compton went on to utilize the topographical skills he had learned while working for the Ordnance Survey in producing 'highly-finished coloured views' of the 'romantic country' of the 'Cambrian Hills', which were widely published.[52] The career of the surveyor Robert Kearsley Dawson (1798–1861) mirrors the Ordnance Survey's own shift from a superficially military to an unashamedly civilian identity. After working for the Ordnance Survey in Ireland in the late 1820s, Dawson was recalled to England in 1831 to map boundaries of parliamentary boroughs for the Reform Bill. William Mudge's personal biography and surveying career – his origins in a family known for the richness of its cultural contacts and his superintendence of a military cartographic project whose scientific and public utility he continually stressed, to the extent that it was eventually detached from the military and re-established in the Office of Works – perfectly encapsulated the interchange of military and civilian worlds in the late eighteenth century. It is that exchange that leads directly to Mudge's presence in Nicholson's nineteenth-century prospect poem.

The best-known invocation of William Mudge in Romantic-period literature displays similarities to Nicholson's poem and was a possible influence on that later composition. As in 'The Vale of Ilkley', in this earlier poem Mudge is placed in the position of the elevated observer of a wide-ranging national prospect. Similarly also, the specifically military aspects of his professional identity are sidelined in favour of his scientific intervention. When William Wordsworth came to compose 'Inscription: Written with a Slate-pencil on a Stone, on the Side of the Mountain of Black Comb' in 1811, he had already referred to Mudge in an unpublished tour as the 'best authority' on Lake District topography. This was a sentiment he would later reiterate in his *Guide to the Lakes*, in which he explicitly designated Mudge an 'experienced observer' and referred to 'that experienced surveyor, Colonel Mudge'.[53]

Wordsworth's 'Inscription' informs a 'bold Adventurer' about a 'geographic Labourer' who had previously ascended 'this huge Eminence':

> on the summit whither thou art bound,
> A geographic Labourer pitched his tent,
> With books supplied and instruments of art,
> To measure height and distance; lonely task
> Week after week pursued![54]

As noted, Wordsworth subsequently identified the geographic labourer to Isabella Fenwick as William Mudge, about whose professional visit in 1808 to the mountain and the surrounding area, in the company of his Ordnance Survey team, Wordsworth had acquired information from the rector at Bootle in Cumbria, Rev. Dr James Satterthwaite, during a visit there in 1811.[55] From Black Combe's summit, Mudge is granted a view of 'the grand terraqueous spectacle': an equal, wide survey of British landscape that another of Wordsworth's Black Combe poems fleshes out in greater detail:

> from the summit of BLACK COMB (dread name
> Derived from clouds and storms!) the amplest range
> Of unobstructed prospect may be seen
> That British ground commands: – low dusky tracts,
> Where Trent is nursed, far southward! Cambrian hills
> To the south-west, a multitudinous show;
> And, in a line of eye-sight linked with these,
> The hoary Peaks of Scotland that give birth
> To Tiviot's Stream, to Annan, Tweed, and Clyde . . .
>
> (Poems, I, 303)

In the 'Inscription', Mudge initially appears aligned to the rural labouring figures of Wordsworth's poetry, such as the leech-gatherer of 'Resolution and Independence' who is 'About the weary moors continually / Wandering about alone and silently'. Mudge appears as a 'Labourer' who has 'Week after week pursued' a 'lonely task', occasionally enjoying a privileged 'glimpse (but sparingly bestowed / On timid man) of Nature's processes / Upon the exalted hills'. At the end of the poem, however, Wordsworth calls into question Mudge's credentials as a commentator on landscape and united nationhood. Wordsworth imagines the Ordnance Survey's trigonometric efforts thwarted by a simple cloud, which turns 'the whole surface of the out-spread map . . . invisible', causing 'total gloom' to descend, in which Mudge 'sate alone, with unclosed eyes / Upon the blinded mountain's silent top!'. Nature makes a mockery of what the historian of science Sven Widmalm calls the 'quantifying spirit' of eighteenth-century geographical science. Ultimately, rather than praising Mudge as an idealized political commentator on landscape, nation, and geographical or scientific 'truth', Wordsworth's poem ends up linking him more clearly with the Enlightenment attitudes that the poet disparages – in cartographical language – in *The Prelude* as attempts to 'range the faculties / In scale and order, class the cabinet / Of their sensations'.[56] Wordsworth's Black Combe inscription utilizes the Ordnance Survey and Mudge specifically as vehicles through which to articulate scepticism about cartography's capacity adequately to represent 'Nature's processes'.

Sightlines, 1798–1810

Though not frequent in Romantic-period texts, invocations of the Ordnance Survey's William Mudge can be recognized by scholars of cartography's wider cultural resonance as marking a departure from earlier literary representations of map-makers. Surveyors most often appeared in eighteenth-century literature in the guise of privately employed estate surveyors, untrustworthy interfering agents coming between landlords and their tenants. William King's poem *The Toast: An Heroick Poem* (1732) warned that 'whate'er *that* Surveyor / For his Profit projects, or the *other* shall swear; / Be abortive their Plots!'.[57] In Fanny Burney's *Cecilia* (1782), an estate surveyor figured as the simple facilitator of improvements to a private estate, but in Maria Edgeworth's novels the role is invested with sinister ulterior motives.[58] In *Ennui* (1809), the estate mapper is 'a low man', an 'odious surveyor', who exchanges places with Lord Craiglethorpe and dupes a woman into falling in love with him.[59] In *The Absentee* (1812), the dishonest estate surveyor facilitates the absenteeism of the landlord and, instead of simply measuring land in order to calculate rent, appropriates that land from the rightful tenants.

The land agent informs long-standing tenants that '*your* little place [is] no longer yours, I've promised it to the surveyor' (*Tales of Fashionable Life*, II, 220–1). Even when the map-maker was not a privately commissioned employee, the figure was still frequently associated with insensitive alterations to landscape or the state's encroachment on private property. John Clare aligned 'surveyors' with 'modern savages' – philistines who 'have lately dug up several foundation stones of the Abbey ... for the purpose of repairing the parish roads'.[60] In Walter Scott's *Guy Mannering* (1815), it is an 'English surveyor' who is behind a recommendation for a 'proposed road' to 'go clear through the main enclosures at Hazlewood, and cut within a mile, or nearly so, of the house itself, destroying the privacy and pleasure ... of the grounds'.[61]

Literary representations of William Mudge differ significantly from such typical eighteenth-century appearances of map-makers. Though Wordsworth's portrait in his 'Inscription' is complex, depictions of Mudge generally transform the map-maker from petty, conniving provincial employee into eminent servant of the state. Mudge's cultural visibility up to the end, in 1820, of his directorship of the Ordnance Survey paved the way for the appearance in literature of map-makers as indisputably political figures on the international stage. However, it is largely in generic, unnamed or fictionalized form that the map-maker appears in texts post-1820, whereas the appearance of Mudge as a named cartographical celebrity in texts from the 1790s to 1820 is striking and almost without parallel in terms of public interest in specific surveyors.

The Ordnance Survey's work in Ireland from the 1820s to the 1840s under Mudge's successor, Thomas Colby, during which it (in)famously engaged in researching and translating Irish place names, helped to cement the OS's reputation as an institution with explicit cultural and political relevance. This led to its adoption by a number of contemporary writers as a mechanism for reflecting on translation and linguistic standardization. Barry MacSweeney's 'Pearl's Poem of Joy and Treasure' (1997) aligned the Ordnance Survey with 'the true height of the law'; the maps' anglicization of place names 'twine[s] my tongue'. Hugh MacDiarmid characterized the Ordnance Survey as a weak, superficial form of geographical representation incapable of capturing national and regional cultural nuances that go 'deeper than Ordnance Surveys divine'.[62] Most prominently, Brian Friel's play *Translations* (1980) fictionalized the Ordnance Surveyors' activities in 1830s Ireland to show how the map-makers' brutal translation of Ireland's place names 'into the King's good English' left its residents 'imprisoned in a linguistic contour which no longer matches the landscape ... of fact'.[63]

These contemporary literary deployments of the Ordnance Survey as an encapsulation of tensions between region and centre, between Westminster and the identities of Scotland and Ireland, and between standard English and regional dialect and Gaelic cast the Ordnance Survey map-maker as an explicitly political figure but also as a faceless servant of a ham-fisted imperial state or, in Friel's case, of a 'bloody military operation' (Friel, *Translations*, 36). MacSweeney and MacDiarmid's poems reference the institution as a whole, rather than personalizing it in the personae of individual map-makers. Friel's play largely offers fictional surveyors, although the character of Lieutenant Yolland is likely to be a transposition of the military engineer William Yolland, who was overlooked for promotion to the Ordnance Survey's directorship in 1847.

The depersonalization of the literary map-maker continued to characterize poetry that evoked the Ordnance Survey as part of a critique of cartography as a reductive means of representing landscape, following the example of Wordsworth's Black Combe inscription. Robert Graves's 'Lost Acres' mourns the 'acres of the mind' – the affective and psychological layers with which landscape is overlain in the mind – that are 'always again lost / By every new Ordnance Survey'.[64] Anne Stevenson's 'Salter's Gate' also evokes the Ordnance Survey in terms of what its maps omit rather than what they (choose to) capture, referring to 'that lost corner of the ordnance survey'.[65] Sean O'Brien's 'Special Train' aligns the OS with middle England: focusing on the council estate, he writes of the working-class 'country / Known neither to us nor the Ordnance Survey'.[66] In such inscriptions, the Ordnance Survey appears as a depersonalized, faceless organization whose political and cultural significance predominantly lies in its reductive standardization of landscape, national identity and language.

The disappearance of the specific (named or implied) Ordnance Survey map-maker from literary depictions after William Mudge's death in 1820 can be attributed to a number of shifts. Mudge was unusual in respect of the cultural prominence of his family name and connections, and – as the first, famous director of a national mapping project – he benefited also from the exposure his pioneering development of instruments, techniques and organizational structures in the Ordnance Survey brought him (innovations his successors were tasked mainly with revising, rather than sweeping away). Newspapers showed far greater interest in Mudge than in succeeding directors, and Mudge himself carved an unusually large space in print culture through his open publication of the 'Accounts' of the Ordnance Survey's progress and of the maps themselves. Literary writers' loss of interest in individual Ordnance Survey map-makers and directors may have been the result of the disaggregation of military and civilian culture into fully separate spheres, as military employment became professionalized in the nineteenth century; in the long term, it may also have been bound up with the Ordnance Survey's changing identity, from celebrated military-scientific project to bureaucratic government department.

The fall from visibility of the particularised Ordnance Survey mapmaker may also have reflected a shift in natural science in which, as Lorraine Daston and Peter Galison argue,

> men of science began to fret openly about a new kind of obstacle to knowledge: themselves. Their fear was that the subjective self was prone to prettify, idealize, and, in the worst case, regularize observations to fit theoretical expectations: to see what it hoped to see. (Daston and Galison, *Objectivity*, 34)

Daston and Galison describe how those who aspired to 'objectivity' in the mid-nineteenth century began to emphasize 'the importance of effacing their own personalities and developed techniques that left as little as possible to the discretion of either artist or scientist, in order to attain an "objective view"' (Daston and Galison, *Objectivity*, 34–5). In the late eighteenth century, a 'cult of the genius of observation' (*Objectivity*, 238) ensured that the idiosyncratic talents of men like Mudge – who had the technology and judgement necessary to manage the vast number of observations conducted from trig points across the country and to rationalize error into neat data sets – were celebrated. However, Daston and Galison argue that, after Mudge's death, observation and scientific atlases began to efface the individual, skilled observer in favour of an aspiration to 'automatism' – the production of images apparently untouched by human hands.

Mudge's appearance in Wordsworth's Black Combe poems, his *Guide to the Lakes* and his unpublished tour, and in Nicholson's 'The Vale of Ilkley' occurred during a brief historical moment between 1798 and 1820. In that window, Romantic-period fascination with the representation of landscape coincided with the valorization of scientific observers, the unhindered mutual exchange of influences between military and civilian spheres and the heightened cultural currency of visual and textual constructions of a unified national landscape during the Revolutionary and Napoleonic wars, against the backdrop of the Anglo-Irish Union. In the midst of this coincidence of cultural strands, the birth of the Ordnance Survey in 1791 and its rise to prominence in the late 1790s resulted in the propulsion of Mudge, its director, to a certain degree of professional and cultural fame. Radiating out like the sightlines that diverge from each trig point in the Ordnance Survey's own triangulation, the resonances of Mudge's presence in Romantic-era texts extend from what is, at first sight, a minor literary detail to illuminate major historical changes in British civilian and military culture.

Notes

1. *Oracle and Public Advertiser*, 3 March 1798, 3.
2. William Roy, 'An Account of the Trigonometrical Operation, Whereby the Distance Between the Meridians of the Royal Observatories of Greenwich and Paris has been Determined', *Philosophical Transactions of the Royal Society* 80 (1790): 111–614, 262; hereafter *Philosophical Transactions*.
3. Out-letters from Master-General, Board of Ordnance, and Commander in Chief, National Archives, WO 46/22, 1791–2.
4. For reference to the 'Duke of Richmond's Survey,' see *Lloyds Evening Post*, 25 July 1792, 91. For references to the 'General Survey', see 'Lights on the Coast', *Sussex Weekly Advertiser*, 8 and 15 April 1793, cited in *The Old Series Ordnance Survey Maps of England and Wales*, 8 vols., eds. J. B. Harley and Yolande O'Donoghue (Lympne Castle, Kent: Harry Margary, 1975–92), I, xxv ; and 'The General Survey of England and Wales', *Times*, 2 November 1816, 1. For reference to the 'British Survey', see Joseph Portlock, *Memoir of the Life of Major-General Colby* (London: Seeley, Jackson & Halliday, 1869), 192. For reference to the 'Trigonometrical Survey', see Surveyor-General's Minutes, National Archives, WO 47/118, 12 July 1791. For the initial intentions of the trigonometrical surveyors and their early progress, see Rachel Hewitt, *Map of a Nation: A Biography of the Ordnance Survey* (London: Granta, 2010), 114–43.
5. It seems that the term 'Ordnance Survey' was first used to refer to the project in 1801, when William Mudge wrote the name on one of the draught interior surveys; see Thomas Budgen, 'Exeter', Ordnance Surveyors' Drawings, British Library, OSD 40 (1801), 3; however, Mudge's annotation could have been added at a later date. The phrase first appeared in print in Aaron Arrowsmith, *Memoir Relative to the Construction of the Map of Scotland* (London: W. Savage, 1809), 5. 'Ordnance Survey' appeared on the 1810 'Ordnance Survey of the Isle of Wight and Part of Hampshire' but was relatively slow to be adopted as the principal moniker of the cartographical endeavour.
6. Dugald Stewart, *Elements of the Philosophy of the Human Mind*, 3 vols. (Edinburgh: Ramsay, 1792–1827), II, 205.
7. The accounts of Mudge, Williams, and Dalby appear in *Philosophical Transactions* 85 (1795): 414–591; and *Philosophical Transactions* 87 (1797): 432–541; Mudge's further updates appear in *Philosophical Transactions* 90 (1800): 539–728; and *Philosophical Transactions* 93 (1803): 383–508.

8. William Mudge and Isaac Dalby, *An Account of the Operations Carried on for Accomplishing a Trigonometrical Survey of England and Wales; From the Commencement in the Year 1784, to the End of the Year 1796* (London: Bulmer and Faden, 1799).

9. *Times*, 16 January 1818, 1.

10. 'The Ordnance Survey of England and Wales', *Daily News*, 28 December 1848, 3.

11. Lorraine Daston and Peter Galison, *Objectivity* (New York: Zone Books, 2010), 34–5.

12. William Wordsworth, *The Fenwick Notes of William Wordsworth*, ed. Jared Curtis (London: Bristol Classical Press, 1993), 29.

13. For histories of the eighteenth-century longitude debate, see Dava Sobel, *Longitude: The True Story of a Lone Genius Who Solved the Greatest Scientific Problem of His Time* (London: Fourth Estate, 1996); and Derek Howse, *Nevil Maskelyne: The Seaman's Astronomer* (Cambridge: Cambridge University Press, 1989), 40–52, 74–84, 124–6. Thomas Mudge's part in the longitude debate is covered by Howse, 170–7, and by Thomas Seccombe and David Penney, 'Thomas Mudge (1715/16–1794)', *Oxford Dictionary of National Biography*, www.oxforddnb.com/view/article/19486 (accessed 21 January 2018).

14. Accounts of Thomas Mudge's endeavours to ascertain longitude at sea, and his son's defence of those efforts, can be found in Thomas Mudge, *A Description with Plates, of the Time-Keeper Invented by the Late Mr Thomas Mudge* (London: Printed for the author, and sold by Mess. Payne, Cadell and Davies, Rivingtons, Dilly, and Richardson, 1799); and in documents in the Royal Society's archives, MM/7/91, MM/7/94, MM/7/100, MM/7/114, and MM/7/117–19. *Times* (30 April 1793 and 10 April 1798) also reported Thomas Mudge Jr's efforts.

15. Joseph Banks, 'Observations on Mr Mudge's Application to Parliament for a Reward for his Time-Keepers', Royal Society, MM/7/100.

16. See William Mudge, 'An Account of the Trigonometrical Survey, Carried on in the Years 1797, 1798, and 1799', *Philosophical Transactions* 90 (1800): 666.

17. Charles Robert Leslie, *Life and Times of Sir Joshua Reynolds*, 2 vols. (London: John Murray, 1865), I, 8.

18. Zachariah Mudge, *A Sermon on Liberty* (London: F. Knight, 1790), 34.

19. Joshua Reynolds, *The Works of Sir Joshua Reynolds*, 3 vols. (London: Cadell & Davies, 1798), I, xxxiii.

20. Stamford Raffles Flint, *Mudge Memoirs: Being a Record of Zachariah Mudge, and Some Members of his Family* (Truro: Netherton and Worth, 1883), 81.

21. See also James Boswell, *The Life of Samuel Johnson*, 2 vols. (London: Charles Dilly, 1791), I, 347.

22. 'Legal Papers Regarding Case of Hugh Debbeig vs Lord Howe', National Archives, TS 11/944/3436, f. 1, 5 February 1782.

23. William Roy, *The Military Antiquities of the Romans in North Britain* (London: Society of Antiquaries, 1793), i.

24. Daniel Paterson, *A New and Accurate Description of the Roads in England and Wales, and Part of the Roads of Scotland* (London: Longman, Rees, Faden, 1803), xviii.

25. See Hewitt, *Map of a Nation*, 147; and Thomas Vincent Reynolds, 'Queries Humbly Submitted to General the Duke of Richmond Relative to the Compilation of a Military Map of the Southern District', National Archives, OS 3/5.

26. Henry Phipps to William Mudge, National Archives, Ordnance Survey Letter Book, OS 3/260, f. 131, 2 September 1811; cited in Charles Close, *The Early Years of the Ordnance Survey* (Newton Abbot: David & Charles, 1969 [1926]), 57.

27. *Weekly Register*, 21 August 1799, 572; http://tinyurl.galegroup.com/tinyurl/4 zzVs5 (accessed 31 January 2018).

28. *Caledonian Mercury*, 6 July 1815, 3.

29. *Times*, 28 May 1817, 3.

30. See *Times*, 2 November 1816, 1; 16 January 1818, 1; 16 July 1818, 3.

31. See *Times*, 2 October 1821, 2.

32. Peter Pindar, *Peter's Prophecy; Or, the President and Poet; Or, an Important Epistle to Sir J. Banks, On the Approaching Election of a President of the Royal Society*, 4th ed. (London: G. Kearsley, 1788), 32.

33. 'Exhibition at the Royal Academy', *Morning Chronicle,* 22 May 1795, 3.

34. Jules Verne, *Meridiana: The Adventures of Three Englishmen and Three Russians in South Africa* (New York: Scribner, Armstrong & Co., 1874), 38.

35. William Dearden, ed., *Poems by John Nicholson, the Airedale Poet* (London: W. H. Young, 1859), 136.

36. John Barrell, *English Literature in History 1730–80: An Equal, Wide Survey* (London: Hutchinson, 1983), 14.

37. John Hughes, 'A Monumental Ode. To the Memory of Mrs. Elizabeth Hughes' (1714), from *Poems on Several Occasions*, 2 vols. (London: J. Tonson and J. Watts, 1735), II, 101.

38. Robert Dodsley, 'Agriculture: A Poem', *Trifles* (London: J. Dodsley, 1777), 110.

39. *The Works of James Thomson*, 4 vols. (London: A. Millar, 1757), I, 109.

40. Erasmus Darwin, *The Botanic Garden* (London: Joseph Johnson, 1799), 78–9.

41. See Anna Seward, *The Poetical Works of Anna Seward, With Extracts from Her Correspondence*, ed. Walter Scott (Edinburgh: J. Ballantyne and Co., 1810), 362–5.

42. 'The Ordnance Survey of England and Wales', *Daily News*, 28 December 1848, 3.

43. John Langton, 'The Industrial Revolution and the Regional Geography of England', *Transactions of the Institute of British Geographers* 9:2 (1984): 145–67, 147.

44. See Leonore Davidoff and Catherine Hall, *Family Fortunes: Men and Women of the English Middle Class, 1780–1850* (London: Hutchinson, 1987), 18.

45. See James Harrington, *The Common-Wealth of Oceana* (London: J. Streater, 1656), 60; John Sinclair, *The Statistical Account of Scotland. Drawn up from the*

Communications of the Ministers of Different Parishes, 21 vols. (Edinburgh: William Creech, 1791–9).

46. Henry Beeke, *Observations on the Produce of the Income Tax* (London: J. Wright, 1799), 8–9.

47. For a discussion of the rhetoric of truth and accuracy in Enlightenment geodesy, see Sven Widmalm, 'Accuracy, Rhetoric, and Technology: The Paris-Greenwich Triangulation, 1784–1788', in *The Quantifying Spirit in the Eighteenth Century*, eds. T. Frängsmyr, J. L. Heilbron, and Robin E. Rider (Berkeley: University of California Press, 1990), 179–206. For the emergence of the language of the 'normal' in the context of the rise of statistics in the early nineteenth century, see Ian Hacking, *The Taming of Chance* (Cambridge: Cambridge University Press, 1990).

48. Neil Ramsey and Gillian Russell, 'Introduction: Tracing War in Enlightenment and Romantic Culture', in *Tracing War in British Enlightenment and Romantic Culture*, eds. Neil Ramsey and Gillian Russell (Basingstoke: Palgrave, 2015), 1–16, 1–2.

49. See Neil Ramsey, 'Exhibiting Discipline: Military Science and the Naval Military Library and Museum', *Tracing War in British Enlightenment and Romantic Culture*, 113–131, 121.

50. See also *Times*, 10 June 1800, 1.

51. See Arthur Hill, *Plans for the Government and Liberal Instruction of Boys* (London: G. and W. B. Whittaker, 1822).

52. See Thomas Compton, *The North Cambrian Mountains, or a Tour Through North Wales, Describing the Scenery and General Characters of that Romantic Country, and Embellished with a Series of Highly-Finished Coloured Views, Engraved from Original Drawings* (London: Thomas Compton, 1817).

53. William Wordsworth, *The Prose Works of William Wordsworth*, 3 vols., eds. W. J. B. Owen and J. W. Smyser (Oxford: Clarendon Press, 1974), II, 302; William Wordsworth, *Guide to the Lakes*, ed. Ernest de Selincourt (Oxford: Oxford University Press, 1977), 8. Compare Wordsworth's reference to Mudge with Thomas James Mathias's reference in the satirical poem *The Shade of Alexander Pope on the Banks of the Thames* (1799) to the 'keen decisive labours' of Major Rennell, the director of a map of India in the 1760s and 1770s and author of *Memoir of a Map of Hindoostan* (1782). Mathias celebrates 'the works so long and so eagerly expected by the learned, from that consummate Geographer, and most accurate investigator, Major James Rennell' (73).

54. William Wordsworth, *Poems*, 2 vols. (London: Longman, Hurst, Rees, Orme and Brown, 1815), II, 285–6.

55. See John Wyatt, 'Wordsworth's Black Combe Poems: The Pastoral and the Geographer's Eye', *Signatures* 3 (2001), http://d3mcbia3evjswv.cloudfront.net/files/Signatures_Vol3.pdf (accessed 25 January 2018); Michael Wiley, *Romantic Geography: William Wordsworth and Anglo-European Spaces* (Basingstoke: Macmillan, 1998), 30, 158.

56. William Wordsworth, *The Prelude, 1799*, 1805, 1850, eds. Jonathan Wordsworth, M. H. Abrams, and Stephen Gill (New York: Norton, 1979), II (1805), ll. 229–33.

57. William King, *The Toast. An Heroick Poem* (London: 1747), 158. The poem first appeared in Dublin in 1732.

58. Frances Burney, *Cecilia; or, Memoirs of an Heiress*, 3 vols. (London: T. Cadell, 1782), I, 120.

59. See Maria Edgeworth, *Tales of Fashionable Life*, 3 vols. (London: Joseph Johnson, 1809), I, 143–53.

60. John Clare, *The Natural History Prose Writings of John Clare*, ed. Margaret Grainger (Oxford: Clarendon Press, 1983), 227.

61. Walter Scott, *Guy Mannering; or, the Astrologer*, 3 vols. (Edinburgh: James Ballantyne, 1815), II, 230.

62. Hugh MacDiarmid, 'The Borders', in *Complete Poems: Volume II*, eds. M. Grieve and W. R. Aitken (Manchester: Carcanet, 1994), 1427. See also Hugh MacDiarmid, 'Scotland', in *Complete Poems: Volume I*, eds. M. Grieve and W. R. Aitken (Manchester: Carcanet, 1993), 366.

63. Brian Friel, *Translations* (London: Faber, 1981), 30, 52.

64. Robert Graves, *Collected Poems* (New York: Oxford University Press, 1975), 76–7.

65. Anne Stevenson, *Collected Poems of Anne Stevenson, 1955–95* (Oxford University Press, 1996), 156.

66. Sean O'Brien, *Cousin Coat: Selected Poems, 1976–2001* (London: Picador, 2001), 121.

CHAPTER 3

The British Atlas

Britton and Brayley's National Survey

Stephen Daniels

The atlas as a cartographical format is more than a collection of maps. A range of scholars, including literary historians and historical geographers, have shown how atlases – usually large luxury volumes – are complex cultural artefacts, comprising a range of genres of both image and text, displaying portraits and landscapes as well as plans and surveys to project the interests of their patrons, promoters, subscribers and purchasers.[1] Such magnificent volumes are expressly emblematic as well as empirical in showing and telling the past and future of the world they depict, along with its present state, displaying its mythical and material constitution. Since the 1595 edition of Mercator's *Atlas* – an account of the creation and form of the whole universe – the Titanic figure of Atlas himself, supporting the globe, has been part of the format's own history and mythography as a bearer of meaning. This applies equally to works of smaller territorial scope, like national atlases. The present chapter examines a much smaller, cheaper, plainer, less elaborately iconographic atlas than those that usually attract scholars' attention – and a more functional one too, in that it was issued to supplement a topographical publication and was meant to be read not simply to aid contemplation of a national territory but also as a means of physically navigating it.

As is well known (and as the previous chapter by Rachel Hewitt has reminded us) the early nineteenth century marked a major cartographic shift in terms of the establishment of vital national scientific survey projects such as that of the Cassinis in France and of the Ordnance Survey in Britain. However, in the early part of the century a range of alternative map forms, and methods for making them, continued to exist. The subject of this chapter, then, concerns an alternative form of national survey to that of the Ordnance Survey, one that is speculative, not state-funded; redraws existing maps rather than making new ones; frames an extensive letterpress of topographical description; and coordinates many other illustrations of sites and scenery, some of which are incorporated in its town plans.

The British Atlas was published as a part work from 1804 to 1809 to accompany *The Beauties of England and Wales*, a serial county-by-county topographical work begun in 1801 under the co-authorship of John Britton and Edward Wedlake Brayley using the methods of documentary survey, with the topographer working on foot. This aspect of the map-making process – involving close engagement with the full cultural topography of each region – radically distinguishes the *Atlas* from its more formal counterparts. *The British Atlas* comprised finely drawn and engraved maps of the counties of England and Wales; two general maps of England and Wales showing the main roads, rivers and canals (Figure 3.1); and plans of twenty-one cities and towns, inset with vignettes and armorial bearings. The maps and plans were engraved in quarto and could be folded and mounted to bind up with the octavo volumes of *The Beauties*. A separate single volume of *The British Atlas* was issued in 1810. This was a much slimmer volume than envisaged. While a 'complete set of county maps' was published, as the title page announced (fifty-eight in all, including four of the Ridings of Yorkshire), the plans scarcely covered the 'Cities and

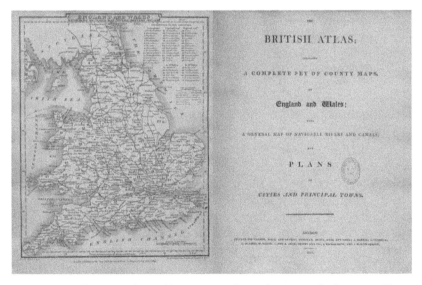

Figure 3.1 John Roper, directed by E. W. Brayley, Index Map and title page to *The British Atlas* (1810). University of Nottingham Libraries – Manuscripts and Special Collections.

Principal Towns'. Only a fraction of the projected urban plans were produced: just fifteen county towns and nine cathedral cities were issued (none in Wales), with some notable places of this kind missing (including York, Salisbury, Truro, Lincoln, Nottingham and Warwick). Among those commercial and industrial towns whose size and growth astonished readers of the 1801 census, Liverpool and Manchester's plans were shown, but there were none of Leeds, Birmingham or Bristol. The total outlay for *The British Atlas* exceeded £4,000, but, before *The Beauties of England and Wales* had been completed, the urban plans were abandoned, largely owing to production costs. Indeed, the price of each number of the *Atlas*, containing three maps, was more than that of each number of the *Beauties*, which contained letterpress and three views; copies were soon being sold off at a loss.[2]

   Together with other map projects of John Britton, the fate of *The British Atlas* – critically well-received but not commercially successful – was a familiar story of speculative, culturally ambitious cartography in the early nineteenth century.[3] It was part of a wider problem of the cost of finely drawn and engraved graphics, including views of various kinds, used to illustrate topographical publications. This chapter examines *The British Atlas* in both graphic and textual terms in the context of the production of *The Beauties of England and Wales*; it also addresses the relations – both contentious and convivial – among the project's various partners and contributors, including writers, artists, patrons, publishers and the two co-authors themselves.

Map-Work

In his recollections of his early life in London – first as an apprentice cellarman newly arrived from a north Wiltshire village, then as attorney's clerk, theatre performer, journalist, and, eventually, topographical author and publisher – John Britton identified geographical knowledge, through maps, text books and travel narratives, as part of a wider self-taught education that expanded the limited horizons of schooling in his native village. To prepare for a two-volume work entitled *The Beauties of Wiltshire* – a precursor to *The Beauties of England and Wales* – Britton took a walking tour of a county which he didn't much know beyond his native region around Chippenham (he had never been to Salisbury or Stonehenge) and which was divided into two contrasting topographical regions: the downlands to the south and the claylands to the north, as different as 'chalk and cheese', as the Wiltshire saying went. What helped Britton envision Wiltshire as a geographical formation was an unannounced visit to the Whig palace of Bowood House. The Marquess of Lansdowne allowed Britton into the library and let him leave with a copy of one of the finest specimens of county cartography: the expensive five-volume folio *Andrews' Map of Wiltshire* (John Andrews and Andrew Dury) – though His Lordship did not offer Britton a lift back to Chippenham, twelve miles away, to relieve the heavy load. Britton learned to travel light with the best small maps he could afford, two or three cheap guidebooks, a pocket compass, pencils, paper and a small portable camera obscura. As well as learning to draw on his travels, he altered and corrected the maps, taking them into the shops of William Faden and John Carey on the Strand, where the revisions were 'consequently inserted into new impressions of their respective plates'.[4]

For Britton, maps were part of a literary and graphic tradition, including pictorial views, statistical tables and narratives of national events in particular places, that helped reform topography as a genre, accessible to a widening public. At the same time, he was conscious that the popular appeal of cartography, through the proliferation of cheap, sometimes crudely produced and inaccurate maps, compromised its cultural status in some literary and artistic circles. 'Map-work' was a dismissive academic term for topographical view-making – a perception against which Britton campaigned as he sought recognition for documentary survey as the framework for high-minded, wide-ranging cultural imagery and associations.[5]

Beauties and Delineations

The success of *The Beauties of Wiltshire* led to a more extensive national work, *The Beauties of England and Wales*, published by Vernor and Hood, a prolific publishing house that focused on low-cost, cheaply illustrated volumes, including (as advertised on the wrappers of each number of *The Beauties*) literary anthologies, guidebooks and reissued literary classics, such as the works of Oliver Goldsmith. Initially planned to be completed in six volumes over three years, the work eventually ran to twenty-five volumes, of increasing length, over sixteen years. Britton undertook authorship in partnership with his Clerkenwell friend and fellow autodidact E. W. Brayley, an enameller by trade. After producing six volumes over six years together, their partnership came under strain, and they wrote under separate authorship before both withdrew from the work in 1811 when it was sold to another publisher, with the remaining counties written by a number of different authors.[6]

From the beginning, despite the commercial success of the work – and in some measure because of it – Britton was in continual dispute with the publishers. Vernor and Hood were keen to capitalize on the success of several publications with 'Beauties' in their titles ('beauties' of character and literature, as well as of scenery). They envisaged a rapid project: a monthly part work, of three prints and thirty pages of letterpress, largely focused on '[Gentlemen's] *Seats and Wood Scenery*', with the text copied, abridged and adapted from published sources, and with little or no new illustration. Britton and Brayley insisted on widening the focus to include a range of locations and forms of knowledge, including ancient history, modern commerce, biography, geology, agriculture, art and architecture, with illustrations of 'celebrated remains of antiquity' and 'the grand productions of nature'. Moreover, they would make new field observations and archival investigations, off the beaten track:

> No place of British ground is so steril [sic] as to want a claim on the feelings and taste of the investigator . . . The walk of Topographical Literature is not calculated for confinement to the dry indiscriminate antiquary and the geneaologist . . . The description of a particular place may be rendered the inspiriting centre of intelligence. (Brewer, *Introduction*, xiv)[7]

In contrast to 'hasty and illiterate compilations, without any attempt at originality, or comparative examination', in which authors followed one another 'like the blinded horse in a mill', the work would be revelatory (Brewer, *Introduction*, xiv). The authors planned to travel extensively to key sites, including libraries and archives, and establish a network of local contacts and correspondents so as to secure information through social introductions and newspaper advertisements, by letter and through responses to a standard questionnaire survey. Many of the correspondents were the traditional sort for topographical works: clerics, schoolmasters and booksellers, keen to contribute to a national work beyond their localities, with a smaller group of gentry and merchants who gave access to their collections and were offered volume dedications. The work took advantage of recent national state surveys: it collected information from the first national census of 1801, the Board of Agriculture's county volumes and the early work of the Ordnance Survey.

Conscious of the inadequacy of the main title *The Beauties of England and Wales* to explain the work, the authors subjoined a secondary one: 'Delineations, Topographical, Historical and Descriptive'. The term 'delineation' assumed a powerful currency in the documentary and eyewitness culture of the time in the context of the clear, systematic and detailed spatial exposition and display of a number of material sites that included the human body as well as buildings and landscapes. Brayley's and Britton's title echoed John Aikin's liberal view of the nation in *England Delineated* (1788) and its epistemology of laying the landscape open, making it accessible to a wide audience, charting a middle way between abstruse theory and dry detail, between entertainment and instruction, and providing '*outline maps* of knowledge' in textual as well as graphic form.[8]

After travelling together on a walking tour of the west of England and Wales to prepare for the undertaking, and then to the counties of Bedford, Berkshire and Buckingham for the first volume in the work's alphabetical order (conveniently close to their London base), Britton and Brayley went their separate ways for the subsequent volumes on more widely spaced counties. In February and March 1802, Britton travelled to Cornwall and Devon; in July, Brayley went to Cambridgeshire and Derbyshire, and later in the year to Durham. The authors used the wrappers of each number to report on the progress of the work (and the lack of it), citing the travails of the topographer as a mark of authenticity. Thus, in the wrapper of the tenth part for March 1802, Brayley explained, 'The present number has been delayed in consequence of my own indisposition, and the absence of Mr. Britton, who, for the sole purpose of obtaining original and accurate information, undertook, in the most inclement season of the year, to make a journey through the counties of Cornwall and Devon, in the former of which he is yet conducting his researches' (Brewer, *Introduction*, x–xi).

Though he was meant to undertake only a share of the writing, Brayley did most for the early volumes, assuming responsibility for the 'literary department' of the work. As well as editorial matters like correspondence, Britton concentrated on illustration – initially his own, then that of others; he commissioned new work when he could, selecting subjects, securing drawings and superintending engraving. This was a sensible move, as Britton was an accomplished draughtsman with a keen eye, while Brayley was the better-read partner, with a highly retentive memory, and a more assiduous scholar, with a prose style unaffected by the fine writing for which Britton had been criticized in previous publications. Brayley could walk and study for hours on end; his was a remarkable range, both in terms of the distance and landscapes covered and in terms of his fields of expertise, from medieval manuscripts to scientific treatises. However, this arduous work came at a cost. He fell into the customary habit of the topographical writer of amassing too much material to process effectively, taxing his powers of discrimination and exposition and turning his volumes into heavily textual, and sometimes pedantic, works. 'I have often known, and sometimes scolded him', Britton recalled, 'for the time and labour he bestowed on the unravelment of a disputed or doubtful point of history, the discrepancy of previous writers, and the verification of a name, date, or event'.[9]

While around 600 engravings were produced for *The Beauties of England and Wales*, the ratio of text to illustration went beyond that originally projected. Moreover, the monthly issue of views was often out of sequence with that of the text, which meant that the relevant views pertaining to a volume were sometimes published years later, at which point they could be placed in sequence in the pages of permanently bound volumes. The authors never secured the budget for the quantity and quality of illustration they envisaged, and the expedients compromised Britton's artistic direction and principle of impartiality. The work of over sixty artists was used. Many drawings were loaned for engraving by local residents, including examples by amateurs as well as the work of professional artists. The team of engravers grew impatient with the publishers, largely for late payment, and copperplates were borrowed or gifted by local worthies, on the assumption that their properties would be featured in the text. Such sourcing of illustration was conventional in topographical works, but it challenged Britton and Brayley's progressive principles of independence and originality.

Maps and Plans

Launched after the first, highly profitable, phase of *The Beauties of England and Wales*, and with an increasing number of publication partners to share the risk (seven are listed on the title page, including the major house of Longman), *The British Atlas* reframed *The Beauties* as a work of delineation in a more visual, objective, systematic and coordinated way. None of the maps was made from newly commissioned surveys; all were redrawn from existing maps, albeit ones prized for their detail and accuracy, and done according to a standard, uniform template across the whole territory. Details such as Roman roads were added by the Bath antiquary Thomas Leman, who provided text on Roman Britain for volumes of *The Beauties*, while armorial bearings for the town plans were supplied by Sir George Naylor. The maps were largely (re)drawn by George Cole (with one map and plan credited to Britton) and engraved by John Roper. Britton and Brayley were separately credited for directing the cartography, largely on the basis of particular volumes of *The Beauties* for which they were respectively responsible. The *Atlas* was a fine achievement and worked as more than an illustration to *The Beauties* (hence its publication as a free-standing volume). As already noted, however, it remained incomplete, with relatively few town plans, and in places it was beset by problems of legibility and articulation.[10]

The county maps were reduced from existing works loaned by William Faden, who took a part share in *The British Atlas*. Geographer to the king and supplier of maps to the Crown and Parliament as well as to the paying public, Faden's name added a lustre to the enterprise. While some of the maps were from Faden's own commissioned surveys, notably those of Kent and Norfolk, many were updated from earlier prestigious, multi-sheet county maps, the copperplates of which Faden purchased at auction and which he continued to sell individually at a premium. While Faden's stock included a comprehensive coverage of county maps, his catalogues reveal a much shorter list of town plans, which helps explain why *The British Atlas* has so few.[11]

George Cole also worked from other maps, including county maps by Faden's rival John Carey. Carey's *New and Correct English Atlas*, first issued in 1787 and continually revised, was a landmark, a consciously modern work and the most original survey since Saxton's *Atlas* of 1579. It emphasized circulation through road and water transport and did so with geographical accuracy, visual economy and fine delineation. If Saxton's *Atlas*, as Richard Helgerson has argued, provided a spatial template to represent the transfer of power from court to country, Carey's provided one that illustrated the transfer of capital from country to city and to commercial and industrial interests, which extended through circulation beyond estate and county boundaries (Helgerson, 'The Land Speaks', 50–65). No less important as base maps for the *British Atlas* were the county maps that Carey produced for Richard Gough's 1789 revision of Camden's *Britannia*, which displayed more antiquarian material, though with Carey's customary clarity.[12] Gough was the leading figure of the Society of Antiquaries; he was also a consciously modern, reformist authority who saw maps – along with other documentary views and illustration – as enlightening and improving 'the wilderness of obscurity' of much antiquarianism. In phrases that became a leitmotif for Britton's project, Gough complained of 'incorrect pedigrees, futile etymologies, verbose disquisitions, crowds of epitaphs, lists of landowners, and such farrago, thrown together without method, unanimated by reflections' by those 'fit only to pore over musty records, and grovel among ruined walls, shut up in closets from the commerce of life, and secluded from information even in their own way'.[13]

Different audiences for the maps – scrutinized both by tourists unfamiliar with a location and by local people who knew the terrain – gave rise to a number of design problems. Standard page dimensions for places of such disparate size and shape required a variety of scales. As reviewers noted, this resulted not only in problems of legibility but also in false impressions, as smaller, densely settled counties such as Rutland were shown – even at small scale – with wide open spaces, while larger counties such as Lincolnshire, with areas of sparse settlement, were shown crowded to the point of confusion. The county maps were uniformly coded to mark traces of ancient Britain, so, in addition to turnpike and mail coach roads, distances from London and between main towns, and places returning MPs, the map marked ruined abbeys, encampments, Roman roads and settlements. The layering and enumeration of administrative divisions, hundreds, half-hundreds and liberties over all the other information further compounded the compression of information, and design decisions inevitably led to some locational inaccuracies. It was perhaps a little churlish for one reviewer to complain of 'an appearance of confusion' in the map of Essex while also demanding that it show a greater number of ancient sites, including barrows and memorial stones, and chiding 'Mr Britton, well known as an indefatigable pedestrian' on the issue of the exact location of various geographical features and on various perceived lacunae.[14]

The urban plans of *The British Atlas* are composite portraits of places, with vignette views, coats of arms and compass roses as well as detailed street and field patterns. Hand-coloured copies are particularly striking as iconic urban images. Many are plans of cities in the technical and traditional sense of that term, denoting the site of a cathedral, and indicate the antiquarian direction Britton and Brayley took in later volumes of *The Beauties*. The vignettes are engraved after the work of some of the artists who provided full-page views for county volumes, and most are an integral part of the cartographic design. The plan of Northampton is an image of civic virtue, almost an ideal town; the composition is based on a 1749 map of the town marketed by Faden, now updated with new information and detail. A panorama of the town drawn by George Shepherd is placed along the lower part of the plan, with some of the key buildings picked out in black on the map, including contemporary ones such as the General Infirmary and dissenters' meeting houses, as well as medieval churches. Panorama and map are aligned so that we look, as it were, both in plan and elevation, seeing both the compressed view, via an approach to the town from the south, and the open display on the map within the encircling boundary of the former town wall (marked by river, remaining masonry and ditch) – an open mix of streets, gardens, orchards and meadows, including the 'Elysian Fields' to the north of the town. The related text tells how great fires cleared the medieval timber buildings, making for a newly planned town with all streets well paved and lit and 'a promenade of healthful exercise' named Paradise Walk.[15] As Britton acknowledges, much of this information was supplied by a Northampton man, the Unitarian George Baker – a 'worthy and zealous topographer' who, as well as making his collections accessible and offering a friendly welcome to the author, impressed his ecumenical vision on the letterpress and plan (Brewer, *Introduction*, xii).

Vignettes for four of the main cathedral cities were engraved after drawings by Edward Dayes and designed to be more integrated into the layout of the plan itself. That for Durham shows a soaring scenic elevation to complement the hachured plan, aligned to the flow of the River Wear. The plans for Hereford, Gloucester and Worcester display Dayes's views of the cathedrals in relation to the River Severn, with that for Hereford (Figure 3.2) focusing on the commercial infrastructure of the river. Considered in conjunction with the text for the Hereford volume, the view of the cathedral sidesteps one of the major architectural controversies of the time. The west front famously collapsed in 1786, bringing down much of the tower, and James Wyatt's restorations provoked outrage in national antiquarian circles (though not as much concern in the city or county themselves). Britton's text is more mindful of the national discourse: it finds the restoration, which detracts from 'the sublimity of the original design', 'extremely incongruous to the principles of the style it pretends to imitate' and blames the 'inadequacy of funds' raised in the city as well as the 'want of skill in the architect'.[16] Dayes' view faces judiciously west, the offending restored front facing away from the spectator, though the truncated squatness of the tower is evident enough. (In the view by John Varley facing the relevant passage of text in the volume, the tower is crowned with recently added battlements and pinnacles.) The censure of the cathedral authorities in the text extends to a neglected interior, with its prize treasure, the 'ancient *Map* of the world, on vellum . . . within a frame ornamented by foliage . . . discovered under a pile of lumber', which is 'even now sufficiently neglected': 'the whole is so thickly covered in dirt, that the full design cannot be traced' (*The Beauties of England and Wales: Vol. 6*, 470).

The year 1805 was the annus mirabilis of Britton and Brayley's national survey. The first full year of *The British Atlas* saw a third of the maps and

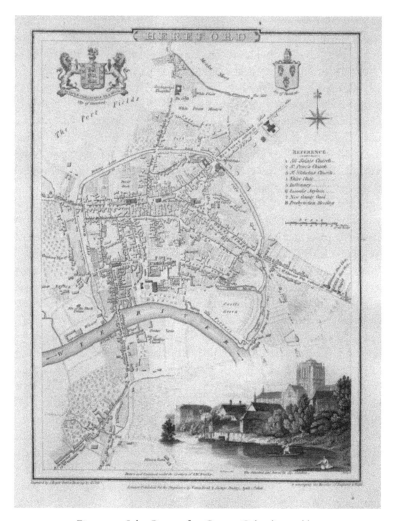

Figure 3.2 John Roper after George Cole, directed by
E. Brayley, *Hereford*, from *The British Atlas* (1810). University of Nottingham
Libraries – Manuscripts and Special Collections.

plans published, many synchronized with volumes of text and illustrations.
The sixth volume published that year – containing Hampshire,
Herefordshire and the Isle of Wight – represents the pinnacle of the
editorial partnership and, at this critical period of the war with France
(the year of the Battles of Trafalgar and Austerlitz), the high point of *The*

Beauties as patriotic topography. The numbers for Hampshire and the Isle of Wight are particularly attuned to their locations' strategic position: a long cross-Channel history is given, and, in a lengthy entry for Portsmouth and its recent dock development, Britton's former opposition to the war is duly and dutifully buried. (During a visit to the port at the end of his pedestrian tour of 1798, Britton found himself in a lodging house with grieving women who had been informed they had lost husbands and sons in the Battle of the Nile (Britton, *Autobiography*, 138–9).) The title-page epigraph to the sixth volume is a passage assembled from *A Poetical Address to the Right Honourable Edmund Burke* (1791) by Britton's friend, the Wiltshire cleric William Lisle Bowles – a work that contrasts '*Gallia*'s ravaged shore' with '*Albion*'s happier plain':

> fairest Isle, whose verdant plain
> Springs beauteous from the blue and billowy main;
> In peaceful pomp whose glittering cities rise,
> And lift their crowded temples to the skies;
> Whose streams reflect full many an attic pile,
> Whose velvet lawns in long luxuriance smile;
> Whose navy on the broad brine awful rolls;
> Whose commerce glows beneath the distant poles:
> Thee! O my country! all my soul reveres
> And admiration swells with ripening years.[17]

Just as the sixth volume of *The Beauties of England and Wales* was published, however, the partnership between Britton and Brayley began to break down. From this point onward they undertook to produce separate volumes under individual authorship.

The Beauties of Lancashire

In September 1805, Britton traversed the country from west to east for the volume on Lancashire, Leicestershire and Lincolnshire, which was published in 1807. Its stated aim – with a sidelong glance at Brayley's unfinished volume on Kent – was to produce the monthly eight parts 'regularly and punctually', 'without delay'. The very speed of production owed much to the contribution of a network of over fifty correspondents, who supplied information, illustrations and text; access to a major source for Leicestershire, compiled by his friend John Nichols; and the assistance of another author, the Rev. John Evans, in writing the text for Lincolnshire. In the circular letter to correspondents, Britton identified the hallmarks of the work as 'brevity, perspicuity and selection', its aim being to 'give a pleasing and familiar picture of the *geography*, *statistics* and national peculiarities of England in the aggregate, and of its parochial characteristics in particular' – a 'familiar picture' here meaning one of popular, convivial appeal (Brewer, *Introduction*, xvii).

In his introductory text, Britton explained that this volume was the first to be written under his name alone, and he set out his principles in doing so, characterizing the work as an extension of the communication he enjoyed with his 'intelligent correspondents' who wrote '*freely* and *fully*' when they were confident their 'favours will be properly appreciated':

> It has long been a maxim with me, that the writer and reader should perfectly understand each other; that there should be no reserve or ambiguity in the former, nor suspicion or doubt with the latter. A mutual cordiality and confidence should exist, and then the one would pursue his labours with comfort and pleasure to himself, whilst the other would read with additional advantage and delight.[18]

Lancashire fulfilled this principle. Thirty named individuals are thanked for 'personal civilities' as well as much 'useful information' that went to make a work completed in three parts between May and August 1807. The wrappers for each number included progress reports that amounted to a conversational, correspondence-like forum in which organizations like the Liverpool Corporation as well as individuals were thanked for specific contributions; material was invited on locations that were in preparation; and explanations were given for why certain information could not be incorporated in time for the printers as the 'sheet [was] worked off'. While the 300-page account of the county was 'necessarily concise to a certain degree', it was 'more copious and circumstantial' than any other such publication, based on 'personal survey ... communications of kind and intelligent correspondents [and] original documents', together with the 'careful examination and advantage of every preceding literary work' (*The Beauties of England and Wales: Vol. 9*, iv). The national imperative was clear, for the 1801 census revealed Lancashire as a county of 690,000, second only to Middlesex – its spectacular growth largely fuelled by commerce and industry, as charted by tables of statistics.

Lancashire is envisaged as a county with open 'avenues to wealth and commerce', principally through its network of waterways, as shown on the large map of navigation in *The British Atlas*, with references also made in the text to other canal maps on sale from Faden. It was precisely navigation that put the county in the vanguard of map-making, which extended beyond its county boundaries in coordinated trigonometrical surveys, eastward to Yorkshire and south to the Midlands. A corollary of this spatial matrix in the text is the assumption that this is territory only imperfectly known and that it is a field for original delineation. So the text begins around Lancaster, with the claim that 'few of the county towns in England ... have been more neglected by the Historian, or more inaccurately described by the Topographer' (*The Beauties of England and Wales: Vol. 9*, 51). At this point, a new monumental ancient and modern history is depicted, framed by an illustration of a recently revealed Roman altar (shown on the title page in splendid antique isolation) and, in the absence of an urban plan, by two views of the town: one after a painting by Julius Caesar Ibbetson of Brookbank's shipyard with a large vessel on the stocks, loaned by local MP John Dent; and another by William Daniel of Rennie's viaduct with a view of the town. Doubtless in deference to Dent, a Tory anti-abolitionist, Lancaster's trade is neutrally described as 'West Indian', though Britton's liberal sentiments become more pronounced as the text moves further south. In the section on Liverpool, the effects on Atlantic trade of the 'devastating and calamitous war' are tabulated, as is the increasing tonnage of slave-trade ships in the eighteenth century before the recent 1807 Act of Abolition, as a reminder of the 'cruelty, injustice, and ignominy' of a trade that certain recent publications on the city were minded to forget (*The Beauties of England and Wales: Vol. 9*, 197).

One of Britton's Manchester-born correspondents strongly influenced the work. George Ormerod – aged twenty-one and on the verge of gentlemanly independence and a career as an antiquarian author – supplied Britton with some of his own drawings, including two views of Manchester College, one of which features in the plan of the city. In a letter that Britton published, Ormerod wrote: 'I always considered your "Beauties" as not intended to enter into deep disquisitions applicable only to the antiquary, or addressed merely to the local vanity of certain county inhabitants; but, as a popular work for general entertainment and utility ... a focus to collect the scattered rays of information' (Brewer, *Introduction*, xii).

The plan of Manchester (Figure 3.3) makes the town's 'present state' plain to see. Based on a new survey by local surveyor Richard Thornton, the map of 'Manchester and Salford' shows not just the 'crowdedly filled' areas along the main waterways but also the built environment striking outward along the main roads in newly marked streets on the suburban periphery that was fast appropriating the fields. If Manchester College is still marked as the civic centre, it is offset and diminished by the town's expansion and 'progressive augmentation'. The inset vignette of the

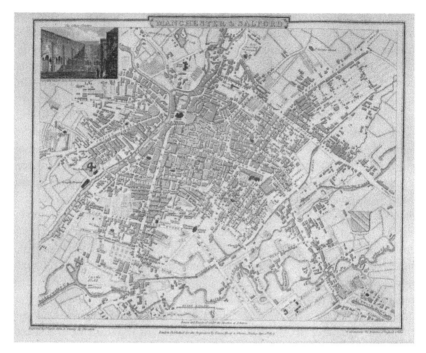

Figure 3.3 John Roper, from a survey by Richard Thornton, directed by John Britton, *Manchester & Salford*, from *The British Atlas* (1810). University of Nottingham Libraries – Manuscripts and Special Collections.

College cloisters (after Ormerod's drawing) is positioned on the map on the fields of Salford, relatively close to the building itself, but – unlike the vignettes of smaller county and cathedral towns – it is relatively small (to the point of illegibility) and not an integral part of the topographical design. Rather, it is pasted on as a small window into history. And unlike the heraldic coats of arms on plans of county towns, which are prominently displayed on the white space of the page, that for Manchester is placed half-hidden on the fields to the south-east of the map, its stripes echoing newly constructed streets.

The Beauties of Kent

In contrast to Britton's Lancashire, Brayley's text for Kent proved to be a massive, time-consuming undertaking. Cartographically, it had the advantage, for its accompanying *British Atlas* map, of being able to draw

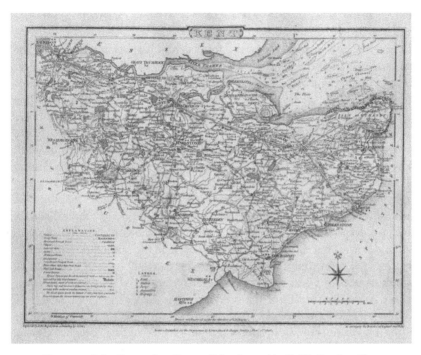

Figure 3.4 John Roper after George Cole, directed by E. W. Brayley, *Kent*, from *The British Atlas* (1810). University of Nottingham Libraries – Manuscripts and Special Collections.

on one of the most famous county surveys – a reduction of Faden's 1801 map of Kent, the first for the Ordnance Survey (Figure 3.4). Here was a patriotic peninsular image of the British bulwark against the threat of Napoleon's empire; the map shows a densely settled land, with pronounced hachuring and sea-depth contours off the coast – a graphic representation that clearly revealed the county's shape and structure.

The text was published in seventeen monthly parts (many delayed) up to the end of 1807, its 800 pages spreading over two volumes, with the majority of its illustrations issued well after the text. These included modern-style coastal views of Margate and Ramsgate in 1812, commissioned by new publishers when Brayley had withdrawn from the work, together with some pictures published years before. The very attraction of Kent as a subject proved a source of authorial anxiety. Kent had long been upheld as a strategic county for the nation as a whole – rich in history and antiquity, agriculture and industry, and coastal commerce, as well as being a bulwark of military defence. Now, with the progressive enrichment of the county through metropolitan expansion, together with the external pressure of war in the form of the Napoleonic Blockade, the national profile of the county was at its height. Kent was already the most described and depicted county in Britain, with a vast literature for Brayley to appraise as he made his own observations and solicited information from residents. This was a much less rapid reconnaissance than Britton's Lancashire. The contrast in speed in the production of the two works brings home a contrast as if between an old and a new England, with Brayley's exploration of Kent's deep topography marked by a high density of medieval history and literary allusion, with scarcely any of the 'geography and statistics' that characterized Britton's social mapping of Lancashire. Canterbury alone is given 275 pages, layered with antiquarian and anecdotal detail, with only a cursory engagement with the place as a modern working city. While Dayes's view of the landmark entrance of the city – St Augustine's Gate – displays the patriotic sight of men loading barrels of beer, the text simply notes that the scene is 'strangely disfigured by the smoke and steam of the brewery'.[19]

Brayley's 'Kent' is dedicated to Samuel Egerton Brydges, founder-editor of the magazine The Topographer (1789–1801). Avoiding 'weighty discussions' on topography as a form of knowledge, this publication emphasized the uncelebrated lives of 'men eminent for their descent' who 'yet have never been raised to the honor of nobility'. 'At this time,' Brydges remarks, 'every year produces an inundation of new men, that over-run almost every county in the Kingdom [and] destroy the venerable mansions of antiquity'.[20] Brydges's anti-Jacobin novel Arthur Fitz-Albini (1798) charted the same cultural terrain, following the travails of a sensitive, ancestral landowner without fortune or title and lamenting the rise of democratic systems and the decline of hereditary culture at the hands of book-hating squires and metropolitan bankers who were buying into ancient estates. Many readers, including some of Brydges's neighbours, recognized the novel as a lightly fictionalized account of the cultural values and situation of the author himself. Brydges ruined himself financially in rebuilding Denton Court as an Elizabethan-style mansion, stocking it with rare books and persuading his brother to press a claim to the extinct Chandos peerage on the supposition that their father – the grandson of a Canterbury grocer (as critics were pleased to report) – represented a cadet branch of the ducal family. Following his brother's death in 1807, Brydges himself adopted the title, though in 1803 the House of Lords had ruled the family claim unfounded, with suspicions that Brydges had altered parish registers.[21]

On the dedication page, Brayley affirms Brydges's claim to the peerage, reporting later in the work that the 'few Lords then present' in 1803 had ruled that the claim was '*suspended*' until 'additional proof on one or two points' was supplied (*The Beauties of England and Wales: Vol. 8*, 1074). Moreover, Denton Court occupies a key place in Brayley's survey of Kent. His sojourn there emboldened him to criticize the style of the standard authority on the county from which he had derived much information – the revised edition of Edward Hasted's twelve-volume *History and Topographical Survey of the County of Kent*, published between 1797 and 1801: 'Mr Hasted, whose details of the scenery of Nature are generally deficient, has been more particularly unfortunate in his descriptive accounts of the contiguous parishes of Wootton and Denton than elsewhere'. Brayley emphasizes that, far from being '*wild* and *dreary*' and lying '*obscurely* and *unfrequented*', the seat of Denton Court was two miles from Canterbury and only six from Dover, on 'the great road to the *Continent*', with the turnpike road from Folkestone to Hythe running 'across the grounds directly in front' (*The Beauties of England and Wales: Vol. 8*, 1075).

Brayley's other main correspondent in Kent was Mark Noble, rector of Barming near Maidstone. Noble was a more established figure in Kentish society than Brydges, having been presented with his living by the king in 1784. He was well networked with the county aristocracy, enjoyed wealth and was possessed of sufficient leisure to pursue antiquarian researches in fields as diverse as the genealogies of European royal families, biographies of regicides and an account of the coinage of the episcopal Palatines of Durham. As the *Gentleman's Magazine* noted, these works 'procured for him the reputation of industry and application, if not of perspicuity and correctness', and his manuscript works greatly outnumbered his published volumes.[22] Among Noble's large collection of papers bequeathed to the Bodleian Library are a series of letters from Brayley concerning preparations for the Kent volume of *The Beauties*. Characteristically crammed with anxious enquiries and often hurriedly written, the letters to Noble reveal how arduous Brayley found the work. He is frequently apologizing for not visiting Barming as planned, owing to the time taken in writing and travelling or to having been in general 'fettered by occurrences', which included bouts of illness and a broken axle shaft on his chaise, whose repair was botched by 'a blundering wheelwright and stupid blacksmith'.[23] The deeper Brayley went into Kent (the county itself as well as the literature on it), the more he confessed he struggled to 'realise my own conceptions' and exercise some discrimination in marshalling the abundance of material: 'I find the Beauties of Kent so attractive, I do not know how to leave them.'[24] Noble helped Brayley in a number of ways, making introductions, distributing his questionnaire to neighbouring aristocrats and answering his many questions on the locality, though Noble's tendency to answer in general terms provoked Brayley to press for further particulars, such as verbatim transcriptions of epitaphs, the precise source of the claim that Henry V had made cannonballs from stones in the vicinity of Maidstone and 'the exact *mineralogical* description of Kentish Ragstone'.[25]

We learn from these letters that a six-month period of illness from January to June 1807 prevented Brayley from writing much, if anything. Brayley details his steps to recovery: he adopted a vegetarian diet and sought a new residence away from the foul air of central London, though this deprived him of easy access to libraries (he owned few books), which was one reason he canvassed support to be nominated as a member of the Society of Antiquaries. Finally in 1808, Brayley was able to send Noble the full volume on Kent before he turned to Middlesex – 'a troublesome county', he declared, for 'the vast mass of material relates to London' (he was eventually forced to abandon the volume).[26] Brayley's final letter to Noble would be written eight years later in 1816, from an address off Fleet Street; it enclosed a prospectus for John Preston Neale's volume of views of Westminster Abbey, for which Brayley wrote the letterpress. Brayley put the lapse in correspondence down to 'an illness of some years and many *disastrous Embarrassments*'; no longer a 'pursuer of the "Beauties" of the land', he wrote, he was now 'almost a daily sojourner among the *Tombs of Westminster Abbey*'.[27]

Strength and Independence

When the publisher Thomas Hood died in 1811, *The Beauties of England and Wales* was sold to John Harris on the understanding that he would take over all management and speed up production. Britton and Brayley seceded from the business, with Britton relinquishing his status as shareholder and his control over illustration. The pace of production increased significantly, with the remaining seven volumes produced between 1812 and 1816 at almost twice the previous rate, with more publishers taking a share of a work that was sustaining high sales. Nine more authors were commissioned to write the remaining fifteen English counties, and two were commissioned to deliver on North and South Wales.

Near the completion of *The Beauties of England and Wales*, one of its publishers, Baldwin, Cradock and Joy, reissued the accompanying county maps that had hitherto appeared as *The British Atlas* in a work on 'a new plan', entitled *English Topography* (1816). The title page has a couplet from Bowles's *Poetical Address* to Burke, which – as already noted – had been quoted at greater length as the epigraph for the sixth volume of *The Beauties of England and Wales*. *English Topography* was produced in difficult financial circumstances after the war, in the context of the 'depressed state of our manufactures and the languishing state of our commerce', at a time when Britain was seeking to regain its 'STRENGTH and INDEPENDENCE'.[28] One element of the project was an aspiration to extend the number of urban plans; in the end, however, this ambition was reserved as a 'future opportunity' for a separate volume that never materialized. *English Topography* was authored by Joseph Nightingale, whose literary commissions included later volumes of *The Beauties of England and Wales* (he completed Middlesex and undertook Staffordshire, Somerset and Shropshire), though Britton regarded him as an uncritical compiler. Nightingale is defensive in the Preface to *English Topography* in the face of critics who charged him with merely paraphrasing published work and whom he thought might deny him, a well-travelled writer, 'a "right of way" through the Republic of Letters'. *English Topography* is, however, impressive as a concise work of 'historical and statistical description' (including new information on population growth between 1801 and 1811) that draws on original sources, with succinct text on each county following each map. What makes the page of tiny typeface navigable are the short paragraphs under standard rubrics such as 'Name, and Early History', 'Air, Land, Water, and Natural Productions', 'Eminent Persons, and Titles', 'Manufactures, Trade, &c.' and 'Table of Towns'. The text does not therefore offer a topographical tour, least of all the kind of rambling tour that in a stylistic as well as a spatial sense characterized some of the later volumes of *The Beauties of England and Wales*; rather, *English Topography* works as a compact, trenchant, comparative gazetteer, with displays of information that complement its maps.

The republication of *The British Atlas* as part of *English Topography*, and the decision to abandon its completion, mark a wider decline of the format of county-atlas-with-urban-plans. The developments that hastened that decline are apparent in *The British Atlas* itself, as it revealed the capacity of the county as a rapidly changing cultural formation and graphic image to disclose transformative nineteenth-century geographical developments that cut across such traditional boundaries. County maps and plans continued to be issued on occasion, often garishly coloured, either as antique maps or as cartographic images fast fading into curiosities that no purchaser was seriously expected to consult as up-to-date guides. This may seem an ironic – if familiar – fate for a project that had begun with a progressive impulse, but, like *The Beauties of England and Wales*, *The British Atlas* represents the past: even on publication, its format recalled the cartography of the previous century.

In the introduction to this chapter I emphasized the cultural complexity of the atlas as a cartographical format, published in conspicuously large, luxurious volumes, made for the libraries of wealthy patrons and customers, attracting scholarly attention by virtue of their aesthetic and political significance, articulated in often elaborately iconographic combinations of image and text. *The British Atlas* seems, on the face of it, a very *different* work: plainer, shorter, unfinished, commercially produced in a volatile market, with changing partnerships. This helps explain why such atlases have hitherto attracted little scholarly attention in terms of their form, content, making and meaning. *The British Atlas* stands in this tradition, but it was produced with higher production values than most in terms of accuracy, information and design. Beginning publication as a serial publication four years after the start of *The Beauties of England and Wales*, *The British Atlas* sought to capitalize on the commercial success of *The Beauties*, supplement its improving quality of illustrated views and enhance the articulation of the project as a national work in progress. While redrawn and engraved from existing surveys, the maps and plans express the subtitled values of 'delineation' ('delineations topographical, historical and descriptive') over those of the publisher's main title, 'beauties'. The style was not entirely plain, and the town plans in particular were more elaborate, with vignettes and cartouches, but all graphics aimed to be clear and concise to accompany the reading of the text in the comfort of modest homes – or even on the road in transit – at a time when British topography was a patriotic pursuit. The appearance of *The British Atlas* as a single volume in 1810 with all the county maps (but only a fraction of the urban plans) represents not just unfinished business but the breakdown of the editors' partnership and their departure from *The Beauties of England and Wales* – Britton for a more lucrative and prestigious career in finely illustrated publishing, Brayley for a penurious path of occasional research and writing. In 1812, as secretary of the Literary Fund, Britton succeeded in obtaining funds for a now destitute Brayley, securing for him in 1825 a permanent post as librarian of the Russell Institution, close to Britton's villa in Bloomsbury. Brayley's own publishing career revived, as, ultimately, did his authorial partnership with Britton, though topographical publishing no longer commanded the commercial and cultural esteem it had at the height of the success of *The Beauties of England and Wales* and during the ambitious beginnings of *The British Atlas*.

Notes

1. See Veronica Della Dora, 'Performative Atlases: Memory, Materiality and (Co-)Authorship', *Cartographica* 44:4 (2009): 241–56; Richard Helgerson, 'The Land Speaks: Cartography, Chorography and Subversion in Renaissance England', *Representations* 16 (1986): 50–85; Peter Barber and Tom Harper, *Magnificent Maps: Power, Propaganda and Art* (London: The British Library, 2010), 92–3. I wish to acknowledge that the research for this chapter was supported by a Leverhulme Major Research Fellowship.
2. T. E. Jones, *A Descriptive Account of the Literary Works of John Britton, FSA* (London: For Subscribers to the Testimonial, 1849), 38–9.
3. See Stephen Daniels, 'Mapping the Metropolis in an Age of Reform: John Britton's London Topography, 1820–1840', *Journal of Historical Geography* 56 (2017): 61–82.
4. John Britton, *The Autobiography of John Britton, FSA* (London: Charles Muskett, 1850), 319–20, 354–5.
5. The term 'map-work' was coined by Henry Fuseli as part of his dismissal of topographical view-making in his lectures as Professor of Painting at the Royal Academy. See John Knowles, ed., *The Life and Writings of Henry Fuseli*, 3 vols. (London: Henry Colburn and Richard Bentley, 1831), II, 217. For Britton's response to Fuseli, see John Britton, *Fine Arts of the English School* (London: Longman, 1812), 65.
6. See John Brewer, *The Beauties of England and Wales: Introduction to the Original Delineations, Topographical, Historical and Descriptive* (London: John Harris, 1818), v–xxxiv. The best modern study of the publication is a chapter in A. J. Kennedy, 'British Topographical Print Series in Their Social and Economic Context, c.1720–c.1840' (unpublished PhD thesis, Courtauld Institute, University of London, 1998), 126–56.
7. See also Jones, *A Descriptive Account*, 29–38.
8. See Stephen Daniels and Paul Elliott, '"Outline Maps of Knowledge": John Aikin's Geographical Imagination', in *Religious Dissent and the Aikin-Barbauld Circle, 1740–1860*, eds. Felicity James and Ian Inkster (Cambridge: Cambridge University Press, 2010): 94–125. On 'delineation' more widely, see Sam Smiles, *Eye Witness: Artists and Visual Documentation in Britain, 1770–1830* (Aldershot: Ashgate, 2000).
9. John Britton, 'Edward Wedlake Brayley, Esq.', *Gentleman's Magazine* 44 (December 1854): 582–6.
10. See David Smith, *Antique Maps of the British Isles* (London: Batsford, 1982), 125–7.
11. See William Faden, *Catalogue of Geographical Works Published by William Faden* (London: Faden, 1822); Andrew Macnair and Tom Williamson,

William Faden and Eighteenth-Century Landscape (Oxford: Wingatherer, 2010), 1–62.

12. See Thomas Chubb, *The Printed Maps in the Atlases of Great Britain and Ireland* (London: The Homeland Association, 1927), 247–53; Catherine Delano-Smith and Roger J. P. Kain, *English Maps: A History* (London: The British Museum, 1999), 106–8.

13. Quoted in John Britton, *An Essay on Topographical Literature* (London: Wiltshire Topographical Society, 1843), xii.

14. *Eclectic Review* 1 (1805): 868–9.

15. John Evans and John Britton, *The Beauties of England and Wales; Or, Delineations Topographical, Historical, and Descriptive, of Each County*, vol. 11 (London: Vernor, Hood & Sharpe, 1810), 136.

16. E. W. Brayley and John Britton, *The Beauties of England and Wales; Or, Delineations Topographical, Historical, and Descriptive, of Each County*, vol. 6 (London: Vernor & Hood, 1805), 461.

17. See William Lisle Bowles, *Sonnets, and Other Poems*, 7th ed. (London: T. Cadell, 1800), 122–3.

18. John Britton, *The Beauties of England and Wales; Or, Delineations Topographical, Historical, and Descriptive, of Each County*, vol. 9 (London; Vernor, Hood & Sharpe, 1807), iii–iv.

19. E. W. Brayley, *The Beauties of England and Wales; Or, Delineations Topographical, Historical, and Descriptive, of Each County*, vol. 8 (London: Vernor, Hood & Sharpe, 1808), 888.

20. [Samuel Brydges], 'Preface', *The Topographer* 1 (1789), i–viii, iii.

21. See K. A. Manley, 'Sir Samuel Egerton Brydges (1762–1837)', *Oxford Dictionary of National Biography*, www.oxforddnb.com/view/article/3809 (accessed 1 September 2018).

22. See Gordon Goodwin, 'Mark Noble (1754–1827)', *Oxford Dictionary of National Biography*, www.oxforddnb.com/view/article/20221 (accessed 1 September 2018).

23. E. W. Brayley, letters to Mark Noble, 1 August 1806–27 December 1808, Bodleian Library, MS. Eng. Misc. d.159.

24. Bodleian Library, MS. Eng. Misc. d.159.

25. Bodleian Library, MS. Eng. Misc. d.159.

26. Bodleian Library, MS. Eng. Misc. d.159.

27. E. W. Brayley to Mark Noble, 5 November 1816, Bodleian Library, MS. Eng. Misc. d.164, f.47.

28. Joseph Nightingale, *English Topography; Or, A Series of Historical and Statistical Descriptions of the Several Counties of England and Wales* (London: Baldwin, Cradock & Joy, 1816), n.p.

CHAPTER 4

Mapping Invasion
Cartography, Caricature, Frames of Reading

Damian Walford Davies

Conceptual Coordinates

It is ground I thought I knew well from many visits over the years –
a peninsula *manqué* (peninsula itself meaning 'almost-island'), five miles by
three-and-a-half, extending in a series of cliffs, bays, and coves into
Cardigan Bay on the north coast of Pembrokeshire in Wales. Called
Strumble Head in English (the first element possibly from 'storm' and
'bill' – that is, headland) and Pen-caer in Welsh ('fort headland', named for
the Iron Age encampment on the summit of the outcrop of Garn Fawr in
its western reaches), it is an ancient landscape of Neolithic tombs and
Bronze Age standing stones, Iron Age settlements, churches of ancient
foundation, small farms, narrow lanes, and high hedges. Geologically, this
is volcanic territory, igneous extrusions having cooled to a series of bare or
furze-covered ridges from which spectacular vistas open out. It remains an
area of sparse population, seemingly cut off from the activity of Goodwick
ferry terminal and the town of Fishguard to the south-east.

I walked this ground for a day in March 2018 with the aid (if that is quite
the word) not of an Ordnance Survey map but of an example of late-1790s
commemorative cartography – or chorography, given its local, particularist
focus – that renders the peninsula uncanny. My contention in this chapter
is that such a defamiliarization was precisely the effect the map would have
had at the moment of its publication on 11 February 1798. I examine the
complex work accomplished by this still little-known and manifestly
underexplored map – *A Plan of that Part of the County of Pembroke called
Pen-Caer and the Sea Coast Adjacent* – 'delineated from actual Survey' by
a local land surveyor, Thomas Propert, about whom, beyond this particular map, we know very little. I analyse the series of startling effects his map
both consciously and unknowingly generates. I also identify the contiguous disciplines, discourses, genres, and graphic scripts – both metropolitan
and distinctly local – that make up the text's rich laminations. By thus

historicizing, deconstructing, and theorizing the map (all things that the verbal-visual icon itself accomplishes), the chapter makes a case for this multi-genre text of semiotic superfluity as a sophisticated cartographic response to a traumatic event and its aftermath.

The very ground of the Propert map is paradox. Offering what might be called a cartographic telling (the map relishes, and is troubled by, the oxymoron), this text is committed equally to the values of scientific mensuration and pictural distortion. It is compelled to fix and endlessly restage history, to exorcise and forever rehearse trauma. It is also concerned simultaneously to localize and internationalize the series of events it represents so that the chorography it offers – underpinned by 'local values' – is part of an implied wider geopolitical atlas.[1] I will also argue that the map pioneeringly collapses the distinction between cartography and caricature, geography and the grotesque, triangulation and terror. It advertises its technicism only to trouble its credentials with a commitment to what might be called a cartographic phenomenology. Further, the map's ideological positioning – indeed, partisanship and posturing – is recursively undercut by its play of signs, both internal and intertextual. This is a map that is interested in calibrating the resonance of ground *in the wake of* the events and social and political relationships it plots and narrativizes. In this sense, the chapter intervenes in discussions of the conflicted genetics of the cartographic imagination in the 1790s. At this time, 'knowing' a territory was (necessarily) a complex amalgam of Enlightenment calculation and haptic happenstance – a negotiation between strict cartographic codification and 'obscurity, imagination and emotion', in which clarity and control were tested by 'idiosyncrasy, individualism and disorientation' that neither the process of map-making nor the finished map-text could disavow. This is because there can be no such thing as a cartography that is not both 'subjective' and 'persuasive'.[2]

One would not expect the sophisticated effects I ascribe to Propert's map to materialize in what seems the product of provincial expertise. But that is itself a prompt to take this map as a case study in historicized literary-cartographic reading. Cultivating a self-awareness, inherited from Romantic New Historicist debates, concerning how precisely to delimit 'context', the chapter explores the interpretative challenge and temptation Propert's map poses both for the late-1790s reader and tourist-user and for the contemporary Romanticist fieldworker. Since the deconstruction of the map as a fit object of enquiry for a 'theoretically informed geography' and 'rhetorical close reading' in the 1980s, we have been trained to bring to cartographic texts a hypersensitivity concerning the contours of their absences, the wider networks in which they signify, their inveterate meta-phoricity and allusive dimensionality, and the 'valuative' nature of their rhetorical distortions.[3] As inheritor of metacritical debates concerning some of the methodological excesses of New Historicist readings, the Romanticist also brings to that analysis a self-consciousness concerning the limits of interpretative possibility – a self-consciousness this present chapter seeks to uphold.

Geo-historical Coordinates: In the Field

The map whose conceptual work and phenomenological effects I have noted is a response to the last invasion of mainland Britain, which took place – as is well known – on the afternoon of 22 February 1797 when a heterogeneous but well-armed French force of between 1,200 and 1,400 conscripts and regulars landed on Carregwastad Point on Strumble Head's northern coastline. The work, from the 1920s, of such historians as David Salmon, E. H. Stuart Jones, Roland Quinault, Richard Rose, and J. E. Thomas – each, with various degrees of revisionist energy, sifting myth from available fact, aware of the episode's lacunae and contending narratives – has given us a portrait of three days in which invasion fears, harboured since 1793, were finally realized.[4] These authors have also emphasized the invasion's cultural, political, and psychological legacy in the form of a series of recriminations that culminated in a Welsh treason trial in September 1797. What is clear is that the invasion – though swiftly contained and involving no military exchange with British troops – cannot be dismissed as 'French farce and Welsh flannel' (Quinault, 'The French Invasion', 618); it visited violence on Strumble Head and was traumatic at local and national levels. As the resonant event that the cartographic subject of this chapter seeks to represent, the invasion is worth rehearsing and conceptualizing as a prelude to an ekphrastic-historicist reading of Propert's map that focuses on its compelling pictural prompts and strategies of narrativization.

Why the *descente* on Wales in the service of a *chouannerie* or popular uprising was launched at all is still a question worth asking, given that it was initially conceived – together with an attack on the north of England from the North Sea – as a diversion 'to the main effort against Ireland' that had already foundered in December 1796 in the stormy waters of Bantry Bay. Wales was itself never the primary objective of the attack; that was to be Bristol, and, if that proved too heavily defended, then Chester and Liverpool 'from a *point d'appui* on the shores of Cardigan Bay' (Stuart

Jones, *The Last Invasion*, 64). The concern of the government was with fortifying other potential points of attack – 'the Firth of Forth, the Humber, and the Downs, and the Channel ports', together with 'Dover, Portsmouth, Portland, Torbay and Falmouth', and Cork in Ireland (154). Thus the Pembrokeshire landing was utterly unanticipated in the place where landfall was eventually made, and the shock rendered Strumble Head weird ground.

Masterminded by General Louis Lazare Hoche, who harboured a deep hatred of Britain, having defeated a British-aided émigré landing at Quiberon in the summer of 1795, the Wales expedition was led by *Chef de Brigade* William Tate – whose age at the time remains ambiguous, with documents referring to him as sixty, over seventy, and forty-three years old, this last now being generally accepted (Thomas, *Britain's Last Invasion*, 60). An American, possibly of Irish stock, he had convincing enough anti-British credentials, having served in the American War of Independence, to be entrusted with the project by Hoche and to be courted by Theobald Wolfe Tone. And yet, in the light of the fact that more than half the invading force were, as Hoche noted, irregulars 'from all the prisons in my district', 'picked convicts from the galleys', and royalists captured at Quiberon ('banditti', 'sad blackguards', 'desperadoes', as Tone noted in his journal), it is hard not to believe that the French Directory regarded them as dispensable – *enfants perdus, mauvaises sujets* – and the *descente* (merely) as a means of spreading terror and alarm and of testing the allegiance of the local populace (Stuart Jones, *The Last Invasion*, 55–6).

Tate's orders on landing were to live off the land and seek to foment a peasant insurrection and as *grande* a *peur* as possible. Technically called the Deuxième Légion des Francs, his force – which also comprised 600 well-trained (and characteristically tall) regular grenadiers, together with a number of Irish officers – was dubbed *La Légion Noire*. The name derived from the fact that they were clothed in British uniforms captured at Quiberon that had been dyed a dark brown – 'brown', as John, Duke of Rutland noted in one of the first touristic accounts of the invasion, 'being the only die *[sic]* that red will take. There was . . . a sort of reddish cast in it, which had a very ugly appearance.'[5] Uncannily, British infantry red was returning to Britain 'grotesquely-dyed' (Stuart Jones, *The Last Invasion*, 123) and seeking vengeance – a material element of the switchback ideological currents and uncanny layerings registered, as we shall see, by Propert's map of the invasion.

Having sailed up the Bristol Channel as far as Porlock, the fleet – comprising two large, state-of-the-art frigates (*Vengeance* and *Résistance*), a corvette (*Constance*), and a lugger (*Vautour*) – abandoned the attack on Bristol and sailed around south Wales into Cardigan Bay. Skilfully negotiating challenging topography, Tate effected a landing up steep cliffs at Carregwastad Point around 4 p.m. on 22 February 1797 – a day 'more than ordinarily mild and serene for the season of the year', as the topographical writer James Baker noted in an illustrated pamphlet that emerged with impressive speed.[6] A local farm, Trehowel (well stocked by its tenant, John Mortimer, against his imminent wedding), was commandeered as head-quarters, and the French fleet under Commodore Jean Joseph Castagnier soon departed. Thus began a series of French movements and troop dispositions across the peninsula involving random (and alcohol-fuelled) plundering of the headland's farmhouses and the inland deployment on the morning of Thursday, 23 February, of two advanced guards. These movements and accompanying actions were to be registered on the Propert map, whose graphic codes simultaneously paralyse and animate them. The first French detachment, of around 800 men, moved a short distance south from their camp to the ridge of rocky outcrops called Carn Gelli, possibly with a picket guard positioned along a narrow lane leading towards Trefwrgi farm, up which any opposing British force may have chosen to march into the peninsula. The second detachment tracked south-east to occupy another vantage point – a concept with which the Propert map would reflexively play – on the plateau atop the rise of Garn Wnda. The French *tricolore* was raised on both eminences in an attempt to rally the local inhabitants (Rutland, *Journal of a Tour*, 135); over this largely treeless coastal landscape the invading force also carried banners emblazoned with the Tree of Liberty.

Famously called from a ball at Tregwynt mansion on the evening of 22 February, twenty-eight-year-old Lieutenant-Colonel Thomas Knox, commander of the Fishguard Fencibles – a volunteer reserve force – took up a defensive position with his troops (around 160 men) south-east of the peninsula in Fishguard Fort, to which he called down a detachment of the Fencibles that were stationed north, at Newport. Later facing charges of cowardice and incompetence, he would have cause to regret his decision – provident as it may have been – to retreat south the following (Thursday) morning. At noon that day, his force was met along the road to the county town of Haverfordwest by the balance of the British units, raised by the county's landowning grandees, advancing from the south; until the uncon-ditional French surrender on Friday, the combined corps of around 600 would be the sole defence force mustered against the invasion. This comprised Captain James Ackland's Pembrokeshire Fencibles (93 strong);

the troop of Castlemartin Yeomanry cavalry (43 men, also all volunteers) led by John Campbell, Lord Cawdor, who assumed overall command at this point on the country road; Lieutenant-Colonel John Colby's detachment of the Cardiganshire militia (around 100 men, raised by ballot and semi-professional); and a complement of around 150 naval men and revenue service officers from south of the 'Landsker' – the cultural dividing line between the 'Welshry' in the north and the English-speaking south of the county. Propert's map is alive to the social and cultural divisions in evidence, that afternoon, on the road.

It is fair to suppose that on the Thursday – the first full day of the *descente* – inhabitants who had fled from their farms as French order broke down would have been met by others whom adventurism, curiosity, fear, and anger had mustered on the peninsula's fringes. Credible contemporary accounts are clear that many were armed with farm implements – a fact registered in a caricature by an unknown artist, issued promptly in March 1797 in London, entitled *A Fishguard Fencible*, which conflates local inhabitant and local volunteer in the form of the metropolitan stereotype of a squat, leek-sporting Welsh volunteer holding not a musket or sword but a short 'reaping hook'.[7] It is an image that both lionizes and ironizes the terrifyingly ad hoc defence of the realm – as does the Propert map, as we shall see. On Strumble Head, there was lethal contact between the French and the local inhabitants, even if there were no fatal engagements between the two bodies of troops. Two Welshmen were killed near Garn Wnda, with an encounter near Carngowil farm resulting in the death of a French soldier, who is said to have been buried in the field opposite Carn Gelli (it is still known today as Parc y Ffrancwr – 'The Frenchman's Field').[8] Strumble Head became a landscape of postmortem obscenity: the Duke of Rutland, who in the summer of 1797 was the guest of Lord Cawdor at his seat in the south of the county, records that the French 'manner of burying their dead was savage in the extreme':

> After digging trenches, they threw the bodies in without ceremony. One of the bodies happened to be too long, and would not readily fit the grave dug for it. 'Laissons nous faire', cried the soldiers. 'Nous vous montrons la manière dont nous les enterrons sur les frontières [Let us do it. We will show you how we bury them on the frontiers']; and jumping upon the neck of the dead man, they broke it, and then doubled it back upon the body. (Rutland, *Journal*, 138)

Strumble Head, indeed. Horrific violence was visited on women also. At Caerlem in the western part of the peninsula, Mary Williams, who some accounts claim was two months pregnant, was shot in the leg and raped by a French soldier – or raped and afterwards shot in the leg. The government provided her with 'compensation'. The account of another rape – 'of a virgin sixty years old' – is also credible (Thomas, *Britain's Last Invasion*, 84–5; Rutland, *Journal*, 132). Elsewhere, a British trooper, loading his pistol, accidentally killed a local woman (Stuart Jones, *The Last Invasion*, 141). Eight French soldiers drowned, it seems, on landing; thereafter, no more than three or four died on each side. Though the invasion's casualty list is small, the shock and horror to which the *descente* gave rise – captured by the Propert map – should not be underestimated.

By dusk on the Thursday, their backs still to the sea, the French knew it was time to treat. The letter of unconditional surrender arrived at Cawdor's headquarters in Fishguard at 9 a.m. on Friday, 24 February, with the surrender itself famously received on the expanse of Goodwick Sands. Part of Cawdor's troops were drawn up on the Bigney, high above the beach, with the populace ranged round on the heights as spectators (the women in their red flannel shawls, which is likely to have given rise to the myth of a *ruse de guerre* by which the French were led, before the surrender, to mistake local women for British regulars). Propert's cartography was itself about to adopt that spectatorial position and surveilling stance. The march of the French rank and file – guarded within a moving parallelogram of British soldiers – to jails and church interiors in Pembroke and Haverfordwest (and thence to the horror of the Portsmouth hulks) was a countywide spectator event.

The news reached London on the Friday. A run on the county banks – occasioned by invasion panic – pressurized banks in London and in turn the central bank, leading to the Bank of England actually 'suspending cash payments' (Stuart Jones, *The Last Invasion*, 165). In Pembrokeshire, fear prevailed, manifesting itself in claims of further sightings of French ships. Not surprisingly, the invasion also occasioned an urgent national debate about the need to shore up coastal defences – 'to put the coasts above insult', as the émigré General Dumouriez put it in the context of the next great invasion scare of 1803–5.[9] In 1797–8, the Pembrokeshire landing also pre-cipitated a 'national mobilization' in the form of the second highly successful volunteering movement of the 1790s. As Mark Philp notes, 'in the first three months' of 1798, 'the number of volunteers doubled from 25,000 to 50,000, and their numbers then doubled again in the following three months', which gave the government some idea of 'the potential for the emergence of a mass army of the nation'.[10] As J. E. Cookson has emphasized, the reserve corps were, in the government's eyes, 'maddeningly incohesive' both within companies and as a composite body of troops. Further, they were regarded 'ambivalently' in the context of a necessary wartime 'improvisation' by a state whose military reforms had not yet brought such units under central control and coordination.[11] We will see that the Propert map thrives on the registration of such ambiguities.

The legacy of the 1797 invasion was one of personal and sectarian recrimination. Baited by his fellow Irishman Charles Hassall (who harboured a grudge), Lieutenant-Colonel Knox immediately found himself having to justify his conduct as commander of the Fishguard Fencibles. It is significant that, towards the beginning of his detailed rebuttal, published in 1800, Knox invokes the surveyor's method of triangulation as he seeks to emphasize the knowledge and judgement he demonstrated during the crisis. Here, the rhetoric of technical mensuration, together with the control, authority, and power it signals, join with other strategies of persuasion (such as detailed narrative and the inclusion of primary documents in an appendix) as Knox seeks to clear his name:

> A sufficiently accurate idea may be gained of the relative situation and circumstances of the part of the country connected with this subject, by considering Haverfordwest, Fishguard, and Llanunda, as forming a triangle, of which a line drawn from Haverfordwest to Garnvaur, a rock of considerable height ... on the western side of Llanunda parish, and from thence continued northward to Strumble Head will be the hypothenuse [sic].[12]

Here, Knox establishes a baseline for his defence of his military judgement and professional integrity by appropriating the cartographer's baseline and trigonometric calculations. Propert's map of 1798 can be said to register – and to be itself technically and conceptually motivated by – a Knoxian trigonometric anxiety.

What seemed to the residents of Strumble Head and the home secretary alike to be an unaccountable choice of location for the invasion immediately gave rise to rumours of collusion by local dissenters. Such circulating narratives were given impetus by the inescapable fact that there was indeed a startling 'degree of interaction' – enforced or otherwise – between locals and elements of the invading force (Davies, 'Terror, Treason and Tourism', 253). Sectarian distrust and bigotry – shared by at least some of the landowners who commanded troops during the invasion – crystallized in substantive charges of treason against two extra-parochial civilians: Thomas John of Little Newcastle, a yeoman farmer and Baptist; and a farmer and elderly Presbyterian, Samuel Griffith of Poyntz Castle.

I suggest it is going too far to claim that this 'was an example of the State at work on a local level', as Davies claims; more accurate is simply to acknowledge that the prosecutions 'were initiated locally, not from London'.[13] Both defendants spent more than six months in Haverfordwest jail, where they were shown to the touring Duke of Rutland. He clearly found 'the Welsh Anabaptists' ('state criminals') looking the part he wanted them to play: Thomas John 'seemed as desperate and determined a villain as ever was seen' (Rutland, *Journal*, 161). A True Bill being found against the defendants in April, they were brought to trial on 7 September 1797; the case collapsed when the Crown witnesses – perjured French officers of *La Légion Noire* – refused to rehearse the evidence they had been suborned to give in their depositions (which survive). J. E. Thomas's semi-revisionist history of the landing holds open the possibility that treasonous complicity between the defendants and the French might well have taken place, though the balance of scholarly opinion remains against this view.

One who emphatically believed the charges were fake was William Richards (1749–1818), a Particular Baptist (and professed kinsman of defendant Thomas John) who had been ministering in Kings Lynn since 1776 but who was present in the area during the invasion. Richards published a powerful defence of the prisoners and an indictment of the sectarianism of their enemies in a Welsh-language pamphlet – dated 24 December 1797 and published in Carmarthen – entitled *Cwyn y Cystuddiedig a Griddfanau y Carcharorion Dieuog* (The Complaint of the Afflicted, and Groans of the Innocent Prisoners). A key intervention in Wales's own inflection of the 1790s pamphlet war, it is a sophisticated allusive and ventriloquial performance ('D—n him! we must look sharp, and take care of him').[14] As I shall argue, the pamphlet's discourse of monstrosity and apocalypse is legible in the cartographic ideograms of Propert's map, whose distortions threaten to unplot the Enlightenment credentials and disfigure the mathematical formulae of its professed 'actual survey'.

The spectatorial elements of the invasion – the utility of high vantage points in surveilling the surrounding terrain, the curiosity-driven forays into the peninsula by inhabitants seeking a 'visual' on the enemy, the surrender-as-staged-spectacle in the natural amphitheatre of Goodwick Sands – ensured an afterlife for the invasion in the form of a touristic experience that grafted invasion narratives onto the topography of Strumble Head. The uncanny presence of the French on the peninsula turned the local inhabitants themselves into tourists in their own defamiliarized terrain. Thus began a culture of creative commemoration and curation in which the invasion's contested meanings, for various groups, were emplaced. As Davies puts it, the invasion 'was packaged for consumption from the start' (250). We have seen how James Baker was first to market with a pamphlet offering visual representations of key moments in the invasion; the Duke of Rutland's sortie, *de haut en bas*, into the orbit of post-invasion Pembrokeshire in the summer of 1797 was emphatically as a tourist tour-writer. One source, not implausibly, recounts how a French soldier's corpse on the cliffs below the landing point was picked clean, 'bone after bone and joint after joint', to yield gruesome souvenirs – a tourist version of the French soldiers' grim boast, 'Nous vous montrons la manière dont nous les enterrons sur les frontières'.[15]

Further, certain accounts detail how the landing place quickly became a gravitational site for the local population every summer (Quinault, 'The French Invasion', 637) and how tourists, both British and French, were led by residents (valued as eyewitnesses) to nodal points at which they found themselves involved as participants in quasi-re-enactments of the invasion's principal episodes. As voyage-writer Richard Ayton and his partner, the artist William Daniell, noted (recording a visit of 1813): 'We were as much as possible made actors in the living scene, by having all its parts unfolded to us in the order and in the places in which they successively happened.'[16] Traceable here is the way in which accounts of the invasion – graphic, literary, rehearsed in the field – sought to narrativize a phenomenon that in many ways resisted the holism, connectedness, and teleology (the triangulation, one might say) that narrative seeks and implies. Though spiced with irony, Ayton and Daniell's account of their visit betrays their acknowledgement of the ways in which the invasion had created traitorous roles to inhabit: 'though we were seen prying about the neighbourhood under very suspicious appearances, making the coast the peculiar object of our attention ... yet we had not the least reason to conclude that we were looked upon as traitors' (I, 127). The work of writing Strumble Head and rendering it graphically – precisely also the work of the cartographer – become ambivalently bound up with, and an uncanny rehearsal of, the operations of the *descente* itself. Thomas Propert's own survey of the peninsula is similarly complicit, troubled as it is by the politics of its own triangulation.

Responses: Spectators, Performers, Maps

Cartographic representations were among the first textual responses to the event. Appearing in London on 20 March 1797, less than a month after the episode it depicts, *A Plan of Fishguard Bay, Near Which the French Landed*

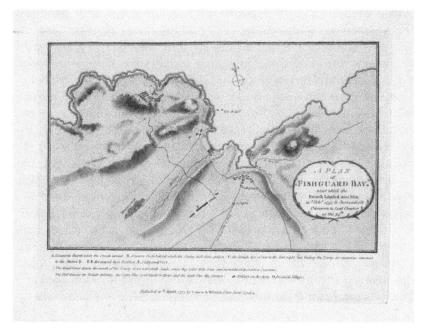

Figure 4.1 *A Plan of Fishguard Bay, Near Which the French Landed 1200 Men*
(20 March 1797); by permission of Llyfrgell Genedlaethol Cymru/National Library
of Wales (Map 6466).

1200 Men (Figure 4.1) was published by the firm of Laurie and Whittle
(who also issued graphic 'drolls' designed by Isaac Cruikshank). The
cartographer-author is not known. Drawn to a relatively large scale of
c. 1:31,680 and attractively colour-washed in greens and browns, it is
indebted to a tradition of battle maps. Mapping a rudimentary, broad-
brush 'narrative' of the invasion (its legend identifying troop movements)
onto a harbour town and a peninsula whose northern coastline blooms in
three imprecise, more-or-less-equal headlands, it has the quality of a sketch
and makes no claim to cartographic accuracy. It captures with some vitality
the arterial nature of the principal roads and the land's corporeality. At the
same time, however, it has a static quality (which the formulae of all maps
produce, even as their other graphic codes chafe against it) that does not give
an urgent impression of any 'insult' being visited on the British coast.
Rather, the map seems to contain and diffuse that insult, down to the visual
rhetoric of the cartouche, sinuously enclosed by a wreath of victory bays.[17]

Soon afterwards, on 15 September 1797, Laurie and Whittle published
*The Invasions of England and Ireland, With All Their Civil Wars Since the
Conquest* – an invasion map drawn by J. Enouy that updated John Speed's
1627 map of the same title. The update includes the *descente* on Wales,
which is identified by text placed in Cardigan Bay and by the symbol of
numbered ships in full sail off a clearly marked 'Strumble Hd'. A second,
coloured edition was published in 1801.[18] A propagandist French version,
by Antoine-François Tardieu, of the Enouy map was published in 1798; it
augmented the number of invasions and again proudly marked the
Strumble Head landing (as invasion number 45).[19] In the Enouy and
Tardieu maps, the British and Irish coasts bristle with hostile ships.
Picturally iconized on this map, on a different plane from the map's
cartographic work, these vessels are not marshalled simply to fill 'embar-
rassing blank spaces' (as was ordinarily the case on maps, where ships
appeared as pictorial staffage).[20] Rather, they are representations of actual
terrorizing agents – the insulting *Vengeance* and *Résistance* of their day.
Thomas Propert was about to take Laurie and Whittle's invasion maps into
dynamic new rhetorical territory.

Triangulating Thomas Propert's Plan

While Thomas Propert's *A Plan of that Part of the County of Pembroke called
Pen-Caer and the Sea Coast Adjacent* (Figure 4.2) has often been cited in
accounts of the invasion, it has never been subject to sustained critique
from the perspective of a critical social geography.[21] Its conflation of
cartography and caricature has gone unremarked, even though it is
a map that begs a historicized ekphrastic response – a reading of its graphic
codes in the context of the circulating cultural discourses of the 1790s.
Further, what has not been identified are the ways in which Propert's
chorography is alive to the phenomenological and psychogeographical
effects of the invasion – the imbrication of terror and terrain that is the
descente's lasting legacy. As already emphasized, the map evinces the
plurality and fluidity of graphic codes and visual genres deployed under
the guise of a cartographic survey-to-scale whose manifest content and
epitexts are at pains to emphasize its planimetric 'truth' and loyalist
politics. Propert's London-published text trumpets a mimetic attachment
to ground and a politics of loyalist commemoration; it is dedicated 'To the
Right Honourable Lord Cawdor' by Propert as His Lordship's 'most
obedient & obliged Servant', and a copy was owned by George III
(Salmon, 'The French Invasion of Pembrokeshire', 206). However, this

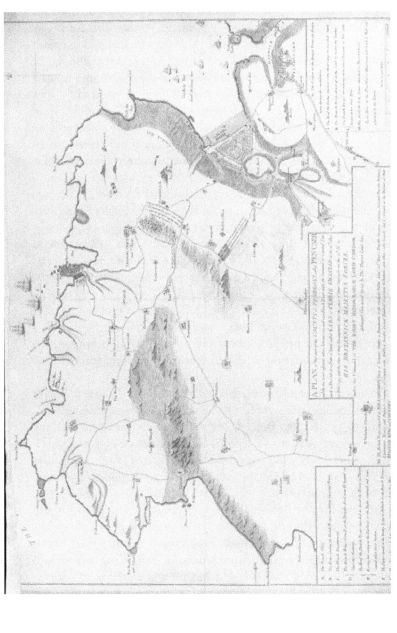

Figure 4.2 Thomas Propert, *A Plan of that Part of the County of Pembroke called Pen-Caer and the Sea Coast Adjacent, where between 1200 and 1400 French Troops under the Command of General Tate, made a Descent on a Point of Land called Garn or Cerrig Gwastad on the 22nd Day of Febry 1797* (11 February 1798); by permission of Llyfrgell Genedlaethol Cymru/National Library of Wales (Map 10823). (The dedication to Lord Cawdor has been cut from this copy).

text cannot fail both to register a welter of conflicted post-invasion ideological positions and to destabilize its own manifest discourse.

Almost everything we know about Thomas Propert himself is on his
map, drawn at a scale of *c.* 1:12,069 or 5.25 inches to the mile. Relatively
sizeable as a material object at twenty-nine by twenty-six inches, it is meant
to be hung as a commemorative icon while, importantly, also being
entirely practical in the field as a working map. Propert identifies himself
in his text as a 'Land Surveyor' and as a native of 'Llanryen near Haverford
West' – the village of Llanrhian, seven miles south-west of Strumble Head.
The years of his birth and death (1759 and 1810) had to be discovered by
consulting his gravestone and parish records.[22] He may well have been an
eyewitness of the invasion; at any rate, the map he creates becomes just
such a (conflicted) witness.

As noted, the map announces that it is 'delineated from actual Survey'.
Propert would certainly have been familiar with the principles of trigonometric calculation and is likely to have measured his territory by 'traverse'
using his sixty-six-foot Gunter's chain, taking 'shots' with a theodolite to
distant features and vantage points. This would have given him a general
framework that could then be filled in with interior measurements. On the
summits where the French had raised their flag, Propert – also seeking
geographical knowledge – raised his theodolite. Sites where the *tricolore*
flew became trig points. Propert's act – no less than that of the French –
was one of cultural and military power and interpellation; it brought the
local cartographic remembrancer into an uncannily proximate relation to
the enemy.

The strategies of Propert's cartography constitute what William J. Smyth
terms '"accents" or "dialects" within a wider framework of representation'.[23]
On his map plate, the peninsula is buttressed from below by flanking
rectangles containing the map's legend. This locates objects and nodal
locations, together with troop companies, movements, and dispositions
over time ('D The British Troops formed on the Turnpike Road near
Fishguard on Thursday evening'; 'F – The Piquet Guard of the Enemy
lying in Ambush for the British Troops'). Thus the chorography is also
calibrated in time, constituting an invasion chronotope. Within a plinth-like
outline that invades the map-space itself, Propert gives the map's descriptive
title, which rehearses the invasion in brief, from landing to the surrender to
'His Britannick Majesty's Forces' (not a regular among them, of course).
Field boundaries are drawn in, together with thirty-six farms, the great
majority of which were 'plundered by the Enemy'. The peninsula's high
ground is represented on a bird's-eye/oblique plane as hachured

agglomerations of small eminences. Written onto the landscape itself are identifications of sites of violence ('In this Field ... one Frenchman was killed & two others mortally wounded'), together with the location of the advanced guard on Garn Wnda. In these places, the narrative inscriptions have the force of epitaphs-in-situ, formally moulded as they are to the field contours and around the elliptical shape of the rock outcrop. The hachured area to the east, around Goodwick Sands, has a strangely pathophysiological appearance, its globular forms seen as if in cross-section. The peninsula's western and northern coastlines appear as a series of shadow-outlined headlands (smoothed and pointed) and coves and bays (both angular and hollowed out), with areas of shading stretching inland, representing expanses of bracken-covered ground. And out in 'The Irish Channel' (which links the peninsula and its coastal waters to that invasion site *manqué* out west, Bantry Bay), boldly and representationally detailed in a bird's-eye view are the four French ships, together with a series of small boats bristling with men and muskets moving south to their landing point at Carregwastad. The map brings home the shock of the invasion – the 'incomprehensible' nature of the event (as the *Chester Chronicle* described it).[24]

Issued at a time when rumours of French invasion rafts, 'worked by machines, windmills, horsemills' (Franklin and Philp, *Napoleon*, 36–7, 48), were circulating, this image-text possesses a hallucinatory quality. It is both chart and picture. It flattens out but also offers perspectival 'views'; its epitexts and scalar values highlight its status as the product of professional geodesy, yet it has a compositional eerieness. It has cartography's 'fixing' quality but is also committed to the *kinetic* – to the passing of time and to narrative progression in its detailing of troop movements and its 'telling' of an event whose material conclusion is known but whose episodes the map endlessly rehearses. The legend in the boxes near the base offers the map's user a chronological, loyalist-teleological outline of the invasion; however, one's reading of the map is not dogmatically bound by any such bearings. The map offers us the opportunity to read/experience those February days in anachronistic, dislocated sequences of our choosing. Propert's plan is a community map focused on a particular tract of land, but it is also a monitory atlas and is to be read relationally and archipelagically: *all* British coastal tracts are vulnerable, and the viewer (wherever she may be) is asked imaginatively to consider 'What uproar and what strife' and what 'Carnage and screams' may now be 'stirring / This way or that way' (to cite Coleridge's invasion poem, 'Fears in Solitude', written two months after the publication of Propert's map) in her own locality.[25]

Propert's is also a text of multiple generic laminations and conflations.
With self-ironizing effect, it brings together eighteenth-century traditions
of battle maps and 'news cartography', eyewitness 'cartographic journal-
ism', the commemorative map, the estate map, military chorography,
wider discourses of civic thanks – and crucially, I suggest, the visual scripts
of graphic satire and political caricature.[26] This latter allegiance is pivotal to
the ways in which Propert as caricature-cartographer responds, with
recourse to the grotesque, to the invasion. The evidence points to
a *conscious* design on Propert's part to recombine – with acutely topical
resonance – two traditions of 'landscape representation' that since the early
seventeenth century had diverged: the 'cartographic tradition of the topographical map drawn to uniform scale' and pictural mappings that
belonged to the realm of art (see Harvey, *Topographical Maps*, 164–73).[27]
What Propert innovatively and indeterminately combines are not just the
'map' and the 'view' but the map, the scripts of metropolitan graphic satire,
and defining elements of the wider literary and visual response to the
invasion.

I suggest that the flotilla of boats disgorged from the French ships off
Strumble Head's north coast in Propert's map carries into the text's
political field 'the earliest print alluding to the possibility of a French
"armada"': James Gillray's famous comic map of 5 November 1793,
*A New Map of England and France. The French Invasion; – or – John
Bull, Bombarding the Bum-boats* (Figure 4.3), in which, in M. Dorothy
George's description, George III as John Bull, in the shape of England and
Wales, 'issues a blast of excrement ... which smites a swarm of [French]
"Bum-Boats" extending from Ushant to the mouth of the Seine' ('Bum-
Boats' being a scatological pun on 'bumboats' – small service craft).[28]
George's military defecation drives the boats back into the very face of
France. Gillray's map politicizes a tradition of 'droll caricature maps' that
grotesquely anthropomorphize the outline of the British coast in male and
female forms – for example, the series of 1793 drolls entitled *Geography
Bewitched!*, of which there were separate versions representing England and
Wales, Scotland, and Ireland (George, *Catalogue, 1793–1800*, 64–5). It also
extends contemporary comic representation of excretory salvos of various
kinds from sociopolitical into geopolitical territory.[29] Propert's deployment of Gillray's visual and verbal puns in his own invasion map sees the
French bumboats of February 1797 (carrying the refuse of French prisons)
expelled from their mother ships, unmet by any counter-blast from the
Welsh shore. My tracing of Propert's allusion to Gillray lends added weight
to the now orthodox assumption that the 'social and geographical'

Figure 4.3 *James Gillray, A New Map of England and France. The French Invasion; –
or – John Bull, Bombarding the Bum-boats* (5 November 1793).

audience for political caricature 'stretched beyond the London elites'
through networks of inland trade, portfolio-lending, and strategies of
pirating, emulation, and adaptation.[30]

Creative interchange between caricature and cartography should not
seem surprising. Both rely on respective corpora of likeness, caricature,
emblem, and icon (and the traffic between these) that depend for their full
meaning on the viewer's ability to read relationally.[31] This is emphatically
not to argue that, in the case of the Propert map, the interchange leads to
a stable ontology. In Propert's text, there is an active representational
struggle between cartography and caricature, geodesy and the grotesque,
in the representation of the northern coastline of Stumble Head, with each

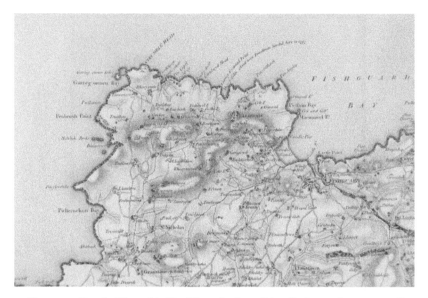

Figure 4.4 Detail of Strumble Head from the first edition Ordnance Survey map of
Pembrokeshire (1819); Pembrokeshire Archives and Record Office.

script ironizing – unmapping and counter-mapping – the other. Despite
its different scale, the first Ordnance Survey map of the area (published in
August 1819, based on a survey conducted in 1809) – which records the
invasion site – instructively reveals the extent to which Propert's delineation of the coastline differs from the precise geographical contours of the
peninsula (Figure 4.4).[32] I do not believe we are dealing here with anything
so simple as cartographic error or accidental distortion on Propert's part.
Nor do I believe that *pareidolia* is in play – that is, the perception of
'patterns or images, in random or vague arrangements of shapes, lines,
colours, etc.'[33] – though the very fact that this possibility arises testifies both
to cartography's representational schizophrenia and to the reality of different viewers' visual responsiveness and suggestibility.

With this in mind, it pays to highlight three sections of the coast and ask
the viewer/reader to encounter them anew in another frame of vision and
from inflected compass angles. At stake are our perceptions of the cap-
aciousness of 1790s cartography and the parameters of our own
deconstructionist-materialist reading of Romantic-period maps. Three
monstrous profiles can be seen to emerge, their visibility enhanced by
Propert's sophisticated shading effects on the body of the peninsula itself.

The first profile, on the western coast, is a canine or lupine head, disturbingly horned; the second, on the north coast, human but ghoulish; and the third, to the east, a witch-like female profile with hooked nose and flying hair, the mouth open (Figure 4.5 (a–c)).[34] It seems as if it is into the throat of this last that the enemy is disgorging itself. The debt to grotesque caricature – including caricature invasion prints such as Gillray's *The Tables Turn'd* of March 1797, in which Charles James Fox is figured as the devil celebrating the *descente* on Wales (visible behind him), with Pitt in his claws – renders 'bewitched' and invasion-hexed both the peninsula that the map is representing and the codes of the map-text itself (see George, *Catalogue, 1793–1800*, 338). Propert's chorography intervenes innovatively in metropolitan graphic satire both by folding back the scale map into caricature and by playing caricature off against the claims of the technical scripts of formal cartographic work. Though Propert's map was certainly not displayed alongside the Gillray, Cruikshank, and Rowlandson prints with which it is in complex dialogue in the multi-pane windows of a Hannah Humphrey, a Samuel Fores, or a William Holland in London, it is partly there, I suggest, that it belongs.

In what direction, however, is this *agon* between cartography and caricature tending in the map? If we accept that the Strumble Head littoral does offer itself as monstrously figured in Propert's plan, what does that horror signify? How is it positioned ideologically and whose purpose is it serving? The map appeared during the 'crisis of 1798', marked by 'a renewed campaign of pro-government propaganda' whose aim was to emphasize 'the horrors of a Jacobin conquest, appeal to national unity and thereby promote patriotic enlistment' (Donald, *The Age of Caricature*, 174). Propert's outwardly loyalist map certainly takes its place at the heart of this political project, with lupine, ghoulish, and witch-like topographical profiles incarnating traumatic local memories of the violent *descente* and motivating (playing to) the pleasing terror of a wider audience's fears concerning an invasion and the threat posed by the Jacobin/dissenting enemy within. Propert's map troubles scientific mensuration with a discourse of monstrosity that is also strongly evident in contemporary Welsh-language ballads (a genre that had, by 1797, been 'taken over by reactionary voices') that respond to the Strumble Head invasion.[35] In these songs, the emphasis – as in the newspaper coverage of what Löffler describes as a 'media event' – is firmly on the concerted loyalism of the peasantry, even as the linguistic and cultural otherness of the Welsh populace within a wider British polity is emphasised (Löffler, *Welsh Responses*, 16). In these popular songs, the French are figured as *bleiddiaid*

(a)

(b)

(c)

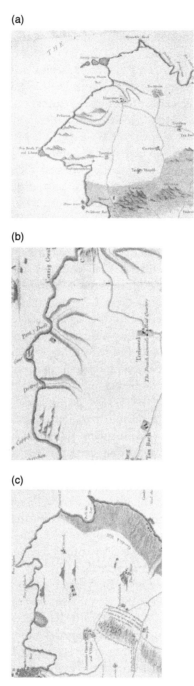

Figure 4.5 (a–c): Details from Figure 4.2: (a) wolf; (b) ghoul; (c) witch.

blin (vicious wolves), *hyll ellyllon* (hideous ghouls), 'Gog and Magog', 'gruesome', a 'ferocious, accursed host', 'perverse', 'loathsome', 'vile', 'savage', 'ugly', 'ravagers', and 'voracious dragons'.[36] As the only female-identified profile on the map, the head of the 'witch' can be seen as an ideogram that gestures at representations in 1790s graphic satire of gorgonic French females (Burke's 'revolution harpies of France, sprung from night and hell') and the *Mariannes*-made-monstrous visible in a work such as Thomas Rowlandson's *The Contrast, 1792 – Which Is Best?*. Crucially, at the same time, the profile inscribes the trauma of the peninsula's female victims: the screaming Mary Williams of Caerlem, shot and raped; the older unnamed woman, also violated; and the woman killed by friendly fire. Thus Propert's chart figures not only French but also specifically male violence visited on the female bodies of the peninsula. Land and people have been feelingly and phenomenologically surveyed.

Such grotesquerie signals in multiple directions – as it does in 1790s caricature (especially in the hands of a master of ambiguous codes such as Gillray), in which, as Ronald Paulson puts it, revolutionary times are seen as 'a process of regressional transformations' and where the question to wrestle with is: 'where [do] the subversive implications stop'?[37] Energizingly divided against itself in the ways already noted, Propert's map articulates conflicting political messages. Distorted in the direction of monstrous caricature, Propert's cartography does not solely demonise the savage French. Where the subversions stop is a (guilty New Historicist) question worth posing.

Strumble Head's wolf, ghoul, and witch – a headland of heads – offer themselves as a caricatural-cartographic comment on the very exaggerations and distortions of the *loyalist* response to the invasion that led to the September 1797 treason trial of the scapegoat dissenters, John and Griffith. As Ian Haywood remarks, 'Gillray makes the point that loyalist fantasies of Jacobin conspiracy have more in common with caricature than with the truth: politics and caricature have converged into an aesthetic of distortion, demonization, defamation and violence'.[38] Thomas Propert's achievement – his contribution to 1790s print culture – is to have brought chorography and caricature together in a teasing and traumatic conflation that reflexively undercuts reactionary 'violent fantasising' (Haywood, 'The Dark Sketches', 434), loyalist triumphalism, and hysteria – while also registering the genuine panic and alarm occasioned by the invasion. Mark Philp reminds us that 'caricatures trade directly on ambiguities and slippages in symbolism and reference ... They encourage us to fear [the enemy] but also to be aware of the threat that national defence poses to our traditional liberties' (Philp, 'Introduction', 13). So with Propert's map: what is figured as also unnatural are loyalist recriminations against the dissenters (in Blakean and Southcottian fashion, William Richards's pamphlet constructs their accusers as 'the five beasts and their kin'); Pitt's counter-terror; state invasions of privacy; and the 'penetrating loyalist gaze' (Löffler, *Political Pamphlets*, 273; Haywood, 'The Dark Sketches', 435).

Further, the violent forms taken by Propert's cartography encode an enduring anxiety concerning the ambiguous relation in which the British volunteer forces (whose allegiance was a major concern) stood vis-à-vis a recently restive population whose opposition to the French was more a 'contingent, spontaneous, local response' than an ideological commitment (Davies, 'Terror, Treason and Tourism', 260). In 1795, the Pembrokeshire militia had been deployed to discourage a riot over the high price of food by armed colliers from the village of Hook; during the succeeding winter, the very volunteer forces that were to meet the French invasion had been ordered to 'parade on market days' to discourage any further local disturbance (Stuart Jones, *The Last Invasion*, 209). Far from being a 'collective triumph' – as Quinault has it (641) – that brought together the populace, gentry, aristocracy, and tenantry (and the Welsh and English), the British 'success' against a French force that was itself multi-ethnic and multilingual was achieved in the face of deep internal political and cultural distrust and socio-economic fracture.[39] Such fissures are figured by the internecine codes of Propert's text.

There is a further recursiveness to the map's allegiances. As loyalist tool, Propert's 'plan' both knows and does not know that it shares the very strategies and aims of the state's panoptic gaze in its attempt to record, capture, and lay bare both the enemy's and British citizens' movements. This is an equation in which cartographic plotting is bound up with a response to political plots. And as already emphasized, the map's chronic self-lacerating, self-unplotting rehearsal of the invasion cannot compel a teleological reading of the recent event; rather, the invasion is made available for viewing as a series of episodes that one may well find oneself rehearsing *backwards*, or more likely haphazardly (counterfactually, even), ending with the arrival of the *Vengeance* and the *Résistance*, not the surrender on the beach. At work here also is retrospective collusion: Propert would have been well aware that his map is the very text that Hoche and Tate needed to effect a more successful terror.

As we – cartographers and Romanticists both – have long recognized, all maps are persuasive and propagandist, connected to a world phenomenologically apprehended not through 'mimetic bondage' or 'transparence' but through formulae of distortion and through the rhetoric of verbal and graphic representation (Harley, 'Deconstructing the Map', 234, 239). As this chapter has argued, Propert's map offers a particularly layered example of such a 'social play of images present and absent' (Pickles, 'Texts', 211) in the context of the circulating discourses of the day and a psychogeographical engagement with the post-invasion ground it mediates. What emerges at this late moment in a revolutionary decade is a text that reveals the permeability of the boundaries between disciplines and ways of viewing the world that at first seem oppositional. This otherwise unknown local surveyor's anniversary map shows cartography's ability to critique its claims to scientific truth and unitary historical memory. Propert's plan works through paradox: it is a trigonometric caricature; a loyalist-Jacobin profession of faith; a system of signs that both affixes and unravels meaning; a chronotope that both ossifies and animates history; a technical work that represses lived experience while at the same time inscribing trauma; and a guide that effaces its effects even as it powerfully interpellates the viewer-reader.

It is by this map that I navigated the peninsula in March 2018 in a post-*descente dérive*. Light was fading as I reached the field where the French soldier is buried, and, a short distance south, the junction from which the killing lane towards Trefwrgi leads south-east, where the French posted the picket guard. More than all the histories, scholarly discussions, and creative retellings of the invasion, it was Propert's map that brought home to me the trauma of those three days in February 1797; the network of contending meanings, images, and narratives – venous as the peninsula's own lanes – that it generated; and the ways in which our scrutiny of the literature and culture of the Romantic period is a test of our responsiveness to precisely those effects that make this unsung but paradigmatic 1790s map the richly disorientating cultural pun it is.

Notes

1. J. Brian Harley, 'Deconstructing the Map', in *Writing Worlds: Discourse, Text and Metaphor*, eds. T. J. Barnes and J. J. Duncan (London: Routledge, 1992), 231–47, 242. Harley's chapter is revised from a previous version published in *Cartographia* 26:2 (1989): 1–20. I thank Claire Orr and Mary Robinson, archivists at the Pembrokeshire Archives and Record Office, Haverfordwest, for their assistance; and Christopher Jones and Mary-Ann Constantine for discussions of the map that is the subject of this chapter.
2. See Rachel Hewitt, 'Mapping and Romanticism', *Wordsworth Circle* 42:2 (2011): 157–65; John Pickles, 'Texts, Hermeneutics and Propaganda Maps', in *Writing Worlds*, eds. Barnes and Duncan, 193–230, 197.

3. See Pickles, 'Texts', 193; Harley, 'Deconstructing the Map', 242, 235.

4. See David Salmon, 'The French Invasion of Pembrokeshire in 1797: Official Documents, Contemporary Letters and Early Narratives', *West Wales Historical Records* 14 (1929): 127–207; David Salmon, 'A Sequel to the French Invasion of Pembrokeshire, *Y Cymmrodor* 43 (1932): 62–92; David Salmon, 'Histories of the French Invasion of Pembrokeshire', *Cylchgrawn y Gymdeithas Lyfryddol Gymreig/Journal of the Welsh Bibliographical Society* 5:1 (1937): 41–8; E. H. Stuart Jones, *The Last Invasion of Britain* (Cardiff: University of Wales Press, 1950); Roland Quinault, 'The French Invasion of Pembrokeshire in 1797: A Bicentennial Assessment', *Welsh History Review/Cylchgrawn Hanes Cymru* 19:4 (1999): 618–42; Richard Rose, 'The French at Fishguard: Fact, Fiction and Folklore', *Transactions of the Honourable Society of Cymmrodorion*, N.S. 9 (2003): 74–105; and J. E. Thomas, *Britain's Last Invasion: Fishguard, 1797* (Stroud: Tempus, 2007). See also Phil Carradice, *The Last Invasion: The Story of the French Landing in Wales* (Griffithstown: Village Publishing, 1992); Hywel M. Davies, 'Terror, Treason and Tourism: The French in Pembrokeshire, 1797', in *'Footsteps of Liberty and Revolt': Essays on Wales and the French Revolution*, eds. Mary-Ann Constantine and Dafydd Johnston (Cardiff: University of Wales Press, 2013), 247–70; and, for a summary, 'Welsh Battlefields Historical Research: Carregwastad Point, Fishguard (1797)', http://battlefields .rcahmw.gov.uk/wp-content/uploads/2017/02/Carregwastad-Point-Fishguard-1797-Border-Archaeology-2009.pdf (accessed 21 June 2018).

5. John Henry Manners (5th Duke of Rutland), *Journal of a Tour through North and South Wales, The Isle of Man, &c.* (London: J. Triphook, 1805), 133–4.

6. James Baker, *A Brief Narrative of the French Invasion, Near Fishguard Bay* (Worcester: J. Tymbs, 1797), 1.

7. See Peter Lord, *Words with Pictures: Welsh Images and Images of Wales in the Popular Press, 1640–1860* (Aberystwyth: Planet Books, 1995), 73.

8. For its precise location, see https://historicplacenames.rcahmw.gov.uk/place names/recordedname/e18eb407-4d9d-4151-812e-6a214db04c78 (accessed 26 March 2018).

9. Mark Philp, 'Introduction: The British Response to the Threat of Invasion, 1797–1815', in *Resisting Napoleon: The British Response to the Threat of Invasion, 1797–1815*, ed. Mark Philp (Aldershot: Ashgate, 2006), 1–17, 6.

10. Alexandra Franklin and Mark Philp, *Napoleon and the Invasion of Britain* (Oxford: The Bodleian Library, 2003), 13.

11. J. E. Cookson, 'The English Volunteer Movement of the French Wars, 1793–1815: Some Contexts', *Historical Journal* 32:4 (1989): 867–91, 882, 869.

12. Thomas Knox, *Some Account of the Proceedings that Took Place on the Landing of the French Near Fishguard, in Pembrokeshire ... And of the Inquiry Afterwards Had Into Lieut. Col. Knox's Conduct* (London: A. Wilson, 1800), 14–15.

13. Both claims are from Davies, 'Terror, Treason and Tourism', 257.

14. Marion Löffler, ed., with Welsh-to-English translation by Bethan Mair Jenkins, *Political Pamphlets and Sermons from Wales, 1790–1806* (Cardiff: University of Wales Press, 2014), 267.

15. H. L. ap Gwilym (H. L. Williams), *An Authentic Account of the Invasion by the French Troops … on Carrig Gwasted [sic] Point, Near Fishguard, 1797* (Haverfordwest: Joseph Potter, 1842), 31. This account is in other respects mythographic, presenting as fact many of the apocryphal stories that have become part of the invasion narrative. See also Quinault, 'The French Invasion', 637.

16. Richard Ayton and William Daniell, *A Voyage Round Great Britain: Undertaken Between the Years 1813 and 1823 … With a Series of Views*, 2 vols. (London: Tate Gallery and the Scolar Press, 1978), I, 125.

17. For two other maps drawn in response to the invasion, see Salmon, 'The French Invasion of Pembrokeshire', 145–7; and *Map of an Area Extending from Tregwynt to Fishguard following the French Invasion of Wales in 1797* (National Library of Wales, MS Estate Maps, Map 7532 134/1/46), likely to have been made decades later.

18. See Walter Goffart, *Historical Atlases: The First Three Hundred Years, 1570–1870* (Chicago, IL: University of Chicago Press, 2003), 203–4.

19. For a discussion of its propagandist credentials, see https://digital.library.cornell .edu/catalog/ss:8245857 (accessed 5 April 2018). See also Goffart, *Historical Atlases*, 204.

20. P. D. A. Harvey, *The History of Topographical Maps: Symbols, Pictures and Surveys* (London: Thames and Hudson, 1980), 173.

21. The map records the following as dealers/printers: 'Mr R. Brown Historical Gallery Pall Mall London'; 'Mr Eadon Charing Cross'; 'Mr Owen Strand'; and 'Mr Williams Cornhill'.

22. His gravestone on the outer wall of the chancel of Llanrhian church gives the date of his death as 7 July 1810; parish records in the National Library of Wales, Aberystwyth, reveal he was buried the following day. See also Kathleen Lewis, *In the Steps of St Rhian: A History of the Church and Parish of Llanrhian* (1962), n.p., www.northdewislandchurches.org.uk/wp-content/uploads/2015 /06/In-the-Steps-of-St-Rhian.pdf (accessed 21 April 2018). The only other cartographic work of Propert's currently traceable is *A Rough Plan of Several Roads in the Parish of Letterston and St Dogwels* (17 December 1787); National Library of Wales, Map 7537. It is possible Propert was a relation of Lieutenant John Propert, who served with the Fishguard Fencibles during the invasion.

23. William J. Smyth, *Map-Making, Landscapes and Memory: A Geography of Colonial and Early Modern Ireland* (Cork: Cork University Press, 2006), 63.

24. Marion Löffler, ed., *Welsh Responses to the French Revolution: Press and Public Discourse* (Cardiff: University of Cardiff Press, 2012), 160.

25. S. T. Coleridge, *Fears in Solitude … To Which Are Added, France, An Ode; and Frost at Midnight* (London: J. Johnson, 1798), 3.

26. For news cartography, see Ruben B. Van Luijk, 'Maps of Battles, Battle of Maps: News Cartography of the Battle at Neerwinden, Flanders, 1693', *Imago Mundi* 60:2 (2008): 211–20.

27. For a different modality of this aim to bridge painting and map – also with Wales as its ground – see Ralph Hyde, 'Thomas Hornor: Pictural Land Surveyor', *Imago Mundi* 29:1 (1977): 23–34; and Peter Otto, *Multiplying Worlds: Romanticism, Modernity, and the Emergence of Virtual Reality* (Oxford: Oxford University Press, 2011), 266–82.

28. Draper Hill, *Mr Gillray, The Caricaturist* (London: Phaidon, 1965),53n.; M. Dorothy George, *Catalogue of Political and Personal Satires Preserved in the Department of Prints and Drawings in the British Museum, Vol VII, 1793–1800* (London: Oxford University Press, 1942), 41 (No. 8346).

29. See M. Dorothy George, *Catalogue of Political and Personal Satires Preserved in the Department of Prints and Drawings in the British Museum, Vol VI, 1784–1792* (London: Oxford University Press, 1938), 848 (No. 7980); George, *Catalogue, 1793–1800*, 422 (No. 9172); and Richard Newton's *Treason!!!* (19 March 1798), in David Alexander, *Richard Newton and English Caricature in the 1790s* (Manchester: The Whitworth Art Gallery and The University of Manchester/Manchester University Press, 1998), 51–2.

30. See Alexandra Franklin, 'John Bull in a Dream: Fear and Fantasy in the Visual Satires of 1803', in *Resisting Napoleon*, ed. Philp, 125–39, 127; Diana Donald, *The Age of Caricature: Satirical Prints in the Age of George III* (New Haven, CT: Paul Mellon Centre/Yale University Press, 1996), 19–21.

31. See Shearer West, 'Wilkes's Squint: Synecdochic Physiognomy and Political Identity in Eighteenth-Century Print Culture', *Eighteenth-Century Studies* 33:1 (1999): 65–84.

32. See J. Brian Harley, *et al.*, *The Old Series Ordnance Survey Maps of England and Wales, Vol 6: Wales* (Lympne Castle: Harry Margars, 1992), xi, xv.

33. *Oxford English Dictionary*, 2nd ed., 20 vols. (Oxford: Oxford University Press, 1989), continually updated at www.oed.com/.

34. The distortion of the coast into the witch-like profile may also have been prompted by the fact that topographical features on the peninsula bear the names Carreg y Wrach ('The Witch's Stone') and Cnwc y Wrach ('The Witch's Knoll').

35. Ffion Mair Jones, '"The Silly Expressions of French Revolution … ": The Experience of the Dissenting Community in South-West Wales, 1797', in *Experiencing the French Revolution*, ed. David Andrews (Oxford: Voltaire Foundation, 2013), 245–62, 261.

36. Ffion Mair Jones, ed., *Welsh Ballads of the French Revolution, 1793–1815* (Cardiff: University of Wales Press, 2012), 158–63, 170–6, 178–84, 196–239.

37. Ronald Paulson, *Representations of Revolution (1789–1820)* (New Haven, CT: Yale University Press, 1983), 200, 189.

38. Ian Haywood, '"The Dark Sketches of a Revolution": Gillray, the *Anti-Jacobin Review*, and the Aesthetics of Conspiracy in the 1790s', *European Romantic Review* 22:4 (2011): 431–51, 440.

39. For a comment on the linguistic and cultural composition of the French force, see Rutland, *Journal*, 142.

PART II

Cartographic Encounters

CHAPTER 5

Producing and Protesting Imperial Mapmindedness
Multimodal Pedagogy and Feminist Frustration in Sarah Atkins Wilson's Geographical Primers

Carl Thompson

> By referring to maps, as you read, you may obtain ideas of geography, and of the situation of countries, much more correctly than from systems or lessons learned by heart, and thus procure an extensive and various knowledge of natural history – of facts, *not* fiction – which you may find of use every day of your life.
>
> Sarah Atkins Wilson, *The India Cabinet Opened*[1]

Romantic-era Britain saw a dramatic increase in map production and map use. The period witnessed a diverse array of cartographical endeavours both at home and abroad; examples include the Ordnance and Geological surveys of Great Britain, the detailed mapping of India by James Rennell and later through the Great Trigonometrical Survey, and the innumerable new maps produced by explorers such as James Cook. These and many similar projects collectively made the modern map, constructed on Enlightenment scientific principles, not just a ubiquitous, familiar tool but a central, even foundational, mechanism for conceptualizing space and territory and for analysing and acting in the world. Indeed, maps and map-making emerged in this period as master tropes for knowledge in general and for any form of knowledge production. As a result, maps increasingly informed many Romantic-era disciplines and professions both literally and metaphorically. Examples include what Matthew Edney has termed the 'cartographisation of the military' across the period and, in geology, composition of the first stratigraphical maps by William Smith and George Bellas Greenough.[2]

The increasing production and use of maps led in turn, it has been argued, to an escalation in not only map literacy but also *mapmindedness*: 'the internalization of a map-like view of the world' so that individuals – and perhaps society as a whole, in its collective discourses – 'think about

space in map-like ways, even if they are not looking at a map at the time'.[3]
Using maps and, more profoundly, thinking with and through cartographical representations thus became, as one analysis puts it, a widely shared
'tacit knowledge' in the Romantic period.[4] People acquired this knowledge
in part through more frequent handling of maps. However, it is a form of
technological determinism to assume (as some scholarship does) that it was
simply greater circulation of maps that increased the degree and prevalence
of mapmindedness in the British population. Rather, mapmindedness had
also to be cultivated and inculcated; people had to be directed – and
disciplined – towards this new mode of 'geo-epistemology' and the new
forms of 'geographical subjectivity' flowing from it.[5]

   The present chapter considers a small corpus of texts which show this
disciplinary project in action, at an early stage of the educational process. In
the 1820s, the writer Sarah Atkins Wilson (1801–63) launched a long-
running career with a series of geographical primers aimed at children.
This was a genre already well established as a staple branch of Romantic-era
educational literature. All the works in this prolific tradition – by Priscilla
Wakefield, Catherine Hutton, Barbara Hofland, Mary Anne Venning and
others – were intended to produce powerful mental maps of the world and
its diverse human populations. However, the majority of them neither
offered their readers any actual maps nor made much reference to cartographical representations in their narratives. Wilson's primers similarly do
not give their readers actual maps to peruse. However, they stand out from
many other texts of this type because of their emphasis on using maps
during lessons and for the insights they consequently yield as to how maps
might figure in the education of children in this period. To a greater extent
than her predecessors, Wilson takes us – through more fleshed-out frame
narratives – into the Romantic-era nursery and domestic schoolroom,
thereby revealing contemporary pedagogic strategies. Such fictive depictions inevitably give an idealized account of these strategies and so should
not be read as straightforwardly factual, documentary records of teaching
methods and outcomes. Yet Wilson's texts presumably reflect contemporary practice. Given their popularity, moreover, they probably helped to
shape later teaching and learning, suggesting ways in which lessons and
reading might be supplemented with map-based exercises and activities.

   Demonstrating   diverse   methods   for   cultivating   mapmindedness,
Wilson's books simultaneously inflect and align this attitude with what is,
broadly speaking, an imperialist outlook and agenda. In this regard
Wilson's geographical primers share the general ideological tenor of most
publications in this branch of Romantic-era children's literature, as recently

explored by Megan Norcia.[6] The complementarity and intimate entanglement in the period of what we might call map training and empire training has again been recognized by scholars; as Edney writes, 'ideas of "empire" and "map" have, in the modern world at least, developed together and in reference to each other'.[7] Yet many discussions exhibit a technological determinism which sees maps (and mapmindedness) as innately generative of imperialist attitudes. Without denying that some aspects of the modern, scientifically constructed map strongly encourage a dominating and acquisitive sensibility, this chapter will argue that Wilson's publications implicitly suggest that the linkage between 'map' and 'empire' had *also* to be instilled and cemented in Romantic-era youth. Maps feature in Wilson's texts as just one element within a larger multimodal pedagogy that incorporates diverse representational technologies and discursive modes, including artefacts, picturesque visual illustrations, games and interactive familial conversation. Only through the balancing and blending of these supplementary materials and strategies are children guided to the desired learning outcomes, which include the symbiotic meshing of map and empire.

The extent to which an imperialist agenda is not necessarily inherent in the seemingly scientific maps of the Romantic period, or in the mapmindedness generated by such maps, is also indicated by moments in Wilson's texts which suggest alternative ways of understanding and responding to maps. There is a curiously paradoxical or 'doubled' aspect to many of Wilson's primers: even as they offer map training in the service of empire training, they simultaneously evince occasional frustration and discontent towards both maps and empire. Such moments of apparent ambivalence about the imperial project are common in nineteenth-century geographical primers by women. These works reflect, Norcia argues, women's ambiguous social and civic status in this period and their conflicted awareness that the supposedly emancipatory, civilized empire they are promoting in fact limits their own freedom and public agency. For the reasons outlined, Wilson, more than her predecessors, demonstrates – or generates – a cartographic dimension to this ambivalence; in her hands it is not only empire but also the modern, scientific maps, and the mapmindedness these images generate, that are simultaneously promoted *and* protested.

Sarah Atkins Wilson and Early Nineteenth-Century Geographical Primers

Geographical primers and textbooks proliferated in the Romantic period as part of a more general burgeoning of instructional literature for children.

Much of this educational literature was produced by women. Such works represented a comparatively uncontroversial route by which women might demonstrate learning and establish professional authorial careers – activities which in other contexts might provoke chauvinist outrage but here were sanctioned by women's traditional role as mothers and educators. Geographical instruction was no exception in this regard. As noted earlier in reference to Wakefield, Hofland, Hutton, Venning and others, women authored many elementary textbooks and introductions to the discipline. This branch of pedagogical literature had the further attraction that it constituted a form of armchair travelling at a time when actual travel to regions beyond Western Europe was still difficult for most British women. It was presumably some combination of these motives which attracted Sarah Atkins when she began her writing career in 1821. Born in 1801 and raised as a Quaker, Atkins changed both name and creed in 1829 when she married the Anglican clergyman Daniel Wilson and simultaneously joined the Church of England. As well as adopting a new surname, Sarah was rechristened Lucy; thereafter it is unclear which forename she used. Her literary career was already under way, but she published anonymously throughout her life. Today different libraries catalogue her publications under various combinations of her first and last names. Here I refer to her, in a clumsy but necessary compromise, as 'Sarah Atkins Wilson'.

Wilson was just twenty when her first book, *The India Cabinet Opened: In Which Many Natural Curiosities Are Rendered a Source of Amusement to Young Minds* (1821), was published by John Harris and Son, a firm well-known for juvenile and educational material. The same year she also published with Harris *The Fruits of Enterprise Exhibited in the Travels of Belzoni* and, with the Quaker firm of Harvey and Darton, *An Evening in Autumn; or, The Useful Amusement*. These books addressed multiple topics, but all stand squarely in the genre of geographical 'primer' (i.e. introduction or elementary textbook), having as their main, framing concern the discussion of different regions of the world. Wilson then published at least ten more educational books in the 1820s. Some have other disciplines as their principal interest: for example, antiquarianism in *Relics of Antiquity, Exhibited in the Ruins of Pompeii and Herculaneum* (1825), and natural history in *Grove Cottage* (1822; usually printed with *The India Cabinet* in later editions), *Botanical Rambles* (1822) and *The Juvenile Rambler* (1825). Yet as these titles illustrate, diverse forms of travel and mobility were often foregrounded, giving many of these texts a geographical dimension, and geography was again the primary concern of *Real Stories, Taken from the Lives of Various Travellers* (1827). Most of these publications were commercially successful. *The India Cabinet* ran to at least five editions; *Fruits of Enterprize* went through nine editions by 1841 and was still being reissued in the 1870s, apparently in its fourteenth edition. By the end of the 1820s, then, Wilson had established herself as a respected 'brand' in children's literature. Although her name never appeared in print, later publications are often credited on their title pages as being 'by the author of', variously, *The India Cabinet*, *Fruits of Enterprize* and *An Evening in Autumn*.

Like children's educational literature more generally, Romantic-era geographical primers could follow a variety of formal models. Here it is useful to extend Norcia's pioneering work on the genre as a whole by disaggregating the diverse stylistic and educational strategies authors might pursue and identifying subtle differences in approach, ideology and influence. Thus Mary Martha Sherwood's *Introduction to Geography: Intended for Little Children* (1818) is non-narrative in form, offering for a range of key terms and places (e.g. land, water, continent, isthmus; Europe, England, France) simple factual definitions and appropriate Biblical quotations. In contrast, works such as Priscilla Wakefield's *A Family Tour Through the British Empire* (1804), Catherine Hutton's *The Tour of Africa* (1819) and Barbara Hofland's *Alfred Campbell, the Young Pilgrim: Containing Travels in Egypt and the Holy Land* (1825) presented information in a more entertaining way. Their volumes offered a redaction of contemporary travel accounts by diverse authors but with the observations and experiences ascribed to imaginary travellers, around whom a fictive travel narrative was organized. Other writers, however, took issue with the fictional traveller strategy. Maria Hack prefaced *Winter Evenings; or Tales of Travellers* (1818) with a warning about what she perceived as the likely effects of 'all those travels where real descriptions are interwoven with a succession of imaginary adventures':

> In a little while, some unlucky question or observation elicits the unwelcome truth, that the favourite hero is only an ideal personage. A re-action immediately takes place in the mind of the youthful reader, who indignantly discards the whole, as an imposition on his credulity.[8]

Hack therefore recounted the actual travels of real-life figures like Captain Bligh, John Byron and Antonio de Ulloa. However, she mediated these narratives through another well-established mode of Romantic-era educational literature, the family conversation in which a fictional authority figure (usually a parent) unfolds information and stories in response to questions from one or more children. The dialogue form, Hack suggested, gave scope for 'explaining difficulties, without interfering with the narrative' and was 'generally agreeable to children' (I, ix).

Hack's *Winter Evenings* was a major influence on Wilson; as we shall see, in places Wilson even seems to plagiarize Hack. The two women were perhaps friends who shared ideas and approaches (both, significantly, were Quakers who subsequently converted to Anglicanism); alternatively, Wilson was unscrupulous about reworking the older author's material. Either way, Wilson's 1820s books mostly follow the Hack model, retelling the activities of real travellers via fictional family conversations between parents and children. (The exception is *Relics of Antiquity*, where Wilson instead weaves a fictional first-person travelogue out of factual accounts.) However, while Hack's 'Mrs B.' in *Winter Evenings* generally stays focused on the specific travel tale she is telling, Wilson's authority figures digress more frequently and more widely, interweaving a greater range of related topics and source texts. In addition, Wilson develops her frame narratives more fully than Hack, giving more information about her fictional families and thereby offering insights into how maps might feature in Romantic-era schooling.

'Open the Maps': Producing Imperial Mapmindedness

All of Wilson's geography primers convey the usefulness of having maps to hand as a supplement to lessons and reading. In the epigraph at the beginning of this chapter (which echoes similar advice in Hack's *Winter Evenings*) Wilson insists explicitly on 'referring to maps ... as you read'; elsewhere her texts offer many examples of children making good educational use of a range of maps.[9] In *Grove Cottage* we see one child 'with the globe before her, busy in passing the quadrant of altitude over Quebec, in order to find its distance from London'.[10] In *Botanical Rambles* and *An Evening in Autumn*, children explore the world using 'travelling-maps' (i.e. folding maps); in *Fruits of Enterprize* the youngest child plays with a 'dissected' or jigsaw map, a popular form of educational puzzle (as discussed in Siobhan Carroll's Chapter 6 in this volume).[11] Wilson also more or less begins her authorial career with a curious cartographic image. A few pages into *The India Cabinet*, her fictional children, while on holiday, encounter 'the *geographical lichen*', so-called 'because it bears a resemblance to the lines of a map' (*IC*, 4): the map, it seems here, is a "natural" as much as a human construct.

These examples give just passing glimpses of children using maps; elsewhere, map use is more fundamentally woven into lessons. In *The India Cabinet*, the central premise is that children learn about the world through exploring the natural historical and ethnographic material (such as rocks, shells and fossils) contained in a cabinet of curiosities maintained by their mother. Consideration of these items, however, is accompanied by scrutiny of 'several maps on rollers ... hanging up in the next room' (*IC*, 33). Similarly, in *An Evening in Autumn* the subtitle's 'useful amusement' is a quiz in which children trace the origins of various commodities (such as sugar, paper and tea) using wall maps; as one child pronounces, 'Let us first unroll the great map and search for them' (*EA*, 15). And in *Fruits of Enterprize* and *Real Stories, Taken from the Lives of Various Travellers*, which follow Hack's example in having a mother redact for her children contemporary travel accounts, the children again track the various journeys spatially, using a map of Egypt in the former case, an atlas in the latter.

Wilson never identifies the specific maps her children use, unlike Hack who in *Winter Evenings* mentions 'Smith's Atlas' (presumably Charles Smith's 1808 *New General Atlas*) and 'MacKenzie's map of Iceland' (from Sir George Mackenzie's 1811 travelogue *Travels in the Island of Iceland*) (I, 8; II, 186). However, Wilson does give, in *Fruits of Enterprize*, a much more detailed depiction of children engaging with cartographical representations. *Fruits* is principally a retelling of Giovanni Belzoni's *Narrative of the Operations and Recent Discoveries within the Pyramids, Temples, Tombs and Excavations of Egypt and Nubia* (1820), although extensive supplementary material is also woven in. The narration of Belzoni's adventures begins with 'maps ... laid open on the library table', then one of the children, Emily, assiduously follows Belzoni's route in a very tactile fashion, repeatedly putting her finger to the map's surface (*FE*, 3). The dialogue is punctuated with interjections such as 'I have traced the course of the Nile from Cairo, with my little finger, upon the map, until it has brought me to [Carnac]' (*FE*, 28) and 'My finger is following him up the Nile, and now it stops at Benisoeuf, a long way south of Cairo' (*FE*, 223). Emily also points out to her mother and the other children the location of key sites, asks for clarification regarding places she cannot find, and reflects on the usefulness of maps. In this way, she resembles Lucy in *An Evening in Autumn*, who similarly acts as chief surveyor and place finder in the group, thereby prompting an older child to call her affectionately 'her little *gazetteer*' (*EA*, 89).

This constant correlation of story to map obviously works to promote greater map literacy and the tacit knowledge of how to handle modern cartographical representations. Yet this cartographization of stories, lessons and games also has more subtle effects. The emphasis Wilson and Hack put on maps is presumably part of their commitment to 'facts, *not* fiction', as the epigraph above puts it; that is, to a pedagogy which rejects the fictive devices sometimes used by other educational writers (e.g., the fictional traveller strategy outlined earlier). Inherent here, however, is the assumption that maps – or at least modern, Western maps – are wholly objective documents that simply transcribe the world as it is. This is certainly how Wilson appears to construe the maps she references and how she accordingly presents them to children. In *Operations and Recent Discoveries*, Belzoni finds several errors in J. B. B. D'Anville's 1765 map of Egypt, the principal guide he is using in the field; this prompts wry comments such as 'on our arrival at the spot where the bay ought to have been, we found that it did not exist'.[12] In her redaction Wilson's 'Mrs A' mentions Belzoni's use of D'Anville's map but elides any reference to its inaccuracies. No doubt this elision chiefly reflects the need to reduce and simplify Belzoni's lengthy narrative. However, it also contributes to a broader development that Edney discerns taking place across the late eighteenth and early nineteenth centuries: the 'normalization' of the assumption that maps are 'thoroughly unproblematic documents prepared by European cartographic science' ('Irony of Imperial Mapping', 41). For Edney, this increasing trust in maps went hand-in-hand with a growing veneration that regarded both maps and cartography as 'icon[ic] of European science and order' (42). As he writes elsewhere, maps became in this period potent 'metaphors for both the process of scientific research and the ideal of the ordered state of nature', while 'surveying was lauded as the application of rational methods to practical ends' ('British Military Education', 18). As we shall see, these are assumptions both reflected and promoted through Wilson's pedagogic use of maps. More fundamentally, however, Wilson's lessons make modern cartographical representations seem epistemologically foundational, a vital, primary means of anchoring different forms of knowledge about the world.

Wilson's maps are also foundational tools in an immersive, multimodal pedagogy. As the children track journeys and commodities across cartographic space, the movement of their eyes and fingers is supplemented by other media and technologies. In *Fruits*, they are shown the 'very large folio volume' (*FE*, 94) of plates published to accompany Belzoni's *Operations and Recent Discoveries* and so correlate map positions with picturesque visual images recording what Belzoni saw at key sites. In *The India Cabinet*, map use is combined with visual and tactile inspection of specimens and commodities from the region under discussion. These correlations of map, visual image and material object are combined with the authority figure's supervising conversation, which guides children as to how they should understand the relationship not only between different representations and objects but ultimately between different regions and cultures. The inter-action of these different media creates a more powerful 'virtual' experience for Wilson's fictive children, as they themselves assume the role of global explorers, traversing a miniaturized world via the map and at key junctures seeing what real-life travellers saw, touching what they touched. This imaginative identification is encouraged by Wilson's authority figures and finds most resonant expression in the way Wilson's children in *Fruits* replicate the activities of explorers by adding information to the household's maps. Thus Emily is at one point advised to 'put a little mark with your pencil' (*FE*, 87) to indicate a place mentioned by Belzoni but currently missing from their map; elsewhere she comments, 'I have made a dot with my pencil, and shall not forget that it is intended for [the ancient city] Berenice' (*FE*, 191). Here the children are not merely pretending to be surveyors – they are actively contributing to the household's stock of cartographic knowledge.

The drawing and copying of maps was by the 1820s a well-established educational technique, dating back at least as far as William Faden's *Geographical Exercises* (1777), which combined drawn maps with blank versions children could fill in themselves. However, in Wilson's frame narratives this exercise becomes a more compelling form of virtual travel and role play. Here maps interpellate children into the roles of surveyor and explorer; furthermore, they help to invest these roles with an air not only of adventure but also of morally worthy, altruistic endeavour. As noted earlier, this period saw maps become increasingly emblematic of, and invested with, what Edney terms 'the ideal of the ordered state of nature' ('British Military Education', 18). Such orderliness is strongly promoted in Wilson's texts, which propound a pedagogy notably – indeed ostentatiously – devoted to taxonomic classification and the concomitant principles of careful organization and conceptual (and literal) tidiness. This is most powerfully emblematized in the eponymous India cabinet of Wilson's first book. Here every class of specimen or artefact has its dedicated place or drawer, with individual items 'ticketed', 'numbered' and recorded in a notebook which itself arguably exemplifies the importance of a disciplined, orderly approach to both knowledge and the wider world. Certainly Wilson's narrative emphasizes the tidy appearance of pages 'neatly ruled with red ink into separate divisions', each division being given 'a number, – No. 10, No. 16, No. 24, – and so on' (*IC*, 31). Other texts do not fashion such a striking symbol of what one might regard as intellectual 'good housekeeping', but this attitude is everywhere apparent, as Wilson's children sit in well-run, middle-class households and are repeatedly taught to apply the taxonomic principles of Linnaeus and other scientists to the wider world. The accumulation and extension of knowledge thus takes on a domesticating aspect – an emphasis partly intended, one suspects, to legitimate the pronounced female interest and expertise in science, exploration and global affairs frequently on show in these texts, both from Wilson herself and from the fictional mothers and daughters she depicts.

This is the larger ethos and agenda that frames the map training outlined in Wilson's texts. Even though several of Wilson's primers – most notably *The India Cabinet* and *An Evening in Autumn* – invite children to consider the global circulation of valuable commodities, Wilson mostly elides any consideration of the commercial agendas and potential financial profits underpinning the journeys she recounts (of both goods and travellers). Instead, Western mobility is consistently depicted as an exercise in disinterested curiosity and rational enquiry, while the accumulation of Western knowledge about other regions is presented as the advancement of all human knowledge and so understood as an intrinsically virtuous, beneficial activity that constitutes a form of enlightened stewardship of the planet. These assumptions in turn attach to the maps used by Wilson's children – so that it is taken for granted that these are ideologically neutral, universally useful cartographic images – while also being greatly strengthened by the maps' apparent scientific precision, their impression of meticulous spatial representation. Also germane here is that Wilson's map lessons implicitly involve introducing children to the principles of longitude and latitude, since coordinates are given on several occasions – for example, when Berenice is located in *Fruits of Enterprize* through identification on the map of 'that point of land projecting into the sea, called Cape Lepte, a little beyond the 24th degree of latitude' (*FE*, 191). Children thus learn to situate specific places within an abstract, universalized conception of space, in which location can be plotted mathematically and the world exhibits an underlying geometric order – this order being given striking visual expression by the grid-like graticules that would have been employed on many of the maps used by Wilson's children.

As Wilson wrote her books in the 1820s, cartographer Edward Quin was at work on *An Historical Atlas: In a Series of Maps of the World as Known at Different Periods* (1830). Here the limited extent of Western geographical knowledge in earlier epochs was expressed visually by having small areas of known, mapped terrain surrounded by swirling dark clouds, representative of regions then little known in Europe. Wilson and her original audience probably never saw this striking cartographical device (though readers of later editions might have done). However, the way maps feature in her pedagogy must have fostered a similar sense of mapping as both outcome and agent of Enlightenment, working to push back dark clouds of ignorance and disorder. Simultaneously – and partly as a consequence of this strong association with Enlightenment and order – Wilson's map lessons probably inculcated a sense of empowerment, entitlement and superiority in British children. As William Rankin notes, maps offer their users a 'detached view from above', creating 'a miniature version of the world ... with the messy complexities of reality simplified and reduced to a legible system of lines and colours' (*After the Map*, 2). Wilson's children are being trained to conceptualize the world from, and position themselves in, this commanding, all-surveying perspective. Often, moreover, children are depicted with multiple maps laid out in front of them, allowing them to bring different, geographically distant regions quickly and easily to hand. In this way, Wilson's map training encouraged a transcendent, panoptic and mobile selfhood, one that felt enabled and licensed to move effortlessly around the globe. And if we accept Beryl Markham's suggestion that 'a map says to you, ... "I am the earth in the palm of your hand"', it also encouraged a sense of power and imaginative possession over the regions depicted cartographically (qtd. in Edney, 'Irony of Imperial Mapping', 24). In *Botanical Rambles*, revealingly, Charles and Ellen look through travel maps until they are led to declare 'we have journeyed completely round the world, we have explored Europe from north to south, searched the interior of Africa, visited America and traversed the sandy deserts of Arabia' – whereupon Charles suggests that they should now play at being 'Zenobia, Queen of the East, and ... Aurelian, the Roman Emperor'.[13]

This panoptic, transcendent tendency is reinforced by other features of these texts. The India cabinet's accumulation of specimens and artefacts similarly works to miniaturize the wider world, bringing the planet's productions into the domestic space and laying them out for inspection by the household. Additionally, in that text's frame narrative and elsewhere in her primers, Wilson's authority figures frequently describe – and so have their students, and the text's readers re-enact imaginatively – ascents to hilltops and mountain summits which culminate in wide-ranging prospect views, or what Mary Louise Pratt has described as 'monarch-of-all-I-survey' scenes.[14] A panoramic breadth of vision is further generated by the digressive tendency in Wilson's authority figures, who routinely branch out from discussion of any given region to note similarities or contrasts elsewhere in the world. Thus Mrs A's narration of Belzoni's Egyptian experiences incorporates observations about the Greenland Inuit, the bamboo huts of Peru, 'Laplanders' (i.e. the Sami of Northern Scandinavia), and many other exotic or 'savage' regions or cultures. Here Wilson shows not only breadth of knowledge but also considerable authorial skill as she deftly splices together her source materials.

Map use thus functions as an important, metonymic tool in a larger project of encouraging children to roam intellectually and imaginatively around the whole planet. Similarly, it helps to inculcate in British children the belief that they can hold much of the world in their hands – whether in map form or as material artefact – and definitively categorize and comprehend the key features and productions of diverse regions. It is the latter tendency, of course, that gives these texts an imperialistic dimension. That said, Wilson's influence and agenda is better described as proto-imperialistic. She nowhere suggests that Britain or any other European power should assume colonial control of the territories she describes; in many cases her works discuss regions in which Britain had no colonial ambitions at this date. Moreover, her works are not so emphatically racist as many other contemporary geographical primers. Barbara Hofland, for example, can barely mention Arabs and many other ethnicities without derogatory comment; in contrast, Wilson sometimes praises other cultures, and her children are occasionally reprimanded for over-hasty criticisms of a range of racial 'others'. Yet with these caveats, her primers undoubtedly encouraged British children to feel morally and intellectually superior to many other populations around the world. If the intellectual project repeatedly pursued by Wilson's educators is one of global taxonomy across many different aspects of the natural and human world, with regard to cultural variation that taxonomizing drive repeatedly seeks not just to classify but also to hierarchize difference. Here it is illuminating to return to the epigraph at the start of this chapter. Children should refer constantly to maps as they read, Wilson suggests, to procure 'an extensive and various' factual knowledge of the world. Immediately, however, she offers the following example of what this entails:

> For instance: in reading the account of the South Sea Islanders, we are led to compare their ingenious yet simple works, with the elegance and utility of the manufactures of the more polished nations of Europe and Asia, and are thus enabled to form an idea of the difference between the rough productions of the uncultivated mind, and those which are the result of science and art. (*IC*, 95)

A reflection on the usefulness and apparent facticity of modern Western maps thus morphs instantly into a hierarchical value judgement about the technological and intellectual superiority of 'polished' over 'uncultivated' nations. From this lesson in developmental differences, it is just a short step to a further lesson, or message, subtly but repeatedly propounded by Wilson's primers: namely, that the 'civilized', developed nations of the world – and often more specifically the British – stand firmly on the side of progress, science and good governance and so are morally obligated to extend these blessings to the wider world and to 'uncultivated' populations. And again, Wilson's conspicuous foregrounding of maps serves a rhetorical as well as practical function in promoting this attitude. Edney remarks that in the nineteenth century 'Europeans came to use mapmaking as a crucial marker of difference between themselves and the peoples they subordinate throughout the world' ('Irony of Imperial Mapping', 41). Wilson's texts never explicitly articulate this distinction, yet the pedagogical programme she outlines undoubtedly works to consolidate this impression both of maps and of Europe and its 'others'.

Protesting Imperial Mapmindedness

In such ways, then, Wilson's emphasis on maps assists an incipient imperialism that is persuaded of its moral rectitude in making interventions elsewhere in the world. At the same time, however, one implication of Wilson's educational texts is that empire training does not necessarily flow from map training. A key feature of Wilson's projected, multimodal pedagogy is the guiding, interpretative narration provided by a mother or similar authority figure. In this way, it is the teacher who largely determines the process of cathexis by which emotional investments and associations are attached to both different regions of the world and their cartographic representations, a process Edney sees as central to the formation of a specifically imperial mapmindedness ('Irony of Imperial Mapping', 32). The empowered, proto-imperialist 'geographical subjectivity' sketched in the last section may derive to some extent from the use of maps as a foundational mode of 'geo-epistemology', yet Wilson's fictional lessons suggest that maps alone are not enough to generate this outlook: further parental guidance must be given. Without this guidance, would the children's map use in itself generate a proto-imperialist sensibility? Or might maps be a route to alternative imaginings of the world and its inhabitants, if construed and interpreted differently or situated in an alternative pedagogy?

We are here in the realm of counterfactual speculation, since the dialogues crafted by Wilson depict parents firmly in control of the teaching scenario, leading children quickly and without protest to the desired learning outcomes. Yet, in Wilson's work as in many other female-authored geographical primers in this period, one can discern glimmerings of ambivalence, frustration and discontent in relation to some of the assumptions and associations sketched in the last section. These dissonant notes are not sounded explicitly but instead manifest themselves – as Norcia suggests of women's geographical primers more generally – through subtly 'disruptive moments' and 'sublimated critiques of imperial closures' (*X Marks the Spot*, 4, 22). And with Wilson, as with the other authors discussed by Norcia, many of these moments of disruption and discontent seem to reflect, or arise from, women's complex relationship to the knowledge-generating, supposedly civilizing and implicitly imperializing agenda these texts generally espouse. Travel to the far-flung regions described by many of Wilson's authority-figures was in this period largely the preserve of men. Similarly gender-marked, and so off-limits to most women, was the production of new, original knowledge in science and surveying (as opposed to synthesizing accounts for educational purposes, in the manner of the geographical primer). These are gender demarcations which Wilson's primers at times endorse and promote yet, on other occasions, implicitly question and protest – and this ambivalence in Wilson has a subtle but significant cartographic dimension.

Here is important to remember the basic fact that all maps reduce a three-dimensional reality to a simplified mono-planar representation. This is a key part of their rhetorical power, their illusion of presenting information clearly and unproblematically. As Bruno Latour writes, in 'a flat surface of a few square meters' there is apparently 'nothing hidden or convoluted, no shadows, no "double entendre"' (qtd. in Edney, 'Irony of Imperial Mapping', 25). Yet of necessity, cartographic representations must flatten the world. The maps Wilson's children are using, moreover, probably also flattened the world in a second, additional sense. By this date, conventions were emerging in Western mapping for indicating degrees of altitude and slope in landscapes, through the use of hachures, contour lines or similar graphic devices.[15] However, Wilson's children mostly consult maps depicting entire countries or continents; at this scale, contour lines or equivalent devices would not have been included, although major mountain ranges might have been indicated graphically or textually.

The viewer's position in relation to these two-dimensional representations is implicitly one of elevation, with the landscape spread out beneath them. This correlates with the marked interest in scenes of elevation and ascent in Wilson's frame narratives, which recount a variety of hill- or mountain-climbs culminating in panoramic, map-like views. Belzoni is described making one such climb in *Fruits of Enterprize*, for example, while *The India Cabinet*'s opening chapter recreates a family ascent of a mountain in the Lake District. From one perspective, these narrated mountain-ascents are entirely consonant with, and complementary to, Wilson's emphasis on map use, with both acculturating children to a commanding viewpoint on the wider world. However, these hill climbs also suggest an inadequacy or absence in the cartographical representations that Wilson is generally so keen to promote: namely, their lack of a vertical axis, due to their two-dimensionality. That lack is further foregrounded by the narrative attention frequently given in Wilson's texts to accounts of descent and to episodes which emphasise depth, enclosure or entrapment in a range of underground spaces. After opening with a mountain ascent, for example, *The India Cabinet* closes with a description, in its last full chapter, of an underground salt mine in Poland where a whole community lives permanently in 'a kind of subterraneous republic' (*IC*, 141). In *Real Stories, Taken from the Lives of Various Travellers*, the penultimate tale recounts an Alpine ascent which was abandoned after three expedition members were swept away and buried 'at a great depth in the snow'; throughout the account, Wilson emphasises the 'chasm[s]', 'fissure[s]' and 'crevice[s]' which often open up in the glaciers surrounding Mont Blanc.[16] Perhaps most strikingly, *Fruits of Enterprize* follows Belzoni's *Operations and Recent Discoveries* in foregrounding prominently the explorer's wanderings through the labyrinthine catacombs of the pyramids – an underground setting later reprised in Wilson's depiction of Herculaneum and Pompeii in *Relics of Antiquity*. For all that her fictive lesson plans put such emphasis on map use, Wilson's own imagination seems powerfully drawn to the third dimension, and to upwards and downwards trajectories, that maps inevitably elide from view.

Rather than just neatly, unproblematically supplementing each other, then, Wilson's multimodal yoking of maps and narrative storytelling often produces subtly discordant moments which necessarily – though also perhaps inadvertently – highlight the limitations of cartographic representation. Simultaneously, the dissonance at these moments often seems informed and further strengthened by a gendered discomfort with aspects of the intellectual and imperial projects elsewhere associated with mapping. As noted earlier, Wilson begins *An India Cabinet*, and therefore her literary career, with an account of a family climbing a mountain in

Cumbria. This episode largely conforms to contemporary gender norms regarding mobility and intellectual authority. The mother of the family and her daughters begin the ascent, but they stop climbing before the summit; only the father and eldest son reach the highest point and so achieve (as Wilson emphasizes) the most panoramic view of the surrounding countryside. After this initial nod to conventional expectations, however, Wilson's texts often problematize rather than confirm contemporary gender roles. Among Wilson's children the girls are just as intelligent as, and often more curious and widely read than, the boys; as we have seen, they are twice presented as better map-readers. And like the boys, the girls sometimes voice a desire to see for themselves the exotic scenes depicted by Belzoni or evoked by items in the India Cabinet. These expressions of female wanderlust generally go unanswered by Wilson's authority figures – yet Wilson's texts do offer, implicitly or explicitly, role models who suggest that such activities are possible and appropriate for women.

In *Fruits*, we learn that the eldest daughter Laura's favourite writer is Elizabeth Smith. A remarkable polymath who died when only thirty, Smith (1776–1806) published translations of the German writer Klopstock and the Biblical book of Job, but she was probably best known – certainly to younger readers – through the posthumous volume *Fragments in Prose and Verse by the Late Miss Elizabeth Smith, ... with Some Account of Her Life* (1808). Perusing this text, Laura would have encountered a young woman capable of matching men in knowledge-gathering ascents to mountaintops, since it includes a lengthy account of Smith climbing Snowdon, making geological and botanical observations in the process.[17] Smith's mountaineering also has a counterpart in Wilson's *The India Cabinet*. If this volume opens with an episode in which only men climb to a mountain summit, later in the narrative Wilson interpolates another mountaineering episode drawn from Fréderic Lullin de Chateauvieux's *Lettres écrites d'Italie en 1812 et 1813* (1816). Here Chateauvieux recounts climbing Vesuvius during an eruption only to meet, just before the summit, an Englishwoman, accompanied by two guides. 'Florinda', as she is dubbed, then accompanies Chateauvieux to view the crater. This undertaking prompts one child, Ellen, to declare that she 'scarcely like[s] Florinda ... She had almost too much courage for a woman, – especially an Englishwoman!' (*IC*, 78). However, the group is instantly guided by their mother to think Florinda's motives 'as laudable and as good as *Monsieur C—'s*', and eventually she is accepted as a heroic, praiseworthy exemplar.

With Elizabeth Smith and 'Florinda', Wilson offers role models who suggest that education, science and adventurous travel are compatible with

female respectability: an implicitly feminist message that is of a piece with
the sheer abundance, indeed surplus, of learning on show in Wilson's texts.
Yet the feminist aspirations embodied in Smith and Florinda also seem
tempered, at various junctures in Wilson's texts, with a more disconsolate
recognition that such agency, mobility and authority is not yet feasible for
British women. Especially resonant here is the subtle gendering Wilson
gives to the tunnels and catacombs through which Belzoni crawls in *Fruits
of Enterprize*. These scenes conjure an eerie sense of stasis, decay and
claustrophobia. Mrs A recounts, for example, how after crawling through
'passage[s] of fifty, a hundred, three hundred or six hundred yards' Belzoni
would 'seek a resting place, and contrive to sit' (*FE*, 102). However,

> when his weight bore on the body of some decayed Egyptian, it crushed in
> immediately. He would then naturally have recourse to his hands to
> sustain his weight, but they could find no better support, so that he
> would sink altogether among the broken mummies, with a crash of
> bones, rags, and wooden cases, which raised such a dust as sometimes
> left him motionless a quarter of an hour, waiting till it subsided again. (*FE*,
> 102–3)

The ghoulishness here is well calculated to pique children's imaginations
and was possibly one reason for this volume's popularity. Yet the sense of
claustrophobia is also gendered insofar as the text must necessarily emphasize, in repeated acts of inadvertent punning, that the principal occupants
of these dark, confined spaces are 'mummies'. At one juncture, Wilson's
Mrs A asks her children, 'you know what mummies are[?]', and receives the
answer: 'the bodies of dead persons, which have been wrapped up in a great
many bandages to preserve them' (*FE*, 36). Here is a Gothic counterpart to
nineteenth-century conceptions of women as 'Angels of the House': an
anxious projection of women as figures trapped within narrow, constrictive
limits, so 'wrapped up' and 'preserve[d]' by over-protective attitudes that
they are in effect embalmed. This definition of 'mummies', moreover, is
a direct plagiarism from Maria Hack's *Winter Evenings*. There are several
moments in Wilson's books where she loosely follows what was clearly an
important precursor text for her: here, however, Hack's exact phraseology
is reproduced, suggesting that this description made a powerful impression
on Wilson.

In an illuminating study of nineteenth-century spatial imaginings,
Siobhan Carroll suggests that enclosed, underground settings sometimes
function as a spur to colonialization, being figured as spaces with potential for domestication and assimilation within Enlightenment structures

of knowledge.[18] Wilson's subterranean spaces, however, often seem to shadow and problematize the Enlightenment project and so belong to a more troubling, dissident tradition also traced by Carroll. The entombments in ice described in *Real Stories* are not a setback to be heroically overcome but, instead, lead to the expedition being abandoned; the underground settings in *Fruits of Enterprize* chiefly convey a fearful, centuries-old stasis and stagnation. Especially significant in the present context, moreover, is the challenge these vivid, psychologically charged descriptions pose to the maps foregrounded elsewhere in Wilson's narratives, and which are generally figured as quintessential metonyms and symbols of Enlightenment rational enquiry. Like the narrated mountain ascents, Wilson's frequent renderings of descent and enclosure imply an inadequacy in the map's two-dimensional representation of space. Yet much more emphatically than the motif of ascent they suggest that the map's inevitable simplification of reality may have dangerous, repressive and falsifying aspects. If the flat surface of a map promises, as Latour suggests, full visibility and surveillance of a terrain, Wilson's underground spaces remind us that this is an illusion and that the real world in fact contains folds and fissures, hidden spaces and secret histories, which most maps elide. Simultaneously, they connect this cartographic elision with other forms of social and intellectual exclusion. In their constant slide from taxonomy to hierarchy when fashioning mental maps of human difference, Wilson's narrators implicitly distribute races and cultures along a vertical axis, with some firmly located in a lower, inferior position. Does the horror of underground entrapment expressed in her narratives articulate an unconscious unease at such dismissive judgements? Certainly these episodes of descent and enclosure often suggest a gendered unease. Wilson's enclosed spaces frequently have an air of uncanny domesticity, eerily echoing the scenes of domestication elsewhere in these texts. When describing the Polish salt mine in *The India Cabinet*, for example, Wilson picks out 'the immense number of little huts, hollowed out of the salt' in which 'many of the miners are born and live all their days' (*IC*, 141–2). In *Fruits* the children are encouraged to imagine themselves crawling alongside Belzoni in the catacombs and occasionally finding 'a more commodious place ... perhaps high enough to seat yourself' – although as Mrs A immediately exclaims:

> But what a place of rest! surrounded by bodies, by heaps of mummies in all directions, which, previous to being accustomed with the sight, would impress upon the mind disgust and horror. (*FE*, 101–2)

Moments such as these, in which domesticity is variously entwined with or mirrored by scenes of claustrophobia, even horror, arguably reflect inherent tensions in Wilson's project of engaging with the wider world and transmitting geographical knowledge while ostensibly keeping to the domestic sphere culturally prescribed at this date for women. In this regard, moreover, maps potentially have a poignant duality for Wilson and the eager female students she depicts. They are a key medium for knowledge about far-off regions and offer a tantalizing, miniaturized glimpse of the world beyond the home – yet it is also likely they will only ever be consulted within the home rather than actually used out in the field. This was almost certainly the case for Wilson herself; although the extent to which she personally travelled over the course of her life is unclear, it is very unlikely that she ever went beyond Western Europe to the more far-flung regions frequently described in her books.[19] In this context, the map perhaps becomes less a tool than a taunt: offering only a simulacrum of a world that will never be encountered in reality, it represents a project of knowledge production – and a prospect of travel – from which women are largely excluded.

These are some of the ambiguities and ambivalences that ripple through Wilson's strongly map-focused pedagogy. It must be stressed again that the lines of implicit critique here – of both maps and the proto-imperialist outlook seemingly associated with, and generated from, map use – are never developed in any detailed, coherent or explicit fashion. The principal aim of Wilson's primers, and their author's conscious intention, is undoubtedly to promote what I earlier dubbed 'map training' and 'empire training'. These texts thus offer a striking illustration of the wider tendency in this period identified by William St Clair, whereby a flood of new geographical works and travel accounts encouraged British readers to take 'all geography . . . into their consciousness' until 'there was nothing in the world which the British did not feel was partly their own'.[20] In similar spirit, Mary Louise Pratt claims that the late eighteenth-century vogue for geography and travel writing generated in Europe a new 'planetary consciousness' which fostered an increasingly proprietorial or curatorial stance towards regions deemed backward or uncivilized (*Imperial Eyes*, 15, 29–30). There are perhaps few better examples of how this new sensibility was formed and disseminated than Wilson's early works, an oeuvre which also highlights the role maps might play, both functionally and symbolically, in nurturing such a Eurocentric outlook.

Yet with Wilson, as with many other female writers in this period, the effort to square geographical, scientific and civic interests with her gender's marginalization and limited mobility produces what Norcia has felicitously termed '*subterranean* traces of discontent and frustration' (*X Marks the Spot* 25; my emphasis). A project of global domestication, one senses, is not wholly appealing to those who experience, and inhabit, an enforced domesticity. As a result, the strategy of maternal and authorial narration intended at one level to complement map use – and to complete the symbiosis of map training and empire training – works at another level to undermine both pedagogical endeavours. One consequence of these texts' multimodality is that the affective and figurative resonances, the greater detail and, as it were, 'thicker description' afforded by narrative, point up the abstractions and occlusions inherent in cartographic representation. And in a context in which Enlightenment cartography plays such a central role, both practically and rhetorically, in the construction of empire as careful, benign stewardship, this recognition of any map's inevitable inaccuracies and inadequacies cuts to the core of not just the cartographic but also the imperial project. Wilson's books thus hint, almost despite themselves, that maps are more equivocal emblems of Enlightenment and empire than her narrators acknowledge. Additionally, these further dimensions to Wilson's writing remind us that maps may be received and responded to in complex and diverse ways. Contrary to a simplistic technological determinism which views modern maps as always and inevitably generative of an imperialist outlook, in Wilson we have an example of how the 'geographical subjectivity' they foster (or, in St Clair and Pratt's terminology, the individual and collective 'consciousness') may also be conflicted, multidimensional and non-unitary, combining in an uneasy balance acceptance and resistance, endorsement and critique.

Notes

1. Sarah Atkins Wilson, *The India Cabinet Opened* (London: Harris and Son, 1821), 94–5; hereafter *IC*.
2. Matthew Edney, 'British Military Education, Mapmaking, and Military "Map-Mindedness" in the Later Enlightenment', *Cartographic Journal* 31:1 (1994): 14–20, 14.
3. Uttal, David H., 'Spatial Symbols and Spatial Thought: Cross-Cultural, Developmental, and Historical Perspectives on the Relation between Map Use and Spatial Cognition', in *Symbol Use and Symbolic Representation: Developmental and Comparative Perspectives*, ed. L. Namy (Mahwah: Erlbaum, 2005), 3–23, 10; David H. Uttal, 'Seeing the Big Picture: Map Use and the Development of Spatial Cognition', *Developmental Science* 3:3 (2000): 247–86, 249.
4. Camilo Arturo Leslie, 'Territoriality, Map-Mindedness, and the Politics of Place,' *Theory and Society* 45 (2016): 169–201, 180.

5. For the concepts of 'geo-epistemology' and 'geographical subjectivity', see William Rankin, *After the Map: Cartography, Navigation, and the Transformation of Territory in the Twentieth Century* (Chicago, IL: University of Chicago Press, 2016), 2.

6. See Megan Norcia, *X Marks the Spot: Women Writers Map the Empire for British Children, 1790–1895* (Athens: Ohio University Press, 2010).

7. Matthew Edney, 'The Irony of Imperial Mapping', in *The Imperial Map: Cartography and the Mastery of Empire*, ed. James R. Akermen (Chicago, IL: University of Chicago Press, 2009), 11–46, 12.

8. Maria Hack, *Winter Evenings; or Tales of Travellers* (London: Darton, Harvey and Darton, 1818), I, v.

9. Sarah Atkins Wilson, *An Evening in Autumn; or, The Useful Amusement* (London: Harvey and Darton, 1821), 67; hereafter *EA*. For the equivalent advice in Hack, see *Winter Evenings*, I, 102–3.

10. Sarah Atkins Wilson, *Grove Cottage* (London: Harris and Sons, 1823), 46.

11. Sarah Atkins Wilson, *The Fruits of Enterprise Exhibited in the Travels of Belzoni* (London: John Harris, 1821), 131; hereafter *FE*.

12. Belzoni, *Narrative of the Operations and Recent Discoveries within the Pyramids, Temples, Tombs and Excavations of Egypt and Nubia* (London: John Murray, 1820), 325.

13. Sarah Atkins Wilson, *Botanical Rambles* (London: Baldwin, Cradock and Joy, 1822), 70–1.

14. Mary Louise Pratt, *Imperial Eyes: Travel and Transculturation* (London: Routledge, 1992), 197–205.

15. For the multiple conventions used for depicting relief in Romantic-era maps, see Julia S. Carlson, *Romantic Marks and Measures: Wordsworth's Poetry in Fields of Print* (Philadelphia: University of Pennsylvania Press, 2016), 61–5.

16. Sarah Atkins Wilson, *Real Stories, Taken from the Lives of Various Travellers* (London: Harvey and Darton, 1827), 157.

17. See Henrietta Maria Bowdler, ed., *Fragments, in Prose and Verse: by Miss Elizabeth Smith. With Some Account of Her Life and Character* (Bath: Printed by Richard Cruttwell, 1809), 100–8, 127–31.

18. Siobhan Carroll, *An Empire of Air and Water: Uncolonizable Space in the British Imagination, 1750–1850* (Philadelphia: University of Pennsylvania Press, 2015), 146–84.

19. Our principal source of information about Wilson's life are the sermons preached at her funeral. These present her as a retiring, home-loving individual, while also emphasizing that in later life she was active in missionary circles and maintained an extensive correspondence with Christian missions around the world. See H. Venn, *Sermons Preached on the Occasion of the Death of Mrs Wilson* (London: Seeley, 1863). Given contemporary patterns of travel it is probably safe to assume that she never went beyond the standard British and continental itineraries of the day. Any journey to more exotic locales would almost certainly have been recorded in her funeral notices. Interestingly,

Wilson's son later judged her 'a missionary at heart' – but in practice this was a role only he, rather than his mother, was able to take up. See E. F. Wilson, *Missionary Works Among the Ojebway Indians* (London: SPCK, 1886), 13.

20. William St Clair, *The Reading Nation in the Romantic Period* (Cambridge: Cambridge University Press, 2004), 233–4.

CHAPTER 6

Romantic Board Games and the 'World in Play'

Siobhan Carroll

In the wake of J. B. Harley's groundbreaking argument that 'maps are pre-eminently a language of power', historians of cartography have come to pay particular attention to the political and social affordances of the map form.[1] In the Romantic period, maps have come to be seen as drivers of what Jordan Branch refers to as a newly emergent 'territorialized national identity' and as constructors of what Ron Broglio portrays as a nationalist 'sense of self and space'.[2] The Romantic period also arguably witnessed the emergence of a new mode of interacting with maps, one that was, at least ostensibly, oriented around pleasure, entertainment, and play.

During the eighteenth century, British publishers capitalized on a growing market for educational toys with board games and puzzles aimed at teaching geography, birthing what the narrator in Sir Walter Scott's *Waverley* characterizes as 'an age in which children are taught the driest doctrines by the insinuating method of instructive games'.[3] To *Waverley*'s narrator, the educational game form, like that of the historical romance, is a suspect rival to traditional history, representing a departure from the rules and regulations that constitute a 'well-governed child-hood' and preparing the way for the protagonist's flirtation with Jacobite insurrection. To Samuel Taylor Coleridge, on the other hand, common educational games such as dissected maps produce an imagination that is perhaps *too* well governed by authority. In *Biographia Literaria*, he famously compared the act of 'taking the pieces of a dissected map out of its box' to readers' slavish devotion to authorial vision when encountering the 'painting of local imagery' in poetry.[4] To Coleridge, the physical assembly of a dissected map and the mental assembly of a poet's landscape were problematic acts that stripped the player and reader of imaginative agency. And yet Coleridge also encouraged the playing of geographical games at home, helping to shape a generation of children who would, as Sara Coleridge later proudly declared, learn to see 'the map [as] a sort of game'.[5]

What did it mean to associate a map with a game? Did encouraging Romantics to 'play' with maps reinforce maps' disciplinary function, as Coleridge's remarks suggest? Or did they instead fulfil the worst fears of *Waverley*'s narrator, by encouraging their players' participation in subversive acts of cartographical imagination? In the following chapter I take up these questions as they relate to some of the best-preserved artifacts of Romantic cartographical play: geographical board games. One of the first and the most popular forms of educational games aimed at children, the geographical board game almost single-handedly transformed the board game from an eighteenth-century gambling device into a nineteenth-century form of family entertainment. Commercially produced games from this era allow us to track the emergence of a Romantic version of what Mathew Kaiser has described as a Victorian 'world in play'.[6] To speak of a 'world in play', he suggests, means both 'a world in flux' and a 'world that throws itself headlong *into* play, *inside* it, where it constructs a parallel universe, a ludic microcosm of itself' (1). And yet the 'experience of a world unhinged from a past' that Kaiser attributes to the Victorians was, if anything, more profoundly experienced in the Romantic age of cultural and political revolution (1). That experience, I argue, birthed games that attempted to control and mediate Romantic social and spatial transformations. In examining geographical board games, we can see how publishers struggled to reconcile the illusion of fixity and permanence suggested by a map with spatial, political, and social change. The mechanism of the game itself – its relationship to chance and unpredictability – ultimately came to be seen as a useful, though potentially disempowering, device for structuring players' relationship to a world in flux.

Cartography and the Geographical Board Game

The eighteenth century witnessed the beginnings of a so-called 'cult of childhood'.[7] Parents and professional educators were encouraged to follow through on the implication of John Locke's 1693 'Fancy ... that *Learning* might be made a Play and Recreation to Children'.[8] Of the various subjects that commanded parents' – and therefore publishers' – attention, geography was thought to be one of the most valuable for children to learn but also, potentially, one of the most vexing to teach. The extensive memorization the subject required could mean that it was perceived as 'dry and uninteresting to the youthful mind', unless, as the *Literary Chronicle* observed in 1827, it was alleviated by the 'combination of amusement with instruction' afforded by a 'Geographical Game'.[9]

Geographical board games appear to have originated in France with the 1645 publication of *Le Jeu du Monde* by Pierre Duval, the 'géographe ordinaire du Roi'. As with its successors, this spiral race game, which had players land on circles containing maps, was modelled on the well-known European gambling game, the 'game of goose'. As demand for geographical education grew, British parents gradually became more accepting of the devices, providing publishers replaced dice with a *totum* or *teetotum* – a spinning top made of bone, wood, or paper.[10] However, it was not until the 1790s that educational board games started to make a regular appearance in publishers' catalogues. The turbulence of the post-revolutionary period arguably accelerated the adoption of French educational methods, as refugees such as the Abbé Gaultier (the author of a popular British textbook on geography and an advocate of teaching through play) opened schools in Britain. Thus, whereas there is little evidence of the widespread use of geographical board games in Britain at the beginning of the eighteenth century, by the 1790s a Romantic educational gaming culture had taken root.

The late eighteenth century's growing demand for geographical board games proved especially useful to publishers specializing in cartographical productions. As Mary Pedley has observed, map-makers and publishers could easily struggle to recoup the costs of surveying, engraving, and printing a map.[11] Geographical board games might require maps, but, because they were often intended to teach geographical concepts like latitude and longitude, they did not necessarily require the *latest* maps. By creating educational games, publishers could thus get yet more use out of an engraved plate even as public demand for a particular map dwindled. From the outset, then, geographical board games were inextricably tied to maps, providing certain maps with educational afterlives that outstripped their original utility and teaching a generation of middle- and upper-class children how maps were to be viewed and used.

During the period from 1787 to 1840, the most common form of cartographical board game used a map, on which was superimposed a racetrack, as a game board. As in the 'game of goose', players would race each other along the track, propelled by chance, until a lucky player reached the winning destination and ended the game. In eighteenth- and early-nineteenth-century geographical games, players were typically encouraged to interact with the map on which the race track was superimposed, memorizing the facts associated with the real-world locations on which their game piece landed. From 1770 onward, when players finished a game they could fold up the game board, which was printed on paper backed by canvas or linen, and – just as though they held a portable travelling map in their hands – insert it into a slipcase designed for easy packing and travel. As material objects, then, British geographical board games reproduced maps, encouraged tactile interaction with the maps they displayed, and positioned geographical game boards as tools that would help players negotiate the physical world. They directed the reading of maps, drawing attention to certain places and omitting others, and constructed in their players' minds and bodies a sense of how such maps were to be read. As such, they serve as useful records of the ways in which Romantic cartographical imaginations were structured.

Thomas Jefferys and Games of Empire

The writings and early geographical games attributed to Thomas Jefferys (1719–71), the geographer to the king, illustrate the degree to which maps – and the games that taught young players to read them – could be politicized. Jefferys – one of the most important figures in eighteenth-century English cartography – is thought to have previously involved himself as a cartographical monitor of French encroachments on English territorial claims, providing careful readings of French maps in *The Conduct of the French, With Regard to Nova Scotia* (1754) that decried a persistent 'geographical depredation' in French representations of their North American possessions.[12] In *The Conduct of the French*, he claims that French cartographers such as Guillaume Delisle had evidently been instructed to expand the size of French possessions and 'to curtail the limits assigned by the English to Nova Scotia', in order to build public support for war (45). By deliberately introducing errors, he explains, cartographers could induce 'persons whose enquiries go no further than the maps . . . to believe the late encroachments of his nation . . . to be just' (50). Fully aware that maps are, as Harley has argued, 'inherently rhetorical images', Jefferys's pamphlet highlights the way in which French – and presumably English – maps can develop public investment in territorial possessions and can be used to generate support for, or undermine, imperial expansion (Harley, 37).

Jefferys's remarks provide a telling frame through which to view the early geographical games attributed to him. His *Royal Geographical Pastime: Exhibiting a Complete Tour Round the World* (1768) is among the earliest surviving English board games, and, as one might anticipate, it wears its English patriotism on its sleeve. The map of the world, we are told, has been 'drawn upon a Stereographic projection, of which LONDON is the centre' – a departure from many of the English games that followed it (which tended to place Europe, but not necessarily England, at the centre of their cartographical representations of the world).[13] Unlike other games, which frequently commenced in London, the *Royal Geographical Pastime* begins in the '1. AZORES, or Western Islands – subject to Portugal' and finishes at '103. LAND'S END – being the first pleasant place in England which is seen by mariners in their return from long voyages, and is equally wished for by the players'. On this board, England and the realm of the domestic are positioned as overlapping spaces of respite that exist *outside* the realm of play, as stable homes to which one longs to return after an interval spent in the world of gameplay and the stimulating, wearying world of international competition that it signifies. Unlike later games, which depict England as part of this world of competition, *The Royal Geographical Pastime* erects a boundary between the national and personal domestic and the 'world in play' it models, a symptom, perhaps, of eighteenth-century discomfort with the importation of worldly 'play' into the sanctified space of the home.

In playing *The Royal Geographical Pastime*, one learns to read the map of the world in terms of individual and global competition. Spinning an eight-sided *totum*, players race along one of three tracks – 'The Tour round the World', 'The British Empire in America', and 'The Russian Empire with their Discoveries in America' – pausing at various locations to review their relationship with England and, in many instances, to call to mind the slights and injustices perpetrated by England's European rivals. The pains inflicted by the latter are often reinforced by the rules of the game, which penalizes the player with a loss of two turns if they land on 'AMBOYNA, remarkable for the cruelty of the Dutch, when they extirpated the English from this island'. Likewise, the player who lands at 'PONDICHERRY . . . the principal settlement of the French in the East-Indies, taken by the English [in the] last war, but restored at the peace of 1763' loses a turn as they contemplate the wisdom of that restoration. The unlucky player thus experiences English territorial setbacks as personal losses and as incidents that interfere with his or her chance of winning the game. He or she is also arguably encouraged to look on military ventures as a means of restoring England's lost pride. Of 'MANILLA [sic]', for example, we are told that it was 'taken from the English by the Spaniards in 1762, who ransomed it from plunder. The ransom, however is not yet paid.' Such allusions to less-than-satisfactory outcomes of the Seven Years War (1756–63) suggest that England has unfinished business still to address, business associated with specific cartographical locations with which the player becomes painfully, repetitiously familiar.

While players are encouraged to read the map of the world as a zone of competition among European powers, the presence of non-European populations is occasionally acknowledged. True to its geopolitical obsessions, the *Royal Geographical Pastime* is less interested than its Victorian successors in the morality of natives, instead assessing groups in terms of their potential as allies: it is more important that players know that the 'Moskito Indians' are 'in alliance with the English' than it is for them to know their state of moral development. The game's most negative characterization belongs to the Chinese, whose Great Wall is dismissed as a 'monument of the Chinese grandeur and cowardice'. To fall back on defences, however well built, is not the model this expansionist game wishes to encourage.

In such descriptions, the game reflects attitudes bred by the Seven Years War. Originating in Britain's desire to expand its North American colonial markets, the war embroiled all the European great powers, the Mughal Empire, and the Central American Miskitu, among other participants (though not China, whose attention during the 1760s was preoccupied by the Afghan Empire).[14] The Seven Years War had proved a military triumph for Britain and had firmly established in Britons' imagination a sense of the martial value of indigenous allies and of Britain's navy, even as it also resulted in the dramatic expansion of Britain's Empire.

Composed following the end of the Seven Years War, and before the losses of the American War of Independence, the map of *The Royal Geographical Pastime* suggests an expansionist trajectory for Britain. It represents with absolute confidence the mountain ranges and rivers of as-yet-unexplored sections of North America and Africa, and it allows the '*fortunate*' player to skip ahead via a navigable version of Britain's much longed for 'NORTH-WEST PASSAGE into the South Seas'. Reminded of the national value of explorers' discoveries and of England's lost ownership of certain places by the game's place descriptions, the player is encouraged to view the British Empire as poised for military and navigational expansion – an expansion in which the game system makes them feel personally invested.

Mapping the Romantic World

If eighteenth-century games such as *The Royal Geographical Pastime* encouraged players to interact with a mapped world that was essentially knowable, the political, social, and scientific revolutions of the Romantic era demanded a different perspective. *Bowles's Geographical Game of the*

World in a New Complete and Elegant Tour, through the Known Parts thereof, laid down in Mercator's Projection (c. 1797) appears to crib many of its descriptions, though not its cartography, from *The Royal Geographical Pastime*.[15] In doing so, it usefully registers some of the cultural shifts that took place in the wake of Jefferys's 1770 foray into educational gaming. Eschewing *The Royal Geographical Pastime*'s overt patriotism, *Bowles's Geographical Game* does not boast of centring its map on London. Instead it advertises its adherence to the Mercator projection (which gained popularity for its utility in navigation) and its depiction of 'known' rather than conjectured geographical features. In cartography and in its characterization of places, it shows itself to be a decidedly post-Cook production, advancing a vision of British identity as rooted in scientific professionalism. While the game continues to remind its players of certain injustices committed against England – in Manila, one is now required to '*stay three turns, to find out . . . why the ransom money is not yet paid to the English, who took this place from the Spaniards in 1762*' – the North-West Passage has vanished, and, in its place, inscriptions such as '*Coast little known*' and '*Continuation of this Coast unknown*' highlight areas where Britain's cartographical knowledge is incomplete. That said, the map does not display the same empirical fastidiousness when it comes to representing the interiors of continents: Africa is represented as being known in its entirety, complete with mountain ranges and rivers. Rather than reflecting an investment in geographical science for science's sake, then, the game reflects a preoccupation with a nautical future for Britain and, potentially, the game's players.

Indeed, the British Empire of *Bowles's Geographical Game of the World* is a decidedly maritime one. Patriotism in this game requires a post-war attentiveness to the welfare of imperial (and particularly naval) labourers. Unlike in other games, in which players are asked to imagine themselves as privileged tourists, in *Bowles's Geographical Game of the World* both 'Ladies and Gentlemen' are encouraged to imagine themselves as navigating the world as sailors. They must '*stay one turn, to be shaved by Neptune*' on their first crossing of the Line, and they are punished with death on encountering '*a most perilous Whirlpool . . . for keeping so bad a look out*'. Unlike *The Royal Geographical Pastime*, the penalties of the game also emphasize the costs of advancing empire. Players now lose a turn '*to assert the Rights of the British Crown*' in Nootka Sound and lose three turns searching for the North-West Passage. At such moments, *Bowles's Geographical Game* tempers the strident expansionism of its predecessor for an audience that had grown wary of the sacrifices demanded by empire.

War-weariness also suffuses the 1790s games published by John Wallis, an affiliate of the Newbery publishing circle who, along with his son Edward Wallis, would become one of the most significant figures in the early-nineteenth-century board-game industry. Wallis had begun his career as a publisher of maps, but, during the 1780s, he was drawn into the burgeoning children's publishing scene. There he became known as a 'vigorous [provider of] games, puzzles, and other juvenile amusements' and as one of the most popular producers of board games on either side of the Atlantic.[16] When the narrator of *Waverley* rails against children being taught history and arithmetic via a 'new and complicated edition of the Royal Game of the Goose', it is likely to be a Wallis game that is attracting his ire (*Waverley*, 12).

Like *Bowles's Geographical Game*, the games produced by the Wallis family positioned themselves against the jingoistic geographical games of an earlier era. Sometimes this positioning may have been unconscious, as in the choice of map that forms the game board of *Wallis's Tour of Europe: A New Geographical Pastime* (1794).[17] Based on John Wallis's 1789 *New Map of Europe Divided into Its Empires, Kingdoms, &c.*, the *Tour of Europe* game board takes no notice of revolutionary France's fluctuating wartime borders, instead positing an eternal, ideal Europe which the player can imagine visiting for pleasure rather than military necessity.[18] Doubtless, Wallis's decision to republish a 1789 map as a game board was a financially astute one, allowing the recoup of prior costs and the production of profits not dependent on an up-to-date version of 1790s Europe's volatile borders. But in practice, *Tour of Europe* instils in its young players' minds a vision of a Europe as it should be – a vision that, following the imminent rise of Napoleon, would seem increasingly at odds with the Europe of contemporary politics.

In its place descriptions, *Tour of Europe* encourages nostalgia for a lost era of cosmopolitan communication and travel. The sidelining of revolutionary politics inherent in its reproduction of Wallis's *New Map of Europe* is continued in its descriptions of places, most notably in its characterization of 1794 Paris as a 'famous city' full of 'curiosities' that reward the tourist's gaze, rather than as the seat of dangerous political ferment. True, the player may lose turns in St Malo in Brittany after being 'taken up for a spy', but they will shortly be 'set at Liberty' once their position as a privileged tourist is understood. Here, and elsewhere in the game, revolutionary politics are, at best, only glancingly acknowledged while the pleasures and privileges of an era of cosmopolitan peace are nostalgically recalled. The tourism routes suspended by war are preserved by the game, which whets players' appetites for travel to inaccessible destinations and implicitly promises that European tourism will one day resume.

The game's investment in international circulation is also (but more subtly) indicated in the organization of its racetrack. Unlike other games of its period, *Tour of Europe* requires the player to follow the pathways taken by trade and communication around the world, starting not from London but from Harwich, 'this being the station for the packet notes to go to Holland'. Players are asked to trace the routes 'where the English packets go in times of peace' across a map haunted by war. The player is penalized not only for traditional sins such as overindulgence in drink ('go back to Abo and stay there one turn') but also for viewing the landscape with a military eye. Thus, to contemplate 'the excellent harbour and fortifications of the city' of Dantzic is to lose a turn. This subtle anti-war stance also surfaces in the game's recollection of historical events, where it tends to emphasize the costs rather than the glory of war. The game remembers the youthful Charles XII of Sweden (a possible role model for military-minded youth) for his defeats ('almost his whole army killed or taken prisoners') rather than for his victories. The game is similarly reluctant to celebrate English martial heroism, taking perfunctory note of four English victories, of which only two come from the last ninety years. If Jefferys's game attempts to inculcate jingoistic fervour in its players, *Tour of Europe* works to the opposite effect, suggesting that *too* great an interest in war leads to personal loss.

Via its cartography and its place descriptions, *Tour of Europe* encourages its players to view the map of Europe as signifying a region of pleasure, curiosity, and sociality that has been temporarily lost to war. In getting players to trace suspended routes with their fingers and familiarizing them with the attractions of certain destinations, the game attempts to inculcate in its players a desire to visit in reality the places elite Britons once engaged with via play. In *Tour of Europe,* geographical gameplay thus emerges as a means both of meditating on the pointless repetitions and losses of warfare and of preserving and promoting among the upper-middle class the practices and culture of cosmopolitan sociability.

Napoleon and the Romantic World in Play

Walker's New Geographical Game Exhibiting a Tour Through Europe (1810; see Figure 6.1) usefully illustrates the Romantic board game's response to a slightly later era of geographical and political uncertainty.[19] Published by the well-known Darton family, this geographical game features

Figure 6.1 *Walker's New Geographical Game Exhibiting a Tour Through Europe*
(1810). Special Collections, University of Delaware Library, Newark, Delaware.

a reproduction of the map of Europe included in the 1797 *Atlas* to *Walker's
Elements of Geography* (1788), a popular educational text of its day.
Coloured in 'the Dutch manner', with mountain ranges (the 'natural'
borders of Europe) shown in profile view, the game board emphasizes
borders and cities rather than navigational features or trade routes (Pedley,
The Commerce of Cartography, 68). The latitude and longitude featured on
the *Atlas* version of this map are omitted, suggesting that the primary
purpose intended for this game lay not in educating children in abstract
geographical principles but in the geopolitical knowledge needed for polite
conversation. The playing track – a thin white line – is not always easy to
see, nor is its convoluted path around Europe necessarily intuitive. To
correctly place one's counter, one must follow the track with one's finger,
skimming over mountain ranges and oceans, reproducing, in its geo-tactile

pleasures, the kind of armchair geography practised by Cowper in *The Task*, in which the reader discovers 'countries . . . . While fancy . . . Runs the great circuit, and is still at home'.[20] The game's rule book, which suggests that one view one's markers as 'servants' accompanying the traveller around Europe on a trip from London to Athens, reinforces this class-bound sense of ease in travel – a sense of ease that is belied by the war-torn European landscape described in the rule book.

For while *Walker's New Geographical Game* invokes the pleasures of imagined travel, certain aspects of it – such as its emphasized borders and anxious place descriptions – suggest that the game format is being used to corral the fluctuations of a Romantic 'world in play'. Rather than printing information on the game board, as in the previous examples, *Walker's New Geographical Game* transfers its rules and place descriptions to a pamphlet rule book, which could be more easily and inexpensively revised and reprinted to keep up with geopolitical events. Even so, the game struggles with the challenges of teaching geography in the midst of the Napoleonic Wars. At times the 1810 pamphlet frets over the accuracy of its representation of places like Toledo, reminding players that 'it would be impossible, during the present state of things in this part of Europe, to be perfectly correct as to particulars. Some time must elapse ere the different provinces are sufficiently settled, to allow of geographical accuracy' (11). Of Buda (the western part of present-day Budapest), we learn that 'at this period the Russians are fighting in the neighbourhood' (22). What the outcome will be, and how the border-to-be-memorized should be drawn, is as unsettled as the outcome of the players' own chance-based game.

Where the game feels on firmer footing is with the subject of Napoleon, a 'despotic' (7) upstart whose success represents a disruption to the class hierarchy the game supports. The rule book reminisces about the glories of Versailles before reminding players of the 'remarkable changes, produced by the revolution', which has placed the palace into the hands of a man 'who, from a private station, without claim to distinction, has raised himself to a throne, once the hereditary right of princes' (7). As presented in connection with a chance-based race game – a genre, Roger Caillois has argued, in which 'winning is the result of fate' rather than merit – Napoleon's rise is constructed as the product of luck, the outcome of an unfortunate spin of the teetotum rather than of any admirable characteristic that Napoleon might possess.[21] To speak of the changes instigated by revolution in a game where players' changes in fortune are driven by the 'revolutions' of a spinning top is also to invite comparison of gameplay with Romantic geopolitics. In this context, the board game becomes an ideologically useful lens through which to view social upheaval: a lens that both preserves the possibility of an overarching providential order – a game, after all, has an author and a clearly defined structure – and also suggests that the setbacks affecting individuals and nations are attributable to the operations of indifferent chance.

If *Walker's New Geographical Game* suggests that the individuals' relationship to the external world is mediated in part by chance, it simultaneously locates another potentially more trustworthy mediator of one's relationship to the social and geopolitical world in cultural capital. As with many games of its type, the acquisition of cultural knowledge is the raison d'être of *Walker's New Geographical Game*. The importance of culture is reinforced not only by the advertising of the game but also by its characterizations of the various nations over which the player passes: by starting in London and ending in Athens, the game suggests a connection between these two great metropolises of learning. One travels through time from the pinnacle of civilization – London – through a Europe in danger of cultural backsliding to Athens, where one reflects on how a city once known for learning is now 'inconsiderable when compared with its former splendour' (24). Athens at least *is* considered, whereas the entire continent of Africa is explicitly excluded from gameplay with a note inscribed on the game board explaining that the 'inhabitants of Africa are deprived at present of all arts and sciences, by which the human mind remains torpid and inactive, [and so] a gloomy sameness every where prevails'. To be uncultured is to be excluded from the zone of movement and play, to be perceived as a subject unworthy of representation, and – specifically in the case of Africa, where the description is printed on the game board rather than on the more ephemeral pamphlet – to be incapable of change. Regarding Africa, the game board further makes the suggestion that spending educational time on that continent would be harmful, as 'to dwell long upon the manners of this Country … besides that it could afford little instruction … would be disgusting to every lover of mankind'. The player is thus taught to skim past Africa and to dwell instead in and on centres of European culture such as Milan, where the player is forced to stay '*three turns to see the immense library of books*' (17).

To penalize with culture and learning may seem like a counterintuitive strategy for an educational game, but it is consistent with the Romantics' conflicted attitude towards games and the 'world in play' they represented. Indeed, beginning in the Romantic era, we see an increase in the number of games that, unlike many of their eighteenth-century predecessors, pitted social values and game penalties *against* each other. Like Coleridge and the narrator of *Waverley*, Romantic game creators seemed increasingly concerned that players might too closely subscribe to the game boards' model of a chance-based world. The counterintuitive penalties in games such as *Walker's New Geographical Game* thus appear to encourage a kind of critical literacy in geographical gameplay. Even as they experience the vagaries and injustices of a chance-based game, players are implicitly encouraged to adopt cultural attitudes and practise behaviours that may not necessarily be rewarded.

The cultural investment of *Walker's New Geographical Game* is continued in its representation of the Napoleonic Wars, which it frames as a battle over European cultural identity. The same set of instructions that bewail Napoleon's usurpation of aristocratic rule express concern over the fate of cultural artefacts that have fallen into French hands: Innsbruck, we are told 'could boast of many costly specimens of genius, but whether these have survived the predatory irruption of the enemy has not been yet ascertained' (17). Napoleon is actively trying to make Paris a new cultural capital, enriching it 'with the spoils of other capitals' and assembling within it 'most specimens of taste and judgment formerly scattered over Europe' (7). This goal is opposed to the logic of the game's London-to-Athens racetrack, which implicitly positions London as the proper heir of classical greatness.

The map, racetrack, and rules of *Walker's New Geographical Game* thus serve to frame the fluctuations of war and social mobility, suggesting a proper order to the world and a trajectory of history that may not be reflected in the daily news. At the same time, the chance-based nature of actual gameplay allows players to experience unpredictable, unmerited departures from order within a temporally bounded instance. An unworthy player – one who is less versed in geography, who is younger, or who comes from a lower social stratum – may win a game that 'worthier' players, shipwrecked by unlucky spins of the teetotum, struggle to complete. At the game's conclusion, one may contemplate the gloomy prospect that British civilization might one day experience the same decline that befell that of the Athenians; but then the game is over. Order is restored: scores are reset to zero; the map is returned to its slipcase. When the cartographical board is brought out for another game, all players will again begin on an even footing in London, traveling to Athens, across a Europe whose permanence is assured by the clear borders of the game board's map. In playing such a game, one learns that the rewards of gameplay are fleeting and that the successes of those who set themselves against Britain – as Napoleon does, and as Fergus, the 'desperate game' player, does in *Waverley* – will inevitably be undone by a reversal of fortune (318). The potential of a board game to consistently generate new narratives, with new winners and losers, makes it a safe space within which Britons can contemplate their worst fears – the possible defeat of Britain by Napoleon – and reassure themselves that Napoleon's victories will have no lasting consequence.

The Spatial World in Play

Even as continentally oriented games such as *Walker's New Geographical Game* nervously balanced representations of geopolitical fluctuation against assumptions of cartographic stability, instability in Europe encouraged the rise of domestic tourism and, with it, a subgenre of game aimed at representing the landscapes of British tourism. While geopolitical instability was not depicted as a potential threat in these games, the spatial changes occasioned by industrialization and global trade were at odds with a Romantic ideal of British identity rooted in place. Geographical tourist games addressed these changes in their imagery and game systems, frequently adopting the counterintuitive strategy practiced in *Walker's New Geographical Game* of penalizing Romantic 'virtues' and rewarding the 'vice' of participation in a cosmopolitan marketplace.

Whereas early games representing Britain tended at least to imply the possibility of tourism, games that actively encouraged a tour of Britain arrived relatively late on the scene. *Wallis's New Geographical Game Exhibiting a Complete Tour through Scotland and the Western Isles* (1792) is one such game.[22] Its perspective, unsurprisingly, is Anglocentric: longitude is given as distance 'from London', and players begin the game at Berwick, 'the principal entrance from England into Scotland'. The track also enters Ireland, where the player visits a variety of towns, the chief virtues of which appear to be their access to the British mainland: 'Londonderry', we learn, is 'a town in Ireland, where the traveller must pay one counter to get back to Scotland, at Whithorn, No. 46'. Unlike most other geographical games of the 1790s, *Wallis's … Complete Tour through Scotland* attends closely to the mechanics of travel, instructing its players where they should book transport and accommodation. Unlike others of its type, the game applies penalties that roughly correlate with the actual costs of travel, requiring players to pay counters to ride ferries and to see ruins – a game mechanic that would be exaggerated in later Wallis games like *The British Tourist* to satiric effect.

Where *Wallis's … Complete Tour through Scotland* most stands out, however, is in the sequencing of its racetrack. Whereas in most geographical games one encounters the numbered locations along the racetrack in a consecutive order, in this game one encounters numbered places out of order, and some places have no relation to the racetrack whatsoever. Thus, the player might follow the track from '31' to the next numbered location, '58', or might pay a counter to travel to number '32', 'Col Island', which is unconnected to the racetrack, using their financial capital to indulge in a touristic departure from the beaten path. While technically a penalty mechanism, place numbers that send the player away from the track create a slightly different game for diverted players, who must scour the map for their next plausible destination and who may benefit by being advanced to places closer to the end of the game. Such departures from geographical contiguity and numerical sequencing suggest that the game is constructing the mobilities of domestic tourism as being different from, and having more agency, than the kinds of travel circuits inscribed in continentally oriented games.

As the nineteenth century dawned, cartographic games began to lose market share to panoramic games, which replaced the game board's map with a circular racetrack of framed illustrations, usually featuring prospect views of well-known buildings or landscapes. The purported educational function of these games remained similar to that of their cartographical cousins, but as titles such as John and Edward Wallis's *Panorama of Europe* (1815) suggest, the pleasures suggested by these games lay in the views they offered of select localities.[23] In Wallis's games in particular, the arrangement of square, window-like images side by side along the track suggested a perspective increasingly influenced by railway travel rather than travelling maps. This connection is made explicit in *Wallis's Locomotive Game of Railroad Adventure* (1835), in which the game track, and the images it consists of, are linked together by metal pipes and bolts.[24]

Despite its title, *Wallis's Locomotive Game* also reveals the continuation of Romantic board games' suspicion of the changes they invoke. Rather than celebrating advances in speed and technology, and new connections to far-flung places on the globe, *Wallis's Locomotive Game* instead highlights moments of stoppage and friction. The excitement of the railway journey is ascribed not to speed and motion but to incidents such as going 'OFF THE RAIL' ('Be thankful you were not killed' [6]), the apparently frequent hazard of 'PIGS RUN OVER' (pay 'one for the poor fellow you have made into pork' [10]), and 'LINE FLOODED' ('it would be a pity you should be drowned through your impatience to get the Game' [11]). Swift circulation is associated both with real-world commerce – ('you made a good bargain by being first in the market!' [6]) – and with the rapidity of gameplay. The game's frequent admonition that players should give their in-game profits to real-world charities suggests both that the game designers wished to inculcate charitable attitudes in their players and, perhaps, that they anticipated players would use the game to gamble with real money, as board game critics had feared. More than many of its predecessors, *Wallis's Locomotive Game* thus walks a fine line between endorsing and criticizing a 'world in play', seeking to capitalize on players' interest in a brave new world of spatial and commercial circulation even as it portrays that world as less than attractive.

   Edward Wallis's *The British Tourist: A New Game* (1820) similarly links fast motion, commerce and gameplay together in ostensive opposition to Romantic values.[25] The game, which charts a tour from 'PROSPECT HOUSE, HERNE' (3) to 'HIS MAJESTY'S COTTAGE, WINDSOR' (11), propels the players through a chain of sedate views of cottages and great houses within an English-dominated national landscape. While the game's opening and closing destinations suggest a celebration of British domesticity, the energy of gameplay is opposed to the tranquillity of the landscapes depicted – and to the penalties applied. As in *Walker's New Geographical Game*, the player is penalized for the virtues the game might be expected to reward. The desire to '*view . . . fine ruins*' (3) leads to punishment after punishment, most devastatingly near the end of the game track, when the opportunity to take '*steam-boats up the river Wye*' sends the player all the way back to 'No. 9' in order to see '*Tintern Abbey*' (9). Meanwhile, players who engage superficially with place are rewarded. The player who lands on '12. A FARM-HOUSE at BROOMFIELD', benefits if he was '*born in London*' as he '*will be at a loss for amusement, and must therefore spin again*' (4). The cosmopolitan dullard enjoys an advantage, while players uncorrupted by the global metropolis are doomed to enjoy this rural sojourn. In *The British Tourist*, as in other games published by the Wallis family, to immerse oneself in the locations one visits, to admire 'fine paintings and statues' (6), or to elevate one's soul through aesthetic contemplation of the landscape is to risk losing the game. At the close of the Romantic era of board games, in other words, we can see the emergence of a board game form that encouraged players to identify a proto-globalized world of technological and spatial change with the structures of chance-based gameplay. At the same time, these games also taught players to hold themselves apart from that world, to understand its rewards as fleeting and its values as morally suspect. In this manner, late Romantic board games encouraged opposition to, rather than compliance with, the disciplinary functions of a game system identified with fluctuation and change – a perspective that would gain new traction in the Victorian era, in novels and memoirs that depicted individuals at the mercy of economic and social transformations as disempowered members of a 'world in play'.

Legacies

In an 1843 letter, the Victorian hymn writer Frederick William Faber described his first sight of the legendary leaning tower of Pisa. 'Knowing what to find', he had set out for Cathedral Square, only to be surprised by his reaction to the famed structure.[26] Rather than recollecting the Italian history he had so painstakingly learned, he found himself instead remembering the hours he had spent playing a 'geographical game with my mother' (182) in the 1820s. Mentally transported back to his Romantic childhood, 'away went buildings, art, history, Pisa, Italy, and the whole concern; my eyes saw, but reported not what they saw. I was in England' (182). The kind of restorative mental travel claimed by poets such as Wordsworth and Coleridge is here triggered not by an exercise of poetic imagination but by the lingering power of the Romantic 'geographical game' to shape Victorian perceptions of space.

Victorians' recollections of geographical games indicate that not only their perceptions of place but also their experience of uncertainty and instability was inflected by their early cartographical gameplay. Recalling how he was forced into international circulation to earn his living, George Augustus Sala characterizes his lack of agency in terms familiar to his Victorian readers: propelled by 'the great whirling teetotum of life' which 'spun round [and] fell, spent, athwart a spot on the map marked "United States of America"', he first travels to the United States; when 'round again went the teetotum', he must travel to Cuba.[27] The sense of 'intellectual and visual mastery' that scholars have claimed is implicitly promised by maps does not quite fit Sala's experience of bewildered, chance-driven travel.[28] And so, in mapping out his journey for his readers in a series of essays, Sala invokes a familiar object that unites cartography with powerlessness and geography with uncertainty. For him and for other Victorians, the lessons learned from geographical games served as a useful preparation for a world in which the stability promised by maps could be hard to find.

It is in such recollections that we can find our best evidence for the lingering impacts of Romantic play culture. For while archives hold occasional examples of game scores and handwritten amendments to rule books, for the most part the geographical play culture of the Romantic period was, like play itself, treated as an ephemeral experience. In the artefacts of surviving board games, we can trace out a trajectory of board-game evolution in which the decidedly nationalist and disciplinary games of the eighteenth century paved the way for a more ambiguous form in the early nineteenth. In these games we can see their creators' struggle to apprehend, and then take advantage of, the subversive nature of gameplay, as they learned to associate the unpredictability of board games' chance-based, ephemeral narratives with the rapidly changing nature of contemporary politics, markets, and spaces. This instability was at odds with the fixed world implicitly promised by the maps that so often did double-duty as Romantic game boards. In the board game form, however, publishers found a means of uniting cartography with unpredictability and of training readers to read maps as stable representations of a world in play. Prepared by such training, a generation of children grew up thinking of play as an instance within which one could sustain cultural values suspended by real-world politics and see 'themselves' as pursuing courses of action that they were simultaneously encouraged to condemn. In the Romantic era, to play thus became a way to experience and also resist revolutionary change – to adopt a kind of double consciousness, in which one was part of a world governed by both providential destiny and amoral chance. In viewing a map, a Romantic child saw not only an opportunity to practise visual mastery or to rehearse national catechisms but also a seemingly static object that in fact represented an unpredictable world of motion, fluctuation, and play.

Notes

1. J. B. Harley, *The New Nature of Maps: Essays in the History of Cartography*, ed. Paul Laxton (Baltimore, MD: Johns Hopkins University Press, 2001), 79.
2. Jordan Branch, *The Cartographic State: Maps, Territory and the Origins of Sovereignty* (Cambridge: Cambridge University Press, 2013), 163; Ron Broglio, *Technologies of the Picturesque: British Art, Poetry, and Instruments, 1750–1830* (Lewisburg, PA: Bucknell University Press, 2008), 51.
3. Walter Scott, *Waverley*, ed. Claire Lamont (Oxford, Oxford University Press, 2008), 12.
4. Samuel Taylor Coleridge, *Biographia Literaria*, ed. Adam Roberts (Edinburgh: Edinburgh University Press, 2015), 307–8.
5. Sara Coleridge, *Memoir and Letters of Sara Coleridge*, Vol. 1 (London: Henry S. King, 1873), 92.
6. Matthew Kaiser, *The World in Play: Portraits of a Victorian Concept* (Stanford, CA: Stanford University Press, 2012), 1–2.

7. Norma Clarke, '"The Cursed Barbauld Crew": Women Writers and Writing for Children in the Late Eighteenth Century', in *Opening the Nursery Door: Reading, Writing and Childhood, 1600–1900*, eds. Mary Hilton, Morag Styles, and Victor Watson (London and New York: Routledge, 1997), 91–104, 101.

8. John Locke, *Some Thoughts Concerning Education* (London: Printed for a Society of Stationers, and sold by J. Baker at the Black Boy in Pater-Noster-Row, 1710), 155.

9. 'British Geographical Game', *The Literary Chronicle* (December 1827), 825.

10. See Johanna M. Smith, 'Constructing the Nation: Eighteenth-Century Geographies for Children', *Mosaic* 34.2 (2001): 133–48.

11. Mary Pedley, *The Commerce of Cartography: Making and Marketing Maps in Eighteenth-Century France and England* (Chicago, IL: University of Chicago Press, 2005), 73–95.

12. Thomas Jefferys, *The Conduct of the French, with Regard to Nova Scotia* (London: T. Jefferys, 1754), 46.

13. Thomas Jefferys, *The Royal Geographical Pastime: Exhibiting a Complete Tour Round the World, by T. Jefferys* (London: Thos. Jefferys at the Corner of St. Martins Lane, 1768). For an image of this game, see https://exhibits .stanford.edu/heckrotte/catalog/db093zb9430.

14. See Daniel Baugh, *The Global Seven Years War, 1754–1763: Britain and France in a Great Power Contest* (Harlow, UK: Longman, 2011), 1–16.

15. *Bowles's Geographical Game of the World: In a New Complete and Elegant Tour Through Known Parts Thereof, Laid Down on Mercator's Projection* (London: Printed for the proprietors Bowles & Carver, No. 69 St. Paul's Church Yard, 1797). Unpaginated game board.

16. Linda Hannas, *The English Jigsaw Puzzle, 1760–1890: With a Descriptive Check-List of Puzzles in the Museums of Great Britain and the Author's Collection* (London: Wayland, 1972), 34.

17. *Wallis's Tour of Europe: A New Geographical Pastime* (London: John Wallis, 16, Ludgate St, 1794). Unpaginated.

18. By 1794, France's military success in the post-revolutionary wars had resulted in three significant border expansions, as France acquired territories in the present-day Provence-Alpes-Côte d'Azur region. John Wallis, with Archibald McIntyre (engraver), *Wallis's New Map of Europe Divided into Its Empires Kingdoms &c: From the Latest Astronomical Observations* (London: John Wallis, 1814).

19. *Walker's New Geographical Game Exhibiting a Tour through Europe* (London: W.& T. Darton, 1810). Unpaginated game board and rule book.

20. William Cowper, *The Task and Selected Other Poems*, ed. James Sambrook (London, Longman, 1994), 4, 116–19.

21. Roger Caillois, *Man, Play, and Games* (New York: Free Press of Glencoe, 1961), 119.

22. *Wallis's New Geographical Game Exhibiting a Complete Tour through Scotland and the Western Isles* (London: John Wallis and Elizabeth Newbery, 1792). For an image of this map, see https://brbl-dl.library.yale.edu/vufind/Record/ 4165335.

23. *Panorama of Europe. A New Game* (London and Sidmouth: J. & E. Wallis, 1815).

24. *Wallis's Locomotive Game of Railroad Adventure* (London: Edward Wallis, 1835). Unpaginated game board and rule book. For an image of the game, see http://collections.vam.ac.uk/item/O26370/walliss-locomotive-game-of-railroad-board-game/.

25. *The British Tourist: A New Game* (London: E. Wallis, 1820).

26. John E. Bowden, *The Life and Letters of Frederick William Faber, D.d.* (London: J. Murphy, 1869), 182.

27. George Augustus Sala, *Under the Sun; Essays Written Mainly in Hot Countries* (London: Robson & Sons, 1872), 42.

28. Christian Jacob, *The Sovereign Map: Theoretical Approaches in Cartography Throughout History*, trans. Tom Conley (Chicago, IL: University of Chicago Press, 2006), 99.

CHAPTER 7

Carto-tactual Subjects
Promoting the Education of the Blind in Romantic-Era France and Britain

Julia S. Carlson

A map has the power to create in a given space ... a 'window' that opens onto another space, suited to a form of intellectual and visual mastery different from everyday empirical perception. A map is a technical and artificial widening of the visible field, of what can be thought and what can be uttered. It is also a space of anticipation, of predictability, of omniscience tied to the very fact of the synoptic gaze.

Christian Jacob, *The Sovereign Map*[1]

John Alston's 1839 map of the British Isles presents, to a sighted reader, a shock of blank expanse – a field of white, 21 inches high, 16 ½ inches across. Closer inspection reveals protrusions, grey-hued from the impress of the thick sheet: marks of latitude and longitude along the map edge and a mix of letters and lines within, upraised above the surface for reading with the hands (Figure 7.1). A simple cartouche identifies the BRITISH ISLANDS but, with no colour wash to distinguish figure from ground and no shade lines to uplift coasts from sea, their forms are not directly manifest. Lacking visual cues for synoptic apprehension, the sighted reader seeks out land-marks and deciphers land marks: ENGLISH CHANNEL in Roman capitals at the bottom of the map; the SHETLAND ISLES at the top, their cragged forms limned by continuous upraised outline. Longer stretches of sinuous coast prove problematic. Is that a peninsula or a bay? Which side is land and which sea? The stable identification of land as land requires the reading of a name or, in the absence of a name, the tracing of a complete and bounded figure – such as the jutting toe at the bottom of the map which borders, in dashed lines, an area bearing the single place name EXETER, which itself borders an area spanned by letters spelling BRISTOL. Information is writ uniformly large to optimize legibility – LONDON, NORWICH, EDINBURGH, ABERDEEN – and reduced to a minimum.

171

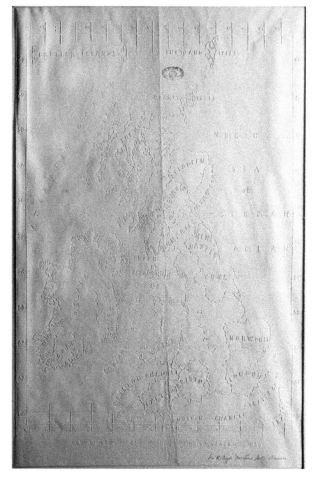

Figure 7.1 *British Isles*. Printed at the Asylum for the Blind, Glasgow, 1839. By permission of National Archives (MPI 1/63).

Simply emblazoned ENGLAND, a north–south swathe of land subsumes the industrializing Midlands and, with WALES to its left, makes a centring touchstone for westerly exploration: to the WESTERN ISLANDS bracketing the mainland above and to the jagged fragment featuring CORK, DUBLIN, and BELFAST below. A matrix of medieval cities and towns held firmly in place by the border graticule, the British Islands emerge within the supervening rational organization of parallels and meridians as a homogenous and historic entity: complex yet coherent, fractured yet fitting.

That Scotland is so richly represented on the upper reaches of Alston's map, with ten place names to England's ten, is apt. 'Printed at the Asylum for the Blind, Glasgow', the map marks Scotland's leading role in the education of the blind in Britain and the role of maps, as both tools and symbols, in this democratic movement. In August 1839, Alston sent the map to Lord John Russell, secretary of state for the Home Department, with a plea for support of the Asylum's Printing Fund. He had mailed an initial request in June, accompanied by a copy of the Book of Genesis printed in raised Roman letters, but had received no reply. Writing again in August, Alston claimed that this sample of his 'Maps for the Blind' was the first of its kind to be printed in Britain and 'very superior' to those being printed in Boston at the New-England Institution for the Blind.[2] Alston's hope that it would convince Lord Russell to aid his 'exertions on behalf of the blind' was satisfied in September when the government granted the Glasgow Asylum, of which Alston was honorary treasurer, £400 for the printing of tactile works – principally, the first complete edition of the Bible in relief (1837–40).[3]

The map 'sufficiently impressed' (*Maps*, 228) government officials, as Rose Mitchell and Andrew Janes have concluded, but what had it communicated, and had it made a different impression than the embossed book? Russell's papers do not reveal, but Alston had invoked both maps and text in his argument for the humanity of the blind and the necessity of their education with palpable media. 'They are rational and immortal beings', he asserted in reports on the work of the Glasgow Asylum,

> and capable of all the enjoyments which others feel from the cultivation of their moral and intellectual powers. It therefore becomes not only a reasonable but incumbent duty, to employ every means for cultivating the moral and intellectual faculties of the unfortunates deprived of sight, and storing their minds with general knowledge. . . . If, for instance, we wish to teach them the art of reading, letters must be prepared palpable to their touch. If we wish to communicate to them a knowledge of the surface of the earth, globes and maps must be prepared, with the divisions, &c. &c., in relief.[4]

More than an example of tangible means for cultivating the 'moral and intellectual powers', the map was a powerful argument for the existence of faculties still not generally recognized in 1830s Britain, when blindness was popularly associated with dependency, mendicancy, and self-interest.[5] No tabula rasa, the map that gradually focuses the British Isles offers also a picture of a mind stored 'with general knowledge' and capable of conceiving of and caring about a world external to itself. It is an emblem of the epistemological and moral value of tact that gains force by disrupting the 'synoptic gaze' (*The Sovereign Map*, 99) and challenging the scopic relations between mind and world that modern geographical maps both inscribe and represent.

As my reading suggests, Alston's *British Isles* would have offered the home secretary no transparent window on the portion of the world he was appointed to supervise. Denuded of visual signals that produce the illusion of external reality (inked print, colour washes, shade lines), the map would have made salient the semiotic components by which it functions while also foregrounding their difference from conventional cartographic renderings of space. No 'signified without a signifier' that 'spreads out the . . . world before the eyes of those who know how to read it' – the defining feature, for Christian Jacob, of an 'effective map' (*The Sovereign Map*, 11) – Alston's tactile prototype may even have brought to Russell's mind European cartography's fundamental assumption of sighted users and its increasing reliance upon specialized visual instruments. Supreme among these were the angle-measuring theodolites being used in nationwide trigonometrical surveys occurring across Europe in the wake of Cassini's *Carte Géometrique de La France* (1744–93), a set of large-scale standardized maps, based upon precision triangulation, which set an international standard for accuracy, comprehensibility, and legibility (Jacob, figure 19).

In 1791, the sudden availability of a state-of-the art theodolite had catalysed the Ordnance Survey of Britain, the modern nation's defining cartographic venture (see Chapter 2).[6] By the systematic measurement of a network of imaginary triangles plotted across the landscape, the Board of Ordnance aimed to establish geographical 'truth'. The 'Situations of all the material points would be truely fixed with regard to one another and thence the Great Outlines of the Country would be truely determined', promised military engineer William Roy when promoting a survey of England employing high-powered visual instruments and trigonometrical calculation (qtd. in Seymour, 7). As it happened, the scope of the project gradually evolved to encompass all of Britain. By 1809 the primary triangulation covering England, Wales, and southeastern Scotland was completed; in 1824 the Ordnance Survey was extended to Ireland; and, in 1838, after public pressure from scientists, societies, and agriculturalists, the long-neglected triangulation of Scotland was resumed. Thus the 'Great Outlines' that the Ordnance Survey ultimately aimed to determine were still being derived when, in 1839, Alston made the outlines of the British Islands perceptible to blind and low-vision users.[7]

In doing so, Alston inscribed a haptic epistemology upon a technology of representation that derived authority from an underlying ocular rationalism. Before the widespread adoption of triangulation, topographical features were positioned by the error-prone method of dead reckoning – measurement by ground traversal with a perambulator, timer, or chains.[8] Triangulation reduced 'actual measurement on the ground to a minimum', diminishing the influence of the unwieldy body and producing the most accurate framework for map-making.[9] The analytical eye of the theodolite powered the process: Jesse Ramsden's telescopically enhanced instrument 'was capable of observing more than 70 miles with no more than 2 seconds of arc error' (Owen and Pilbeam, 7). Since distances between points were trigonometrically derived from these measurements, and since each triangle interlocked with others, calculations were reciprocally correcting. Geometrical law thus controlled the surveyors' ordering of space, but the high-precision theodolite was the prime mover: '*Theo – theos* – something to do with a god', as its etymology is speculatively derived in Brian Friel's dramatization of the Ordnance Survey of Ireland.[10] As the subversive Irish farmer in *Translations* who nightly removes and repositions the Englishmen's theodolite recognizes, the maps constructed upon its measures – at six times the scale of the maps of England and Wales – could function as tools of imperial control, abetting the exploitation of resources and the surveillance and management of populations.[11] They presented a totalizing 'God's-eye view' unavailable to the human eye.[12]

How disruptive was Alston's map to the ocular ideal that governed modern geographical maps? Whereas Friel's play construes the OS maps of Ireland as spaces 'of omniscience tied to the very fact of the synoptic gaze' (Jacob, 99), critiquing their epistemology and the imperialism it supported, Alston's map proffers a perceptual modality that is haptic and incremental but remains, at base, a 'construct of vision' – a compilation of 'numerous observations into an image of space' (Edney, 72). Considered operationally, the map could even be said to bolster the powers of vision in its extension of enlightenment to 'unfortunates deprived of sight' (*Statements*, 8). Considered rhetorically, however, as an intervention in the discursive context of August 1839, the map gave cultural and political value to tactual experience. Tactile remediation disabled vision and defamiliarized the cartographic, confronting the reader with the powers of touch and raising, in its raised outlines, a novel impression of mind as well as of nation. Great Britain, Alston estimated, contained 'nearly 18,000' 'Blind persons', a heretofore overlooked but 'interesting class of our fellow-creatures' who could now place themselves in this larger social and political context (*Statements*, 24, 23). As a production of the printing press, Alston's map offered the possibility of circulating this tangible projection of an inclusive and charitable Great Britain on a national scale.

If Alston's map represented an unprecedented extension of tactility as a mode of British geographic knowledge and communal feeling, it nevertheless had antecedents in eighteenth-century Europe. Originally handmade for a wealthy few, tangible maps attracted the attention of French intellectuals who, in essays, articles, exhibitions, poems, and engravings, strategically employed them to challenge the assumption that vision was necessary to the formation of humane, civilized personhood. In this chapter, I examine the ways in which blind women and men interacting with maps became, in depictions aimed at the sighted, potent images of tactual subjectivity and participation in the public sphere. Tangible maps of various forms and media did not merely challenge prevailing stereotypes of the blind, linking touch with sensibility, intelligence, imagination, and mutuality. Beginning with Diderot's account of maps made with wire, wax, and wool and concluding with Scottish map-makers' experiments in print, I show how they spurred a democratic educational movement that spread from France to America and to Britain and, in recasting personhood, society, and nation, helped to change the status of blind people around the globe.

Model to Map, Touch to Tact

The tangible map entered European discourse in an addition to Denis Diderot's 1749 *Lettre sur les aveugles à l'usage de ceux qui voient* (*Letter on the Blind for the Use of Those Who Can See*). In the *Letter* Diderot had engaged a philosophical question about the relations between visual and tactual perception posed by William Molyneux and addressed in the second edition of the *Essay on Human Understanding* (1694). As articulated by Locke, 'Molyneux's Problem' supposes 'a Man born blind, ... taught by his touch to distinguish between a Cube, and a Sphere of the same metal'; it further supposes 'the Cube and Sphere placed on a Table, and the Blind Man to be made to see'. Could he, Locke asks, 'by his sight, before he touch'd them ... now distinguish, and tell, which is the Globe, which the Cube'?[13] Locke, along with Molyneux, thought not. Because tactual and visual sensations differed, their relation could be apprehended only by experience. Others believed their relation directly perceptible. Thomas Cheselden's 1728 account of his surgical correction of a young boy's cataract-induced blindness fuelled empirical investigation of the question, but, as William Paulson observes, it enshrined the moment of revelation when bandages were removed and the subject's visual interpretations of globe and cube could be interrogated (37, 57).

Diderot's intervention in the 'Molyneux-Cheselden tradition' of speculation and experiment turned attention from the 'cured' to the perceptions and understandings of the blind. Beginning with his arrival at the home of the 'man-born-blind of Puiseaux' to find him 'using raised characters to teach his son to read', the *Letter* is pervaded by Diderot's admiring notices of sensory perception gleaned from his interactions with a man living comfortably with his blindness.[14] Although the tactual, auditory, and olfactory senses of the 'man-born-blind' are keen, his compelling accounts of vision and specular reflection support Diderot's alignment of the blind with abstract thinking as epitomized, in the *Letter*, by Nicholas Saunderson, late Lucasian Professor of Mathematics and lecturer on optics at Cambridge. Diderot's fascination with what one can think, learn, and teach using tactual symbols and technologies is illustrated by his inclusion of six full-page diagrams of Saunderson's tablets for making arithmetical calculations and describing rectilinear shapes, across which his fingers would run 'with surprising agility' as he clarified concepts for his sighted pupils (189). Diderot proffers the possibility, only partly ludic, that the fingertips may do the thinking when they are the source of a person's 'principal sensations and all of his knowledge'; they may even be the seat, contra Descartes, of the 'soul' (183). The frontispiece to Saunderson's 1740 *Elements of Algebra*, which Diderot would have known from his reliance on the text's biographical introduction, suggestively pictures the eyeless professor with fingers and thumbs in searching contact with the rings and hoops of his armillary sphere (a model of the movements and positions of celestial objects). Although the *Letter* equivocates on the matter of dualism, Diderot's appreciation of the epistemological powers of touch is patent: 'With practice, touch can develop and become more sensitive than sight' (197). His pragmatic call for a 'language for touch' is likewise clear: with codified signs, the blind could correspond, and 'men-born-deaf-dumb-and-blind', instead of languishing in 'feeble-minded' isolation, could 'acquire ideas' (184–5).

For Martin Jay, the *Letter* constitutes an 'implicit challenge to the primacy of vision assumed by earlier students of [Molyneux's] problem', particularly the Lockean sensationists who maintained Descartes's 'faith in the linkage between lucidity and rationality'. In *La Dioptrique*, Descartes had called vision 'the noblest sense' and praised the inventions – telescopes and microscopes – that 'augment its power'.[15] Thus the man of Puiseaux's apparently anti-Cartesian response to the question of 'whether he would like to have eyes' is as slippery as it is provocative:

'I'd just as well have long arms, as it seems to me that my hands could teach me more about what's happening on the moon than your eyes or telescopes can, and besides, eyes stop seeing well before hands stop touching. It would be just as good to improve the organ I already have, as to grant me the one I lack.' (176)

Hands may indeed be more reliable than the eyes lauded by Descartes, but the ludicrous image of telescopic arms suggests their support of an equally abstract mode of knowing – one that distances sensations from soul, nerves from ideas.[16] This is reinforced by Diderot's more serious speculations about the man-born-blind's capacity to reason about astronomical bodies by a form of suppositional self-augmentation. Sensation 'occupies . . . an extended space' of skin, Diderot theorizes, which he 'is able to enlarge or reduce by making the affected area larger or smaller'. In touching a small rounded object, 'he could even make a body as large as the earth's sphere, were he to suppose his fingertip as large as the sphere and feel its full height, width and depth' (182). As with Saunderson's fingering of his model of the celestial sphere, the principal organ of touch is an avenue for astronomical and geometrical reasoning.

According to Jennifer Riskin, Diderot's *Letter* mounts a critique of 'sensation without sensitivity' by enforcing an eighteenth-century stereotype of the blind as lacking in sympathy and moral sentiment because of their visual ignorance of the experience of others (20, 50–4): 'I suspect them, in general, of being inhumane. What difference can there be for a blind man between a man urinating and shedding blood without a whimper?' (Diderot, in Tunstall, 179). However, scholars writing from positions within disability studies who condemn the charge of 'emotional solipsism' (Riskin, 20) overlook Diderot's later addition to the *Letter*, which forthrightly rejects the representation of the blind as inhumane rationalists by profiling a blind map-reader and, indeed, map-maker.[17] At the outset, Mélanie de Salignac challenges Diderot's claim that the blind, 'to whom the symptoms of suffering are invisible, must be cruel. "Do you imagine", said she, "that you hear a cry of pain as I do?"' When Diderot reminds her that some people '"suffer in silence"', Salignac insists that she '"should soon discover them and pity them all the more"'.[18] The profile bears out her claim, relating the process whereby her senses had been trained from 'earliest youth' to navigate the world with confidence and concern for others:

> She knew by the feeling of the air whether the weather was cloudy or fine, whether she was walking in a square or a road, in a road or a cul-de-sac, in an enclosed or open place, in a vast apartment or a small room. She measured

the space by the sound of footsteps or the echo of voices. When she had gone over a house, its plan remained in her head, so that she would warn others of little obstacles or dangers in their way. 'Take care,' she would say, 'the doorway here is low; you will find a step there.' (150)

The passage introduces the idea of the mental map ('its plan ... in her head') produced not by sight but by sound, motion, and feeling. Salignac's particularly exquisite physiological sense of touch ('the feeling of the air') here coincides with a form of social and moral 'tact' recently conceptualized by Baron d'Holbach as an instinct for virtue and by Voltaire as a 'delicate sense of what is fitting and proper in dealing with others'.[19] Rather than inwardness, the plan in the head of the blind woman figures spatial and social outwardness ('"the doorway here is low; you will find a step there"') and a correspondingly keen discrimination of characterological contours. Salignac 'noticed a variety in voices which we have no conception of', by which she identified and never forgot people, and was charmed not by visual beauty but the 'fine qualities of the heart and intellect' (151). Tuned to a finer affective channel, Salignac might very well discover silent sufferers and '"pity them all the more"'.[20]

Salignac's sensitivity and sensibility exceeded the system of signs developed by the sighted for the sighted, although it was with such signs, modified for the touch, that her senses had been trained and with such signs that Diderot communicates her humanity and cultivation. 'She had been taught music by notes in relief placed on raised lines on a large board' and now heard 'imperceptible' variations of 'inflexion' conveying feelings no words had been invented to express (152, 149). With cut-out letters Salignac had learned the alphabet; now she read books, printed for her by Prault on one side of the page, by feeling the impressions left on the verso. She wrote by pricking letters into a sheet of paper with a 'needle or pin', and she 'read the communication' that answered hers 'by passing her finger-tips over the slight roughness formed on the back of the paper' (154).

However impressive these semiotic adaptations, it is Salignac's tangible maps that focus Diderot's gaze and elicit his eyewitness testimony: 'I have seen the maps in which she studied geography', he asserts. 'The parallels and meridians were made of wire; the boundaries of kingdoms and provinces of embroidery in linen, silk, or wool of various thicknesses; the rivers and streams and mountains of pins' heads of various sizes; and cities and towns of drops of wax' (152–3). What Diderot observes is not the translation of a two-dimensional into a three-dimensional code but the remediation of a visual marking system into varied textures, thicknesses, sizes, and solidities. In this robust transformation of medium and sign, mountains are marked not by hachures but by varieties of pins' heads; administrative orders are designated not by width or form of line but by species and thickness of fibre. Diderot's close-up view of these not-strictly-standardizable signs substantiates his claim that Salignac could 'discern minute details in shapes of objects which often pass unnoticed by those who have the best eyesight' (150). Unlike the 'palpable notations' Saunderson made with pins of two sizes upon gridded tablets, the media of such maps pertain to home and human dress (linen, silk, wool, pins, wax), evoking social lives and women's activities (embroidery, sewing) while aligning sensation with sensibility and spatial knowledge with material existence. The woman who '"quite easily"' (152) understood the astronomical triangulations and algebraic equations of Nicholas-Louis de Lacaille – which were read aloud by her mother – and who would have made 'progress ... in science' (157) had she lived past twenty-two is located within cultural, intellectual, and civil society, as well as in the natural world, by the material description of her topographical maps. Unlike the house plan in her head, they are a concrete, communicable figure of that keener tact by which she comes to know, and feel, the world outside her mind. They enforce Diderot's challenge to the epistemological sovereignty of vision by correcting the *Letter*'s narrow association between touch and abstract reasoning.

Walking Fingers, Armchair Geographers: Enlightenment Spectacles and Subjects

'I have seen the maps.' Seeing maps that were studied by touch provoked written description, public discussion, and, with other palpable technologies, social change. But geographical maps inspired particular fascination. It was after reading Diderot and gaining first-hand knowledge of tangible media that Valentin Haüy opened in Paris the world's first school for the blind, the Institut des Jeunes Aveugles. In April 1784, Haüy had visited the hotel rooms of harpsichordist and singer Maria-Theresia von Paradis – but not to listen to the touring virtuosa. Described as 'the ambassador of the Viennese *Aufklärung*' who introduced 'Enlightenment Europe to the benefits of tactile pedagogy', Paradis was there exhibiting her pricked writing, playing cards, portable printing press, arithmetic tablets, and geographical maps.[21] In awe, a contributor to the *Journal de Paris* characterized Paradis's first printed work, a letter to the inventor of the press, as 'full of the most delicate & best expressed sentiments'. He described her maps in more detail: boundaries were marked with threads, 'the different orders of cities' with 'grains of glass, more or less coarse', and seas, kingdoms, and provinces with various compositions of sand mixed with glass ('sable glacé').[22] The maps excited 'more curiosity than interest', the second director of the Institute recalled, and were 'much spoken of at the time' while 'eulogiums were lavished upon' the 'learned blind man' (Johann-Ludwig Weissenburg of Mannheim) who had worked to perfect them. The maps' arousing of 'more curiosity than interest' among Parisians speaks to their strangeness and novelty as well their elaborateness of construction: 'the seas and rivers were represented', Sébastien Guillié recalled, 'by pieces of glass, cut with great art'; 'the towns ... by copper nails with round heads of different sizes'.[23] Viewers might have been more entranced by the composition of objects derived from the world they were intended to represent, Guillié signals, than genuinely inquisitive about the pedagogy or the persons they served. If, as Christian Jacob suggests, the 'ambiguous power of the map' resides in the monarchic fantasy of 'totality' and 'closure' it permits alongside self-lost absorption in the 'detail and labyrinth of the world', the tangible maps of Weissenburg and Paradis presented exhibition-goers with the power of ambiguity (326, 327): the wonder of material thickness and the jolt of difference from the clear medium of print. They 'were of no use to those who had their sight', Guillié claimed, 'who could not even guess the purpose of them unless informed of it' (102).

Haüy's visit convinced him of the practicability of tactile pedagogy for all classes, not simply the European elite trained by private tutors.[24] It also reinforced the virtues of visual display and public exhibition for educational and social reform. Blind himself until 'he saw the light in Mademoiselle de Paradis', Haüy declared that the 'wonders' the blind could perform without assistance needed to be seen to be believed.[25] In order to stimulate donations, however, their talents needed to seem socially useful – the ruling criterion for philanthropy in Enlightenment France (Weygand, 82–4). Tangible texts and maps that were also legible to the sighted could mediate these demands. As Haüy explains in his *Essai sur l'education des enfans-aveugles* (1786), published a year after the school's inception, Paradis's hand press enabled her, as composer and compositor, to express her ideas and feelings to the sighted. By likewise 'applying the blind to the art of printing for the use of those who see', he would render the blind, too often 'consigned by destiny to idleness, languor and dependence', 'useful to society': they could practice a waged trade and participate, as artisans, in the print project of Enlightenment.[26] Further, his pupils would themselves be enlightened by books printed in relief – in elevated lettering that was read by hand and which ink could make apparent simultaneously to the sighted. They would print a library of embossed books – some 'on white paper for their own use', others tinged with black – from which they would learn and with which they could teach (239). They would also print maps *in relievo* when a method for doing so was invented (239, 250) because a philanthropic institute could not support the 'great expense' of hand-crafted maps which were 'considerably damaged by the least handling'.[27] Until that time, ordinary maps would continue to be inexpensively multiplied on the school's presses and fitted with wires to mark bound-aries. Claiming that it was 'the form or size of every part of the map' that allowed discrimination, Haüy eliminated the differential texturization Weissenburg had developed (244). To be both legible and attractive to 'sighted masters' and sympathetic observers, an identical map with printed marks intact was pasted over the base map (Guillié, 103).

The *Essai sur l'education des enfans-aveugles*, in which Haüy presented the general plan for the Institute, is recognized as the world's first embossed book. Typeset and printed by the pupils, the object physically realized the utility of the blind. Their educability and humanity, however, were more dynamically displayed in the public exhibitions of literacy that helped fund the free school. Map-reading proved particularly effective. As Haüy reported in the *Essai*, 'the first of our pupils have brought themselves to such admirable perfection in the use of geographical maps, that people see them with surprise, at our exhibitions, distinguish a kingdom, a province, an island, the impression of which is presented to them ... upon a square piece of paper' (244–5). Compared to tactile print, which pupils read 'in slow succession' (233), the contour of 'a kingdom, a province, [or] an island' could be relatively quickly felt and identified in a display of knowledge that suggested both their mastery of the subject and their own rescue from 'obscurity' (228). Thus, if Haüy's simplification of tan-gible maps diminished the maps' curiosity factor, it enhanced their rhet-orical force and entertainment value. From 1785, audiences flocked to concert halls, salons, museums, and the Institute itself (Weygand, 100–2). Part of the appeal was the game-like nature of the cartographic exercise: 'Another blind man made several historical and geographical demonstrations ... and has walked his fingers across the map at the pleasure of the assembly, each time designating the name of the part touched.'[28] Maps afforded a spectacle of enlightenment involving the free play of map-readers' walking fingers and the interactive engagement of onlookers.

Not only exhibitions but also large-format engravings harnessing the symbolic power of geographical knowledge worked to counter pernicious stereotypes of the blind as useless dependents on charity.[29] As Zina Weygand recounts, Haüy had been outraged by a 1771 'burlesque concert' at a Parisian coffeehouse, in which pensioners of the medieval Quinze-Vingts hospice for the blind appeared in dunce caps with asses' ears, sang couplets, and accompanied themselves "'ridiculously on the violin'". The spectacle continued a long tradition of representing the 'partially sighted as the symbolic equivalent of "the fool"', Weygand explains, 'a pathetic reflection of humanity', upon which engravers capitalized by circulating caricatures that heightened the mockery (90, 91).[30] In December 1784, Haüy countered with a promotional engraving for the Institute commemorating the achievements of its first pupil, François Le Sueur, whom Haüy paid as compensation for the begging that his education precluded (Guillié, 57; Blacklock, 256) (Figure 7.2).[31] Pictured 'Age 18, reading with the help of his Fingers', Le Sueur, the caption tells, 'had, until seventeen-and-a-half years of age, relatively no notions of letters'; 'in about three months', however, he 'succeeded in reading, printing, and writing, all in relief characters; and by this means he raised himself to the study of the French language, Arithmetic, Geography, History, Music, &c' (translation mine). A large open book at his fingertips, a musical score, rows of shelved books, and the technologies of tactile writing and printing (screw press, type case, pen, and writing tablet) all index Le Sueur's literacy and industry. But it is the wall-map labelled AMÉRIQUE MÉRIDIONALE, to which his uplifted eyes point ours, that translates this literacy to viewers and performs Le Sueur's release from 'corporeal darkness', 'mental inactivity', and the 'intolerable melancholy' they cause (Blacklock, 234). A table globe atop foldout maps, cascading to books on the floor below, emphasizes his geographical absorption and, with the vast continental outline suspended between globe and head, represents cognitive interiority: subjectivity by virtue of palpably mediated knowledge of the external world.

The facing outlines of man and continent, a reference to Jean-Baptiste d'Anville's renowned map of South America, enforce the subjective and social effects of geographical media. D'Anville (1697–1782) was a recognized *géographe de cabinet*, or 'armchair geographer', who corrected and reissued *La Carte d'Amérique Méridionale* four times between 1748 and 1779, incorporating the latest geographical data regarding the interior while leaving the coasts, which had already been well drawn by Spanish and Portuguese explorers, relatively untouched.[32] As with the continent that the 'armchair geographer' worked assiduously to deliver from obscurity, so with the mind

Figure 7.2 *François Le Sueur, Blind, Age 18, Reading with the help of his Fingers &c,* Gravure de Desmaisons, 1784. Courtesy of Perkins School for the Blind Archives.

that the digital geographer works to fill with knowledge. The young man profiled in the image, and whose angular profile is suggestively re-echoed in the coastlines, is not one of society's 'dead members' but worthy of its recognition (Blacklock, 222). Citing, in addition to d'Anville's map, two articles in the *Journal de Paris* attesting to the man's achievements and listing two print shops where the engraving might be purchased, the wall-sized portrait incorporates the seated man within the indexical print networks of the Enlightenment.[33] Illustrating Haüy's aspiration that 'no man, be he poor or disabled … be kept outside humanity's sphere' (Weygand, 92), the portrait-map suggests that the young geographer, by his own research, writing, and printing, may even further its description.

'Citizens of Nature': Translating and Romanticizing the Map

The tangible map and figure of the blind map-reader entered Britain in a translation of Haüy's *Essai* made by the Scottish poet Thomas Blacklock (1721–91), who had been blinded by smallpox at six months. A '*cause célèbre* in Edinburgh literary circles from the mid-century', Blacklock had been represented by patrons David Hume and Joseph Spence as an embodiment of the 'central values of sentimental culture': 'taste, sensitivity, politeness, and innumerable virtues of character, not least his apparently stoical endurance of his blindness'.[34] After Blacklock's death, his admirers published his poems with an introductory 'Account of the Life and Writings of the Author' by Henry Mackenzie and with the translation of Haüy's *Essay on the Education of the Blind*. Although not embossed, the translation testified to Blacklock's ambitions for an institution to educate the blind. One of the educational methods envisaged was tactile reading, Blacklock, in an article in the third edition of the *Encyclopaedia Britannica* (c. 1790–1), having hailed Haüy's plan for collective education articulated in the 'palpable characters' of a book that he now held 'in his own hands'.[35] Using Haüy's texts, Blacklock marvelled, the blind 'are enabled to form and decypher, not only the characters required in common language, but also mathematical diagrams, arithmetical and geographical processes, and all the characters used in the written language of music'. Disbelievers could visit Paris to 'behold with their own eyes this spectacle so interesting to humanity ('Blind', 298).

The posthumous volume evidenced Blacklock's mastery of written languages but also positioned him as an example of the suffering that Haüy's tactile education was designed to overcome. As Catherine Packham argues, Mackenzie's 'Account' treated Blacklock not only as a 'man of feeling' but also as a disadvantaged object of social sympathy by introducing his poems as moral illustrations of suffering deeply felt and heroically withstood (428, 431). Mackenzie particularly praised Blacklock's 'Soliloquy: Occasioned by the Author's escape from falling into a deep well, where he must have been irrecoverably lost, if a favourite lapdog had not, by the sound of its feet upon the board with which the well was covered, warned him of his danger' – a poem which deplores 'at length the deprivations, horror and dangers of blindness' before achieving resolution in '"piety and resignation to the will of heaven"' (Packham, 434, 435).[36] But the poem's resolution is hard won, as Packham notes, and its account of the world's invisibility more compelling. This begins, I suggest, with the lengthy title sequence of subordinate phrases that formalizes the world's extension beyond the ken of the poet and focuses the matter of its auricular

mediation. It is 'the sound of [his lapdog's] feet upon the board with which
the well was covered' that reveals the proximate abyss – not an emphatic
pause but emphatic paws that convey their meaning with stunning force:
'ERECT with horror stands my bristling hair; / My tongue forgets its
motion; strength forsakes / My trembling limbs; my voice, impell'd in
vain, / No passage finds' (8–11). The poem thus dramatizes the condition
described in the *Encyclopaedia* – and amplified by citations in Mackenzie's
introduction – of being '"perfectly conscious of no space but that in which
he stands, or to which his extremities can reach"' (qtd. in Blacklock, xxi).
In the episode of reach-restricting terror recounted in the poem, not even
the space of the body is navigable; the 'impell'd' voice 'No passage finds' as
sound fails to mediate self and world.[37] '"[O]bnoxious to injury from every
point"', the blind are '"rather to be considered as prisoners at large than
citizens of nature"' (qtd. in Blacklock, xxi).

The inaccessibility of nature is a cause of 'aggregated misery' for the poet
and doctor of divinity, as the 'Soliloquy' reveals:

> FOR oh! – while others gaze on nature's face,
> The verdant vale, the mountains, woods, and streams;
> Or, with delight ineffable, survey
> The sun, bright image of his parent God;
> The seasons, in majestic order, round
> This vary'd globe revolving; . . .
> . . .
>
> To me those fair vicissitudes are lost,
> And grace and beauty blotted from my view.
> The verdant vale, the mountains, woods, and streams,
> One horrid blank appear . . .   (38, 40–5, 59–62)

Following Milton, Blacklock puts '"nature's works"' under erasure; the
'"book of knowledge fair"' written by God is a '"blank"' to his 'wretched
orbs' (Blacklock, 67).[38] The Beauty and Harmony 'transcrib'd / On
nature's form' are 'snatch'd for ever from [his] sight'; in their 'stead,
a boundless, waste expanse / Of undistinguish'd horror covers all' (70–2,
73–4). Bound books are likewise illegible, for the university, that 'sacred
fane / Of knowledge', is 'scarce accessible' (98–9). These are powerful
statements of exclusion from a man celebrated for his study of languages,
sciences, and belles-lettres at Edinburgh and who was made the object of
philosophical speculation for his use of nature imagery.[39] However vivid
such imagery might seem, Mackenzie warns, Blacklock's 'ideas of visible
objects' were derived from sounded words printed in books and not from

any preternatural sensory capacity (Blacklock, xx, xxv). He cites the poet's authoritative *Encyclopaedia* article: '"light reveals external things in all their beauties . . . and in all their varieties"'; only by its medium does the '"whole material and intelligent creation lie in open prospect"' and may '"the majestic frame of nature"' be '"perceived at a single glance. To the blind . . . the visible universe is totally annihilated"' (xxi). With its 'waste expanse / Of undistinguish'd horror', the 'Soliloquy' enacts the foreclosure of the prospect view and prospect poem, the map-like survey of the landscape popularized by John Denham, John Dyer, and James Thomson.⁴⁰ Blacklock's poem may posit the 'vary'd globe' (45), but it is ever 'blotted from [his] view' (60).

Glossed by Mackenzie's citations of Blacklock's prose, the 'Soliloquy' primes readers for the posthumous collection's last word, a poem by one of Haüy's pupils that concludes the *Essay on the Education of the Blind* (259–62). This poem, an ode by M. Huard, counterpoints Blacklock's blank despair by offering palpable media as a route to knowledge, nature, and collective agency. With 'tactile signs' unknown in ancient Greece, the 'hopeless blind' learn to 'construe thought, / To read, to write, and calculate' (39, 38–40). By impressing 'TYPOGRAPHIES', they make 'learneds thoughts embodied shine' (21–2). But it is the manual reading of relief maps that embodies and impassions the blind:

> THOUGH Nature from our darken'd eyes,
> For ever veils her charms sublime,
> The form of earth, and ev'n of skies,
> By Fancy's aid, we figuring climb;
> We trace the rivers to their source,
> Of stars we calculate the course;
> From Europe to th'Atlantic shore,
> Successive journies we pursue,
> Thanks to the hand, whose prudence due,
> Guides us in Geographic lore.   (41–50)

Maps mobilize their interpreters, overwriting the blankness of Nature. 'We' do not see her 'charms' but 'climb' earth's 'form' and 'trace the rivers to their source'. This is not Diderot's rational man-born-blind 'suppos[ing] his fingertip as large as the [earth's] sphere' (182) but rather the prudent hand's moving contact with tangible media stimulating the fancy and projecting embodied subjects into the terrestrial or celestial world. The 'hand' enacts the journeys related in books ('Guides us in Geographic lore') or pursues its own adventures, its niceness of touch opening vast regions of space ('th'Atlantic', 'the skies'). Unlike the accidental assistive technology of lapdog feet and sounding board (which in revealing the vacancy immobilized the man), the hand in touch with the scaled medium activates the imagination and constructs the feel, and voice, of a collective 'we'. Blacklock's self-immured 'prisoners at large' may become 'citizens of nature' through haptic, intermedial exploration in books and maps (qtd. in Blacklock, xxi).[41] The 1793 collection thus animated for English readers the figure of the blind map-reader and gave voice, in the transnational dialogue between blind poets, to a new function and form for the tangible map: the enfranchisement and mobilization of the isolated soliloquizer by the palpable reinscription of 'nature's face' (Blacklock, 40).

Naturalistic Relief, Neural Networks, and National Correspondence

Despite Blacklock's pedagogical recommendations, the organization he helped found 'almost entirely neglected' the mind.[42] Like the other charitable Protestant institutions established in the wake of the Paris school – Liverpool (1791), Bristol (1793), London (1799), and Norwich (1805) – the goal of the Edinburgh Asylum for the Industrious Blind (1793) became moral improvement through the curing of idleness and relief of indigence[43] – not map-making, as at Paris, but, at Liverpool, mop making; at Edinburgh, basket weaving, mattress making, and stocking knitting (Hayhoe, 59).[44] Only after the 1819 translation of Sébastien Guillié's *Essay on the Instruction and Amusement of the Blind* did experimentation with tangible media begin in Britain. In 1827 James Gall (1784–1874) published a primer in a triangular typeface more discernible to the touch than Haüy's round-hand font; in 1835, he founded in Edinburgh the first school 'established exclusively for the education of the Blind', putting Blacklock's agenda into action and making tangible naturalistic maps foundational to his social and educational program.[45]

Gall followed the poet in declaring the 'visible universe' a 'blank' to the blind and emphasizing their 'insensib[ility] to every point of creation, except the little spot on which they tread'.[46] Their 'morbid self-opinionativeness and metaphysical distortion of mind' could be relieved, however, by the 'contemplation of the simplicity and beauty of nature' as physicalized in maps as well as by reading (*Account*, 10). But carto-literacy preceded and supported literacy, Gall theorized, by helping to refashion the manual labourers of the blind asylums as digital explorers. Whereas the interpretation of a letter shape confounds the beginner and causes 'painful anxiety', the '*great general features*' of a map satisfied the mind and stimulated the 'finger'. When it 'has become familiar with the great outlines',

> it will soon begin to make further discoveries of the more minute forms and lines which were at first unnoticed; and this process of discovery goes forward, without effort and without end, until the finger has acquired such a degree of sensitiveness as to enable it to feel even the most delicate indications of form and position. (*Account*, 48, 47–8)

'[S]uperior sensibility' could be cultivated only by 'proper maps' which gave 'a very natural imitation of the countries' they represent, such as those produced by James Gall's son, who developed a process of relief printing honoured by the Scottish Society of Arts (47, 46, 49).[47] Unlike the Bostonian Samuel Howe's maps, which used raised marks to indicate boundaries and natural features, Gall's modelled the rises and falls of the landscape.[48] They showed the 'sea … low and the land high', 'the rivers run[ning] in valleys; and the hills ris[ing] above the land in rugged imitations of their originals' (*Account*, 49). Gall's three-dimensional projections made palpable the 'vicissitudes' of 'nature's face' lamented by Blacklock and gave Britons the opportunity, as Huard put it, 'to figuring climb' the 'form of earth'. More so than the outline maps Haüy devised, they exploited and cultivated touch's particular prowess, as theorized by Bishop Berkeley, in the discrimination of form, magnitude, distance, and orientation.[49]

The curricular goal of this digital exploration was not to represent the 'visible world' to the mind's eye but to strengthen neural and social networks: to establish a 'powerful intercourse … between the mind and the nerves of the fingers' and, thereby, among the blind and between the blind and the sighted (*Account*, 47). It is thus fitting that Gall invokes the geographical overview to figure the alienation of the blind and social possibilities of tactual sensibility: 'They are thinly and individually scattered over the face of the whole country; and their misfortune fixes them to a spot, and compels them to seek retirement in the seclusion of their homes' (*Sketch*, 9). But cartographic exercise would extend their reach by enabling their writing by alphabetic stamps and 'correspond[ence] with their friends by post or otherwise'.[50] Others could then 'read the letter which he has with his own hands written' – a 'pleasure, of the purest' kind (*Sketch*, 88, 89, 90). As construed by Gall, then, the tangible map does not promote the 'intellectual and visual mastery' of a space that it 'objectifies' by 'dissociat[ing] it from the consciousness of the subject' (Jacob, 99). The relief-printed mimetic map rather relieves the abstracted mind by awakening its dormant relation to the hand and putting the embodied subject in contemplative, incremental touch with nature and others, 'draw[ing] more closely together those bonds of humanity and sympathetic feeling' (*Sketch*, 90). The naturalistic – indeed, Romantic – map fosters tact and human contact.[51]

Alston's 1839 *British Isles*, with which this chapter began, is 'thought to be the first tactile map created in the United Kingdom' (*Maps*, 228). According to Gall, however, by 1837 he had published maps of Europe, North America, Edinburgh, and the Eastern and Western Hemispheres, a small-scale specimen of which is included in the *Account* (50, 48–9). Those presented at the Scottish Society of Arts in 1836 'exhibited the outlines of countries, the courses of the rivers, and the ridges of mountains very distinctly, and seemed to possess the strength requisite for insuring their permanence'.[52] If any of these do survive, I have yet to locate them. It would be more accurate to say, then, that, of Britain's first few printed tactile maps, Alston's is the only apparently extant – its survival a testament more to the importance of the archive, and to the map's role in securing funding for the printing of embossed Bibles, than to the superiority of its production process or priority.

Alston's *British Isles* marks not firstness but a ninety-year history of impressing the public with the moral and epistemological value of touch and the educability and humanity of the blind. The inkless impression also registers technological, ideological, and rhetorical change. While it realized Haüy's goal of printing maps *in relievo*, it did so by subordinating the interests of sighted readers, which Haüy's system of pasting ink-printed maps atop wire-fixed maps had protected.[53] Also, instead of profiling an individual former-beggar in a decorative cartographic print – a promotional strategy that risked spectacularization and exceptionalism – Alston mobilized the border graticule to make a novel statistical-graphical argument for socio-educational reform. Using ratios of the number of people 'afflicted with Blindness' per 100 members of the population, which increased in proximity to the equator and the Poles (as the German geographer Johann August Zeune had determined), Alston estimated a population of 'nearly 18,000' 'Blind persons' who would benefit from tactile education, 'Great Britain being situated between 50 and 60 degrees of latitude' (*Statements*, 23–4). The 'careful marking of latitude and longitude in the margins' (*Maps*, 228) of a map with little interest in delineating individual areas with mathematical accuracy can thus be understood as a strategy of national re-representation: a way of figuring forth, and coalescing, those English, Irish, and Scottish 'unfortunates' to demonstrate the 'expediency' of their education (*Statements*, 8, 7). The visual discipline's fundamental tools, projection and the plane coordinate system, took a feeling turn. Instead of relating locations on the map surface to the earth, the graticule related Britons to a 'class of our fellow-creatures' (*Statement*, 23). Whereas Gall's printed maps worked to refine tact so the blind could write themselves into the hands and hearts of the nation, Alston's performed their assimilation and urged the sighted to patriotic duty. Like their handcrafted European progenitors, early British printed tactile maps aimed to reorganize self, society, and nation – with integration, not domination, as the goal.

Notes

1. Christian Jacob, *The Sovereign Map: Theoretical Approaches in Cartography throughout History*, trans. Tom Conley, ed. Edward H. Dahl (Chicago, IL: University of Chicago Press, 2006), 99. I wish to thank Noëlle Roy of the Musée Valentin Haüy, David Weimer of the Harvard Map Collection, and Jennifer Arnott and Jennifer Hale of the Perkins School for the Blind for their research assistance, helpful comments, and conversation.
2. On Samuel Gridley Howe's maps, see David Weimer, 'A Touch of the Sighted World: Tactile Maps in the Early Nineteenth Century', *Winterthur Portfolio* 51 (Summer/Autumn 2017): 135–58.
3. John Alston to John Russell, 15 August 1839, National Archives, HO 102/47, MPI 1/63; Rose Mitchell and Andrew Janes, *Maps: Their Untold Stories* (London: Bloomsbury, 2014), 228.
4. John Alston, *Statements of the Education, Employments, and Internal Arrangements, Adopted at the Asylum for the Blind, Glasgow*, 6th ed. (Glasgow: Printed by George Brookman, 1839), 7–8.
5. Heather Tilley, *Blindness and Writing: From Wordsworth to Gissing* (Cambridge: Cambridge University Press, 2017), 1.
6. *A History of the Ordnance Survey*, ed. W. A. Seymour (Folkestone, Kent: Dawson, 1980), 21–2, 4.
7. The Principal Triangulation of Britain, including Ireland, was completed in 1853. By 1882 OS topographical maps of England, Wales, Ireland, and Scotland had been published. On 'Scottish agitation' for the survey, see Christopher Fleet and Charles W. J. Withers, 'A Scottish Paper Landscape', *National Library of Scotland*, https://maps.nls.uk/os/6inch/os_info1.html.
8. They were then fitted to the mapmaker's graticule by a handful of astronomical determinations which needed to be repeated for accuracy but often were not. Matthew Edney, *Mapping an Empire: The Geographical Construction of British India, 1765–1843* (Chicago, IL: University of Chicago Press, 1990), 18.
9. Tim Owen and Elaine Pillbeam, *Ordnance Survey: Map Makers to Britain Since 1791* (Southampton: Ordnance Survey, 1992), 11. On triangulation, see also Edney, 104–10.

10. Brian Friel, *Translations* (London: Faber and Faber, 1981), 11.

11. On the Irish Survey, see Seymour, 79–98, and Hewitt, 245–88.

12. Edney, 72; Jacob, 325–6.

13. Quoted in Marjolein Degenaar and Gert-Jan Lokhorst, 'Molyneux's Problem', *The Stanford Encyclopedia of Philosophy* (Winter 2017), ed. Edward N. Zalta, https://plato.stanford.edu/archives/win2017/entries/moly neux-problem/. Locke, Molyneux, and their opponents assumed 'that the senses worked together to transmit whole impressions of a multifaceted external world'; Jessica Riskin, *Science in the Age of Sensibility: The Sentimental Empiricists of the French Enlightenment* (Chicago, IL: University of Chicago Press, 2002), 25. On the Molyneux problem, see Riskin, 36–48; William R. Paulson, *Enlightenment, Romanticism, and the Blind in France* (Princeton, NJ: Princeton University Press, 1987), 27–38; and Mark Paterson, *The Senses of Touch: Haptics, Affects and Technologies* (London: Bloomsbury, 2007), 37–57.

14. Denis Diderot, *Letter on the Blind for the Use of Those Who Can See*, trans. Kate E. Tunstall, in Tunstall, *Blindness and Enlightenment: An Essay* (New York: Continuum, 2011), 172.

15. Martin Jay, *Downcast Eyes: The Denigration of Vision in Twentieth-Century French Thought* (Berkeley: University of California Press, 1993), 85, 71.

16. On the work of the reasoning mind in Cartesian sensation, see Riskin, 27.

17. For example, D. A. Caeton, '"Veux-tu regarder, bourreau!": The Somanormative Dimensions of the Diderotian *Citoyen*', *Journal of Literary & Cultural Disability Studies* 4:1 (2010): 80–2. On Diderot's ironic play, and indictment of the sighted, see Tunstall, 73–4.

18. Denis Diderot, *Diderot's Early Philosophical Works*, trans. and ed. Margaret Jourdain (Chicago, IL, and London: Open Court, 1916), 148.

19. Ewa Lajer-Burchrarth, *The Painter's Touch: Boucher, Chardin, Fragonard* (Princeton, NJ: Princeton University Press, 2018), 13–14.

20. On *tact* as penetration into the unspoken, see Lajer-Burchrarth, 14. On the figure of the 'supercrip' in the *Letter*, but not the Addition, see Caeton, 84–6.

21. Zina Weygand, *The Blind in French Society from the Middle Ages to the Century of Louis Braille*, trans. Emily-Jane Cohen (Stanford, CA: Stanford University Press, 2009), 79, 77.

22. 'Variétés. Aux Auteurs du Journal', *Journal de Paris* 115 (24 April 1784), 504; translation mine.

23. Sébastien Guillié, *An Essay on the Instruction and Amusements of the Blind* (London: Printed for Richard Philips, 1819), 102.

24. It more largely proved 'that a gifted and suitably educated blind person could embark upon a real career that allowed her to play a role in the social and cultural life of her time' (Weygand, 79).

25. Valentin Haüy, 'Bienfaisance. Aux Auteurs du Journal', *Journal de Paris* 274 (18 September 1784): 1159; translation mine.

26. Valentin Haüy, *An Essay on the Education of the Blind*, in Blacklock, *Poems by the Late Reverend Dr. Thomas Blacklock; Together with An Essay on the*

Education of the Blind, trans. Thomas Blacklock (Edinburgh: Printed by Alexander Chapman and Company, 1793), 240, 222, 227.

27. The 'rubbing soon made the sand disappear' (Guillié, 102).

28. 'Variétés. Institut des Aveugles. Aux Rédacteurs du Journal', *Journal de Paris* 338 (26 August 1805): 2376; translation mine.

29. Exhibitions continued after the nationalization of the Institute during the revolution. On its transformations, see Weygand, 121–57; Paulson, 102–04.

30. This event likely made Haüy ambivalent about the curricular inclusion of music (Paulson, 99–101).

31. The Institute had just won the support of the Philanthropic Society.

32. Lucile Haguet, 'J-B d'Anville as Armchair Mapmaker', *Imago Mundi* 62 (2011): 88–105, 93.

33. See Brad Pasanek and Chad Wellmon, 'The Enlightenment Index', *Eighteenth Century Theory and Interpretation* 56:3 (2015): 357–80.

34. Catherine Packham, 'Disability and Sympathetic Sociability in Enlightenment Scotland: The Case of Thomas Blacklock', *British Journal for Eighteenth-Century Studies* 30 (2007): 423–38, 427.

35. 'Blind', in *Encyclopaedia Britannica; Or, A Dictionary of Arts, Sciences, and Miscellaneous Literature*, vol. 3, 3rd ed., eds. Colin Macfarquhar and George Gleig, illust. Andrew Bell (Edinburgh: Printed for A. Bell and C. Macfarquhar, 1797), 298. Although volumes were issued beginning in 1788, all title pages list 1797 as the date of publication.

36. Packham quotes a reference to the 'Soliloquy' in an 1811 article on Blacklock in *The Edinburgh Encyclopaedia*.

37. Sound provides only 'confused and inadequate' ideas of 'extension and interval' ('Blind', 283).

38. Blacklock quotes *Paradise Lost*, Book III, lines 47–50: 'for the book of knowledge fair / Presented with a universal blank, / Of nature's works to me expung'd and ras'd, /And wisdom at one entrance quite shut out' ('Blind', 284).

39. Mackenzie, following Edmund Burke, attributed this aptitude to Blacklock's having listened to poetry from an early age, his memory, and his associations with those 'ideas of sound' (Blacklock, xv–xvii).

40. 'Cooper's Hill', 'Grongar Hill', and *The Seasons*.

41. Similarly, the student of natural philosophy may develop a 'personal intercourse' with nature by becoming 'more intimately acquainted with her laws' ('Blind', 287).

42. Gabriel Farrell, *The Story of Blindness* (Cambridge, MA: Harvard University Press, 1956), 153. The Edinburgh Royal Blind School records that the Asylum 'provid[ed] rudimentary mental arithmetic and recitation of scripture lessons to complement instruction in handcrafts' (www.royalblind.org/our-organisation/our-history).

43. Simon Hayhoe, *Blind Visitor Experiences at Art Museums* (Lanham, MD: Rowman & Littlefield, 2017), 58–9.

44. Women were admitted to the Edinburgh Asylum from 1820. On handcrafting at Liverpool, see David Johnston, *The Uncomfortable Situation of the Blind*,

with the Means of Relief, Represented in a Sermon, Preached in the Tron Church,
Edinburgh, on Tuesday May 15, 1793 (Edinburgh: Printed for the Society for
the Relief of the Indigent Blind, 1793), 25–6.

45. James Gall, *An Account of the Recent Discoveries Which Have Been Made for*
    Facilitating the Education of the Blind, with Specimens of the Books, Maps,
    Pictures, &c. for their Use (Edinburgh: James Gall, 1837), 11, 15. In 1875 Gall's
    school merged with the Edinburgh Asylum to form the Royal Blind School.

46. James Gall, *A Historical Sketch of the Origin and Progress of Literature for the*
    Blind: And Practical Hints and Recommendations as to their Education
    (Edinburgh: James Gall, 1834), 11, 12–13.

47. The Society for the Encouragement of the Useful Arts in Scotland (now Royal
    Scottish Society of Arts). In 1855 James Gall (1808–95) also devised what is
    now called the Gall-Peters projection.

48. On Howe's symbols, see Weimer, 16–9.

49. On Berkeley, see Paulson, 29. Recent studies of tactile map interpretation
    recommend the use of volumetric symbols; see Jaume Gual, 'Three-
    Dimensional Tactile Symbols Produced by 3D Printing: Improving the
    Process of Memorizing a Tactile Map Key', *British Journal of Visual*
    Impairment 32:3 (2014): 83–92.

50. 'Stamps with the letters set with pins' are used to 'press through the paper'
    (*Account*, 16).

51. On naturalistic relief and national community, see my *Romantic Marks and*
    Measures: Wordsworth's Poetry in Fields of Print (Philadelphia: University of
    Pennsylvania Press, 2016), 112–28.

52. 'Proceedings of the Society for the Encouragement of the Useful Arts in
    Scotland', *Edinburgh New Philosophical Journal* 20 (October 1835–April
    1836), 422.

53. The use of the common Roman alphabet, which Gall and Alston favoured
    over a more tangible 'arbitrary' sign system, indicates the assimilating agendas
    of the early educators of blind and low-vision students; see Julia S. Carlson,
    'Tangible Burns', in *The Unfinished Book*, eds. Alexandra Gillespie and
    Deidre Lynch (Oxford: Oxford University Press, 2020), 121–35. On the
    Roman alphabet on Howe's maps, see Weimer, 7.

CHAPTER 8

Wordsworth and Mandelbrot on the Coast of Britain

Joshua Wilner

[I]magination, by which I mean the faculty which produces impressive effects out of simple elements.

William Wordsworth, 'Note to The Thorn', *Lyrical Ballads*[1]

Bottomless wonders spring from simple rules, which are repeated without end.

Benoit Mandelbrot, 'Fractals and the Art of Roughness'[2]

In 1967, Benoit Mandelbrot published in *Science* magazine a brief but groundbreaking article entitled 'How Long Is the Coast of Britain?'.[3] As part of his long-standing and wide-ranging interest in patterns of irregularity, Mandelbrot was well acquainted with a number of complex irregular curves and shapes whose features challenged the resources of standard Euclidean geometry. Indeed, since their discovery by mathematicians beginning in the late nineteenth century, these odd figures had been viewed as a 'gallery of monsters' (the phrase is Henri Poincaré's): capricious freaks of the unmoored mathematical imagination that grounded inquiry in the physical sciences had best steer clear of, even as they precipitated an extended crisis in pure mathematics.[4]

Around 1960 – considerably later than this crisis, and quite independently – the gifted and eccentric British mathematician, physicist, psychologist, and pacifist L. F. Richardson was undertaking empirical work on the measurement of coastlines – as a by-product of his efforts to develop a 'theory of the geographical opportunities for fighting' and, more specifically, of 'contiguity' (i.e. shared frontiers) as a factor determining the likelihood of 'deadly quarrels' arising between nations. Responding to surprising discrepancies in the recorded lengths of national borders, Richardson recognized that the measurement of irregular borders will vary quite widely, as a function both of the unit of measurement used and of the border's degree of irregularity. With, no doubt, a touch of patriotic fondness and some degree of personal identification, he then adduced the erratic western coast of Britain (among the most irregular in the world by his account) as his prime exhibit for what has come to be known as the 'coastline paradox'.[5]

A self-described 'outlier', Mandelbrot recognized in Richardson a kindred spirit.[6] He also recognized in the coast of Britain an eminent and – equally important for Mandelbrot – a *naturally occurring*, visible instance of the kind of peculiar geometrical objects that had bedevilled pure mathematics.[7] Radicalizing the implications of Richardson's observations, 'How Long Is the Coast of Britain?' deciphered in the scribble and scrabble of Britain's western shore the clues to a new geometry of nature organized around the concept of fractional, or 'fractal', dimension. Within a decade, the essay's findings had grown into Mandelbrot's classic work *The Fractal Geometry of Nature*, presented by its author as both a 'casebook' and a 'manifesto' (2). Writing in 1623, at an inaugural moment in what historians of science refer to as 'the mathematization of the world picture', Galileo famously recast in *Il Saggiatore* the medieval topos of the Book of Nature,

> this great book which lies continually open before our eyes (I mean the universe), but cannot be read until we have learnt the language and become familiar with the characters in which it is written. It is written in mathematical language, and the letters are triangles, circles and other geometrical figures, without which means it is humanly impossible to comprehend a single word.[8]

With an acute sense of his own work's historical significance, Mandelbrot begins *The Fractal Geometry of Nature* with a counter-dictum: 'Clouds are not spheres, mountains are not cones, coastlines are not circles, and bark is not smooth, nor does lightning travel in a straight line' (1).[9]

A Romanticist might be tempted to wonder how well L. F. Richardson knew his Wordsworth, for the emblematic status which the western coast of Britain acquires in *The Fractal Geometry of Nature* is strangely anticipated by the privileged position it occupies in Wordsworth's poetry. Rising higher than any point in Britain south of the Scottish Highlands, Mount Snowdon lies only a few miles inland from the western coast of Wales, a coast that figures both prominently and obscurely in the all-but-visionary land's-end prospect that stretches before the poet as *The Prelude* approaches its conclusion:

> I look'd about, and lo!
> The Moon stood naked in the Heavens, at height
> Immense above my head, and on the shore
> I found myself of a huge sea of mist,
> Which meek and silent, rested at my feet:
> A hundred hills their dusky backs upheaved
> All over this still Ocean, and beyond,
> Far, far beyond, the vapours shot themselves
> In headlands, tongues, and promontory shapes
> Into the Sea, the real Sea, that seem'd
> To dwindle and give up its majesty,
> Usurp'd upon as far as sight could reach.
>
> (XIII, 40–51)[10]

This chapter offers a new way of understanding and reading Wordsworth's Snowdon episode in Book XIII of *The Prelude* by applying the mathematical and geometric concept of fractal patterning to the relationship between chronology and rhetoric in the forward-movement of the poetic account. The ascent of Snowdon offers a perfect moment of building to a climax through which to explore such ideas.

Fractal Patterns and Self-Similarity

Because fractal patterns typically exhibit part–whole similarity at diminishing levels of scale (what Mandelbrot terms 'self-similarity'), the idea that fractals have some relation to familiar rhetorical and literary structures such as synecdoche and mise-en-abyme presents itself readily enough.[11] As we will see, however, such identifications tend to emphasize similarity at the expense of difference, thus taking the *fractiousness* out of fractals. In particular, the notion of fractal dimension drops out of the equation. By contrast Mandelbrot observes, on something of a literary-critical note: 'In the compound term *scaling fractals*, the adjective serves to mitigate the noun. While the modifier *scaling* points to a kind of order, the primary term *fractal* points to disorder and covers cases of intractable irregularity' (*FGN*, 18). Or as Wordsworth writes early in *The Prelude* of 'the breath / And harmony of music' – and implicitly of its own strains:

> There is a dark
> Invisible workmanship that reconciles
> Discordant elements, and makes them move
> In one society.   (I, 352–6)

Before proceeding to a consideration of the Snowdon episode of *The Prelude*, then, I want to attempt a brief exposition of the relationship Mandelbrot proposes between self-similarity and fractal dimension, which is summarized in the abstract to 'How Long Is the Coast of Britain?':

> Geographical curves are so involved in their detail that their lengths are often infinite or, rather, undefinable. However, many are statistically 'self-similar', meaning that each portion can be considered a reduced-scale image of the whole. In that case, the degree of complication can be described by a quantity D that has many properties of a 'dimension', though it is fractional; that is, it exceeds the value unity associated with the ordinary, rectifiable, curves. (636)

The argument may be reduced to two moments. In a first moment, Mandelbrot demonstrates that the estimated length of an irregular coastline tends to *grow without bound*, the smaller the unit is by which it is measured. By contrast, the estimated length of a smooth curve *tends towards a limit* (approaches a finite sum) as the unit of measurement decreases, a relationship on which calculus depends. As a result, 'the typical coastline's length ... is so ill determined that it is best considered infinite' (*FGN*, 25).

To offer a slightly mismatched example: were the Rhyd Ddu path by which Wordsworth ascended Snowdon a smoothly curving slope, a child climbing the ridge to the peak would take smaller, and therefore proportionally more, steps than an adult, but both would walk the same distance.[12] Since the path along the ridge in fact involves many rises and dips (not to mention windings) at many different levels of scale, the child's smaller step will have to cover many small ups and downs that the adult will, as we say, 'take in his or her stride', with the result that the child's journey will not only involve more steps but *also* cover a longer distance. Small wonder that Wordsworth and his climbing party pass 'a hedge-hog in the mountain crags' (*The Prelude*, XIII, 24), curled up as if for rest at the side of the path. With its small, lumbering gait, it was a traveller through eternity.

While one may pause at so curious a result, what mainly matters for Mandelbrot is the aporetic conclusion that, since all irregular coastlines are infinite, they cannot be compared with regard to length: 'If one wishes to compare different coastlines from the viewpoint of their "extent", length is an inadequate concept' (*FGN*, 25). The second moment in the argument responds to this impasse with a redeployment of energies: if geographical curves cannot be measured with regard to length, they *can* with regard to their degree of irregularity or ruggedness, though doing so will involve an extensive elaboration of what had been the esoteric mathematical concept of fractional dimension.

As will already be evident, the coastlines or paths in these examples exhibit self-similarity – *comparable structure across differing levels of scale*. As Mandelbrot himself glosses the term in the abstract to 'How Long Is the Coast of Britain', a figure is said to be 'self-similar' if it can be divided into portions each of which 'can be considered a reduced-scale image of the whole'.[13] Examples of such figures abound, but there is nothing inherently non-Euclidean about them (witness the instance of the straight line, which Leibniz proposed defining as 'a curve, any part of which is similar to the whole') (qtd. in *FGN*, 419).

When considered in relation to differences, not only of scale but also of dimensionality, however, the property of self-similarity reveals some complexities which may at first escape notice but which are necessary to explain in mathematical terms here. If we divide a line into, say, three equal parts, each interval is a 'reduced image' of the whole on a scale of 1 to 3. But of course, we have to divide a square into nine equal parts in order to obtain the same scale relation of 1 to 3 between the square and its tiles, and a cube into twenty-seven parts. If we recall that a number to the first power is equal to itself, then we see that in each case the dimension of a geometrical object corresponds to the exponent relating its division into parts to the scaling factor.[14] Since it is possible both to artificially construct and to identify in nature figures for which the exponent is fractional rather than a whole number, it becomes possible to conceive scale relations obtaining within fractional dimensions. And it emerges that, while the western coast of Britain may be infinitely long, its fractional dimensions – the index of its abyssal roughness or texture relative to a smooth, if wandering, curve – is 1.25.

While more by way of clarification needs to be said here, I will limit myself to the following claim: The discordance of dimensions which is the hallmark of fractal form (i.e. the similarity dimensions and topological dimensions of fractal forms are discordant, while for Euclidean forms they are concordant) defies the analysis of differential calculus because it exploits an *irregularity* lurking in the calculus that only emerges as a problem in the face of figures such as *irregular coastlines*. Conceptually, there is a distinction between a point, which has location but no dimensionality, and a unit, which has dimensionality but is transposable as to location. In order to treat a point as the limit of a series of units of decreasing length (and thus the terminus of the division of a curve into ever-smaller parts), the concept of a point as a unit of infinitesimal dimension has to be substituted for the concept of a point as a location. The crucial point for a literary critic to grasp is that the nature of this substitution is *rhetorical*, not *mathematical*: the replacement of one use of the term 'point' by a different use of the same term. With fractal figures, this discrepancy becomes structurally central and generative rather than negligible. This offers a new way of interpreting narrative chronology and rhetorical form across the long poem. So, for example, the sequence of events in *The Prelude* proceeds chronologically but also is shaped by formal or rhetorical considerations. Chronological and formal requirements may reinforce each other but also may interfere, be discordant, with one another. In the so-called *Five-Book Prelude* of 1804, the ascent of Snowdon is the final episode of the poem both chronologically and formally. In later versions it retains its formal finality but is out of order chronologically, particularly in relation to the interpolated books on London and the French Revolution, which biographically it preceded. Wordsworth's indefinite introductory language – 'In one of these excursions, travelling then / Through Wales on foot' (XIII, 1–2) – fudges the difference.[15]

Fractal Epic Poetry

A conceptual system that relates differentiation, iterative progression, and totalization provides Wordsworth's *Prelude* with its structural programme. As is well known, Wordsworth intended in writing *The Prelude* to prepare himself for work of epic compass, work that would speak not of 'the growth of the Poet's mind' – 'a theme, / Single, and of determin'd bounds' (*The Prelude*, I, 669–70) – but 'Of Man, of Nature, and of Human Life' (this the opening line of Wordsworth's 'prospectus' to *The Recluse*, the greater work in view of which *The Prelude* was undertaken). The task of tracing 'the origin and progress of [his] powers ... to the *point* when he was emboldened to hope that his faculties were sufficiently matured for entering upon the arduous labour which he had proposed to himself' (emphasis added) was thus itself to constitute a final, consolidating trial of those powers.[16]

As is also widely acknowledged, the Snowdon episode with which *The Prelude* concludes works as an emblematic recapitulation of this process of becoming-poet, gathering into its story of ascent, to a position of comprehensive vision, the movement of the poem as a whole, in a way that *relates directly to the fractal model* described earlier. M. H. Abrams, for example, describes the passage as 'a metaphor for the climactic stage both of the journey of life and of the imaginative journey which is the poem itself' and readily compares the poet's 'definitive vision' on 'a mountain-top' to that of Moses on Sinai.[17] Writing from a less reverential perspective, Mary

Jacobus nonetheless agrees that the ascent itself 'provides a representation of the entire narrative of *The Prelude*'.[18]

However warranted such an understanding of Snowdon's structural significance, an understanding which Wordsworth evidently shared, it nonetheless proves to be overdrawn, in two related regards. Certainly, when Wordsworth begins the episode by recalling how he 'left Bethkelet's huts at couching-time, / And westward took my way, to see the sun / Rise from the top of Snowdon' (*The Prelude*, XIII, 3–5), it is not hard to detect the allegorical undercurrent with its suggestion of a purgatorial ascent to a point of visionary illumination. But the narrative never arrives at this moment or this place. Instead it *breaks off* with a description of and meditation on the moonlit land's-end scene which spreads before the poet as he emerges from the fog bank though which he has been climbing, what Wordsworth in early draft material refers to as 'the scene / Which from the *Side* of Snowden I beheld' (my emphasis).[19]

Nor, of course, did Wordsworth ever come near to completing *The Recluse*, the vast philosophical and poetic project to which *The Prelude* was meant to lead. That Snowdon tells the story of an *interrupted* rather than a *completed* ascent prefigures, in retrospect, this more encompassing pattern of incompletion. Or, to put the matter more precisely, the way in which the nocturnal scene beheld from Snowdon's slope *eclipses* the traveller's expectation suggests in turn how the writing of *The Prelude* both displaces and exceeds the epic ambitions in which it originates. This is not to say that *The Prelude* ends up taking the place of *The Recluse* as a capstone achievement, but neither is it a compromise formation, mediating between the comprehensive but unattainable scope of epic and the circumscribed intensities of lyric subjectivity, a lyrical epic (as is sometimes said). Rather, the writing of *The Prelude* actively resists location within the basic system of genres, with its attendant model of poetic development, in terms of which both Wordsworth and Coleridge sought to justify it. It is produced within and as a different field of possibilities, one which emerges out of the impossibility of the teleological project of poetic self-constitution.[20]

If Snowdon marks a break – or breaking through – in 'the growth of the poet's mind' rather than a confident and punctual arrival at a moment of completion, what needs further to be understood is that this break occurs as a *function of the very patterns of development that it disrupts*. Surely Abrams is right to see a principle of self-similarity (a term he does not use but which one suspects he would have found serviceable) organizing the relation of life to poem and of poem to final episode. Indeed, nested temporal progressions of this kind are a characteristic and pervasive feature

of Wordsworth's narrative art. They are the formal corollaries of heighten-
ing self-consciousness and appear to verge, in Geoffrey Hartman's powerful formulation, on 'consciousness of self raised to apocalyptic pitch'.[21] It is
a mistake, however, to see these processes as necessarily converging towards
a moment of retrospective self-totalization: the same recursive tendencies
that generate and organize these rhetorical patterns are capable of giving
rise to figural structures which, like the objects of fractal geometry, transport us into regions of thought, of imagination, of representational form,
and of material being that unsettle the limits of those same patterns.

In order to make these claims more concrete, I return now to a closer
examination of the Snowdon episode, with particular attention to the
relation between its introductory narrative and the sublime descriptive
passage that supervenes. On the surface, the former is notably undramatic,
as though to throw into relief the arresting character of the scene which
follows. The lines offer little variation of pace, no change of setting, and
a virtual absence of incident, the 'small adventure' (26) which Wordsworth
does recall – a dog barking at that hedgehog we passed a while back –
serving mainly to measure the depth of the surrounding quietude. The
monotony of the narrative surface veils, however, a complex and charged
transaction between the human figures and the landscape through which
they move. We encounter at first a line of tension or edge between the
inner mood of the travellers, 'full of heart and having faith / In [their] tried
Pilot' (14–15) and the low-hanging mist 'Half-threatening storm and rain'
(13) into which they are about to enter. Once the group begins its ascent,
however, the line dividing inner and outer, mood and landscape, figure and
ground is dissolved, as the obscuring mist becomes the outward extension
of the self-absorption of each of the travellers:

> Little could we see
> Hemm'd round on every side with fog and damp,
> And, after ordinary Travellers' chat
> With our Conductor, silently we sunk
> Each into commerce with his private thoughts.
> (*Prelude*, XII, 15–19)

Yet that initial line of tension has not disappeared completely. It is
displaced, first of all, into the submerged sense of self-division across
which the 'commerce' of internalized dialogue is transacted. And it then
resurfaces as a consolidated and intensely charged front: for what now
emerges at the core of Wordsworth's self-absorption is a kind of combat at
close quarters with the earth itself:

> With forehead bent
> Earthward, as if in opposition set
> Against an enemy, I panted up
> With eager pace and no less eager thoughts.
>
> (*Prelude*, XII, 29–32)

In their progressive consolidation of identity in a sightless and silent labour of ascent, these lines rehearse, then, in a very compressed form, the stages in an *askesis* oriented towards the surmounting of the physical body.

Indeed, the imaginative pressure of this aspiration, which is not only being recalled but is actively at work within the process of narration, is such that when the spell of self-absorption begins to be broken by the moonlight's penetration of the mist, Wordsworth half describes this transition as though it were the continuation of a progression: not a breaking in of light from the outside but a breaking out of light from the poet's tread, as though from a body on the threshold of its transfiguration:

> When at my feet the ground appear'd to brighten,
> And with a step or two seem'd brighter still,
> Nor had I time to ask the cause of this
>
> (*Prelude*, XII, 36–8)[22]

The quickening of the narrative pace – each line a further step, each step a further brightening of the ground – focuses us in, of course, on the brief interval in which Wordsworth is crossing from the mist into the open, moonlit air and propels us, it would seem, towards the instant of illumination, the flash, that ensues. But it also registers the interval of confusion – 'Nor had I time to ask the cause of this' – in which Wordsworth's imagination trips on the verge of hallucinatory projection even as he checks himself with each step.

Nor is this interval of disequilibrium truly corrected in the moment which brings the traveller to a halt:

> For instantly a Light upon the turf
> Fell like a flash: I look'd about, and lo!
> The Moon stood naked in the Heavens at height
> Immense above my head, and on the shore
> I found myself of a huge sea of mist,
> Which meek and silent, rested at my feet.
>
> (*Prelude*, XII, 39–44)

Subliminally the language asks us to take literally the dead metaphor of falling light, as though the light which falls 'like a flash' at Wordsworth's feet had dropped, like a garment, veil, or corona, from the moon which now 'stood naked in the Heavens', a figure which is the inverted and magnified image of the poet's emergence from the mist. Accordingly, there is a sense not only of immense spatial distance but of an abrupt temporal rift separating the moon from the fallen cloud of light (and, be it said in passing, an echo of the Biblical separation of the light from the deep).

A more extended consideration of the scene would show that the aftershocks of this rifting (itself the hyperbolic magnification of the tension which has been working upon itself throughout the preceding narrative, beginning with the low-hanging mist 'Half-threatening rain and storm' and the sallying forth of the travellers, 'Uncheck'd' and 'full of heart' [14]) distribute themselves throughout the rest of the description along both vertical and horizontal axes.[23] They are felt for example in the figure 'A hundred hills their dusky backs upheaved / All over this still Ocean' (45–6), a figure which combines rising up with diving down, particularly if one recognizes the Miltonic echoes, and in a more complex way in the figure of the mimic coastline, which is also a fractal horizon at the uncertain limit of vision, projected by the vapours which 'shot themselves, / In headlands, tongues, and promontory shapes / Into the Sea' (47–9). They are gathered together again most conspicuously in the supplementary but central figure of the

> fracture in the vapour,
> A deep and gloomy breathing-place thro' which
> Mounted the roar of waters, torrents, streams
> Innumerable, roaring with one voice . . .
> (*Prelude*, XII, 56–9)

Here Wordsworth locates 'The Soul, the Imagination of the whole' (65). This striking figure is not only, or even primarily, spatial, but a place where the dynamic split between the downward rush of many waters into the sea and the upward surge into the open of their one voice is concentrated, thus recapitulating, displacing, and condensing the rifting with which the passage begins.

I suggested that the confused question of priority – do I generate the light, or apprehend it? – which opens onto that rift involves not only the relation of the traveller's imagination to his natural environment but also the relationship of the poet's language to the experience it recalls. Along the path of the linear narrative, the shift of temporal scale – so that the metrical progression of the lines shadows the traveller's advancing steps – leads directly to the convergence on an instant: the 'flash' that ensues and thence illuminates or apprehends the space of what Wordsworth calls 'the universal spectacle' (60). At the same time, the downshift moves to collapse the difference between the recollected moment and the moment of its recounting into a single instant. And indeed the interjection 'lo!' seems to mark or pretend to mark this moment of convergence between the reported event and the event of its re-marking. Without entering into further detail, I would simply call attention here to the temporal, grammatical, and semantic indeterminacy of the interjection 'and lo!', which expresses Wordsworth's own wonder but also, and more theatrically, directs the reader's attention to the scene which is about to be unveiled, as though the phrase 'I look'd about, and lo!' were a truncation of 'I looked about, and look!', which in fact it is, since 'lo' is, not only morphologically but also etymologically, both an alliterative transformation of the exclamatory 'O!' *and* an old shortening of the imperative form of 'Look!', thus subdividing the (apparent) pivot from narration to description between an auto-affecting cognition (O!) and a perlocutionary unveiling (Look!).

But the orders of difference we are speaking of are of course incommensurate. The difference between an event and its narration is grammatical before it is temporal, and the wish to render that difference as a measurable relation that could be expanded, contracted, or reduced to an all-but-instantaneous identification, ultimately bespeaks a desire to submit the materiality of language to the control of an homogenizing rationality, in a way not unrelated to Wordsworth's drive, in climbing Snowdon, to surmount his own body. Within the calculus and the techno-scientific project it enables, the result is to occlude, via a logic of the infinitesimal, the rhetorical substitution of a conception of point as the limit of dimension (zero as least number) for a conception of point as dimensionless position (zero as non-number).

In an early draft, Wordsworth compares his liminal experience on Snowdon – at the Old World's western verge – to that of Columbus in the following terms:

> Such power to pass at once from daily life,
> Such power was with Columbus & his Crew
>   they
> When first, ~~far~~ travelled into unknown seas,
>   Needle}
> They saw the Comp}faltering in its office,
> Turn from the Pole.[24]

And indeed, what Wordsworth registers with Snowdon passage is at once a bold and an anxious probe of uncharted territory. But, as with Mandelbrot, the region thus probed does not lie *beyond* the limit of the charted but within the limit itself as a field of investigation, just as Mandelbrot's work does not multiply dimensions but voyages into the conceptual and intuitive interstices of the distinctions by which we delimit them. Nor is this a distinct, a localizable, place or event within the geography or cartography of *The Prelude*; the needle which falters in its office is at once the stylus that traces and the eye that discerns its trembling.

Notes

1. William Wordsworth, Note to 'The Thorn', in *Lyrical Ballads 1798 and 1800*, eds. Michael Gamer and Dahlia Porter (Toronto: Broadview Press, 2008), 287.
2. Benoit Mandelbrot, 'Fractuals and the Art of Roughness', TED, 2010. Retrieved from www.ted.com/talks/benoit_mandelbrot_fractals_the_art_of_roughness
3. Benoit Mandelbrot, 'How Long Is the Coast of Britain? Statistical Self-Similarity and Fractional Dimension', *Science* 156:3775 (1967): 636–8.
4. The phrase is fabled not only because so often cited but also because, though routinely and reasonably attributed to Poincaré, it is not quite what he wrote. See *Science et Méthode* (Paris: Flammarion, 1947), vol. 2, sect. 5, 132–3.
5. Lewis Fry Richardson, 'The Problem of Contiguity: An Appendix to *Statistics of Deadly Quarrels*', *General Systems: Yearbook of the Society for the Advancement of General Systems Theory* 6 (1961): 139–87, 167–8.
6. Benoit Mandelbrot, *The Fractalist: Memoir of a Scientific Maverick* (New York: Pantheon Books, 2012), 228–9.
7. As Mandelbrot acknowledges (referring to Poincaré's landmark work on the three-body problem in *New Methods of Celestial Mechanics*): 'Poincaré recognized that the classic monsters could enter, not into descriptions of visible Nature, but into abstract mathematical physics'. *The Fractal Geometry of Nature* (New York: W. H. Freeman, 1983), 414; henceforth *FGN*.
8. Galileo Galilei and Stillman Drake, *Discoveries and Opinions of Galileo: Including the Starry Messenger (1610), Letter to the Grand Duchess Christina (1615) and Excerpts from Letters on Sunspots (1613), The Assayer (1623)* (New York: Anchor Books, 1990), 237–8.
9. Although *The Fractal Geometry of Nature* makes no reference to Galileo, Mandelbrot makes the connection and the contrast explicit in *The Fractalist*, 233.
10. William Wordsworth, *The Thirteen-Book Prelude*, ed. Mark L. Reed (Ithaca, NY: Cornell University Press, 1991). Unless otherwise noted, all references are to the 1805 text.
11. One of the best-known verbal icons of self-similarity comes from Richardson's earlier work on the mathematical structure of atmospheric turbulence in his *Weather Prediction by Numerical Process* (Cambridge: Cambridge University Press, 1922): 'Big whorls have little whorls that feed on their velocity, and little whorls have lesser whorls, and so on to viscosity in

the molecular sense' (68). As Mandelbrot notes, Richardson's conceit in turn draws on Swift. Although Mandelbrot follows common practice in citing the sentence as lines of verse, Richardson does not in fact distinguish it typographically from the rest of the paragraph in which it is embedded (*FGN*, 402).

12. There are a number of different routes up Snowdon, but the details of Wordsworth's narrative are sufficiently precise to identify his path as the Rhyd Ddu to someone familiar with the terrain. For a map and detailed discussion, see Kenneth Johnston, *The Hidden Wordsworth: Poet, Lover, Rebel, Spy* (New York: Norton, 1998), 268–70.

13. In cases of 'statistical self-similarity', similarity across scales may not be intuitively evident but can be established on numerical grounds. As Mandelbrot notes, 'self-similar figures are seldom encountered in nature (crystals are one exception). However, a statistical form of self-similarity is often encountered' (637).

14. Expressed as a mathematical formula: $N \, 1/S^{D} = 1$, where '1/S' is the scaling factor, 'D' is the dimension, and 'N' is the number of parts into which the figure is divided. Using logarithms to solve for D, one arrives at the following: $D = \log N/\log S$.

15. See Duncan Wu, *The Five-Book Prelude* (Oxford: Blackwell, 1997), 134.

16. Wordsworth provides his own account of the envisioned relationship between *The Prelude* and *The Recluse* in his preface to *The Excursion* (the only part of *The Recluse* to be completed):

> Several years ago, when the Author retired to his native Mountains, with the hope of being enabled to construct a literary Work that might live, it was a reasonable thing that he should take a review of his own Mind, and examine how far Nature and Education had qualified him for such employment. As subsidiary to this preparation, he undertook to record, in Verse, the origin and progress of his own powers, as far as he was acquainted with them. That Work, addressed to a dear Friend [Coleridge], most distinguished for his knowledge and genius, and to whom the Author's Intellect is deeply indebted, has been long finished; and the result of the investigation which gave rise to it was a determination to compose a philosophical Poem, containing views of Man, Nature, and Society; and to be entitled, The Recluse; as having for its principal subject the sensations and opinions of a Poet living in retirement. The preparatory Poem is biographical, and conducts the history of the Author's mind to the point when he was emboldened to hope that his faculties were sufficiently matured for entering upon the arduous labour which he had proposed to himself; and the two Works have the same kind of relation to each other, if he may so express himself, as the Antichapel [sic] has to the body of a gothic church.

William Wordsworth, *The Excursion*, eds. Sally Bushell, James Butler, and Michael Jaye (Ithaca, NY: Cornell University Press, 2007), 38.

17. M. H. Abrams *Natural Supernaturalism: Tradition and Revolution in Romantic Literature* (New York: Norton, 1973), 286.

18. Mary Jacobus, *Romanticism, Writing and Sexual Difference: Essays on The Prelude* (Oxford and New York: Clarendon Press, 1989), 267.

19. See Reed, ed., *Thirteen-Book Prelude*, II, 250, 288 (MSS. WW and W, respectively).

20. In Book III of *The Prelude*, as Julia S. Carlson discusses in *Romantic Marks and Measures: Wordsworth's Poetry in Fields of Print* (Philadelphia: University of Pennsylvania Press, 2016).

21. Geoffrey H. Hartman, *Wordsworth's Poetry, 1787–1814* (New Haven, CT: Yale University Press, 1971), 17.

22. The implicit or subliminal reversal of perspective is again more explicitly registered in cancelled lines from MS. W: 'When that small plot the moving back of earth / That fac'd me as I climb'd' (Reed, ed., *Thirteen-Book Prelude*, I, 392; II, 283).

23. For a more detailed analysis along these lines, see my '"Self-Displacing Vision": Snowdon and the Dialectic of the Senses', *Wordsworth Circle* XXVIII:1 (2006): 27–33.

24. The lines are, again, from MS. W. and may be found in Reed, ed., *Thirteen-Book Prelude*, II, 290, or Wu, *The Five-Book Prelude*, 201–2 (along with footnotes detailing Wordsworth's source).

PART III

Beyond Romantic Cartographies

CHAPTER 9

Deep Mapping and Romanticism
'Practical' Geography in the Poetry of Sir Walter Scott

Christopher Donaldson

> I am an utter stranger to geometry ... My geographical knowledge is merely practical.
>
> Walter Scott, Letter to George Ellis, 30 January 1803[1]

Considerations of geography, cartography, and Scottish Romanticism have tended to focus on the function of landscape and setting as vehicles for exploring national and regional identity. This tendency is apparent in many scholarly assessments of post-Enlightenment Scottish literature and culture, but it is especially evident in recent evaluations of the works of Sir Walter Scott.[2] Collectively, these evaluations have enhanced our understanding of Scott's influence on modern conceptions of Scottish selfhood. Far less attention, however, has been paid to Scott's personal understanding of cartography, and almost no one has considered the relevance of Scott's writings to latter-day developments in geographical thought and practice.[3] The present chapter takes up these neglected topics, and in doing so it undertakes to examine the relation of Scott's early poetry and antiquarian research to the emergence of 'deep mapping' as a field of performance and inquiry.[4]

Do You Know the Way to Erceldoune?

In January 1803, the English antiquarian George Ellis wrote to Scott to express his perplexity about several places mentioned in the *Minstrelsy of the Scottish Border*. Ellis, it seems, had already conferred with John Leyden, a mutual friend who had assisted Scott with collecting Border ballads for the *Minstrelsy*. Ellis had even gone so far as to take Leyden to the cartographer Aaron Arrowsmith to consult the 'best map of Scotland' available (*Letters*, I, 174). But their visit had proved unavailing. Even with

Arrowsmith's maps spread before them, explained Ellis, 'Leyden was unable . . . to trace the several dales and heights which are the scenes of your ancient ballads' (174). Disappointed but undeterred, Ellis had consulted his own library, looking with particular assiduity for the location of Erceldoune, the birthplace of the thirteenth-century bard Thomas the Rhymer, who featured in the second volume of Scott's collection. Here too, however, Ellis found himself stumped, and in his letter to Scott he expatiated on this conundrum: 'In truth, I have never been able to find even *Ercildoune* [sic] on any map in my possession.'⁵ Since a third volume of the *Minstrelsy* was then in press, Ellis implored, would it not be worth 'prefixing to it a good map of the Scottish Borders' as an aid to the inquisitive reader (*Memoirs*, I, 366)? A 'bird's-eye view map', such as the one he had himself produced of the Caucasus, might be most satisfactory (*Letters*, I, 174).

This suggestion intrigued Scott, but, as he noted in his reply, there were 'two strong objections' to Ellis's request (174). The first of these was logistical: the third volume of the *Minstrelsy* would 'be out in a month', and there simply was not time to prepare a map to accompany it (174). The second objection, by contrast, was of a more personal nature, and in explaining it Scott made a noteworthy admission:

> You are to know that I am an utter stranger to geometry, surveying, and all such *inflammatory* branches of study, as Mrs Malaprop calls them. My education was unfortunately interrupted by a long indisposition, which occasioned my residing for about two years in the country with a good maiden aunt who permitted and encouraged me to run about the fields as wild as any buck that ever fled from the face of man. Hence my geographical knowledge is merely practical, and though I think that in the South Country 'I could be a guide worth ony twa that may in Liddesdale be found' yet I believe Hobby Noble or Kinmont Willie would beat me at laying down a map. (174)

This whimsical medley of historical, autobiographical, and literary reference is typical of Scott's correspondence. What is remarkable here, though, is how Scott marshals these references in order to clarify the local source and character of his knowledge of the Borders. The brief autobiographical reminiscence included in this passage is particularly important. In recalling his 'wild' childhood forays into the countryside around his Aunt Janet's home in Kelso, Scott indirectly emphasizes that his 'practical' understanding of the Borders was rooted in personal experience. Like the moss-troopers immortalized in the ballads of the *Minstrelsy*, Scott's 'geographical knowledge' of the Border region was, by his own assertion, immanently empirical. It was an acuity cultivated not in the schoolroom but in 'the fields'. It was an intelligence accrued not simply through reading but through remembering and reciting antique songs such as the ballad of 'Hobbie Nobel', which Scott's seemingly impromptu quotation casually recalls. It was, in so many words, a perspective immersed and embedded in the landscape, and as such it stood at variance with the disembodied and detached 'bird's-eye view' afforded by the sort of survey map that Ellis had in mind.

These differing vantage points are indicative of two contrasting modes of topographical apprehension: one based principally on calculation and geometrical representation; the other on memory and sensory experience. Whereas the former prioritizes the delineation of visible surfaces, the latter is concerned with more than what is merely visible. The former privileges the depiction of the spatially synchronous, whereas the latter is characterized by its preoccupation with what Michael Shanks and Christopher Witmore have called 'the folding of history and time through land and place'.[6] The former finds its archetypal expression in the making of maps; the latter finds its archetypal expression in the telling of tales.

These considerations return us to Ellis's consternation about the location of Erceldoune. For, when viewed in the light of the distinctions made in the previous paragraph, Ellis's failed search becomes far more meaningful. What his eyes missed while poring over his maps is, after all, something Scott would have caught with his ears – namely, that Erceldoune when said in broad Lallans sounds rather like Earlston, the standard modern spelling of the town's name. Earlston is just down the road from Kelso, and for Scott, who passed so much of his youth in the vicinity, the town's ancient and modern names, though distinct in their written forms, would have sounded much the same. Ellis, being an Englishman, could be excused for failing to hear this similarity – and for not being more familiar with the local terrain. But Scott was evidently surprised that Leyden, who hailed from near Hawick, should 'want' sufficient 'knowledge of the ground' (*Letters*, XII, 233). '[Leyden] ought to have known Erceldoune', tut-tutted Scott: 'you will find it in every map. Look for Lauder which is 25 miles S. of Edin[burgh] glance your eye down the Leader upon which brook that Burgh is situated and you will find Erceldoune or Earlstoun [sic] about four miles above its junction with the Tweed' (233). Scott, as this quotation affirms, certainly knew how to 'lay down a map', but this sort of orienteering was only a superficial expression of the much deeper geographical understanding he possessed.

This brings me to the purpose of the present chapter. In what follows I want to explore manifestations of this deeper geographical understanding in Scott's writings about the Anglo-Scottish Border region, and I shall do so by examining indicative examples from both his fictional and his antiquarian works. As my principal example, though, I shall focus on Scott's verse romance *The Lay of the Last Minstrel*, which first appeared in 1805. An offshoot of the *Minstrelsy*, *The Lay of the Last Minstrel* is a remarkably self-conscious poetic experiment. It is a poem steeped in the literary fashions and sensibilities of its era. Even more than this, though, it is a poem that emphatically reflects Scott's antiquarian interests in the attention it devotes to the histories and associations of specific places in the Border region. Setting *matters* in the *Lay*; it is not merely a scenic backdrop, nor is it simply a matter of diegetic emplotment. Rather, the setting is ancillary to an excavation of history and memory in which the narrative of the poem is actively engaged. *The Lay of the Last Minstrel* is, as I mean to show, a literary work that is deeply invested in documenting traces of the past that, though not necessarily visible, have remained palpably present in the landscape of the Borders to this day.

Building on this analysis, I shall then proceed to consider how the geographical attentiveness of Scott's works can help us to historicize the emergence of what, with increasing frequency of late, has been termed 'deep mapping'. In essence, deep mapping is a field of practice and inquiry that aspires to devise and model holistic approaches to the study of space and place. The parameters of this field are not clearly defined, and some of its more vocal advocates have explicitly stated that deep mapping should be 'polyvocal', 'open-ended', 'pluralistic', and thus not 'reducible to any single disciplinary perspective'.[7] But even such deliberately indeterminate assessments do posit some general principles from which the broad outlines of the field can be traced. Specifically, such assessments suggest that deep mapping is a mode of observation, investigation, and interpretation that aims to record and to communicate those aspects of a location, locality, or region that are not, or cannot be, adequately conveyed through conventional modes of cartographic representation. One such aspect is time. Conventional planar maps, though powerful forms of abstract representation, possess a shallow time depth. Synchronicity is essential to the visual logic by which they order the spatial information they display. Deep mapping, by contrast, favours a more layered or palimpsestic approach to spatial representation, one which allows multiple periods in the history of a location, locality, or region to be exposed and examined simultaneously. In practice, deep mapping involves accumulating different kinds of geographical and attribute information, and submitting that information to comparative analysis and inquiry. The aim of such analysis and inquiry is, of course, not only to facilitate considerations of the differences between the past and present characteristics of a given location, locality, or region but also to explore the continuous interplay between past and present that informs how the location, locality, or region in question is perceived, experienced, and understood.

The mode of geographical apprehension apparent in Scott's writings about the Borders is, as I have suggested, commensurate with just this sort of temporally enriched approach to the study of space and place. Accordingly, in this chapter I want to propose that Scott's writings demonstrate that deep mapping, though a development of our own period, is a field of practice that can be brought into meaningful dialogue with the literature and culture of the Romantic age. Key in this context are what (to borrow Rosemary Sweet's phrase) we might call Scott's 'antiquarian instincts': in other words, his enduring fascination with those vestiges of the past that the landscape of one's present time contains or even conceals.[8] I have already touched briefly on this aspect of Scott's writings, and I shall elaborate on it later in the chapter. But before I do so, let me be perfectly clear about my intentions. I am not claiming that Scott's works anticipate or prefigure the deep mapping practices of the present day. Nor, for that matter, am I proposing that his works constitute an act of deep mapping. Rather, my contention is that Scott's writings about the Borders participate in a discourse of antiquarianism that, though it is integrally a product of his era, can be placed into a continuum with deep mapping as a compatible mode of inquiry. In short, as I mean to show, deep mapping is not only an approach that can be productively applied to the study of Romantic literature but also a methodology that accords well with the geographical procedures and preoccupations of one of the most remarkable and influential writers of the Romantic age.

'A Great Meikle Nowt-Horn to Rout on'

The antiquarian foundations of Scott's geographical knowledge were, as I have intimated, laid deep. An avid compiler of ancient songs and oral traditions, he was, even in his youth, also an eager collector of artefacts. This is an aspect of Scott's character famously celebrated in his son-in-law John Gibson Lockhart's *Memoirs of the Life of Sir Walter Scott*, which devotes several pages to describing the holiday 'raids' Scott made in the Borders between 1792 and 1799. During these years, as Lockhart affirms,

Scott took a series of annual tours into Liddesdale with Robert Shortreed, a Roxburghshire native who served as Scott's travelling companion and guide. These tours were, by all accounts, cheerfully desultory rambles, but, as Lockhart suggests, they were not altogether aimless. Scott's interest in Liddesdale was rooted in his fascination with 'the ancient *riding ballads*, said to be still preserved' in the valley (*Memoirs*, I, 194) and equally with Hermitage Castle, a ruined fortress north of Newcastleton that had associations with his own moss-trooper ancestors, including such infamous warriors as Sir Walter Scott, first Lord Scott of Buccleuch (1565?–1611) and Walter Scott ('Auld Wat') of Harden (*c.* 1550–1629?). Accordingly, as he travelled with Shortreed, Scott applied himself in 'gathering' old 'songs and tunes, and occasionally more tangible relics of antiquity' (*Memoirs*, I, 194, 195). Many of these 'relics' became prized possessions, items that Scott later displayed with evident personal pride at his Abbotsford estate. But chief among them all was 'the large old border war horn' (Figure 9.1) that

Figure 9.1 William Gibb, *Plate XXII: Border War Horn*. The horn is displayed here alongside another of Scott's prized antiquities, James VI/I's hunting bottle. Courtesy of the Department of Special Collections, Stanford University Libraries.

Scott received from Dr John Elliot, a local surgeon who shared his passion for antiquities (*Memoirs*, I, 199).

The horn, which had apparently been recovered from the marshes around Hermitage Castle, pleased Scott so much that he 'carried it home ... slung about his neck' so he could 'rout on' it as he rode (*Memoirs*, I, 200). That Scott was clowning about can hardly be doubted. Shortreed certainly thought that he was, and he teased Scott by comparing him to the beggar with 'a great meikle nowt-horn' portrayed in the old Scottish song (200). But given the provenance of the war horn, and its consequent association with Scott's ancestors, it also seems likely that Scott was engaging in a bit of light-hearted historical re-enactment – styling himself, as it were, in the guise of his own 'redoubted moss-trooper progenitors' (*Letters*, I, 22). There is an element of artifice in Lockhart's account of this episode, of course. This portion of the *Memoirs* is, in truth, a rather carefully sifted selection of Scott's correspondence and Shortreed's recollections. The resulting 'portrait' of Scott is, as a contemporary reviewer of the *Memoirs* observed, one conspicuously 'touched with caricature'.[9] Scott appears here as just the sort of romantic adventurer that later figured in his novels: a curious but good-natured, confident but quixotic, passionate but naive young man. Such conflations of Scott's life and works occur throughout Lockhart's biography, but this does not invalidate the significance of the account Lockhart provides. His description of Scott's early antiquarian pursuits may be caricatured, but this does not mean that it should be regarded as necessarily false. Lockhart might have exaggerated features of his father-in-law's personality, but those features belonged to Scott nonetheless. What Lockhart's portrayal of Scott's Liddesdale 'raids' emphasizes is, after all, an aspect of Scott's character that is widely attested to and at which I have already hinted – namely, his interest not just in historical remains but in the sensory awareness of history that those remains could transmit. As one of Scott's more recent biographers has averred, Scott 'loved what he called "technical history", objects that one could handle and which conjured up the past through the fingers that held them'.[10] History for Scott was not just something to be read about but something that had to be grasped with the hand, heard in the ear, and felt underfoot. It was, in short, something to be studied with the senses and, thus, something best studied in situ.

Scott's clowning about on his war horn becomes even more meaningful when it is viewed in the light of these reflections. Rather than being merely a moment of youthful buffoonery, it can be regarded as an early example of Scott's awareness of how the immaterial past could be activated through the embodied perception of its material remains. Once again, the empirical dimension of Scott's knowledge of the Borders is manifest. The horn, as the anecdote from Lockhart's *Memoirs* implies, was valuable to Scott not only as an antique but also for the sake of the experience of holding it and playing it and hearing the noises it made. More than just a tangible remnant of antiquity, such an object was an artefact that could give sensory access to otherwise intangible aspects of the history of the Border region. Key here, of course, was sound.

Horns, as Scott knew, were an integral feature of the ancient soundscape and social geography of the Borders. Like the peal of its civic equivalent, the church bell, the bellow of the horn was capable of resounding across the area inhabited by a community and, in the process, of acoustically consolidating that area as a socialized space. Like the ringing of church bells, the blowing of horns was an act woven into the fabric of Border society. Horns, like church bells, sounded the call to assembly and the call to alarm. Such a sound was a socially cohesive force; it was one which, as Alain Corbin has observed, conditioned 'the habitus of a community'.[11] Such a sound was an auditory signal capable of unifying a settled landscape and regulating its communal life. As Scott affirmed in the commentaries he included in *The Minstrelsy of the Scottish Border*, the inhabitants of the region sounded the horn not only to convene hunts, forays, and pursuits but also to 'raise the country to help' in the event of inroads or invasions.[12] In his 'Essay on Border Antiquities', Scott later elaborated on the history of these practices by connecting the use of horns with the institution of cornage tenure, by which, as Scott surmised, certain barons 'held their land and towers for the service of winding a horn to intimate the approach of a hostile party'.[13] Scott was mistaken about the specifics of this particular feudal custom, but he was nonetheless correct in calling attention to the social duty that those who held towers and lookouts performed by sounding the alarm in the event of an attack. Like beacons set alight to signal oncoming danger, the war horn was a means of sending both warning and a call to arms across the area inhabited by a community and its allies.

The 'winding' of the war horn was clearly an act that appealed to Scott's imagination. What matters here, though, is that Scott's knowledge of the practice was not merely theoretical. It was also based on personal experience. He knew how the weight of such a horn felt in the hand. He knew, moreover, the way its sound carried on the air. Scott's interest in this ancient instrument was, suitably, not restricted to his historical writings: it was also something he chose to express in many of his more imaginative works, most notably in his poetry. War horns figure in a variety of Scott's poems: they appear in works ranging from full-scale romances such as *The Lady of the Lake* to more modest lyric pieces such as 'Lullaby of an Infant Chief'. Nowhere, however, does Scott feature the sounding of the war horn with more poetic force than in *The Lay of the Last Minstrel*, a verse narrative detailing the conflicts occasioned by the murder of his ancestor, Sir Walter Scott ('Wicked Wat') of Branxholm and Buccleuch (*c.* 1490–1552). Among the more powerful set pieces included in this rousing tale of sixteenth-century Border warfare is the alarm that sweeps through the region at the advance of the invading English army. Here the minstrel, our narrator, having described the 'red glare' of the 'beacon-blaze' ignited on Penchrise Pen, turns our attention to a watchman (or 'warder') looking towards the flames from his station on the walls of Branxholm Tower:

> The warder viewed it blazing strong,
> And blew his war-note loud and long,
> Till, at the high and haughty sound,
> Rock, wood, and river, rung around.
> The blast alarmed the festal hall,
> And startled forth the warriors all;
> Far downward, in the castle-yard,
> Full many a torch and cresset glared;
> And helms and plumes, confusedly tossed,
> Were in the blaze half-seen, half-lost;
> And spears in wild disorder shook,
> Like reeds beside a frozen brook.[14]

This stanza, when lifted from the place it occupies in Scott's poem, might initially seem somewhat wooden. The combination of closed couplets and monosyllabic rhymes, though appropriate to the martial subject matter of the *Lay*, might nonetheless strike the ear as rather stiff, especially given the iambic undercurrent that pulls the reader through the first half-dozen lines. But the more one lingers over these verses, the more one begins to notice rhythmic variations that work in tandem with Scott's use of imagery and repetition to heighten the dramatic potential of the scenes depicted. The shifting position of the caesura between the first and second couplet is particularly notable, since it corresponds with the accentual alteration caused by the placement of the stressed initial syllable in lines three and four. Especially in the latter line ('Rock, wood, and river, rung around'), this alteration of accent assumes a para-mimetic importance. It conspires with the resounding effected by alliteration and assonance to enact, analogically, the very action Scott describes. This close connection between form and content becomes all the more apparent in the eighth and ninth lines, where the introduction of an extra syllable brings about a similar effect. Whereas in the former case the superfluous addition of the word 'full' syllabically overfills the line, in the latter case the decision not to syncopate 'confusedly' causes a momentary confusion itself by disrupting the alternation of stressed and unstressed syllables maintained throughout the rest of the stanza.

Such departures from the octosyllabic cadence discernible in these lines hint at one of the more important features of Scott's poem – namely, that its verses are gathered together less by syllable than by stress. Like Samuel Taylor Coleridge's *Christabel*, a poem which exerted a strong influence on Scott, *The Lay of the Last Minstrel* is an elaborate experiment in accentual versification.[15] Like Coleridge before him, moreover, Scott justified this metrical experiment by explaining his desire to develop a style suited to the antique idiom of his poem. As Scott affirmed in the notice he prefixed to the *Lay*, he was quite intentionally attempting to 'partake of the rudeness of the old ballad, or metrical romance', which with its 'occasional alteration of measure' and 'changes of rythm [sic]' (*Lay*, iv) afforded a flexible medium for the expression of different types of action and different 'tones of feeling'.[16] For contemporary readers, who were generally more accustomed to the symmetry and regularity of syllabic metre, this attempt to exploit the irregularity and 'rudeness' of ancient poetry proved highly appealing. Even the often-implacable Francis Jeffrey, though he faulted certain elements of Scott's subject matter, nonetheless applauded the effect the *Lay* achieved by 'adapting' the conventions of antiquated prosody to suit the 'taste of the modern reader'.[17]

But as the stanza demonstrates, *The Lay of the Last Minstrel* is not just distinguished by the sound effects Scott achieved through his use of a deliberately archaic style. The poem is also distinguished by the attention it invests into the role that sounds, such as the warder's 'war-note', played in shaping the social landscape of the Borders in the past. These two endeavours (to convey something of the sound of ancient poetry and something of the sounds of the region where that poetry originated) govern the design of Scott's poem, but the latter prevails in the passage I have quoted. Indicatively, Scott's treatment of the horn in these lines focuses not on its material form but on the effect of its resounding. Very little energy is expended on describing the war horn itself; rather, the emphasis falls on the actions its 'high and haughty sound' excites and elicits. This aspect of the power of the horn is developed further in the subsequent stanza of the *Lay*, wherein the seneschal sends the assembled warriors forth:

> 'On Penchryst glows a bale of fire,
> And three are kindling on Priesthaughswire;
> > Ride out, ride out,
> > The foe to scout!
> Mount, mount for Branksome, every man!
> Thou, Todrig, warn the Johnstone clan,
> > That ever are true and stout—
> Ye need not send to Liddesdale;
> For when they see the blazing bale,
> Elliots and Armstrongs never fail—
> Ride, Alton, ride, for death and life!
> And warn the Warder of the strife.
> Young Gilbert, let our beacon blaze,
> Our kin, and clan, and friends to raise.'
> > > (*Lay*, 85; III, xxvii)

The dramatic force of these lines owes much to the rapid change of the seneschal's addressees and, concomitantly, to the briskness and earnestness of his commands. Collectively, these features contribute to the sense of urgency that builds throughout this portion of the poem. To this end, they work in tandem with other overt stylistic effects, such as Scott's use of repetition and emphatic shifts in metre. Equally important here, though, is the more subtle use to which Scott puts the series of family names and place names that fills out the stanza. This list of surnames and toponyms recalls a mnemonic device commonly employed in ancient ballads and romances, wherein the recitation of proper names often provides anchoring points for the events narrated. Even more than this, though, Scott's deployment of specific names in this stanza achieves two important ends: on the one hand, it outlines the broader setting of this section of the *Lay*; on the other hand, it furnishes the reader with an insight into the way the geography that underpins the setting of the poem was historically organized and perceived.

From Branxholm Tower, near Hawick, the seat of the Scotts; to Lochwood Castle, near Moffat, the seat of the Johnstons; to Mangerton Tower, near Newcastleton, and Prickinghaugh Tower, near Larriston, the strongholds of the Armstrongs and Elliots respectively – the roll call of surnames and toponyms invoked or implied in this stanza conveys the sense of a region defined not by spatial geometry but by a network of family groups. Scott gives us here a terrain measured by the strength of social relations rather than by miles or minutes. The sightlines marked by the

placement of beacons on neighbouring heights, such as Penchrise Pen and
Priesthaugh, are a characteristic feature of this region in that they form
channels of social communication between dispersed clans, septs, and
families. That said, the region Scott depicts in this stanza remains one
constituted less fundamentally by its topography than by the social intercourse and family ties of its inhabitants. If, as John Sutherland has put it,
the *Lay* is 'at its root . . . a family affair', it is not only because Scott's poem
elaborates on a chapter in the history of his own clan but also because the
action and setting of his narrative are defined by the network of his clan's
historical allegiances (*Life*, 100). The final line of the stanza just quoted
('Our kin, and clan, and friends to raise') furthers this impression. This
clause, which artfully combines syntactic equivalence and semantic hierarchy, works in tandem with the geography posited in the preceding verses
to emphasize the radiating network of communities that the riders,
equipped with their own horns, are sent to warn and summon.

  In this passage, then, Scott cues the reader not only into the way the
sounding of the war horn was woven into the ancient social geography of the
Borders but also into the way that geography was historically understood. The
network of family groups to which he refers in the lines I have quoted is of
particular importance in this context, as it intimates how those living in the
Borders conceived of the area around them and under their control. The
ancient communities of the region, as Scott knew, perceived their locality in
terms of kinship and tribal connections as much as, if not more than, they did
by graphic inscriptions, such as maps, charts, or plans. The sounding of the
war horn to warn and to summon support was an integral part of this web of
connections that bound families, family groups, and clans together. What was
crucial for Scott, though, was that this sounding was an act that an artefact like
the Hermitage war horn could help him re-enact. Like the family names and
place names Scott threaded through the verses of the *Lay*, such relics of the
past grounded the history recounted and embellished in his writings within
a knowable locality – one that, though saturated with history and legend,
could nonetheless be explored and experienced in the present day. Such relics
could, moreover, conjure up something of the consciousness that had shaped
perceptions of that locality during earlier epochs of its inhabitation. Scott's
interest in such items, like his interest in the locations with which they were
associated, was guided by just the sort of deeper geographical understanding
that I characterized at the outset of this chapter. It was, in short, a fascination
informed by Scott's preoccupation with the layering of narratives, artefacts,
and local associations that, in their accumulation, had contributed to and
consolidated the identity of the Border region through time.

'Where the Memory of Ancient Battles Still Lives'

The research Scott conducted during his early tours of Liddesdale was far from methodical. But even in their more idiosyncratic moments, such as the occasion of his ride with the Hermitage war horn, these journeys presaged working practices that Scott went on to employ over the course of his career. As a writer he was, by custom, sedulously attentive to the local details of his narratives, and he frequently consulted travel diaries and topographical studies in order to ensure the faithfulness of his accounts of specific places. But fieldwork, such as the sort prefigured in Scott's 'wild' childhood forays and in his youthful Border 'raids', proved equally integral to his later literary pursuits. Notably, in the introduction Scott prefixed to the 1830 edition of *The Lady of the Lake*, he reflected on the 'uncommon pains' he had taken 'to verify the local circumstances of th[e] story', confessing that he had even galloped from Loch Venachar to Stirling Castle in order to ensure that it was 'practicable' for the ride to be completed 'within the time' he allotted for it 'in the poem' (*Poetical Works*, VIII, 9–10).

Scott's willingness to engage in this sort of 'ground-truthing' reflects a well-documented aspect of his authorial practice – namely, his desire to vouchsafe the geographical authenticity of his narratives. What I want to emphasize here, though, is that this desire is also commensurate with Scott's investment in a geographically grounded excavation of the history and memory of the Border region. Scott's fictional and antiquarian writings about the Borders, as I have intimated, are informed not only by his own 'practical' understanding of particular landmarks and locations but also by an appreciation of the function of locality as a support for cultural memory. Indicatively, in his 'Essay on Border Antiquities', Scott described the Anglo-Scottish Border as a 'frontier . . . where the memory of ancient battles still lives' alongside the 'massive ruins' of castles and other mouldering remnants of antiquity (*Border Antiquities*, I, iii). The broader implication of this collocation of the region's tangible and intangible heritage is straightforward: like the ruins strewn about the landscape, the memory retained by the communities of the Borders in their songs and folklore stood in need of recording and conservation. The concern and interest implicit in this statement illuminates the nature of the work Scott undertook in collecting and publishing ancient border ballads and romances – and in responding to the traditions of those ballads and romances in his own literary works.

This impulse to collect and commemorate is an aspect of Scott's writing that has recently received attention from Lucy McRae, whose research into

The Minstrelsy of the Scottish Border specifically attends to the influence of conservation and commemoration on Scott's practices as an editor and compiler of Border ballads.[18] As McRae affirms, Scott's predilection for 'ballads that demonstrated their historicity and regionality' was not merely a matter of taste. Rather, it was an expression of Scott's anxiety about the potential degradation and disappearance of traditional histories pertaining to specific localities in the Border region.[19] Such an assessment is clearly compatible with Scott's own account of his motivations in the *Minstrelsy*, wherein he explicitly acknowledged his desire to record 'popular superstitions, and legendary histor[ies]', which, 'if not now collected, must soon [be] totally forgotten' (*Minstrelsy*, I, cix). What is worth stressing further here, though, is how Scott's editorial practice specifically situated those superstitions and histories geographically. The commentaries and notes Scott included in the appendices and apparatus of the *Minstrelsy* emphatically connect specific ballads with their geographical settings. This is a practice on which Scott would later elaborate in antiquarian tomes such as his *The Border Antiquities of England and Scotland* and *The Provincial Antiquities and Picturesque Scenery of Scotland*, where his descriptions of local customs, traditions, and history were accompanied by illustrations of specific artefacts and landmarks. In this way, Scott's antiquarian writings can be seen to parallel his endeavours as an editor and a poet in works such as the *Minstrelsy* and *The Lay of the Last Minstrel*. Though distinctive, each of these publications participate in what Les Roberts has called 'the production of "deeply" configured spatial knowledge', and it is on this account that one can draw connections between Scott's writings and the modern practice of deep mapping.[20]

The lack of precise definition of the concept of 'deep mapping' is, as I have already suggested, partly a consequence of the exploratory nature of it as a practice. Still, the developing body of commentary devoted to deep mapping does furnish insights into both the interdisciplinary tendencies of the field and its theoretical and methodological underpinnings. Hence, Iain Biggs has characterized deep mapping 'as using practices drawn from literature, performance, and the visual arts to evoke the warp and weft of materials, perspectives, and temporalities that "make up" a place'.[21] Implicit in such assertions is the connection between the recent rise of scholarly interest in deep mapping and a set of complementary currents in cultural geography and in the arts and humanities. I refer here, on the one hand, to the increasing importance of performance-informed approaches within cultural geography and, on the other hand, to the intensification of interest in geographical concepts and methods in the arts and humanities. These two trends have evolved gradually over several decades, but they have undergone a considerable quickening over the past twenty years due to the integration of computational technologies, digital media, and, consequently, new modes of practice across the arts, humanities, and social sciences. Deep mapping, though it is not merely a product of these latter developments, can be – and often is – closely associated with them.[22]

Especially important in this context are geospatial computing applications such as geographic information systems (GIS) and cognate technologies, such as virtual globes, Internet mapping programmes, and locative media that utilizes the Global Positioning System (GPS). These technologies, though they were not originally designed as deep mapping platforms, have been generative and enabling resources for the practice of deep mapping, and they have been widely adopted and adapted to facilitate in-depth explorations of specific places. The appeal of these technologies is broadly based on their ability to support the sort of palimpsestic approach to spatial representation that deep mapping aspires to pursue. This is especially the case with GIS, which are essentially relational databases that organize geospatial information into layers that are cross-referenced with coordinate data and, thus, can be stored, retrieved, and arranged to facilitate the visualization and exploration of the different strata that contribute to and consolidate the understanding of a given location. The coordinates with which these layers are cross-referenced are typically geographical and therefore connect the information to specific locations and features on the surface of the earth. It is equally possible, however, to use non-geographical coordinates, such as generic vector data, to superimpose layers on other surfaces, such as non-geodetic images. Trevor Harris, John Corrigan, and David Bodenhamer, who have collectively published a significant amount of commentary on this topic, have remarked on this analogical relationship between deep maps and GIS. As they contend in one of their more recent publications, the affordances of GIS technology 'provide an organizational framework and a storyboard to navigate through media artifacts of evidence and record and discover latent connections through pathways of alternative readings of the evidence and differing juxtapositions of the materials'.[23] This notion of deep mapping as a process of exposing, exploring, and – indeed – narrating the layers of meaning that inform the identity of a given location, locality, or region is salient, as it gestures to the ancient intellectual pedigree of deep mapping as a practice.

There is, after all, an inherent complementarity between deep mapping and the sorts of antiquarian approaches that informed the works of writers such as Scott.[24] A key point of connection here is the tradition of chorography. Chorography originated in classical antiquity as a category of research focused on inventorying, at length, the features, character, customs, and manners of particular regions. This practice, combining as it does elements of history, geography, ethnography, and natural philosophy, was adopted by early modern scholars as a way of characterizing the intensive investigation of specific localities. A key work within this context, of course, was William Camden's *Britannia* (1586), which, with its subtitle 'a chorographical description' (*chorographica descriptio*), exerted a powerful influence over the subsequent development of antiquarian research in Britain and consequently informed the scholarly culture in which the writings of antiquaries, such as Scott, emerged. Like deep mapping, chorography is a process of recognizing and reckoning the transhistorical character of a region as a landscape persisting through time – and therefore as one populated by markers and memories of the past that exert an abiding influence on perceptions of the character of that region in the present.[25] As Howard Marchitello has observed, chorography is a 'practice of delineating topography not exclusively as it exists in the present moment, but as it has existed historically'.[26] Thus, not unlike deep mapping, chorography is an analytical and descriptive process guided by an awareness of the interplay of past and present on the way in which a given location, locality, or region is perceived, experienced, and understood.

Accordingly, although deep mapping may be a practice aided by digital media, its methods and aspirations are broadly complementary with those of a much older scholarly tradition. This is something that one can clearly see in Scott's antiquarian and fictional works, which, as Michael Shanks has observed, resemble the chorographical research of contemporary antiquarians in the minute attention they devote to detailing 'names and lists, genealogies and toponymies' (*Archaeological Imagination*, 100). In our own time, this aspect of Scott's geographical procedures places him within a lineage of writers who are distinguished by the depth of their engagement with geographical practices. Critical discussions of this lineage have tended to define it as comprising the works of authors such as Iain Sinclair, Wallace Stegner, W. G. Sebald, and William Least Heat-Moon, whose works, though highly diverse, are nonetheless founded on a comparably granular and emphatically empirical understanding of place.

Though they represent an array of distinct perspectives and interests, these writers each promote narrative and storytelling as integral to the practice of deep mapping. They are not all, to be sure, equally self-reflexive about the theoretical implications of their practice. Collectively, however, they affirm the necessity of perceiving how the interweaving of the material and the discursive shapes our understanding of place. Underlying this affirmation is a conviction that the human experience of the physical world is fundamentally informed by the narratives we create about it. Hence, in the writings of Stegner, Least Heat-Moon, and others, various forms of storytelling are employed in tandem with more traditional forms of empirical research in order to trace the threads that weave the material and discursive dimensions of geography together. This kind of experimental practice finds a persuasive justification in much recent scholarship in cultural geography, especially in the non-representational theory of Nigel Thrift, the phenomenologically informed fieldwork of John Wiley, and the social and environmental anthropology of Tim Ingold. As Ingold in particular has insisted, when it comes to the study of geography, narrative is imperative. 'Telling a story', he contends, is 'not like unfurling a tapestry to *cover up* the world, it is rather a way of guiding the attentions of listeners or readers *into* it'.[27]

'A Guide Worth Ony Twa that May in Liddesdale Be Found'

Such a conception of the purpose of storytelling is one especially well-suited to Scott. As Stuart Kelly has recently noted, when Scott started writing poetry he did so not only by wringing stories from the names of specific locations but also by pinning his narratives to particular places. Many of Scott's poems, as Kelly avers, include lines that read like an itinerary or gazetteer.[28] Consider, for example, the lines detailing the aforementioned gallop to Stirling Castle from *The Lady of the Lake*:

> Along thy banks, swift Teith! they ride,
> And in the race they mock thy tide;
> Torry and Lendrick now are past,
> And Deanstown lies behind them cast;
> They rise, the bannered towers of Doune,
> They sink in distant woodland soon;
> Blair-Drummond sees the hoofs strike fire,
> They sweep like breeze through Ochtertyre.
> (V xviii; *Poetical Works*, VIII, 234)

This, to borrow Kelly's expression, is 'poetry as toponomy' ('Show Me the Way to Tillietudlem'). Torry and Lendrick, Deanstown and Doune, Blair-Drummond and Ochtertyre – these are actual places, and Scott made a point of emphasizing that fact by including references to each of them in his footnotes.

Scott's proclivity for amassing place names in his poems, of course, also drew the attention of his contemporaries. Not everyone was complimentary. Coleridge, for one, remarked derisively that 'when you strike out all of the interesting *names* of places' in Scott's poetry, 'you will find nothing left'.[29] The charge lodged here is plain enough: that the only thing poetic in Scott's poems are the intriguing place names they contain. This appraisal is amusing, but it does not quite do justice to the deeper, associative value that Scott frequently attributes to the places named in his poems. These place names, as we have seen, work metonymically to evoke specific historical, familial, or legendary associations. What is more, these named places often occur in sequences that help to establish specific geographical relationships that spread across the lines of verse with as much purpose as, if not more than, the lines which might be drawn to connect place names on a map. The places mentioned in Scott's poems are, in short, much more than 'interesting *names*'. Rather, as Tim Fulford has suggested, these named places enable Scott to situate the reader in the landscape of his poetry while simultaneously investing that landscape 'with a romanticised history'.[30] Scott's invocations of names; his attention to lines of sight and to auditory experience; and his use of syntax and versification to convey these experiences in his verse – these are not simply features informed by Scott's intimate knowledge of the geography of the Borders or his interest in local antiquities. They are also features that invite the reader to see the Border region in the embedded way one well-versed in its local history, lore, and topography might do.

Such an embedded perspective is an essential feature of the geographical knowledge presented in Scott's Border poems. As we saw at the outset of this chapter, Scott attributed his knowledge of the Border region not to maps or books but to the time he spent 'run[ning] about the fields' round Kelso in his youth. What I want to emphasize in conclusion, though, is the way Scott's sense of his 'merely practical' geographical understanding accords with what Tim Ingold has characterized as an inhabitant's point of view. As Ingold observes, 'a person who has grown up in a country and is conversant with its ways knows quite well where he is . . . without having to consult an artefactual map'.[31] Such a person, continues Ingold, 'may be unable to specify his location … in terms of any independent system of coordinates, and yet will still insist with good cause that he knows where he is' (219). 'This', Ingold concludes, 'is because', for such a person, 'places do not have locations but histories' (219). This conception of orienteering, with its appreciation of history qua narrative and personal experience, complements Scott's own sense of his relationship to the Borders. If, as Scott assured George Ellis, he could 'be a guide worth ony twa that may in Liddesdale be found', it was because of the deeply personal understanding of the region that he had cultivated as a young man. Like Kinmont Willie and Hobbie Noble before him, Scott's knowledge of the Borders was an intelligence rooted in a sensory awareness of the texture, character, and grain of the local terrain. If, in inviting the reader to share in this sensory awareness, Scott's writings can be seen to complement the aspirations of deep mapping, then his work as a poet and antiquarian reminds us of the influence that the culture of Romanticism has exerted on the geographical practices of our time.

Notes

1. Walter Scott, Letter to George Ellis, 30 January 1803, in *The Letters of Sir Walter Scott*, 12 vols., ed. H. J. C. Grierson (London: Constable & Co., 1832–6), I, 174.
2. See, for example, Penny Fielding, *Scotland and the Fictions of Geography* (Cambridge: Cambridge University Press, 2008); and Fiona Stafford, *Local Attachments* (Oxford: Oxford University Press, 2010), 135–75.
3. See Michael Shanks, *The Archaeological Imagination* (Abingdon: Routledge, 2016), 43–126.
4. In relation to the writing of this paper, I would like to thank Larry Scott and Tim Noakes of the Department of Special Collections, Stanford University. Thanks are also due to Dr James Butler (Lancaster University) and to Professor Carole Hough (Glasgow University, and PI of the REELS project). The research underpinning this chapter has been supported by the Leverhulme Trust under Research Project Grant RPG-2015–230.
5. J. G. Lockhart, *Memoirs of the Life of Sir Walter Scott*, 7 vols. (Edinburgh: Robert Cadell, 1837), I, 366.
6. Michael Shanks and Christopher Witmore, 'Echoes of the Past: Chorography and Topography in Antiquarian Engagements with Place', *Performance Research* 15 (2010): 97–106, 104.
7. Iain Biggs, 'The Spaces of "Deep Mapping": A Partial Account', *Journal of Arts and Communities* 2 (2011): 5–25.
8. Rosemary Sweet, *Antiquaries* (London: Hambledon and London, 2004), 22.
9. 'Lockhart's Life of Sir Walter Scott', *Tait's Edinburgh Magazine* 4 (1837), 205–20, 214.

10. John Sutherland, *The Life of Sir Walter Scott* (Oxford: Blackwell Publishers, 1995), 46.

11. Alain Corbin, *Village Bells*, trans. Martin Thom (London: Papermac, 1999), 97.

12. Walter Scott, *Minstrelsy of the Scottish Border*, 3 vols. (Kelso: James Ballantyne, 1802–1803), I, 185.

13. Walter Scott, *The Border Antiquities of England and Scotland*, 2 vols. (Longman & Co., 1814), I, lxix. On the institution of cornage, see *Britons, Saxons and Scandinavians: The Historical Geography of Glanville R. J. Jones*, eds. P. S. Barnwell and Brian K. Roberts (Turnhout: Brepols, 2011), 118–22.

14. Walter Scott, *The Lay of the Last Minstrel* (London: Longman & Co., 1805), 84, III. xxv and III. xxvi.

15. See Walter Scott, *The Poetical Works of Sir Walter Scott, Baronet*, 11 vols. (Edinburgh: Cadell & Co., 1830), I, xxii–viii; hereafter cited parenthetically as *Poetical Works*.

16. Walter Scott, 'Essay on Romance', *The Miscellaneous Prose Works of Sir Walter Scott, Bart* (Edinburgh: Robert Cadell, 1834–6), VI, 127–216, 136.

17. Francis Jeffrey, 'The Lay of the Last Minstrel: A Poem. By Walter Scott, Esquire', *The Edinburgh Review* 5 (1805): 1–20, 1.

18. Lucy McRae, 'Walter Scott's *Minstrelsy of the Scottish Border* and the Dynamics of Cultural Memory' (unpublished Ph.D. thesis, University of Edinburgh, 2014).

19. Lucy McRae, 'Local Explanations: Editing a Sense of Place in Walter Scott's *Minstrelsy of the Scottish Border*', *Forum* 3 (2014): 1–12, 2.

20. Les Roberts, 'Deep Mapping and Spatial Anthropology', *Deep Mapping*, ed. L Roberts (Basel: MDPI, 2016), vii–xv, xi.

21. Iain Biggs. '"Deep Mapping": A Brief Introduction', in *Mapping Spectral Traces*, ed. K. E. Till (Blacksburg: Virginia Tech College, 2010), 5–8, 2.

22. See, for example, Roberts, 'Deep Mapping', xi.

23. Trevor M. Harris, John Corrigan, and David J. Bodenhamer, 'Conclusion: Engaging Deep Maps', *Deep Maps and Spatial Narratives*, eds. D. J. Bodenhamer, J. Corrigan, and T. M. Harris (Bloomington: Indiana University Press, 2015), 223–33, 232.

24. Mike Pearson and Michael Shanks, *Theatre/Archaeology* (London: Routledge, 2001), 64–5.

25. See Darrell J. Rohl, 'The Chorographical Tradition and Seventeenth- and Eighteenth-Century Scottish Antiquaries', *Journal of Art Historiography* 5 (2011): 1–18.

26. Howard Marchitello, *Narrative and Meaning in Early Modern England* (Cambridge: Cambridge University Press, 1997), 78.

27. Tim Ingold, 'The Temporality of Landscape', *World Archaeology* 25 (1993): 152–74, 153.

28. Stuart Kelly, 'Show Me the Way to Tillietudlem', *Five Imaginary Scottish Places*, BBC Radio 3 (1 June 2015), www.bbc.co.uk/programmes/b05wytj9 (accessed 31 July 2017).

29. S. T. Coleridge to Henry Crabb Robinson (20 October 1811) in *Selections from the Remains of Henry Crabb Robinson*, ed. E. J. Morley (Manchester: Manchester University Press, 1922), 44.

30. Tim Fulford, *The Late Poetry of the Lake Poets* (Cambridge: Cambridge University Press, 2013), 142.

31. Tim Ingold, *The Perception of the Environment* (London: Routledge, 2000), 219.

CHAPTER 10

Unmapping John Clare
Circularity, Linearity, Temporality

Sally Bushell

It isn't on the map because it's not there; but if you go there, it *is* there and you get a sense of a piece of geography that exists in a world that isn't real and isn't deep topography but it is floating because it's in the mind, it's in the memory, it's in the imagination and it haunts that part of the world.

'Walking, Witnessing, Mapping: An Interview with Iain Sinclair'[1]

What does it mean to 'map' literature critically or creatively from a twenty-first century perspective, and how might we best go about doing so in the light of the new interdisciplinary paradigms for cartography? These are the broader questions underpinning the chapter. In the first half I will be responding to the spatiality of the Late Romantic poet John Clare, indirectly through three readings of his work, with each successive response building on the previous one and each strongly spatial in nature, generating its own maps as part of the argument being made. However, it should be understood that I am not interested in critiquing past models so much as in tracing a developing history of critical and creative remapping of John Clare through key interventions: the anticipatory work of John Barrell in *The Idea of Landscape and the Sense of Place*; the adoption of Barrell's maps by Franco Moretti in *Graphs, Maps, Trees*; and the creative appropriation of Clare by Iain Sinclair. The second half of the chapter will then turn from geography to history in an attempt to 'unmap' Clare, or at least to spatialize Clare anew, by privileging *chronos* over *topos*. It adapts Pierre Nora's concept of *lieux de mémoire* to break free from the dominant circular/linear model in order to articulate a new way of reading Clare's poetry and prose.

The first half of the essay implicitly draws on the practices of critical cartography and applies them *back* onto the literary discipline from which they originated to read *critical* interpretations partly through the acts of mapping they employ. This approach, introduced by J. B. Harley and then developed by others (Mark Monmonier, Denis Wood, Denis Cosgrove) builds upon the work of Roland Barthes and Michel Foucault to understand the map as an object wielding visible and invisible power and capable of being read in ways that language can be read; indeed, this is what allows the application of a 'deconstructive' approach. If we accept the findings of this approach in relation to real-world maps and the field of cartography, then we also need to realize that they can rebound back onto literary studies in relation to analysis of forms of literary and literary-critical mapping.

Mapping Clare: Barrell and Moretti

Let's go back, then, to 1972 and John Barrell's critically canonical chapter on Clare in *The Idea of Landscape and the Sense of Place*. Barrell begins by evidencing the argument that there was a unique practice of open-field farming in only a few areas of the country, of which Clare's village was one. He argues for 'a characteristically open-field sense of space' and that 'the characteristic sense of space which the topography and organization of an open-field parish created was circular, while the landscape of parliamentary enclosure expressed a more linear sense'.[2] In this account, poetry becomes almost a direct expression of place ingrained in, and flowing through, the native inhabitant.

Barrell's method itself might be visualized as concentric. He begins with underlying geological patterns and works inward to historical and agricultural practices generated from that pattern in the soil, then to the shaping of human habitation and lives, and finally to Clare – to his poetry, his language, his syntax. In so doing, Barrell is making the ultimate literary-geographical argument – one of perfect integrity between land and man:

> It is a body of knowledge, a set of details, that Clare has arrived at in this particular place, and not elsewhere. The content of the poem thus becomes the sense of place that the imagery and the language (and I shall argue later the syntax) together express. (131)

Barrell then reads this *particularity of place* off against other established eighteenth-century models (James Thomson, William Cowper) and establishes Clare as having his own distinctive counter-aesthetics, 'not so much of a continuum of successive impressions as of one complex manifold of simultaneous impressions' (157).

Early on in his analysis, Barrell provides two maps of Helpston (Clare's village), as part of his historical introduction, ostensibly to illustrate the effects of enclosure upon the village (see Figures 10.1 and 10.2). The maps

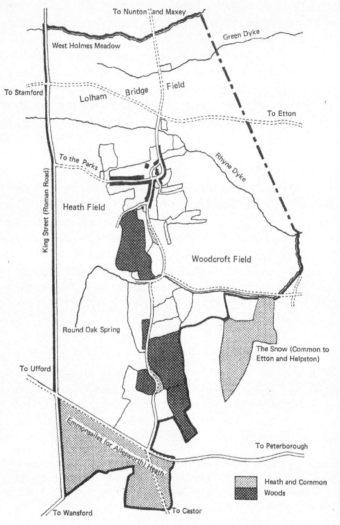

Map 1. A sketch map of the parish of Helpston in 1809, before the enclosure
(approximate scale: 1 mile = 2¼ in.). The irregularly-shaped patches of land
around the village itself, and on either side of the road to Castor, are old enclosures; the rest of the unshaded area within the parish boundary is open-field
arable, with some meadow-land. It is impossible to fix precisely the boundary
of the parish in its north-east corner: it picked its way between the furlongs in
Lolham Bridge Field and in Etton fields (see note 7, page 225).

Figure 10.1 *Helpston Pre-Enclosure* (1809). John Barrell, *The Idea of Landscape and
the Sense of Place, 1730–1840* (Cambridge: Cambridge University Press, 1972), 103. By
kind permission of John Barrell and Cambridge University Press.

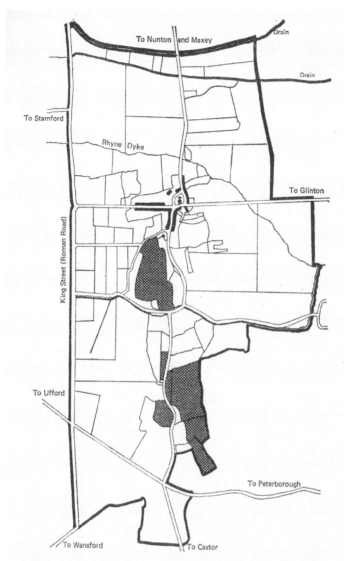

Map 2. A sketch map of the parish of Helpston in 1820, after the enclosure (approximate scale: 1 mile = 2¼ in.). The shaded area is woodland; the unshaded area within the parish is divided into more or less rectangular fields, which would in turn have been sub-divided by their various proprietors (see note 28, page 227).

Figure 10.2 *Helpston Post-Enclosure* (1820). John Barrell, *The Idea of Landscape and the Sense of Place, 1730–1840* (Cambridge: Cambridge University Press, 1972), 107. By kind permission of John Barrell and Cambridge University Press.

are given to an 'approximate scale: 1 mile = 2 ½ inches' (102), and, being the rigorous scholar that he is, Barrell provides a lengthy note explaining that the first map is a composite from various sources.[3] The maps, in other words, are expository: they exist alongside the text to convey the argument more effectively than words alone can do.

At the same time, however, critical cartography makes us all too aware that no map is objective, even if we respond to it as if it is. Mark Monmonier, in *Mapping It Out* (a book intended to encourage those in the humanities to adopt maps and other spatial approaches in their work), discusses the nature and purpose of the expository map. In considering the power of such a map and what it 'adds' to a text, Monmonier states, 'By organizing information chronologically as well as spatially, maps can support a variety of historical narratives address-ing long or short periods of time.'[4] Noting the importance of color, font, and symbol, Monmonier states that 'if location is at all a factor, the map provides a useful structure for allowing isolated facts to form a pattern, either among themselves or in relation to other geographic features' (18).

Barrell's maps work as a pair. In each case the eye is drawn to the darker colours of the boundary roads and the areas immediately round the village, with the symbol of the church at its literal centre. The maps beg to be compared, and, when we do so, we see that the second map formalizes the more innate lines of the first, reinforcing Barrell's argument about the linearity of enclosure, with the roads forming major transverse lines cutting across and down the landscape (as opposed to the informality of the footpath). Of course the major visual difference between them is the interior division of the three large fields, created by the physical imposition of enclosure laws, into 'little parcels' ('Enclosure', line 43) of land in Figure 10.2, as opposed to the circularity of open-field farming in the first map (as well as the loss of common ground). The maps do also display some sleights of hand, however. The use of dotted lines for key routes in Figure 10.1 (as opposed to solid lines in Figure 10.2) encourages us to see the three fields as larger and more open masses than they are (after all, the roads remain in the same location on both maps). Also, although the maps are to act as mirrors to each other, and the boundary outlines are the same size, the representation of the immediate vicinity around the village (which is unchanged) is smaller on the later map in Figure 10.2 than in the earlier in Figure 10.1. This subtly reinforces the idea that the village is central to community life *before* enclosure – a controlling hub – but radically dimin-ished *afterwards*.

As this suggests, Barrell's maps powerfully visualize an historical 'before' and 'after' and so symbolize a spatial reshaping of this world that has significant implications for the poet growing up there:

> As long as he was in Helpston, the knowledge he had was valid, was knowledge: the east was east and the west west as long as he could recognise them by the landmarks in the parish, . . . [But] when the old landscape was destroyed a part of Clare's knowledge was destroyed also. (121–2)

Precisely *because* of their ability to visualize this change so directly, these two maps have acquired a meaning beyond themselves in terms of their literary-critical influence, coming both to shape and to stand for dominant critical readings of Clare himself: the *poet* of before and after; sane and mad; located and lost.

It is easy to move across from Barrell to Franco Moretti, since the latter reproduces the same two maps of Helpston in his second book, *Graphs, Maps, Trees* (2005). The central section of the book in which they appear is that dedicated to 'Maps' and focused upon answering core questions for Moretti's new methodology in relation to literary maps: 'Do maps *add* anything to our knowledge of literature?' and 'What exactly do they *do?*'.[5] To offer a succinct account of the power of his form of literary mapping, Moretti contrasts the same two spatial forms that Barrell had focused on – the circular and the linear – to consider their implications for the interpretation of spatial meaning in literary works. Centring his discussion on Mary Mitford's fictional series *Our Village*, he draws attention to the foregrounding of the road in her narrative but does so in order to reveal that 'then you make a map of the book, and everything changes' (36). He explains that 'the road "from B— to S—", so present at the beginning of the book, has disappeared: narrative space is not linear here, it is *circular*' (37). This opening discussion then leads Moretti into Barrell's account of two geographic systems and the historical change to rural practices (and thus way of life) that are 'so well visualized in his two maps of Helpston' (38).

Where Barrell's use of maps was secondary to his literary-geographical argument, for Moretti maps illuminate spatial meanings in a way not otherwise possible. Thus, there is a sense in which the map triumphs (and must triumph) over the text. He reproduces Barrell's pre- and post-enclosure maps in order to contrast them with Mitford's *Our Village* volumes, which, he points out, reverse the historical trend that Barrell outlines, shifting from a linear to a circular model. This ultimately leads Moretti into perhaps the most important point that he makes in the chapter: that literary maps are fundamentally different from real-world geographic maps in terms of what they need to do. For literary mapping what is of most interest is the *relations between things* rather than their absolute or accurate location. Moretti concludes: 'Diagram: Cartesian space. But diagram of *forces*' (57). In other words, crucial elements of event, narrative, character and dialogue occur between points on the literary map, and those relations are not static and fixed but powerfully dynamic.

Most striking in Moretti's appropriation of Barrell's maps is the lack of any mention of John Clare himself or of the literary-critical purpose of the maps as originally produced. In other words, the maps cease to be expository or to be integrated with a literary-critical argument. They are used purely in terms of the larger historical/social and ultimately spatial shift they record and not at all in relation to the integrated model of landscape, person, and language that Barrell so painstakingly built around them. Rather, it is as if Moretti introduces them only to assert his alternative method of mapping, over and above the earlier model of literary geography that Barrell exemplifies. This highlights both the strength and weakness of Moretti's mapping strategies in relation to literary works: he convincingly asserts the dramatic power of the maps; but he also largely separates map representations from detailed integration with (or analysis of) the texts that generated them. Moretti is able to do this because of the double identity of every map (even the literary-critical) in having both a denotative and connotative meaning. Moretti hijacks Barrell's maps to draw upon their authority within the discipline, their iconic status for literary-geography, but repurposes their original meaning.

Remapping Clare: Iain Sinclair

If critical cartography has potential in relation to literary studies (not least because it already shares a theoretical underpinning with the humanities), literary studies also has much to offer critical cartography. It contains the potential for counter-mapping and unmapping by writers, characters, and readers, as space and place are distorted by subjectivity or real topographies are overlain or displaced by imaginary spaces. Iain Sinclair's work provides a good example of this. Published in the same year as Moretti's book, but undertaking a very different form of literary mapping, is his *Edge of the Orison* (2005). This work of British psychogeography involves a remapping of Clare's escape from the asylum in Epping Forest, as the subtitle makes clear (*In the Traces of John Clare's 'Journey out of Essex')*.[6] Sinclair seeks to apply his own larger method of ambulatory mapping – which has as much in common with contemporary artists such as Richard Long and Hamish Fulton or with cultural geographers as it does with literary criticism – to this particular route out of London.

In an interview with David Cooper and Les Roberts, Sinclair refers back to a map made for his own earlier work *Lud Heat* ('supposedly the book in which I discover my own method') and states:

> All of these things go into a map in a way that it wouldn't be allowed to be if I was actually a topographer, really doing a proper map. It's much more like those medieval maps you see where the things that are important are drawn large. ('Walking, Witnessing, Mapping', 85)

This literary topography has its own distinct identity: subjectively generated, qualitative, but also about the relationships – the forces – between points on the map in a way that echoes Moretti.

Sinclair's inherent interest in embodied creative acts of mapping draws him to Clare but not to the mapping of Helpston (the centre). Rather, he focuses on the terminal act of Clare finding his way back home by heading north out of his London asylum. Sinclair's method, as with *Lud Heat*, involves the transposition of one pattern, one geometry of meaning, onto another, in a model of layers that ultimately asserts the 'floating' spatiality of imagined or remembered space over the actual.

Like Barrell, Sinclair plays off circular and linear models of meaning, but for him the focus is on Clare the walker, his 'circle of memory. Eight-mile walks (from his Helpston cottage) that defined his heart-place and sense of identity' (20) and 'the circle of the landscape in which he had once been anchored' (120). Later when arriving himself in the nearby village of Glinton, which Clare associated with his lost/never love Mary Joyce, Sinclair describes how 'Glinton spire serves a double function. It reminds us of Clare and it reminds us that, as a fixed point on a flat plain, it helped him to organise the circuit of memory: a needle in the compass rose of childhood's mapping' (46). Against this, the linear walk home is his last true walk, 'a fugue of forgetting' (212), as 'he travelled towards the thing that troubled him most: memory' (124).

Once again, two maps are given, at the front and back of Sinclair's book. These present a linear and circular juxtaposition but with a different emphasis from those of Barrell. The map at the front, presenting the routes of 'John Clare' (1841) and 'his pursuers' (2000), has the dotted and plain lines of the two journeys up out of London intertwining and winding around each other. The second map, at the back of the book, entitled 'Edge of the Orison: Peterborough's gravitational field', presents the town in its modern location surrounded by roads and with Helpston off to the north. What are these maps doing? The first map functions almost as a visualization of method, not only in the denotative ambulatory sense (the two routes with 159 years between them that form the spine of the work) but also symbolically, since the walk is the means of Sinclair re-engaging with his wife's own past and search for origins, and this personal narrative is then bound up with that of Clare's hopeless search for his non-existent love. However, since Sinclair explicitly references Barrell on more than one occasion (18, 42), we can certainly also read the linearity of the front map as a kind of challenge to Barrell's account and one that, in an analogous though distinctive way, defines and determines the entire enterprise. In fact, if Barrell was all about the 'before' – explicitly stating that his focus on landscape means he can rest with his 'preference for the earlier poems' (180) – Sinclair is far more about the 'after' – just as Sinclair also offers prose, not poetry; the late poet, not the early – in order to open up his own discrete space for creative-critical appreciation.

Sinclair's second map ostensibly relates to Clare and the limits of his world. Sinclair tells us: 'He pushed his circuits wider – heath, woods, road – until he found himself caught in the coils of Peterborough' (276). But it also functions to connect past and present – 'Peterborough confounds us, as it confounded Clare' (275) – and implicitly works to contextualize the project in terms of Sinclair's own larger body of work. The gravitational field of Peterborough functions as a smaller, regional version of the M25 famously walked by Sinclair in *London Orbital*: 'Peterborough is like a dying star, dragging in debris from the surrounding countryside, swallowing villages and villagers.'[7] As in *London Orbital*, the road is a barrier and the antithesis of what is being attempted – the anti-walk – but it also contains the means of release into an alternative state of being: 'As with any orbital loop, the easy option is to keep going, round and round Peterborough, into highway reverie' (302).

Reflecting upon the three spatial models considered in this chapter, we can see that all three arguments have at their core a dynamic interaction between circularity and linearity and that the later two readings play off the earlier one. Barrell's work offers the most traditional form of literary criticism, but his use of dramatically contrasting maps to help make his case is unusual, and thus he stands as an early, iconic example of effective literary mapping, which makes him attractive to Moretti. Moretti abstracts both the maps and the spatial model from their literary-critical anchors in order to juxtapose the two spatial forms to privilege map over text. Sinclair at first sight seems to privilege the linear over the circular. *The Edge of the Orison* is itself initially visualized as a horizontal image, with Clare heading in a straight line towards the edge (fearful of falling off 'the brink of the world').[8] Actually, however, Sinclair's dominant spatiality for Clare is best conceived of as a kind of bubble on the earth, a circular perimeter of deliberate self-containment that represents the limit-point for multiple, repeated, eight-mile walks taken in any direction from the centre. Not only that, but we see that the same spatial model is right at the heart of Sinclair's own larger map of his lifelong walk-work. In an interview at the Victoria and Albert Museum, recorded by the Literary London Society, he states:

> So for a lot of reasons I really felt, for years, that I wanted to do that walk, Clare's Walk through Epping Forest, back up to Glinton. And the perfect moment obviously came at the end of this M25 tour, which was not resolved, it was a kind of circuit that went nowhere, there was no way out of it – so to break away from London was to follow Clare.[9]

Clare's escape is also Sinclair's.

Unmapping Clare

In the first half of this chapter I have deliberately read Clare *in* and *through* others in order to generate a multilayered response that highlights the range of spatial forms of interpretation embraced by literary studies while also critically interpreting both maps and texts used in those arguments. In the second half, I want to 'unmap' Clare by prioritizing time over space, drawing upon a concept articulated by French historian Pierre Nora – that of *lieux de mémoire* (sites/realms of memory). What I am trying to do here is to employ a temporal model that is also spatial to offer an alternative conceptualization to the linear/circular one that has dominated thus far. I want to come at place through the memory that it embodies. Such an approach chimes with that called for by Simon Kövesi, in the final chapter of *John Clare and Place* – referenced by David Cooper in the next chapter of this volume.[10] Kövesi considers emerging and future ways of remapping Clare – including Sinclair's 'psychomaps' (217) – and looks to new, more creative modes for contextualizing and historicizing his work in ways that chime with my attempt to do so here.

In terms of his own discipline (history), Pierra Nora is an iconoclast who seeks to find a new way of conceiving of the historical that is not predetermined by either a Marxist ideology or a traditional account of history as narrative and event. His orchestration of a multi-volume engagement with sites of memory (*lieux de mémoire*) provides an alternative means of organizing and analysing the past through its own historiography. He offers the following definitions of his influential cultural concept:

> Our interest in *lieux de mémoire* where memory crystallizes and secretes itself has occurred at a particular historical moment, a turning point where consciousness of a break with the past is bound up with the sense that memory has been torn – but torn in such a way as to pose the problem of the embodiment of memory in certain sites where a sense of historical continuity persists.
> There are *lieux de mémoire*, sites of memory, because there are no longer *milieux de mémoire*, real environments of memory.[11]

The concept is quite contradictory and difficult to grasp. In spite of his entire enterprise being centred upon gathering and describing these places as the last haunts of 'true' memory and the last line of resistance to history, Nora views them ultimately as the product of a *failing* society – one so obsessed with historiography that it tries to record and archive everything. Such a society can *only* respond to history-as-memory through these formalized monuments because it has already lost what was most valuable to it: its collective memory. He therefore describes the *lieux* as

> fundamentally remains, the ultimate embodiments of a memorial consciousness that has barely survived in a historical age that calls out for memory because it has abandoned it. (12)

Memory, as a central part of our way of life, is dead, so the *lieux* can only ever stand in for this. Nevertheless, they remain the *only* way in which history continues to be challenged. Nora waxes lyrical when he describes them as

> moments of history torn away from the movement of history, then returned; no longer quite life, not yet death, like shells on the shore when the sea of living memory has receded. (12)

I want to experiment here by taking Nora's model of the loss of shared, lived history and its memorialization in fixed sites and applying it to Clare. This will enable a move from a focus on the predominantly spatial to the spatio-temporal as well as allowing us to consider how adaptable a model of 'memory-history' ('Between Memory and History', 24) might be to a model of 'memory-literature'. The first crucial question to be asked, then, is whether the concept of *lieux de mémoire* only works at the macro level or whether it can be localized in an individual.[12]

At the heart of Nora's account of history is the concept of 'rupture', since he focuses on moments of major change in the relationship between the past and the present that require a re-conceiving of how we 'do' history and that are then embodied in the *lieux*. When we turn back to Clare, we can see that such a model has a natural affinity with his life and work (the two being bound closely together) because both of these are also subject to such a 'rupture' – the 'before' and 'after' that Barrell's maps so powerfully represent and symbolize. Thus, we can return to familiar territory in a new way. But is there one spatio-temporal rupture or many? When the model is personalized, as well as external historical events there is also the individual's response to those events and their effect on personal history. We might say that, for Clare, the first rupture (caused by enclosure) is externally generated, historically occurring during Clare's growth into manhood; the second rupture is both external and internal, as his physical relocation from Helpston to Northborough activates a sense of self-alienation; the third is an entirely interiorized rending of the self that results in mental destabilization (and then incarceration).

If we were to articulate a dominant chronotope (spatio-temporal form) emerging from the critical and creative mappings here considered, we might do so by combining Barrell's sense of Clare as inherently 'local' with Sinclair's emphasis on loss.[13] The base temporality uniting much of Clare's work is that of a unique moment in time and space that either is about to be or already is lost in the real world. This personal chronotope could be compared to the Greek epic theme of *nostos* (homecoming after the Trojan wars) and the powerful feelings bound up with it that are directed towards a place that may or may not still exist (or, for Clare, one to which he can no longer return). Sinclair puts it well when he states:

> Clare is nostalgic about nostalgia, the old wound, the site from which he has been expelled – but where he still lives. Lost muse, (two miles down the road in Glinton). Lost childhood (always present but out of reach). (*Edge*, 44)

If we compare this dominant chronotope to the account of *lieux de mémoire* already described, then we see that *nostos* is also generated by rupture and works as a bridge attempting to reconnect past and present both spatially and temporally. (This is true even for Odysseus, for whom *nostos* acts as both a motivational force, keeping him going through multiple adversities and diversions, and a spatial pull, linking the present self to a past that still exists in space, though it may not in time.) However, *nostos* is informed by both hope and fear, for the Greek hero. With each expression of anxiety about achieving a safe return, that return comes closer. For Clare there can be no such hope, only an increasing move away from actual place and into the memory of it. As quoted already in this chapter, Nora claims: 'There are *lieux de mémoire*, sites of memory, because there are no longer *milieux de mémoire*, real environments of memory' ('Between Memory and History', 7). This is again remarkably relevant to Clare's 'before' and 'after', understood primarily in terms of time rather than space; his personal *lieux* are the last remnants of a way of life that is no longer possible. As Clare's actual 'environment of memory' is destroyed, so he displaces into personal *lieux* where 'memory crystallizes and secretes itself' ('Between Memory and History', 7). 'Swordy Well', 'Langley Bush', even Mary Joyce herself – all are particular sites within that earlier idealized landscape of mind and place that now are *only* held in the mind. For Clare, the 'environment of memory' is not shared, however, or at least not with other humans. He is bewailing not the loss of culture held in memory by a minority group (the peasantry), exactly, as Nora might want him to, but the loss of a place that enabled a certain kind of existence for him within it. As such, he becomes highly representative of the darker side of Romanticism: the celebratory loss of self in and through nature becomes destructive when the internal map no longer has correspondence with the external.

I want to consider the poem 'Remembrances' in the light of this model of personalized temporality. Written after the second major rupture for Clare (the move from Helpston to Northborough), 'Remembrances' sets up a seasonal, temporal, and personal change that cannot be overcome:

> Summer pleasures they are gone like to visions every one
> & the cloudy days of autumn & of winter cometh on.
> I tried to call them back but unbidden they are gone.
>
> (lines 1–3)[14]

The long lines of the poem lend themselves to a mid-line caesura that enhances the dual temporalities present within many of them. This is made explicit in the third line with an explicit attempt to bridge the gap: 'I tried to call them back [/] but unbidden they are gone'. The poet recalls his own earlier self inhabiting the alternative temporality of childhood:

> I thought them all eternal when by Langley bush I lay
> I thought them joys eternal when I used to shout & play.
>
> (lines 6–7)

As the poem unfolds it begins to map out the various 'spots' around Helpston that Clare also describes as being of value to him in his 'Autobiographical Fragments':

> I used to be fondly attachd to spots about the fields and there were 3 or 4 were I used to go to visit on Sundays . . . One of these was under an old Ivied Oak in Oxey wood . . . Two others were under a broad oak in a field called the Barrows and Langley Bush and all my favourite places have met with misfortunes. . . . Lee Close Oak was cut down in the inclosure and Langley bush was broken up by some wanton fellows while kidding furze on the heath. (41–2)

Inevitably the poem alternates between 'then' and 'now', the endless time of childhood and the retrospective loss of the poet in the present:

> By Langley bush I roam, but the bush hath left its hill,
> On cowper green I stray tis a desert strange & chill.   (lines 61–2)

My interest here, however, is not in Clare's attribution of loss to Enclosure that 'like a Buonaparte let not a thing remain' (line 67) – the poem of second rupture thus incorporating the first – but in his naming of local sites as an act of poetic mapping, a listing of his personal *lieux de mémoire* as a desperate attempt to externalize them and so somehow give them a life outside himself. For Clare, the map is always at the largest possible scale, involving the location of these naturalized monuments to his own past self, or what he calls 'the parted places' (*AF*, 161) – particular bushes, trees or brooks.[15] In the course of the poem he lists:

> by Langley bush I lay (line 6)
> by old east wells boiling spring (line 11)
> beneath old lea close oak (15)
> on old cross berry way (line 21)
> on the rolly polly up & downs of pleasant swordy well (line 24)
> in round oaks narrow lane (line 25)
> o'er 'little field' (line 31)

Each particular place is also tied to his own life narrative and small events recalled by him, as the full lines reveal:

> where I used to lie & sing by old east wells boiling spring (line 11)
> when beneath old lea close oak I the bottom branches broke (line 15)
> when jumping time away on old cross berry way (line 21)

Here, it is as if Clare externalizes his own cognitive map of place *through* his poetry. If one were to try and map Clare truly, then, it would require a different form of mapping from any of those so far created for him: a spatial form generated from the internal cognitive map, not imposed from outside – nor even really determined by road and field boundaries. These exist in the world in one way but are also held internally within Clare as a living repository of spatial memory and something stronger – since they enable him not just to map the landscape but also to situate and know himself within it. As place is destroyed, the anchor is loosed, and John Clare drifts away. He is the keeper of those places, until the loss of that map (or the discrepancy between internal map and external place) undoes him, and then his poems become the substitute spaces where all that is left of them, or him, survive.

I stated earlier that there are three moments of rupture that cause Clare to memorialize place in his poetry, but underlying all of these there must be a prior state away from which such rupture occurs – 'true memory' in Nora's terms ('Between Memory and History', 13). In 'Autobiographical Fragments' Clare admits that 'I am foolish enough to have fancys different from others and childhood is a strong spell over my feelings' (69). This 'strong spell' seems to relate to a privileging of the kind of being in the world that the state of childhood offers, which for Clare is poetic in itself:

> There is nothing but poetry about the existance [sic] of childhood real simple soul moving poetry the laughter and joy of poetry and not its philosophy and there is nothing of poetry about manhood but the reflection and the remembrance of what has been … nothing more. (*AF*, 37)

The temporality of childhood is a state of eternal 'nowness' as opposed to one of increasing retrospect – the 'nothing but' of the child falls away into a 'nothing of' for the adult. Clare's spots have much in common with Wordsworth's in this way, being held in a kind of suspended time but also moving increasingly out of reach:

> The hiding-places of my power
> Seem open, I approach, and then they close
> I see by glimpses now, when age comes on
> May scarcely see at all.[16]

However, whereas Wordsworth is content to privilege these internal spots – their imaginative force triumphing over their origins in the world and providing an ongoing source of power within – for Clare their survival *only* within his memory becomes an unbearable burden.[17]

There is a much-quoted section of 'Autobiographical Fragments' in which Clare provides an image of himself straying 'out of my knowledge'

(121). This passage provides both Sinclair with his book title and Barrell with his core argument for locality:

> I had imagind that the worlds end was at the edge of the orison and that a days journey was able to find it . . . so I went on with my heart full of hopes pleasures and discoverys expecting when I got to the brink of the world that I could look down like looking into a large pit and see into its secrets the same as I believd I could see heaven by looking into the water . . . so I eagerly wanderd on . . . till I got out of my knowledge when the very wild flowers and birds seemd to forget me and I imagind they were the inhabitants of new countrys . . . The very sun seemed to be a new one and shining in a different quarter of the sky . . . Still I felt no fear . . . My wonder seeking happiness had no room for it . . . I was finding new wonders every minute and was walking in a new world often wondering to my self that I had not found the end of the old one. (*AF,* 40–1)

However, neither Barrell nor Sinclair, when discussing it, reproduce the *later* part of the description, in which it emerges that this experience is *in no way negative* for the child. Where, for the adult Clare, 'getting out of his knowledge' is distressing to the point of mental collapse, the child 'feels no fear' because he is protected by 'wonder'.[18] Rather, Clare articulates a state of open receptivity – 'finding new wonders every minute' – that relates to a particular temporality *only* able to be unselfconsciously experienced in childhood (the perpetual 'now').

If we return to 'Journey out of Essex' we can see that this distressing episode, too, is bound up with the same idealized temporality for Clare. Clare's account of Mary Joyce as given in 'Autobiographical Fragments' makes clear that the boyhood relationship was both 'romantic or platonic' – Clare describes his feelings as a 'smotherd passion' (87) – and invested with a kind of eternality: 'As the dream never awoke into reality her beauty was always fresh in my memory . . . She is still unmarried' (87). Mary then exists as a human embodiment of the same chronotope that informs the precious topographical sites of childhood. In any personalized map of *lieux de mémoire* we might expect 'home' to lie at the centre, and this is also the concept that most lends itself to embodiment in person rather than place (e.g. the mother often existing as 'home' for the child). In 'Journey out of Essex', however, the journey could only ever end happily if Clare were able to travel backward not only in place but also in time – which is what he is trying to do. Without this, the only possible conclusion is the resulting spatio-temporal anomaly of being 'homeless at home' – in place, but out of time (and so not able to connect with the person who embodies home for him). Home and hope are bound together, pulling the poet forward (*nostos*) but negating each other in the end: 'I soon began to feel homeless at home and shall bye and bye feel nearly hopeless' (265). From this perspective, 'Journey out of Essex' almost becomes readable as a kind of tragic mock-epic. Ironically Clare's is a kind of inverted *nostos* in which he can only exist truly in that place, but the place itself is increasingly out of time.

Conclusions

I want to conclude by reflecting on the two approaches adopted in the first and second halves of this chapter. If we do this, we can see that Nora's model for history could be compared to that of critical cartography; in fact, one could almost call it 'Critical Historiography'.[19] At its most extreme, Nora claims that the study of history does not represent the past so much as supplant it: 'History's goal and ambition is not to exalt but to annihilate what has in reality taken place' ('Between Memory and History', 9). In other words, it finds a new way of reading, even of conceiving of the discipline, by challenging the authority of the positivist model that brought it into being. Thus, the claim to absolute authority is not only misguided but actively destructive of a hidden counter-model. This sense of a 'public face', behind which lies something more authentic and true, also informs critical cartography (for which what is *not* on the map becomes as important as what is).

Where does this leave us once we reapply such models to literary texts? Clare's poetic places do map onto Nora's *lieux*, but they embody a purely personal and individualized sense of history that is not capable of (and would be destroyed by) any actual formal monument substituting for what they represent. Instead, once the sites are no longer there, the *poems themselves* have to become the *lieux de mémoire* – less than what they stand for ('the real simple soul moving poetry of childhood') but better than nothing in a future-world that is out of tune with its own past. The attempt to represent such a place is itself paradoxical, since it becomes the *only* possible way of partially recovering such moments, but it does so knowing that it can never fully do so. Right at the heart of Clare's poetics is a rupture of representation that is always present for poetry – the impossibility of ever being able to capture the moment – because the act of desiring to capture it distorts it, and because 'words are poor receipts for what time hath stole away' ('Remembrances', 131, line 29). Only the time before time can ever be fully free. Perhaps this is what characterizes a literary *lieu de mémoire* rather than an historical one – an utterance that knows it is always at one stage removed from itself, in a disjuncture that can never be overcome.

Can literature succeed, then, where history fails?[20] Is a single text a *lieu de mémoire* in the same way as – say – a major dictionary, a library, or an archive? Or does it actually offer something different? Is it more of a bridge between living memory and an unrecoverable past? I would suggest that poems can function in the way that other memorials might – as crystallizations of a moment of historical shift – and also that, because they are only held in language, they bear an affective power that can allow the reader to understand place anew through the eyes of another. In other words, life *can* be breathed back into memory after all – but through a different *kind* of collective cultural memory, one that literature offers and language enables. After all, isn't that what poetry is all about? Clare seemed to think so:

> The stuff which true poesy is made of is little else . . . It is the eccho [of] what has been or may be . . . When the reader peruses real poesy he often whispers to [himself] 'bless me Ive felt this myself and often had such thoughts in my memory' though he was ignorant of poetry. (*AF*, 9)

Notes

1. David Cooper and Les Roberts, 'Walking, Witnessing, Mapping: An Interview with Iain Sinclair', in *Mapping Cultures: Place, Practice, Performance*, ed. Les Roberts (London: Palgrave Macmillan, 2012), 85–100, 13–14.
2. John Barrell, *The Idea of Landscape and the Sense of Place, 1730–1840* (Cambridge: Cambridge University Press, 1972), 103.
3. See Barrell's notes in *The Idea of Landscape and the Sense of Place*, n.7 on 225 and n.28 on 227. He draws mainly upon two historical maps of 1772 and 1779 for the first map. The second is based on the Award map for enclosure (NRO Map 1089). See also Sinclair's conversation with poet Tom Raworth and Sinclair's description of Barrell as 'pouring [sic] over enclosure maps for Helpston': *Edge of the Orison: In the Traces of John Clare's 'Journey out of Essex'* (London: Hamish Hamilton, 2005), 42.
4. Mark Monmonier, *Mapping It Out: Expository Cartography for the Humanities and Social Sciences* (Chicago, IL: University of Chicago Press, 1993), 204.
5. Franco Moretti, *Graphs, Maps, Trees: Abstract Models for a Literary History* (London: Verso, 2005), 35.
6. Sinclair, *Edge of the Orison*. Sinclair is not the first to do this; see the poet Ronald Blythe's reconstruction of the route as described in 'Solvitur Ambulando: John Clare and Footpath Walking', *John Clare Society Journal* 14 (1995): 17–27, 87–8.
7. Iain Sinclair, *London Orbital* (London: Penguin, 2003), 275.

8. John Clare, 'Autobiographical Fragments', in *John Clare By Himself*, eds. Eric Robinson and David Powell (Manchester: Carcanet, 1996), 40–1; hereafter *AF*.

9. Steven Barfield, ed., 'Psychogeography: Will Self and Iain Sinclair in Conversation with Kevin Jackson', *Literary London: Interdisciplinary Studies in the Representation of London* 6:1 (2008): 1–41, 13.

10. Simon Kövesi, 'Conclusion: Clare as Our Contemporary; Clare as History', in *John Clare: Nature, Criticism and History* (London: Palgrave Macmillan, 2017), 215–37.

11. Pierre Nora, 'Between Memory and History: *Les Lieux de Memoire*', *Representations* 26 (Spring 1989): 7–24, 7.

12. Nora does allow that an individual can himself become a *lieu*. He describes Michelet (the great nineteenth-century French historian) as 'a remarkable *lieu de mémoire* unto himself'; see *Rethinking France: Les Lieux de Mémoires, Vol. 4: Histories and Memories*, ed. Pierre Nora, trans. David P. Jordan (Chicago, IL: University of Chicago Press, 2010), 4, xii. This can also be true of a work, such as Larousse's dictionary (4, 185–203).

13. The term 'chronotope' (literally 'time-space') is that formulated by Mikhail Bakhtin in his long essay on the subject; see 'Forms of Time and Chronotope in the Novel', in *The Dialogic Imagination: Four Essays by M. M. Bakhtin*, ed. Michael Holquist, trans. Caryl Emerson and Michael Holquist (Austin: University of Texas Press, 1982), 184–258.

14. *John Clare: Poems of the Middle Period 1822–1837*, vol. IV, eds. Eric Robinson, David Powell, and P. M. S. Dawson (Oxford: Clarendon Press, 1998), 130. See also Jonathan Bate, 'The Flitting', in *John Clare: A Biography* (London: Picador, 2003), 387–401; and Sara Guyer, 'The Poetics of Homelessness', *Reading with John Clare: Biopoetics, Sovereignty, Romanticism* (New York: Fordham University Press, 2015), 78–100.

15. Despite long interest in Clare as a poet of intimate places and the 'local', none of the maps provided in literary-critical and editorial work function at a scale that allows for this kind of personalized mapping of the self onto the landscape.

16. William Wordsworth, *The Prelude, 1799*, 1805, 1850, eds. Jonathan Wordsworth, M. H. Abrams, and Stephen Gill (New York: Norton, 1979), XI, 330–3.

17. For Wordsworth, this kind of absolute destruction of powerful childhood spaces never occurs, but it is worth wondering what might have happened to his poetics if it had.

18. Later in 'Autobiographical Fragments' Clare uses comparable imagery to describe an adult experience of travelling twenty-one miles away from home, but now he feels alienated: 'I felt quite lost while I was here tho it was a very livly town but I had never been from hom[e] before scarc[e]lly farther than out of the sight of the steeple . . . I became so ignorant in this far land that I could not tell what quarter the wind blew from and I was even foolish enough to think the suns course was alterd and that it rose in the west and sat in the east' (76).

19. Nora states: 'Reflecting on *lieux de mémoire* transforms historical criticism into critical history' ('Between Memory and History', 24).

20. Right at the end of the article 'Between Memory and History', Nora seems to deny the posing of such a question, suggesting that history in its current manifestation has merged with and supplanted literature: 'History has become our replaceable imagination', he states, adding that 'memory has been promoted to the centre of history: such is the spectacular bereavement of literature' (24). These concepts are not fully explicated, however.

CHAPTER II

The Problem of Precedent
Mapping the Post-Romantic Lake District
David Cooper

He made report
That once, while there he plied his studious work
Within that canvas Dwelling, colours, lines,
And the whole surface of the out-spread map,
Became invisible.

William Wordsworth, 'Written with a Slate Pencil on a Stone,
on the Side of the Mountain of Black Combe'[1]

'Mapmindedness'

In a 2009 manifesto for map studies, Martin Dodge, Rob Kitchin, and Chris Perkins argue that there is a need for the work of scholars to be informed by the practices and processes of creative cartographers.[2] Noting the proliferation of maps and mappings in contemporary art practice, the geographers argue that 'creative possibilities . . . ought to inform our studies too, and that we ought not to separate the analytical from the creative' (239). This chapter picks up on this braiding of the artistic and the analytical by examining how creative cartographies can open up critical thinking about mapping, place, and Romantic writing. More specifically, it expands the literary-historical focus of the collection by interrogating how three post-World War II landscape writers – Alfred Wainwright, Sean Borodale, and Richard Skelton – have each embedded maps and mapping practices within their creative responses to a cardinal Romantic site: the English Lake District. This chapter, then, thinks critically about the work of writer-cartographers; but, in turn, it argues that reading *creative* work can facilitate *critical* thinking about place-specific Romantic writing.

There are points of imaginative and formal connection between these three writers whose work, to date, has received surprisingly little scholarly attention. The work of all three is characterized by an attentiveness to the textural particularities of the Cumbrian topography; and they each have a preoccupation with what it means for the human body to move through, up, and across this landscape. Perhaps more importantly, their works are unified by a shared difficult-to-define-ness – a resistance to conventional generic categorization that is evident in their mutual merging of textual and visual, literary, and cartographic strategies. Yet, in spite of these nodes of connection, it is also important to acknowledge that Wainwright, Borodale, and Skelton are radically different landscape writers with radically different creative agendas; and, crucially, Borodale and Skelton – in the work considered in this chapter – are responding to particular commissions. So, although Wainwright, Borodale, and Skelton each gravitate towards maps and mapping practices in order to situate themselves and their work within the intertextual space of the Romanticized Lake District, each displays a different attitude towards what Robert Macfarlane has described as 'the problem of precedent'.[3] What is more, they each conceive of and utilize the figure of the map in heterogeneous ways. Integral to this chapter's literary geographical readings, therefore, is the concept of *map-mindedness*, coined by the cartographic historian P. D. A. Harvey, which is foundational to Damian Walford Davies's theorization of the multiple, slippery ways in which maps and mappings can be framed within literary contexts.[4] Walford Davies's pluralistic understanding of literary maps allows for 'maps and mappings both actual and figurative, textual and graphic'; it takes in 'literal physical entities, verbal chorographies and textual and visual figures' (12). This chapter subscribes to Walford Davies's flexible conceptual framing of creative cartographical practice and, in following this literary geographical lead, will suggest that the work of all three landscape writers raises ontological questions about what might be defined as a literary map. By extension, the critical discussion is informed by a preoccupation with the dialectics of surfaces and depths. Cartographic practice necessarily involves, of course, the flattening of the three-dimensionality of the world onto plane representational space. In the work of these three writer-cartographers, however, the map is a representational space in which tensions between horizontality and verticality, surface and depth are played out as they variously seek to locate their hybrid practices in relation to the Romantic literary history of this particular place.

'Maps Are My Reading': Alfred Wainwright's Performatively Deep Mappings

As Julia S. Carlson asserts, it is important, when examining the spatial history of the Lakes, to avoid placing literary writing and guide books in separate, hermetically sealed spheres of cultural categorization.⁵ As a result, it seems essential, when thinking about post-Romantic Lake District literary map-making, to begin with Alfred Wainwright (1907–91), that 'indefatigable pedestrian' who, between 1955 and 1966, documented a total of 214 high places across the seven volumes of his *Pictorial Guide to the Lakeland Fells.*⁶ Wainwright's famously fastidious practices have shaped the way the Lakes is perceived within the national geographical imagination. Yet in spite of this, Wainwright's oeuvre has, to date, received little literary-historical or cultural-geographical consideration. Perhaps even more surprising is that Wainwright's singular mapping methods have yet to be extensively scrutinized by cartographic historians or critical cartographers. Wainwright's characteristic method is to dedicate several pages to each of the fells that he chooses to document. More specifically, he documents each fell through prose descriptions of natural features and a combination of self-styled 'Illustrations' including topographical drawings, maps, diagrams of ascents, details of the summit, viewfinder panoramas, and ridge routes. Through a range of visualization practices, then, Wainwright exhaustively maps each fell from multiple angles and locations; and the cumulative effect of this multi-perspectival mapping is a textual-cartographic performance of the writer's intimate geographical knowledge of the Cumbrian uplands. Wainwright's difficult-to-categorize work thereby offers a detailed mapping of place: an exhaustive documentation of the uplands that is predicated on both a long-term personal commitment to the landscape and an attentiveness to the textural particularities of each fell. What is more, the 'Illustrations' that feed into this mapping are characterized by cartographic innovation. His 'diagrams of ascent', for instance, blend a series of perspectival shifts onto the one representational plane. The purpose is primarily practical, as Wainwright's intention is to show walkers both the whole route of ascent and the outline of the summit to which they are heading. Yet clearly these diagrams are also creative acts, as Wainwright has necessarily exerted a degree of imaginative energy, as well as practical effort, to envision the Lakeland landscape in this way. Wainwright's 'Illustrations', therefore, are, simultaneously, utilitarian guides, creative cartographies, and egocentric maps. Yet perhaps their defining characteristic is the way that various kinds of depth – perspectival, geographical, temporal, and emotional – are conveyed on the plane surface of the page.

How does Wainwright locate these cartographic innovations in relation to *Romantic* ways of seeing and representing the Lakes? He opens *Memoirs of a Fellwanderer* by asserting that 'the small print and symbols of Ordnance Survey maps [are] always my favourite literature'.⁷ Earlier in his life, the map's integration of verbal and visual signifiers had facilitated the imagining of geographical experiences yet to be had; their synthesis of place names and symbols were read in anticipation of another weekend spent out on the fells. In his self-proclaimed 'Twilight Years', though, maps served as Wainwright's repositories of spatial memories: 'I still sit for hours with familiar maps open before me: I know them so well that the loss of detail doesn't matter, even as a blur they evoke vivid memories of happy wanderings' (1–2). Here, then, Wainwright frames maps-as-texts: they 'have always been my favourite literature. I would always rather study a map than read a book' (*Memoirs*, 73). Yet, in spite of this cultural privileging of the map, Wainwright does intermittently reveal his familiarity with the canon of Lake District landscape writing. In a letter sent to Eric Walter Maudsley in May 1942, for instance, Wainwright meditates on his recent relocation to Kendal from his home town of Blackburn: 'Sometimes I look in the excellent Public Library, a treasury of Lakeland lore, and bring home the books I love best to read.'[8] Wainwright, however, does not mention the eighteenth-century topographical writings of William Gilpin or Thomas West, Thomas Gray or William Hutchinson; nor does he cite Wordsworth or Coleridge, Southey or de Quincey. Instead, he contrarily reserves his enthusiasm for J. B. Baddeley's *Thorough Guide to the English Lake District*, a popular, yet essentially functional, guidebook that was originally published in 1880.[9] Yet, in spite of this apparent eschewal of the region's Romantic past, Wainwright declared, in a separate letter to Maudsley: 'Future generations, when they think of Wordsworth and Southey and Coleridge and de Quincey, will think of Wainwright also.'[10] There is a degree of performativity shaping this knowingly grandiose claim; but, at the same time, it demonstrates that Wainwright *was* conscious of his prospective position in an exclusively male line of Lake District landscape writers.

It is possible to frame Wainwright's performed disinterest – and his valorization of Baddeley's *Thorough Guide* – within a complex entanglement of social, political, and biographical contexts and dislocations.[11] Yet, crucially, Wainwright does not register that Baddeley's own account of the Lakes emerged out of earlier ways of seeing the landscape of the Lakes and earlier modes of cultural tourism. Moreover, Wainwright does not acknowledge that his conceptualization of the area as a bounded, Edenic space – a geographical trope which runs through both his publications and private correspondence – is imaginatively, if unconsciously, indebted to eighteenth- and nineteenth-century constructions of the region. This failure (or deliberate

reluctance) to register that his own landscape practices and aesthetics
are products of the complex layering of earlier cultural responses is
similarly evident when he recollects his first vision of the landscape of
the south Lakes from the relatively modest elevation of Orrest Head
above Windermere:

> We went on, climbing steadily under a canopy of foliage, the path becoming
> rougher, and then, quite suddenly, we emerged from the shadows of the
> trees and were on a bare headland and, as though a curtain had dramatically
> been torn aside, beheld a truly magnificent view. It was a moment of magic,
> a revelation so unexpected that I stood transfixed, unable to believe my eyes.
> (*Memoirs*, 23)

It is a self-mythologizing remembrance that carries clear echoes of
Wordsworth's recollection, in 'Home at Grasmere', of first gazing down
upon the paradisal Vale of Grasmere from an 'aerial' 'station' halfway up
Loughrigg:

> And, with a sudden influx overpowered
> At sight of this seclusion, he forgot
> His haste, for hasty had his footsteps been
> As boyish as his pursuits; and sighing said,
> 'What happy fortune were it here to live!'
> (lines 5–9)[12]

Both Wordsworth and Wainwright turn to the language of the sacred to
recall those epiphanic moments at which they first viewed the environments that they would go on to call home. There is a key spatial distinction, however. That is to say, Wordsworth's lyrical poem is preoccupied
with *verticality* as he remembers looking down into a clearly delimited
space and attempts to unravel his complicated, and at times conflicted,
deep-rooted attachment to a particular *place*. Wainwright, on the other
hand, imaginatively reconstructs gazing *horizontally* across the Cumbrian
uplands and his first identification with the wider *landscape* of the Lake
District. Yet, in spite of this vertical/horizontal distinction, Wainwright
still reinscribes an archetypally Romantic response onto the geography of
this corner of north-west England.

Wainwright frequently frames his own wonder-in-landscape in terms of
love: a word that is, according to Clare Palmer and Emily Brady, central to
this writer's 'environmental identity'.[13] Yet in a letter to W. R. Mitchell,
Wainwright reveals another – inextricably interlinked – aspect of his vision
of the Cumbrian landscape: 'The map of Lakeland had now become a vast
territory for exploration, and I planned my walks as conducting a military

campaign. You remember the war maps, the black arrows of advancing troops, the pincer movements, the mopping-up operations?'[14] Once again, this letter can be read as an epistolary performance. At the same time though, the instinctively militaristic, masculinist imagery reveals much about Wainwright's impulse to perceive the Lakes as a landscape to be conquered. By extension, then, his subsequent map-making, as well as his tireless tabulation of geographical data, can be seen to have surprising, and unsettling, correspondences with the kind of geographical imaginaries and vocabularies more ordinarily associated with colonialist cartographic projects. In his letter to Mitchell, Wainwright goes on to clarify that his 'thoughts were not of war, but utterly at peace' (95). The qualification, though, reads as something of an afterthought. This private letter confirms that Wainwright's mapping project is a sustained – and, at times, even aggressive – act of imaginative appropriation. Emptying the landscape of its Romantic past, Wainwright strives to reclaim, through inventive forms of creative map-making, the Lake District as his own. Yet, in asserting – through a synthesis of cartography and text – the depth of both his geographical knowledge and his long-term landscape-attachment, Wainwright ultimately slips over the surfaces of the region's literary past.

'Walking to Paradise': Sean Borodale's Surface Mappings

In contrast, Sean Borodale's more recent 'Walking to Paradise' (1999) is a textual mapping that is preoccupied with surfaces, of various kinds, but remains underpinned by the artist's acute awareness of both the region's literary history and mapping-as-process. In 1999, Borodale – an artist who moves restlessly between poetry, visual art, and film – was Northern Arts Fellow at the Wordsworth Trust, Grasmere. During this Fellowship, Borodale curated *Walking to Paradise*: a multimedia installation for which four artists – Luke Dickinson, Jane Hill, Kabir Hussain, and Borodale himself – reflected upon the Wordsworths' domestic place-making following their move to Dove Cottage in December 1799. Borodale based his own response upon the 137-mile walking tour of the Lakes undertaken by Wordsworth and Coleridge (and, in part, Wordsworth's brother John) between 30 October and 17 November 1799, during which Wordsworth spotted Dove Cottage for the first time. In preparing 'Walking to Paradise', Borodale retraced the route taken by Wordsworth and Coleridge – a ramble which took them from Temple Sowerby to Pooley Bridge, via Kentmere, Hawkshead, Grasmere, Keswick, Ouse Bridge, Buttermere, Ennerdale, Wasdale, Rosthwaite, Threlkeld, and Patterdale. In the exhibition catalogue, however, Borodale explains how the original 'route was divided into short stretches and their order shuffled, allowing seasonal and chronological irregularities to occur in the final edited shape, in which the original sequence of the Wordsworth-Coleridge tour was restored'.[15] It is a knowingly ludic act in which geographical space is made analogous to a pack of playing cards and through which the reader's expectations of the temporal sequentiality of landscape writing is destabilized. Furthermore, it is a non-linearity that problematizes the sense of teleological progression implied in the title, 'Walking to Paradise', and that similarly underpins the overarching spatial trajectory of Wordsworth's 'Home at Grasmere'. The resultant, 'restored' text consists of the exhaustive field notes that Borodale recorded as he walked through the Lake District landscape. These notes were later transferred from pocketbooks to twelve sheets of paper which were then folded to replicate a series of 800-by-1,100 millimetre Ordnance Survey–style 'Maps' (see Figure 11.1).

Map 01 begins with a sequence of staccato sentences that establish Borodale's methodological approach:

> A circle of stones set into the ground like teeth. One larger stone in the ring, marks scratched over its face, the scratches paler than the stone's weathered crust. Walk. Dark morning. Green levels behind you. Trees uphill, your left-hand view. Copse of black spiky trees. Ounces of pale blue sky. The wind facing you.[16]

Figure 11.1 Sean Borodale, 'Walking to Paradise' Map 01 (1999). The Wordsworth Trust, 2011.R1.14.1.

The reader is not furnished with information that might locate the speaker in either space or time: there are no place names to anchor the text in real-world geography; nor is there any indication as to when this walk was undertaken. Instead, the reader is bombarded with environmental images as Borodale tirelessly notes the phenomena he encounters when moving through the Cumbrian landscape. Yet, amidst what Tim Edensor refers to as the 'flow of experience' generated by the rhythms of walking, the reader is able to discern certain topographical features.[17] The text begins, for instance, with the speaker noting the formation, and telluric rootedness, of a stone circle that stands before him. This is followed by a sentence that zooms in to focus on the 'weathered crust' of the stone that is placed at the centre of this circle – a perspectival shift that signals Borodale's intention to document textural surfaces as he travels through the Cumbrian terrain. The reader may speculate as to whether Borodale is here referring to the late Neolithic Castlerigg Stone Circle near Keswick; but, if that is the case, the text deliberately withholds the precise co-ordinates. It is a method, then, that privileges phenomena over place.

In the exhibition catalogue, Borodale explains his creative process: 'Making studies ... whilst walking is a deliberate attempt to get back to the basics of looking' (15). In other words, he calls attention to his phenomenological impulse to remain unflaggingly attentive to the 'thing-ness of the thing' as the environment unfolds within the immediate orbit of his own body.[18] Over the course of the twelve maps, the speaker's eye is consistently drawn down to the flora and fauna at his feet as he walks across the landscape. In the textual space of just a few lines in Map 03, for instance, he documents 'bougainvillea', 'stiff-petalled sweet peas', 'pine-appleweed', 'red-elderberry umbels', and 'rose-tinted haws'. Moreover, he invariably moves beyond visual perception to record what the phenom-enological geographer Paul Rodaway describes as the 'sensuous geograph-ies' that unfold through the practice of pedestrianism.[19] On the opening lines of Map 01, he responds to the embodied situatedness of being-in-landscape by describing the wind 'filling up your ears': an articulation of a 'kind of intimate geography' (Rodaway, x) in which the boundary between self and world is dissolved. Elsewhere, Borodale demonstrates his interest in documenting 'auditory geography' (Rodaway, 84): 'Wet noises all around you. Ticking, popping, glugging' (Map 01); 'Sound is the changing tempo of falling raindrops which mass up on leaves and fall again bigger' (Map 01). As a result, Borodale onomatopoeically records how his sense of place is shaped, at least in part, by the ways 'auditory phenomena penetrate us from all directions at all times' (Rodaway, 92).

Although the approach is phenomenological, the creative method of notation simultaneously maps back onto the place-specific Romanticism that Borodale is explicitly retracing. Borodale's catalogue notes are prefaced by two epigraphic quotations. The second is Henry David Thoreau's assertion that 'it is the bog in our brain and bowels, the primitive vigor of Nature in us, that inspires our dream' (14). More pertinently, the first quotation is an extract from *Biographia Literaria* (1817), in which Coleridge reflects on his use of the 'pencil and memorandum-book' on his 'almost daily' walks through the landscape: 'I was making studies, as the artists call them, and often moulding my thoughts into verse, with the objects and imagery immediately before my senses' (14). The 1799 walking tour was 'Coleridge's first visit to the north', and Wordsworth's primary intention was to introduce his friend to the 'grand mountain scenery' of his native Cumbria.[20] Throughout the walk, Coleridge carried a pocketbook into which he jotted on-the-spot observations of an always-emerging topography: 'close by my left hand a rocky woody Hill, & behind it, half hidden by it, the violet crag of Grasmere'; 'I climb up the woody Hill & here have gained the Crummock Water'; 'Buttermere comes upon us, a fragment of it – the view enclosed by a huge Concave Semicircle'.[21] By placing the two difficult-to-categorize texts side-by-side, therefore, it becomes evident that there are parallels between the in-the-field note-taking practices of Coleridge and Borodale. To be more precise, Borodale inherits Coleridge's preoccupation with the use of the note – that 'necessarily imperfect and fragmentary' form – to capture the processual, polysensory experience of moving-through-landscape: 'the constant pull', as Borodale puts it, 'of the distance ahead that moves us on' (15).[22] By extension, Borodale follows Coleridge's speculative interest in the possibility of the note as a literary form in its own right, a mode that allows for the textual mapping of the sequentiality of embodied experience.[23]

There are also clear methodological distinctions between the two accounts. Revisiting the 1799 pocketbooks after encountering the nameless landscapes of Borodale's narrative-less 'Walking to Paradise', the reader becomes hypersensitive to Coleridge's predilection for noting the many toponyms that he has been taught by Wordsworth. Read in broadly psychological terms, this textual practice can be understood to be Coleridge's earnest attempt to deepen his understanding of the topography that had such a profound influence on the imaginative growth of his friend and collaborator. Rev. George Hartley Buchanan Coleridge, on the other hand, offers a more practical explanation when he asserts, with excessive confidence: 'No doubt he [Coleridge] intended to make a consecutive narrative of these memoranda, and publish it as a picturesque tour' (137). Ultimately, it is only possible to speculate on the reasons for this toponymical compulsion. What is of greater interest, then, is the way that, through the absence of nomenclature, Borodale's 'Walking to Paradise' draws attention to Coleridge's practice of developing his geographical knowledge and understanding of the Lakes through the identification and documentation of place names. A reading of Borodale's act of creative remapping, therefore, provides a critical context for interpreting the textual geographies located within Coleridge's original pocketbooks.

A reading of 'Walking to Paradise' also opens up questions about the place-specific text that, perhaps surprisingly, does not explicitly inform Borodale's response to the bicentenary celebrations. The vision of a constantly unfolding Lake District landscape, that Borodale borrows from Coleridge, implicitly contrasts with the images of finality that are scattered through Wordsworth's 'Home at Grasmere'. On the one hand, Wordsworth's poem is a retrospective celebration of setting up a new domestic life in a seemingly utopian space. As Raimonda Modiano observes, however, the poet's recollections are almost invariably destabilized by 'a darker vision of Grasmere' in the form of a 'premonition that this newly found Eden is ruled by sacrifice and its corollary, violence'.[24] In other words, 'this paradise holds out the possibility of death as surely as the promise of life, and more disturbingly, cancels the very boundary that separates the living from the dying' (Modiano, 485). Looking back, then, Wordsworth's remembrance of his relocation to Grasmere is characterized by dialectical pulls of space and place, potentiality, and at-homeness. To return to Borodale's practice, the different models of space and spatial experience that are articulated by Coleridge (in 1799) and Wordsworth (in 'Home at Grasmere') are visually encoded in two maps that appear in an Appendix in the *Walking to Paradise* exhibition catalogue. These line drawings map out two journeys: the tour of the Lakes undertaken by Wordsworth and Coleridge in October and November 1799; and the route from Sockburn to Grasmere followed by Wordsworth and Dorothy in the following month. Visually, the first drawing maps out a near-figure-of-eight tour that playfully loops into and back out of the Lakes. The second, however, charts a linear journey with a clear starting point and, most crucially, a final resting place. In other words, the line drawing calls attention to Wordsworth's own retrospective description of the Vale of Grasmere, this 'small abiding-place of many men', as a 'termination, and a last retreat' ('Home at Grasmere', lines 165–6). By extension, these drawings also act as visual reminders of the significant shift that was to take place in Coleridge's geometric imagining of the Lakes: by the time of his walking tour of August 1802, his use of the neologism 'circumcursion' indicates how, following his move to Keswick, the Lakes had become a site of entrapment as well as enrapture.[25]

The question remains, though, as to how 'Walking to Paradise' functions as a series of *material* mappings. Borodale's in-the-moment note-taking encapsulates the phenomenological polysensoriality of being-in-landscape in a way that cannot be achieved via the detached Cartesianism of conventional cartography. By extension, then, 'Walking to Paradise' can be read as an apparent privileging of the textual over the cartographic. This reading becomes problematized, however, when reflecting on the 'spatial event' of reading Borodale's textual maps.[26] During the winter of 1999–2000, the twelve maps were unfolded to form one large text covering the length of a gallery wall in the Wordsworth Museum. The experience of encountering the work within the white cube of the gallery felt – in marked contradistinction to the sense of ongoing movement that characterizes the textual content – disconcertingly static and fixed. Moreover, the visitor was implicitly invited to reflect upon the reading processes as no authorial guidance was offered as to how to approach such a large amount of documentary text. Was the reader expected to begin with Map 01 and to follow the text in a linear manner? Or was Borodale affording the reader the opportunity to pick fragments of text at random in order to create an individual, serendipitous path through this textual thicket stripped of all temporal and spatial markers? The overall effect could be overwhelming as the viewer became lost within the 'forest of signs' – a term that Simon Morley applies to the comparable textual practices of the contemporary artist Fiona Banner – on the gallery wall.[27] In the absence of cartographic conventions – 'signs and collections of signs, laying out in graphical form indications of spatial relationships or placing into spatial context other information with a locational attribute'[28] – the gallery wall was a blur of words.

Today, 'Walking to Paradise' can only be encountered in the reading rooms of the British Library or the Wordsworth Library, Grasmere. In the latter, the reader is permitted to unpack the maps from archival boxes and to unfold them onto the flat surface of the library reading table. It is an experience that acts as a reminder of the embodied, tactile pleasures of traditional map use. In spite of their apparent portability, however, a Borodale map does not function as an '"immutable mobile"' that can contribute to the 'spatial transfer of knowledge'.[29] Rather, once read, the 'Walking to Paradise' map is necessarily folded back into place and returned to the archival box. It is an act that assumes symbolic significance as Borodale's fragmentary words are collapsed in on themselves, compartmentalized, and returned to the stacks. These are yet more words – and lots of them – to be added to the ever-expanding intertext of Lake District literature held within a library that is dedicated to the ongoing legacy of British Romanticism and, more specifically, the poetics of this particular landscape.

The 'Isness' of the River: Richard Skelton's Deep Mapping of Dunnerdale

If Borodale's 'Walking to Paradise' is informed by a preoccupation with surfaces, then the experimental practices of Richard Skelton are based on digging deep – imaginatively, historically, linguistically – into the landscape. Skelton's interest in constructing mixed-form deep mappings of place was first signalled by *Landings*: a body of work, concentrating on Anglezarke Moor in Lancashire, that Martyn Hudson describes as 'one of the most sustained, experimental musical and literary projects of recent years'.[30] In 2008, Skelton relocated – with his partner and creative collaborator, Autumn Richardson – to a cottage at Ulpha, Dunnerdale, in the remote south-west of the Lakes. It is a landscape rich with Romantic associations: Coleridge became lost here during his 1802 'circumcursion'; and, almost two decades later, Wordsworth, in Sonnet XX of 'The River Duddon', was entranced by the water as it flowed through 'The Plain of Donnerdale'.[31] After moving to Ulpha, Skelton and Richardson 'began to close-map the area around their cottage and further up the Dunnerdale valley, making new works out of this old place'.[32] Although it is still a work that characteristically resists rigid generic categorization, perhaps the most conventional manifestation of this excavation of a deliberately circumscribed place is *Beyond the Fell Wall* (2015): 'a distillation', through poetry and prose, of Skelton's 'thoughts and observations on this particular patch of land'.[33] In the same year, Richardson and Skelton published *Memorious Earth*: a gathering of 'written and assemblage works' rooted in 'field work and [extensive] research in the area' following the artists' return to Cumbria in 'late 2011'; a body of work which, significantly, was framed as 'A Longitudinal Study'.[34]

Collectively, these collaborative and sole-authored works present a portrait of place that is disorientingly distant from the landscape aesthetics of Wainwright or even Borodale. Skelton envisions a hard terrain of 'savage remembering': a landscape of fell walls and dwelling places but, at

---

the same time, a territory through which '[w]olf, bear, lynx, cave lion, elk and wolverine once moved' (*Beyond the Fell Wall*, 65). According to Macfarlane, through the eschewal of the imaginative and formal strategies ordinarily associated with 'conventional eco-elegy', as well as the boundless movement 'back through the Holocene and into its prior epochs' and 'forwards to imaginary far futures', 'categories such as the picturesque or even the beautiful congeal into kitsch' in Skelton's deep mapping of place.[35] The overall effect is an unsettling ecological imagining of the Cumbrian landscape that radically disturbs many post-Romantic assumptions about the cultural geographies of the Lake District but that is entirely apposite for the anxieties of the Anthropocene. What Skelton implicitly identifies to be the imperative to look outside and beyond Romanticism is underscored by the ten titles that are listed in the 'Bibliography' for *Beyond the Fell Wall*. It is a list that includes *Dry Stone Walling: A Practical Handbook* and a scholarly article on 'Pollen Analyses from the Deposits of Six Upland Tarns in the Lake District'; but, strikingly, it finds no room for 'The River Duddon' nor Coleridge's Notebooks.

A sceptical interest in cartographic practice informs Skelton's deep historical understanding of place. In *Landings*, Skelton recognizes: 'Maps are vital repositories of place. They enshrine the collective memory – recording not only what is current, but what is deemed worth holding onto from the past.'[36] Here, then, Skelton's interest in conventional cartography is primarily temporal as he suggests that the surfaces of maps can reveal much about the communal handling of history in a particular location. This awareness of the potential of the map is further suggested by the way that the *Memorious Earth* exhibition – shown at Abbot Hall Art Gallery, Kendal, in early 2015 – featured sections of two historic Ordnance Survey maps of Dunnerdale. On one level, these documents simply helped to locate the viewer in a real-world geography; but, on another, their inclusion illustrated how conventional cartographies might feed into a holistic deep mapping of place. Yet, although Skelton does not completely reject the map, he is acutely conscious of what Cartesian cartography does not reveal:

> [Maps] enforce a mon_onymous relationship between name and place – rarely does any location receive more than a single epithet. Yet this fact belies the complex relationship we have with our surroundings, and the many different ways in which we express our sense of place. Shouldn't there be room on maps for local names, folk-names and familial names; for narrative, personality and myth? What happened to the polyonymy of place? (*Landings*, 121)

Here, Skelton articulates a frustration that the material two-dimensionality of the map necessarily leads to a reductively fixed and impoverished toponymical understanding of place. The cartographic naming of places, then, might open up thinking about what has been privileged within 'the collective memory' of a particular landscape; but, at the same time, the limitations of the representational surface result in the marginalization of other forms and acts of naming. Given these preoccupations, it is not surprising that Skelton has emerged as a major figure, 'a keeper of lost words' (*Landmarks*, 181), in Macfarlane's ongoing project to counter the diminishing of contemporary geographical vocabularies.

To frame Skelton's practice as mappings, therefore, necessarily requires a conceptual movement beyond the conventionally cartographic. While living in Dunnerdale, Skelton issued *Limnology*, 'a book' of words about rivers, streams, lakes and other inland waterways' that takes the form of a 'scattering of lists and *text rivers*, and . . . poems'.[37] Central to the project is the 'gathering' of over 1,000 'water-words' from Cumbrian dialect, a linguistic assembling that takes in, as Skelton explains in an unpaginated end note, 'tributaries from Icelandic, Anglo-Saxon, Gaelic, Manx, Irish, Welsh, Old Welsh and Proto-Celtic' and which is then presented in a sequence of visual forms that typographically imitate riverine processes. Skelton revisited and refined this attentiveness to the lost languages of Cumbria's 'inland waterways' in his contribution to 'Wordsworth and Bashō: Walking Poets', a group exhibition held at the Wordsworth Trust in 2014. His first contribution, 'I Know Not Where', is a 'distillation' of 200 key words extracted from Dorothy Wordsworth's *Alfoxden Journals*. The result is a textual mapping of Dorothy's journal entries that invites the reader – as with Borodale's 'Walking to Paradise', which was exhibited in the same space – 'to find their own routes and, in so doing, to write their own topographical narratives'.[38] In 'Still Glides the Stream', his second contribution, Skelton shifts his creative-critical focus to Wordsworth's 'The River Duddon'. In the first part of this work, the artist 'collates all thirty-three original sonnets into a single text and erases each occurrence of a water-word' – ancient terms, 'in the Germanic and Celtic language families, [which] would have been spoken in the British Isles long before Wordsworth's time' (McKay, 128). The second part of 'Still Glides the Stream' is, as Carol McKay puts it, 'a negative image of the first', as the 'lost water-words' – 'a', 'an', 'ar', and so on – produce an etymological mapping of Wordsworth's apostrophic poem (see Figure 11.2). It is a creative work that unconceals the geographic unconscious in Wordsworth's lyric sequence as Skelton digs down to excavate those 'ancient' words that are

Figure 11.2 Richard Skelton. Detail from *Still Glides the Stream* (2014).

indelibly embedded within the sonnet sequence that famously traces the Duddon from source to sea. As a result, Skelton offers a creative mapping that alerts the reader to the possibility that 'The River Duddon' can be read as a poem that is constructed out of the lost, ancient words for water in this particular place.

Clearly, Skelton's creative practice is far removed from uncritically posi-tivist framings of cartography as acts of geographical verisimilitude. 'Still Glides the Stream' does correspond, however, with Denis Cosgrove's asser-tion that cultural geographers have increasingly come to use the term 'mapping' to refer to heterogeneous practices and projects that are loosely based on 'organizing, documenting and representing spatial knowledge in graphic form' (177). Richardson and Skelton have acknowledged: 'Both our written and assemblage work is . . . involved in a critical dialogue with its own contexts and historical precedents' (*Memorious Earth*, 12). In the solo work 'Still Glides the Stream', then, Skelton removes the entanglements of poetic conceits that have often attracted critics to Wordsworth's sonnet sequence, including, for example, the passage of the river as a metaphor for the temporality of human life and the use of the Duddon as an unlikely symbol for the exploration of national identity. Instead, the artist – through the representation of 'spatial knowledge in graphic form' – strips 'The River Duddon' back to topographical and linguistic basics. As a result, Skelton implicitly challenges the critical preoccupation with Wordsworthian '*con-cepts*', rather than '*things*', to draw upon ideas articulated in the introduction to *Memorious Earth*, by mapping 'the *isness*' of the River Duddon that flows through the sonnet sequence of 1820 (12). Skelton's creative mapping, then, offers a way of reading the Romantic text. By extension, Skelton, through this act of creative-critical mapping, situates Wordsworthian Romanticism as a momentary intervention within the long, deep histories of this south-western corner of the Lakes.

Conclusion: Towards Critical-Creative Mappings

A more expansive post-war literary geographical investigation would need to consider the work of a wider range of post-Romantic writers who have turned to maps and mapping practices to situate themselves and their work within the Lakes. This would necessarily involve the exploration of references to maps in a range of texts: from Clive Linley's use of Wainwright's *The Southern Fells* in Ian McEwan's *Amsterdam* to the map that the west Cumbrian poet Norman Nicholson imagines falling out of a carriage window in his allusive poem 'Askam Unvisited'.[39] Such a study would also consider the paratextual maps embedded within the pages of Lake District novels, including the geographical illustrations that Wainwright contributed to Richard Adams's dystopian fiction *The Plague Dogs*.[40] It would involve examining the work of writers – including the Canadian concrete poet bp Nichol – who have played with the possibilities of textual-graphic mappings. As a starting point, however, this chapter has deliberately focused on three landscape writers whose textual mapping practices reveal a range of ways of responding, through word and image, to the Lake District as a Romanticized landscape. Moreover, the work of each writer reveals a contrasting attitude towards the nature of maps. Wainwright develops cartographic innovations to geovisualize his deep personal familiarity with, and love for, the landscape of the Lakes: a performatively egocentric project in which mapping is practised as an act of creative requisition. In contrast, both Borodale and Skelton turn to mappings, of differing kinds, to think about the Lake District as a richly, and perhaps problematically, textualized topography. Borodale self-consciously skims over the surfaces of things in making material maps that retrace a seminal walking tour in the spatial history of British Romanticism. Skelton, on the other hand, expands the definition of the literary map via a deep topo-linguistic reading of Wordsworth's 'The River Duddon'. All three writer-cartographers, then, playfully explore what maps can be and what maps can do. Crucially, though, both Borodale and Skelton gesture towards the ways that creative cartographic practice can open up critical thinking about the Romantic representation of this particular landscape.

This chapter has had a clear place-specific focus. In conclusion, though, it contends that the discussion of post-Romantic mappings of the Lake District has two wider critical implications. First, the exploration of the work of Borodale and Skelton has highlighted how critical thinking can be held, both overtly and latently, within creative practice. By extension, it has indicated how the thinking of the Romantic scholar might be reconfigured through a critical engagement with such imaginative rewritings of Romantic texts – an argument that Simon Kövesi has recently and persuasively articulated in relation to the presence of the life and poetry of John Clare in 'contemporary literary culture'.[41] Second, the chapter has highlighted how a critical atten-tiveness to such creative work might recalibrate the practices of the scholar who is interested in making his or her own maps of Romantic literature. In their manifesto for map studies, cited at the beginning of this chapter, Dodge, Kitchin, and Perkins urged scholars to examine how a critical engagement with creative cartographies might open up new ontological thinking about maps and mapping practices. Crucially, however, they move beyond the purely interpretative to propose that scholars might also *employ* the playfully experimental practices showcased by creative map-makers. As other chapters in this collection illustrate, there has been a proliferation of projects, over recent years, exploring the possibilities and potentialities of mapping Romantic writing through digital technologies. There is still room, however, for such critical literary cartographers to draw upon the imaginative responses to earlier writing that shapes the practices and processes of some creative map-makers. That is to say, there remains scope for creative-critical cartographies to inform the making of new critical-creative maps of Romantic literature.

Notes

1. William Wordsworth, 'Written with a Slate Pencil on a Stone, on the Side of the Mountain of Black Comb', in *Wordsworth: Poetical Works*, ed. Thomas Hutchinson, rev. Ernest de Selincourt (Oxford: Oxford University Press, 1969), 429, lines 20–4.
2. Martin Dodge, Rob Kitchin, and Chris Perkins, 'Mapping Modes, Methods and Moments: A Manifesto for Map Studies', *Rethinking Maps: New Frontiers in Cartographic Theory* (London: Routledge, 2009), 220–43, 239.
3. Robert Macfarlane, 'Extreme Styles of Hunting', *Guardian Review*, 21 May 2005, 35.
4. Damian Walford Davies, *Cartographies of Culture: New Geographies of Welsh Writing in English* (Cardiff: University of Wales Press, 2012), 12.
5. Julia S. Carlson, 'Topographical Measures: Wordsworth's and Crosthwaite's Lines on the Lake District', *Romanticism* 16 (2010): 72–93, 72.

6. A. H. Griffin, *A Lakeland Notebook* (London: Robert Hale, 1975), 50.

7. A. Wainwright, *Memoirs of a Fellwanderer* (London: Frances Lincoln, 2003), 1. This posthumous publication conflates two earlier books: *Fellwanderer: The Story behind the Guidebooks* (1966) and *Ex-Fellwanderer* (1987).

8. Letter to Eric Walter Maudsley, 13 May 1942, in *The Wainwright Letters*, ed. Hunter Davies (London: Frances Lincoln, 2011), 47–51, 49.

9. Hunter Davies notes Wainwright's particular attachment to the 'twentieth edition' of Baddeley's *Guide* which 'appeared in 1935' and featured 'twelve full-colour maps, the sort you pulled out from the pages, plus three very good Bartholomew panoramas drawn in pen and ink'. See Hunter Davies, *Wainwright: The Biography* (London: Orion, 1998), 136.

10. Letter to Eric Walter Maudsley, 10 April 1943, in *The Wainwright Letters*, 70.

11. See Rick Rylance, 'Three North Pennine Journeys in the 1930s: Auden, Trevelyan and Wainwright', *Critical Survey* 10:3 (1998): 83–94.

12. William Wordsworth, 'Home at Grasmere', *William Wordsworth*, ed. Stephen Gill (Oxford: Oxford University Press, 1984),); 174, lines 9–12.

13. Clare Palmer and Emily Brady offer a geo-philosophical analysis in 'Landscape and Value in the Work of Alfred Wainwright (1907–1991)', *Landscape Research* 32:4 (2007): 397–421, 399.

14. Letter to W. R. Mitchell, undated, in *The Wainwright Letters*, 95.

15. Sean Borodale, 'Walking to Paradise', in *Walking to Paradise* (Grasmere: The Wordsworth Trust, 1999), 15.

16. Sean Borodale, 'Walking to Paradise', Map 01 (Grasmere, The Wordsworth Trust, 2011), R1.14.1. Further references to Borodale's work will be given parenthetically in the text and by 'Map' number.

17. Tim Edensor, 'Walking in Rhythms: Place, Regulation, Style and the Flow of Experience', *Visual Studies* 25 (2010): 69–79, 69.

18. Martin Heidegger, 'The Origin of the Work of Art', in *Poetry, Language, Thought*, trans. Albert Hofstadter (New York: Harper & Row, 1971), 15–87, 25.

19. Paul Rodaway, *Sensuous Geographies: Body, Sense and Place* (London: Routledge, 1994).

20. Mary Wordsworth, cited in *Collected Letters of Samuel Taylor Coleridge: Volume I 1785–1800*, ed. Earl Leslie Griggs (Oxford: Clarendon Press, 1956), 542. Volume I of the *Collected Letters* contains Mary Wordsworth's transcription of Coleridge's contribution to a letter written by William to Dorothy Wordsworth dated Keswick, 8 November 1799.

21. *The Notebooks of Samuel Taylor Coleridge: Volume 1, 1794–1804*, ed. Kathleen Coburn (Routledge & Kegan Paul, 1957), entry number 537. Here, 'Grasmere' refers to the fell of Grasmoor in the north-west of the Lake District.

22. Rev. Gerard Hartley Buchanan Coleridge, 'Samuel Taylor Coleridge Discovers the Lake Country', in *Wordsworth and Coleridge: Studies in Honor of George McLean Harper*, ed. Earl Leslie Griggs (Princeton, NJ: Princeton University Press, 1939), 137.

23. Borodale further develops this methodological interest in *Notes for an Atlas* (Dartington: Isinglass, 2003), a book-length poem predicated on a walk through London.

24. Raimonda Modiano, 'Blood Sacrifice, Gift Economy and the Edenic World: Wordsworth's "Home at Grasmere"', *Studies in Romanticism* 32 (1993): 481–521, 482.

25. Samuel Taylor Coleridge, Letter to Sarah Hutchinson, 10 August 1802, in *Collected Letters of Samuel Taylor Coleridge: Volume II 1801–1806*, ed. Earl Leslie Griggs (Oxford: Clarendon Press, 1956), 848.

26. Sheila Hones, 'Literary Geography: The Novel as a Spatial Event', in *Envisioning Landscapes, Making Worlds: Geography and the Humanities*, eds. Stephen Daniels, Dydier DeLyser, J. Nicholas Entrikin, and Doug Richardson (London: Routledge, 2011), 247–55.

27. Simon Morley, *Writing on the Wall: Word and Image in Modern Art* (London: Thames and Hudson, 2003) m 187.

28. Mark Denil, 'Cartographic Design: Rhetoric and Persuasion', *Cartographic Perspectives* 45 (2003): 8–67, 8.

29. Denis Cosgrove, 'Cultural Cartography: Maps and Mapping in Cultural Geography', *Annales de Géographie* 2 (2008): 159–78, 165.

30. Martyn Hudson, 'Archive, Sound and Landscape in Richard Skelton's Landings Sequence', *Landscapes* 16 (2015): 63–78, 66.

31. William Wordsworth, 'The River Duddon', *Wordsworth: Poetical Works*, 300.

32. Robert Macfarlane, *Landmarks* (London: Hamish Hamilton, 2015), 187.

33. Richard Skelton, *Beyond the Fell Wall* (Toller Fratrum: Little Toller, 2015).

34. Autumn Richardson and Richard Skelton, *Memorious Earth: A Longitudinal Study* (Cumbria: Corbel Stone Press, 2015), 8–12.

35. Robert Macfarlane, 'Generation Anthropocene: How Humans Have Altered the Planet for Ever', *The Guardian*, 1 April 2016, www.theguardian.com/bo oks/2016/apr/01/generation-anthropocene-altered-planet-for-ever (accessed 1 October 2017).

36. Richard Skelton, *Landings*, 5th ed. (Cumbria: Corbel Stone Press, 2015), 121.

37. Richard Skelton, *Limnology* (Cumbria: Corbel Stone Press, 2012).

38. Carol McKay, 'Richard Skelton', in *Wordsworth and Bashō: Walking Poets* (Sunderland: Art Editions North, 2014), 128.

39. Norman Nicholson, 'Askam Unvisited', in *Collected Poems*, ed. Neil Curry (London: Faber and Faber, 1994), 38. Nicholson's pair of poems, 'Askam Unvisited' and 'Askam Visited', clearly echo Wordsworth's poems on Yarrow.

40. Richard Adams, *The Plague Dogs* (London: Allen Lane, 1977).

41. See Simon Kövesi, 'Conclusion: Clare as Our Contemporary; Clare as History', in *John Clare: Nature, Criticism and History* (London: Palgrave Macmillan, 2017), 215–37.

CHAPTER 12

Maps without Territory
Disappearing Trelawney Town

Paul Youngquist

It's a bright, soft afternoon in January. My friend Frances Botkin and I are sitting at the Senior Common Room bar on UWI campus near Kingston, Jamaica. She's sipping a rum and water. I'm nursing a Red Stripe. A tall man wearing an African amulet around his neck and a serious look on his face walks up and begins talking to Fran about things I do not understand – Maroons, an invisible hunter, the cost of buses, an Afrocentric fashion show. Before I know what has happened, or exactly how, I've been recruited to help organize a conference he's conjuring to coincide with the annual Quao Day celebration in Charles Town. Fran's done so before and shares his vision of a gathering of scholars in Charles Town's Asafu Yard to encourage communication and exchange among Maroons and academics interested in their traditions. Now it's become the 'Annual Charles Town International Maroon Conference'.[1] Back then it was a leery dream. The tall man dreaming it and charming me into doing likewise was Colonel Frank Lumsden, without whose inspiration such a gathering would never have come to be. I want to thank him (he's among the ancestors now) and his indefatigable administrative familiar, Professor Botkin, for making the dream real and sustaining its increasingly successful recurrence.

Near the end of our conversation that bright day, Colonel Frank did something that in retrospect strikes me as magical: he took from his pocket a well-handled document and started methodically to unfold it on one of the black metal tables nearby. 'See this?' he asked. 'This is a map of Charles Town. It proves Charles Town can never be sold. See all these plots around it? These boundaries and lines? They mark private property. These lots have deeds. They can be sold. But this blank space in the middle is not private property. No deeds to it exist. It's held in common, common Maroon property. Charles Town can't be sold. It's Maroon land. Forever.' At the time, I only dimly understood the point of Colonel Frank's lesson in radical cartography. In retrospect, however, I see it was a bold declaration of indigenous rights, an act of anti-colonial counter-mapping that lays claim not merely to a represented territory but more completely to a whole way of life, grounded in that Maroon common and sustained by collective ownership without deed.

Expropriating Trelawney

Colonel Frank was not wrong to insist on the authority of his map. In his Maroon hands it was a weapon, sharp as a machete and even better for cutting, in the struggle for indigenous rights. Maps after all produce the territories they define. In the long history of Maroon independence, they typically serve the interest of colonial authority, producing territories that limit Maroon influence and confine Maroon agency. As Denis Wood insists, 'the map is a vehicle for creating and conveying *authority* about and over territory'. He goes on: 'The transmission of authority is what maps are *about*'.[2] They link 'territory to other things, advancing in this way the interests of those making (or controlling the making) of the maps' (20). They therefore acquire the ability, in Wood's perilous phrase, '*to perform the shape of statehood*' (31). I want to examine briefly the role maps play in the expropriation and disappearance of the oldest Maroon common of them all in Jamaica – Trelawney Town – not just to illustrate the imperial force of state-sponsored cartography but to demonstrate that such maps also attest to the persistence of the Maroon common they would eradicate.[3] Colonel Frank's counter-map of such a common raises the question, the very troubling question, of authority: if not by the state's, then by what authority does the Maroon common persist, in Colonel Frank's auspicious word, 'forever'?

In 1841, a woman named Mary Brown, with several others, submitted a petition to the Assembly of Jamaica on behalf of themselves and their children. It reads as follows:

> That three of the petitioners, viz.: Mary Brown, Sarah M'Gale, and Mary Ricketts, were among the number of maroons, who were deported from this island in the year 1796: That understanding, on returning with their families to this, the country of their birth, they were to have restored to them the lands at Cudjoe town, in the parish of Trelawny, which they occupied previous to their transportation, petitioners sold off all they owned at Sierra Leone and came here, but although the said lands were unoccupied, they have not the means of re-occupying them.[4]

Jamaican Maroons were escaped slaves who ran away from Spanish plantation owners to establish free communities in the mountainous interior, where

Trelawney Town was the largest settlement. They led the First Maroon War in 1728 and the Second in 1795. When peace was made, however, the Maroons were cheated. The treaty securing their surrender was immediately and summarily broken by then-lieutenant governor Balcarres, and the Trelawney Town Maroons were shipped off on an odyssey that saw them first deposited in Halifax, Nova Scotia, then relocated four years later to the abolitionist colony of Sierra Leone.[5] Mary Brown and her companions were remnants of these original Trelawney Town Maroons. The three lady petitioners returned to their home in Jamaica hoping to recover the Maroon common – Trelawney Town – that the Assembly had, with dubious legality, expropriated over forty years earlier. Their petition was referred to special committee. They then disappear from the legal record. Had Mary Brown and her Maroon friends asked to see a map of the territory in question, Figure 12.1 shows what they would have received. The surveyors Stephenson and Smith drew this map from fresh measurements in 1807. This particular copy dates from 1835 and bears an annotation made in 1837. As its legend indicates, it 'represents fifteen hundred acres of Land in the Parish of St. James formerly possessed by the Trelawney Maroons'.[6] That word 'formerly' does a lot of ideological work. Those 1,500 acres fall into a patchwork of 12 irregular 100-acre plots surrounding a central square of 300 acres. The lines dividing them force the former Maroon common into a new form: private property. Seven of the parcels have owners, attested by the phrase 'belonging to' written within their boundaries in sepia ink. Four still await sale, but nothing indicates that any of them were actually occupied – except the 300-acre square in the middle and the contiguous parcel 12. That space harbours a special purpose, as the inscription in the map's bottom-left corner indicates: 'The ground reserved for use of the troops is shown by the Yellow outline' (St. James 184B). An earlier map, 'surveyed by desire of Lieutenant General George Nugent, Commander in Chief', also attests that those acres are 'reserved for the use of His Majesty's Forces'.[7]

This map of 'MAROON TOWN', the name in block letters smack in the middle of the space reserved for military use, eradicates Trelawney Town by linking private property to state authority, backed by military force. Such a map may, in Wood's words, '*reduce the necessity for*, the application of armed force' (1), but it nevertheless conveys the obvious threat directed at the Maroon common: acknowledge state authority – or else. Only a few years later the Assembly of Jamaica would advance that threat less openly with the Maroon Allotment Act of 1842, which, at least nominally, reclaimed all remaining Maroon lands for redistribution by the state. Maps such as this one construct a Maroon common without territory, 'disappearing' Trelawney Town through the cartographic power of military force.

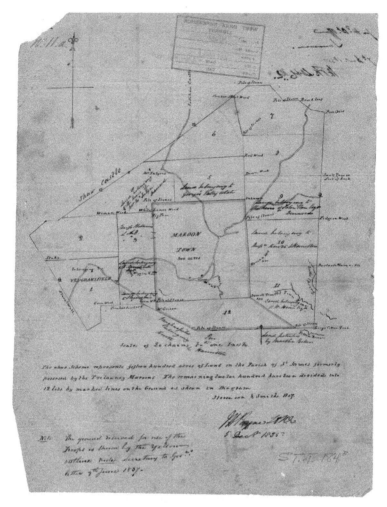

Figure 12.1 *Map of Trelawney Town* (1835). St. James 184B, National Library of
Jamaica, Cadastral Maps and Plans.

A Genealogy of Spaces

Such is the force of proprietary space, the space of ownership and state
authority, performed by this map of Maroon Town. It's a far cry from the
common space originally granted by treaty to the insurgent Maroon
groups Leeward and Windward, in 1738 and 1739. I'd like to trace
a genealogy of this proprietary space in relation to the Maroon common

created by treaty, the better to glimpse the enduring tension that configures the struggle for indigenous territorial independence today. Maps once again prove a potent means of performing state authority, but I'll begin with what could be considered the original act of counter-mapping in this context: the treaty that opens common space in the first place.

In 1738, after eighty years of lightening depredations by guerrilla Maroons, the Assembly of Jamaica – worried for the colony's profitability – sued for peace.[8] Colonel Guthrie negotiated with the great warrior Kojo, leader of the Leeward insurgents, a treaty that would yield another kind of space entirely from the proprietary sort that was constitutive of colonial life. They signed the treaty at a place called 'Petty River Bottom', about three miles east and slightly south of Trelawney Town proper.

I hiked down to the site in the company of Michael Grizzle ('call me Chief'), the self-appointed leader of the resurgent Maroon community at the former site of Trelawney Town, now called Flagstaff. It was a tough hike, a rough descent: past Gun Hill, a sheer limestone dome shagged with bamboo (where the British mounted a swivel gun up top to batter Kojo's warriors into the cockpits); through an open field of banana trees (where Maroons erected a 'throat Castle' during the 1795 insurrection: Colonel Fitch's British head on a pike); and down into thick bush on a rugged dirt and limestone path. Precipitous drops opened left and right. To slip would mean cuts and bruises at the very least. Along the way, with his machete, Chief pointed out examples of cockpit country's native vegetation. Thousands of indigenous plants, he said. Here only. Nowhere else in the world. He reached down and touched an unusual fern, forky with branches bearing short green leaves – one of three species unique to this side of the cockpits.

We settled into a jerky rhythm and hiked for a couple hours, Chief whacking vines and suckers as we tripped along. Even screened by the foliage, the sun was hot. If the terrain didn't do me in, thirst would. I wouldn't make much of a Maroon, I thought. They knew these crenellated steeps intimately, where to find water tucked into impermeable foliage. Up ahead a few paces, Chief suddenly stuck his machete in the ground and scrambled up a few sharp rocks. As I caught up to him I could hear a steady trickling. He tipped a little bottle under a tiny fall, catching water as it spilled. We had arrived at Petty River. Chief scrabbled onto a rocky ledge. 'Up here's the cave with the spring where it starts. Dallas mentions it in his history of the Maroons.[9] A British sentry tracked a Maroon woman to this place. That's how they found Kojo and his people.'

Chief entered the cave and his voice came booming: 'Snake! I see a snake.' I ducked into the cave too, cool and dank. 'Where?' 'There. Boa. Yellow boa! I've never seen a snake in here.' It slithered into a dark crack in the cave's wall. 'A blessing,' I said archly. A lapsed Rasta, Chief Grizzle likes to patter about the glories of Islam, the true spiritual heritage (in his view) of Jamaica's Maroons. For all his talk of Maroon Muslims forsaking pork and white rum, of *salam alaikum* and Kojo bowing east to solemnize the treaty, when revelation came in this sacred place of history it took the physical form of African spirituality. The snake. Obi, spirit of life and healing. 'Definitely yellow boa. I have goosebumps. I have never found one here at Petty River.'

The treaty Kojo and Guthrie signed secures a very strange arrangement, perhaps unprecedented in the annals of colonial encounter. The so-called right of conquest vests the entire island of Jamaica in His Majesty the King of Great Britain, as the map that accompanies R. C. Dallas's *History of the Maroons* (1803) indicates. But peculiarly, the treaty of 1738 cedes, or at least seems to, a portion of that territory to the Maroons in perpetuity. Its Third Article declares that 'they shall enjoy and possess, by themselves and their posterity forever, all the lands situate and lying between Trelawny Town and the Cockpits, to the amount of 1500 acres, bearing north-west from the said Trelawny Town'.[10] The situation here is similar to that of Milton's God in Book VII of *Paradise Lost* when, in creating the world, he absents his presence to secure a space for new creation: 'I uncircumscribed myself retire.'[11] Sovereignty withdraws its sovereign presence to incur a space of freedom, in this case common space, the space of a Maroon common. If this largesse were merely a matter of sovereignty granting rights to subjects, then the law would administrate state authority over proprietary space, as it does through patents granted to proprietors of estates. But the grant here is collective. The Maroons possess these 1,500 acres 'by themselves and their posterity for ever' (qtd. in Dallas, I, 60). The price for this independence? They agree to serve as the island's police force, returning runaways and scotching rebellions. Perhaps in spite of its worst intentions, Guthrie's treaty with Kojo confers collective ownership of that territory, creating in the process an ostensibly inviolable Maroon common beyond the touch of the king's law, save where stipulated by treaty.

Add to this effect the implications of the treaty's Fifth Article, and conditions emerge for the production of a kind of space incommensurable with the proprietary space of colonial commerce. Weirdly, the territory conferred on the Maroons remains both bounded *and* open. Kojo and his people 'shall all live together within the bounds of Trelawney Town', while at the same time 'they have liberty to hunt where they shall see fit, except within three miles of any settlement, crawl, or pen' (qtd. in Dallas, I, 61). Trelawney Town is bounded. Granting that three-mile proviso, the liberty to hunt is unbounded. While the Magna Carta provides precedent for such liberty, territory there remains vested in the sovereign, King John.[12] Here it belongs to the Maroons. The treaty of 1738 creates conditions for the production of a common space both bound by collective possession and open to free mobility beyond its nominal borders. This space is so important to the Maroons that a blood oath secures it. Guthrie and Kojo drank blood, rum, and gunpowder from the same calabash, consecrating that space as sacred, a common space grounded less in the authority of the state than that of the ritual act that secures the treaty. What Barbara Kopytoff says of the treaty, then, can be said of the common space it makes possible too: 'The treaties that were the legal charters for the new Maroon societies became their charters of origin as well, assuming a sacred character that made any attempts to change them an anathema.'[13] As with the treaty, so with the Maroon common it creates: its bounded and open space assumes a sacred character irreducible to state authority.

Mapping the Common

Now back to the maps. Read serially, maps of Trelawney Town record the implacable subjugation of the Maroon common by proprietary space. In an ideal world maps would exist all the way back to 1738. They don't, primarily because the territory in question was not formally surveyed for almost twenty years.[14] But a map from 1776 illustrates the impending fate of the Maroon common at Trelawney Town. A boundary with straight lines at oblique angles surrounds a large space designated 'Trelawney Town' in flowing script. Within it appears more writing that narrates the story of another paradise lost: 'William Downers, 300 acres, Lost in the Negro Town Lands' (St. James 434). The state granteth and the state taketh. Downers's patent provides a fulcrum for Trelawney territory, whose ambiguous boundaries secure the Maroon common. But it's worth observing too what is happening beyond those boundaries. Estates are popping up like mushrooms in 300-acre parcels. The 1750s saw a spate of newly granted patents and the inevitable surveys to fix their boundaries: to the north-west, Lachlan Shaw and James Grant; due west, James Hardimann, Adrian Ried, and James Henry; to the south, Elizabeth Burnard, Samuel Vaughan, and William Curtis. Proprietors of new estates. Harbingers of development. Independent landowners and British subjects.

White people. There goes the neighbourhood. Sometimes literally, as the placement on this map attests of two Furry's Towns, one New and one Old, the former within the boundaries of the 'Negro Town Lands' and the latter two parcels west and slightly north. A smattering of markers labelled 'Furry's Old Town' tell a mute tale of proprietary prerogative and state relocation. They fall mostly within the boundary of a parcel of land belonging to one Mark Hardyman, surveyed (according to the map's legend) on 17 September 1755 – more than fifteen years after the treaty establishing the Maroon common. Two towns bearing the same name, one included in the common and one bounded by proprietary plantation space: this doubling begs for explanation, but the map provides none, beyond a bare narrative of migration insinuated by the slippage from 'Old Town' to 'New'.

A fuller story unfolds in the pages of *The Journals of the Assembly of Jamaica* for the year 1758. It records the petition of Mark Hardyman regarding the trespass of a Maroon and his entourage on lands patented in his name in 1755. Upon surveying the land two years later, according to the petition Hardyman 'found that a negro named Furry, belonging to Trelawney-Town, had separated himself from said town, and built houses and plated provisions, on the petitioner's said land, in the place where the works must have been erected'.[15] The Maroons had an eye for location. Although Hardyman offered Furry £50 to compensate for 'improvements' made to the property, Furry and his people refused, preventing Hardyman from settling it for two bootless years, 'to his very great damage' (77, 66). To settle this proprietary dispute, Hardyman petitions the state, requesting the lieutenant governor of Jamaica 'to command the said Furry and his people to return into their own land' (66). Their settlement within the legally established boundaries of his personally patented parcel occurs in violation of the terms of the 1738 treaty, because 'the petitioner's land, on which said Furry has trespassed, is three miles beyond the limits of the aforesaid 1500 acres as appears by a resurvey made by William Wallace, in compliance with an order of his honour the Lieutenant-Governor' (66). Furry oversteps the boundary of the Maroon common by three miles. Hardyman invokes full force of state authority to redress this violation of proprietary space by errant Maroons: the weight of the king's viceroy and the measure of cartographic practice.

The Assembly of Jamaica responded with a resolution that underscores the Maroons' importance to the island's tranquillity. While it ordered Furry and his followers to leave Hardyman's property, it also resolved to compensate their forced relocation back to Trelawney Town. Thirty acres of provisions would be planted exclusively for their sustenance, and Furry would receive state assistance 'to build houses, and make a town as good as what he shall be dispossessed of . . . and the expense to be incurred by this service shall be supported by the public' (91). In 1758 it was imperative to keep these interlopers happy, given the crucial role the treaty assigned all Maroons in keeping Jamaica's peace and political stability. The state's dispossession of Furry and his unauthorized band of settlers returns them to the Maroon common, reasserting the legal and territorial distance between it and the proprietary space of sugar production. As if to consolidate that distance, *The Journals of the Assembly of Jamaica* records an immediate motion 'that a committee be appointed, to bring in a bill to ascertain the boundaries of Trelawney-Town, and to settle and allot 1000 acres of land for Accompong's Town, and to ascertain the boundaries thereof, agreeably to the several surveys lately made of the same' (91). While proposing to increase the space devoted to the Maroon common by 1,000 acres, this motion subjects Trelawney Town – for the first time since its creation by treaty – to the imperial practice of surveying, recalibrating its open boundaries by cartographic force. As proprietary space encroaches, the Maroon common recedes into its own hitherto ambiguous borders.

The Trelawney Town Maroons still possess their common 'for themselves and posterity for ever' (in actuality about twenty more years). But what of that other element of the space they inhabit, 'the liberty to hunt where they shall see fit'? The proviso allowing them to do so three miles distant from settlements, crawls, and pens becomes effectively impracticable with the development of these properties. The openness and mobility presumed in the liberty granted to track wild pigs – a significant source of Maroon vigour – gets eradicated by dint of development, a familiar means of subjection in the developing world. It is enclosure by gentrification. The bounded yet open space of the Maroon common closes down with the encroachment of those proprietary parcels. In a cruel irony, worthy of colonial cunning, the Trelawney Maroons become complicit with the steady constriction of their mobility. The better they police the surrounding wilds for runaways, as the notorious 9th Article of the Treaty stipulates they must, the safer those wilds become and the more whites move in. The map of 1776 shows state authority trenching upon the sacred by force of patent, development, and capital.

Another map, this one drawn in June 1787, continues this history. But, in fortuitous fidelity to the facts on all sides, it communicates as well a counter-history of the diminishing Maroon common (Figure 12.2). The surveyor's inscription is gouged and sear, difficult to parse completely, but

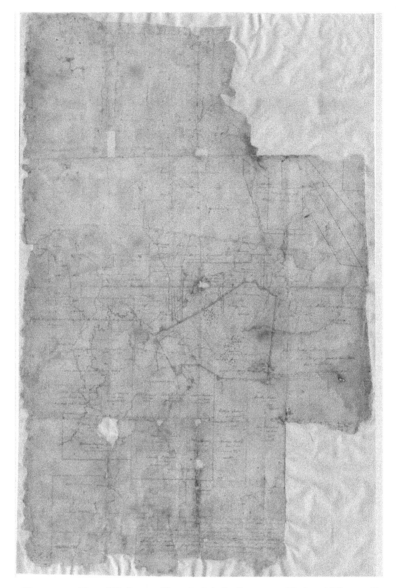

Figure 12.2 *Map of Trelawney Town* (1787). St. James 434, National Library of
Jamaica, Cadastral Maps and Plans.

the gist is clear: the map records a survey undertaken at the behest of Walter Murray Esq., member of the Honourable Assembly of Jamaica, once again to determine the integrity of the boundaries of the Maroons' 1,500 acres. 'I have discovered no trespasses', writes the surveyor, 'upon these lands by any of the neighbouring Settlers', a small miracle given that the map shows the Maroon common now surrounded on all sides by proprietary space.[16] Even the 'Waste Rocky Mountains and Cockpits' due east of Trelawney Town are 'said to have been' (those words scratched out in pencil) 'lately patented by George Robert Goodwin' (St. James 184A). Waste not want not. The Maroons have not been so respectful of their own boundaries: 'their principle dependence are [sic] on lands belonging to David Shaw, to Robert Kennion' and to another not named because of a tear in the paper (St. James 184A). Maroons are property poachers. Whites are not. They're slothful too, as a comment written inside their boundaries indicates: 'Excellent Provision Grounds not much Cultivated' (St. James 184A).

But a finer print – or, in this case, script – testifies to the liberty with which the Maroons inhabit their common. Scattered across the plane of contiguous proprietary spaces are notations that narrate a counter-history of independence. It starts with Kojo's insurgence at 'Conquer We Pass, a defile between precipices where the Maroons made their first stand against Col. Guthrie and were beaten back', eventually to triumph some miles to the south-east 'at a narrow defile where [they] made their last stand, near which ... Col Guthrie encamped during the negotiation by which those people enjoy their present privileges' (St. James 184A).

'Guthrie's Defile' – its name memorializes the debacle of the British passing through it. Maroon fighting strategy was as simple as it was lethal. Draw the tottering enemy into impossibly close quarters and hail them with bullets or hack them with machetes. Guthrie's Defile is a narrow passage winding through a twisted chute of limestone, sharp and shoulder-high with no room to duck for cover. It's a single-file passage too tight for wielding a gun, too cramped for turning to run, a one-way corridor to colonialist hell. Chief Grizzle and I walked through this Maroon maw of slaughter. Thank God we had no enemies. We'd be dead. In a historical sense we already were. I heard the sound of the *abeng*, the Maroon shofar, howling across the cockpits. I saw British foot soldiers picked off like ripe mangoes. The going only got slower as they piled up, until it stopped altogether, the whole column now at the mercy of these wily black warriors, some dressed in vines and branches, some sporting stolen fieldpieces, some hacking heads the way Grizzle hacked vines. Guthrie's Defile. Debacle. Defeat.

The map that names this place may '*perform the shape of statehood*' (Wood, 31), but it registers, too, a not-so-secret counter-history of Maroon mobility, cunning, and insurgence. Some distance beyond the western border marked 'Fine Bottom Lands', a note records their prior claim: 'Old grounds . . . of which the Maroons say Vaughan cheated them'. And further south still, on Rebecca Bernard's parcel, another note marks a place 'said to be Col. Cudjoe's Old Grounds to which the Maroons still pretend a claim' (St. James 184A). Such pretended claims testify to the liberty with which the Maroons inhabited their common, less as measured acreage than as open territory whose borders were the pious fictions of white proprietors and their paper sovereignty. The Maroons moved as they pleased across their common, declaring independence with their feet. This is the counter-history that state-sponsored mapping records in spite of itself, the transgression of proprietary spaces in the name of common liberty.

Uncommon Enemies

Another copy of the map shown in Figure 12.1 bears an ominous additional note in pencil: 'Col. Sandford kild [sic] – just north of King's House and up from James' house' (St. James 184B). Unobtrusive, almost mute, this note heralds the extirpation of the Trelawney Maroons as a people and the expropriation of their common by military force. On the basis of the counter-history these maps record, it seems clear that the underlying cause of Maroon insurgence requires clarification. Most colonial accounts trace the sparks igniting it back to one of several sources: Maroon indignation over the unjust punishment of two accused of stealing pigs near Montego Bay; Maroon irritation at losing their favourite white superintendent, required by treaty to live among them in Trelawney Town; or French agitation by provocateurs of insurrection sent to Jamaica from nearby St Domingo.[17] Without denying the pertinence of these circumstances, it's important where possible to allow the actions of Trelawney Town Maroons to speak for themselves, particularly when recorded in the documentary record. A Maroon counter-memory persists alongside conventional colonial accounts, and it puts their insurgence in another light entirely.

Not Maroon indignation and irritation, not French agitation, but a British colonial policy of proprietary enclosure provides the main impetus for Maroon rebellion in 1795: the relentless encroachment of proprietary space on the bounded yet open space of their common. In *The History of the Maroons,* Dallas makes a similar case in terms of demographic numbers: at the time of the treaty of 1738, the Maroons, in his estimation, 'did not amount to 600'. By 1770, 'they consisted of 885'. Three years later, their numbers had risen by almost 20 per cent to 1028, and by 'the year 1788 had increased to about 1400' (I, 120). Independent Maroons did not suffer the decline in numbers typical of enslaved populations. They reproduced and flourished in Trelawney Town, to the point that their increase would inevitably render 1,500 acres inadequate to sustain them. That the Maroons were aware of this situation, and of the colonial state's de facto policy of enclosure, is the lesson of an account Dallas provides of the first dispute that arose between the Maroons and colonial authority:

> From the time the Maroons were established as a free body, no dispute had arisen with them till the year 1773, when, some surveyors being employed to mark the lines of the adjoining patents, or grants of crown-lands, for the purpose of determining the boundaries of their 1500 acres conceded by treaty to them, they took alarm, supposing an encroachment to be made on their territory, and threatened the surveyors ... From that period no new altercation took place till the year 1795. (I, 128–9)

The Maroons had good reason to view those surveyors as emissaries of enclosure. Any land judged outside the 1,500-acre Maroon common would be deemed proprietary and fit for development. A tradition of territorial insurgence among the Maroons begins here in 1773, with the arrival of those servants of an imperial cartography bent on restricting their common to measurable bounds.

Nearly twenty years later, in 1792, Colonel Montague James and other leading officers of the Trelawney Town Maroons, 'on behalf of themselves and the rest of the Maroons in the said town', petitioned the Jamaican Assembly for more and better land.[18] The terms of their petition mix good husbandry with demographic necessity:

> SHEWETH, That the lands appertaining to the town were originally laid out for 1500 acres, and some time since resurveyed by order of the Assembly, and found to contain that quantity. That great part thereof consist of very high rocky mountains, totally unfit for cultivation. That the rest have been under cultivation ever since the year 1739, and, being of a light texture, are at length become so exhausted, as to be totally insufficient and inadequate to the support of the present number of the maroons, who, in the meantime, are greatly increased. (*Votes*, 7 March 1792)

Rocky ground, leeched topsoil, and abundant birth combine to vitiate the Maroon common. Independence turns carceral, and the Maroons respond as circumstances require, as their petition attests: 'in consequence thereof, trespasses are made on the lands of adjoining proprietors, and a scene of great distress and confusion must ensue, unless measures are taken to prevent it' (7 March 1792). 'Trespass' names the contradiction imposed on the Maroon common by the encroachment of proprietary space. The 'liberty to hunt' granted by treaty, which rendered the bounded common open, becomes a criminalized practice, as does the need to plant provisions on land actually capable of cultivation and now patented to private owners.

The Assembly rejected the petition on several grounds. The first reason was 'because the land they have is still uncultivated, although the soil is exactly the same with that of the adjoining properties, many of which are in a high state of cultivation' (7 March 1792). While it seems unlikely that the Assembly of Jamaica would have granted particularly valuable land to the Maroons in the first place, the claim that 'adjoining properties' share the same soil is topographically preposterous. As visitors today to the site of Trelawney Town (now Flagstaff) can see for themselves, the Maroons living there had the peculiar advantage of *looking down* on their neighbours.

The view from the rooftop of the Flagstaff Visitor's Centre stuns the viewer: 360 degrees of corrugated green, falling westward to the sea, which on a clear day shimmers in the distance. Chief Grizzle built the Visitor's Centre with grant money from the Jamaica Social Investment Fund and USAID. All it needs now is visitors, but it's a long uphill drive on a twisting road from Mobay or Falmouth. Geographically speaking, little has changed since 1795. Much of the Maroons' 1,500 acres was and still is too *vertical* to sustain the 'high state of cultivation' imputed to proprietors working a level field. Combine geographical fact with agricultural necessity (the exhaustion of arable land), and circumstances arise to make insurrection inevitable in the face of state intransigence.

The Assembly remained unmoved. They pointed to 'the very rapid settlement and cultivation taking place in that part of the country' as another reason to refuse any increase in Maroon acreage, an argument that arrogates continuous development to planters and terminal inertia to Maroons (*Votes*, 6 December 1792). They noted too that those feckless tenants 'do not depend on cultivation for the supply of clothes, and other necessaries, they stand in need of', indicting Maroon abstinence from commercial intercourse as a questionably separatist way of life (6 December 1792). But the Assembly's most revealing refusal betrays the true stakes of its territorial game: although by treaty and tradition an independent people, the Maroons could always 'acquire what they want as private property, on leaving the town' (6 December 1792). Become proprietors, or die trying not to: the Assembly's response illustrates with baleful clarity a plan, no less imperial for remaining unofficial, to strangle the Trelawney Town Maroons with the very chains that established the boundaries of their common and where possible turn them into proprietors with property of their own – a consummately British path to liberal citizenship.

Nothing changed in 1792; the Assembly made no concessions. The Maroons continued their increase on land ill-qualified to sustain them, succumbing with every new birth to a colonial policy of assimilation through enclosure. By 1795, their circumstances inevitably worsening, almost any pretext might ignite insurrection: unjust punishment, rebellion abroad, or retirement of a faithful superintendent. Whatever the ostensible cause, the Trelawney Town Maroons declared hostilities against the British in August, set fire to their houses and provision grounds, and withdrew into the nearby and nearly impenetrable mountainous territory known as the 'cockpits'. They would fight to the death to sustain their way of life on a common equal to their needs. An aquatint engraving offers a snapshot of their rebellion. Drawn by Nicholas Robson, etched by J. Heath, and published in London on 5 February 1796 (about a month before hostilities finally ended), it depicts the early skirmish that saw the death of Colonel Sandford but with telling reserve. The violence of war appears here with bated grace, a tension also captured in the engraving's long, descriptive title: 'Maroon Town in the Parish of St. James Jamaica, with a representation of the attack in the Road leading to the Town in which Col Sanford & other respectable Gentlemen were unfortunately killed. Aug. 1795'.[19]

Trelawney Town is the picture's apparent subject. The deadly attack appears in in its margins. As a representation of the Maroon common, the central scene conveys a sense of tranquillity. Scattered across common property, no fences or boundary stones between them, houses of varying size create the impression of a peaceful village nestled among rolling hills in a lush tropical clime. Maybe too peaceful. For all its beauty, something here feels amiss. No one wanders from house to house; no dogs or goats idle on the grass between. When the eye glimpses two black figures, both bearing rifles, in flight in the foreground, the mood shifts abruptly. The village isn't peaceful – it's deserted. Villagers who remain have taken up arms. The reason appears in the distance, at the far end of their common: a regiment of solders, obviously British, standing ready to heed the orders of an officer on horseback. Suddenly the picture erupts with a military violence seething in the shadows of its pastoral appearance: horsemen in

buff and blue descend a steep road to the left, their leaders making
courageous charge with sabres drawn and pistols cocked. But their blood-
lust dupes them. In the shade on the hill behind them, five black fighters
prime their rifles to take hidden aim; those in flight in the foreground do
not run from the horsemen but *toward* a brother sniper hidden behind
a low palm. Death welcomes the British to Trelawney Town as Colonel
Sandford rides his last.[20] Forbiddingly aloof, Robson's image conveys both
the tranquillity of the Maroon common and the hostility hurled against it.
Under such circumstances, the guerrilla tactics of these fighting Maroons
seem not only necessary but honourable, solidarity against enclosure, now
enforced with sabres and guns. That 'respectable Gentlemen were unfortunately killed' advances another kind of petition on behalf of the Maroon
common, this one written in Colonel Sandford's blood.

They buried Sandford near where he fell on the road he rides in the
engraving, still in use today. A Maroon named Charles Shaw (but every-
body calls him 'Shanti') showed me the grave, just beyond a low rise to the
road's left. You'd miss it if you didn't know what to look for: a geometry of
death among the gravel and the scrub – parallel rows of rough stones,
a broken pile of them at the foot. Sanford's body lies beneath: no monument, no plaque, only local memory to embalm it. 'Dis whole place,
Trelawney Town,' said Shanti, his arms wide, 'de whole ting was
a battlefield. We still find shot today.' He held out a smooth white stone
the size of a marble. I must have looked incredulous. 'Trus me. I know
eestory.' He gazed into the foliage overhanging the grave. 'I remember tings.
Stories. From when mi grandfadda drink rum with old Maroons dem.
From Jimmy John bottles. Say dem seen a tall man standing over Sanford's
grave. Wore a red coat with gold button. So tall you can walk between him
legs.' Shanti's eyes lit up as he stared at the air. 'Sandford. Him *spirit*.'[21]
Doomed apparently to haunt the place of his death by Maroon ambush.

The lieutenant governor and the Honourable Assembly responded to
the Maroon insurrection with force, brutality, and guile, requisitioning
regulars meant for the occupation of St Domingo, deploying vicious
bloodhounds acquired from Cuba, and securing Maroon surrender with
a false promise that they could remain on the island. I see no reason *not* to
call the brutal British suppression of the insurrection, with its dogs,
deception, and deportation, a programmatic policy of ethnic cleansing
and cultural genocide.[22] It ended with the transportation of the Trelawney
Maroons off Jamaica to Nova Scotia and the expropriation of their common by the state.[23] Once theirs to possess and enjoy forever, it would
become the site of British barracks, parades, and burials: the Maroon

common turned military bunker. Behind the authority of all those maps looms the ready heavy weaponry of the state.

Common Cause

How then to persist against such force in the struggle for indigenous territorial independence? Chief Grizzle has taken steps to resurrect Trelawney Town. He's legally incorporated an NGO whose name charts his aspirations: 'Trelawny Town/Flagstaff, Nyankopong State, Limited'. 'Nyankopong' means children of God, and 'state' means what you think. Grizzle seeks state-style sovereignty of the sort ostensibly enjoyed today by other Maroon communities for this disappeared town and its expropriated territory. I hope he gets it, but the state of Jamaica acknowledges Maroon sovereignty when it serves Jamaica's interest, a situation made only trickier by the presence of bauxite, the commercial source of aluminium, throughout cockpit county, including the 1,500 acres of Trelawney Town. It might be possible, however, to take a lesson from the original Trelawney Town Maroons. They put less stock in state sovereignty than its sacred equivalent. If, as Kopytoff insists, 'for the Maroons the treaties were sacred agreements, carrying the promise of a new life', then sacred rather than state authority might better guarantee territorial independence in the face of proprietary encroachment, particularly today (46).[24]

Articles 25 and 26 of the UN Declaration of the Rights of Indigenous Peoples lay the groundwork for such a defence. The former declares indigenous peoples to 'have the right to maintain and strengthen their distinctive spiritual relationship with their traditionally owned or otherwise occupied and used lands, territories, waters and coastal seas'.[25] The latter stipulates that states 'give legal recognition and protection to these lands, territories, and resources, ... conducted with due respect to the customs, traditions and land tenure systems of the indigenous peoples concerned' (10). These articles reverse the usual relationship between the state and sacred authority, obliging political sovereignty to serve sacred traditions. A state-sponsored treaty such as that negotiated between the British and the Maroons must acknowledge, where pertinent, its sacred implications – and protect them.

Such a prospect holds out little hope for restitution for Trelawney Town Maroons, the expropriation of whose common in 1796 found a generalized legal equivalent in the Maroon Allotment Act of 1842, formally arrogating to the state all remaining Maroon commons for redistribution back to its erstwhile collective owners as small parcels of private property. But the UN

Declaration of the Rights of Indigenous Peoples nevertheless offers a model for social engagement that disengages the ruling force of state authority. The sacred aspect of the old treaties between the British and the Maroons contests their erstwhile political sovereignty. I advance the sacred here not as an ultimate foundation for some better, because higher, authority but more in the spirit of what Michael Hardt and Antonio Negri, in another *Declaration*, call a 'movement', whose force 'is grounded in specific local situations, such as the indigenous communities ... who demand self-management'.[26]

Hardt and Negri continue:

> This external relationship between movements and governments has the power to set in motion a significant transformation (and diminution) of the directive aspects of government (or state) action. It could, in other words, force the mechanisms of government to become processes of governance; the sites on which different political and administrative wills are engaged can become multiple and open; and the governing function can dilute sovereign power to become instead an open laboratory of consensual interventions and plural creations of legislative norms. (82)

In light of the UN Declaration, Maroon insistence on the sacred character of their treaties with the British offers one such means of transforming the directive force of state authority.[27] The aim here is less to limit than to multiply the possibilities for indigenous life, promoting the common as a legitimate – and sacred – alternative to proprietary space.[28] Kojo's struggle continues, now sacred in view of his victory. I'll therefore close with the prayer that it might inspire new insurgents to resurrect a common 'that they might enjoy and possess, for themselves and posterity for ever'.

Notes

1. The Charles Town International Maroon Conference now occurs annually. I've been privileged to serve with Frances Botkin as co-organizer for a decade. For information on conferences past and to come, see the Charles Town Maroon website: www.maroons-jamaica.com/ct/index.php/conference.
2. Denis Wood with John Fels and John Krygier, *Rethinking the Power of Maps* (New York: Guilford, 2010), 52, 61. See too Matthew H. Edney, *Mapping an Empire: The Geographical Construction of British India, 1765–1843* (Chicago, IL: University of Chicago Press, 1997); especially chapter 1, 'The Ideologies and Practices of Mapping and Imperialism', 1–38.
3. Throughout this essay I will use the antiquated spelling of 'Trelawney' as the one preferred by living descendants of the Trelawney Town Maroons. The more widely used spelling today is 'Trelawny'.

4. *Votes of the Honourable Assembly of Jamaica, 1841–42* (St. Jago de la Vega, Jamaica: Alexander Aikman, 1842), 200.

5. For a full account of the Maroon uprising and its aftermath, see Ruma Chopra, *Almost Home: Maroons Between Slavery and Freedom in Jamaica, Nova Scotia, and Sierra Leone* (New Haven, CT: Yale University Press, 2018); Mavis Campbell, *The Maroons of Jamaica, 1655–1796: A History of Resistance, Collaboration, and Betrayal* (South Hadley, MA: Bergin & Garvey, 1988) and *Nova Scotia and the Fighting Maroons: A Documentary History* (Williamsburg, VA: Department of Anthropology, College of William and Mary, 1990); as well as John N. Grant, *The Maroons in Nova Scotia* (Halifax, NS: Formac, 2002); Bev Carey, *The Maroon Story: The Authentic and Original History of the Maroons in the History of Jamaica, 1490–1880* (Gordon Town, Jamaica: Agouti Press, 1997); and Bryan Edwards, *The Proceedings of the Governor and Assembly of Jamaica in Regard to the Maroon Negroes* (London: Stockdale, 1796).

6. St. James 184B, National Library of Jamaica, Cadastral Maps and Plans.

7. St. James 434, National Library of Jamaica, Cadastral Maps and Plans.

8. For early accounts of the British treaty with the Maroons and its motives, see Edward Long, *The History of Jamaica*, 3 vols. (London: T. Lowndes, 1774), 2, 340–8; and the 'Introduction' to Bryan Edwards, *The Proceedings of the Governor and Assembly*. For a recent assessment, see Kathleen Wilson, 'The Performance of Freedom: Maroons and the Colonial Order in Eighteenth-Century Jamaica and the Atlantic Sound', *William and Mary Quarterly* 66:1 (2009): 45–86.

9. R. C. Dallas, *The History of the Maroons*, 2 vols. (London: Longman and Rees, 1803).

10. Quoted in Dallas, *The History of the Maroons*, I, 60.

11. John Milton, *Paradise Lost*, eds. Stephen Orgel and Jonathan Goldberg (New York: Oxford University Press, 2008), 173.

12. On the relationship between the Magna Carta and the commons in British and American traditions, see Peter Linebaugh, *The Magna Carta Manifesto: On Liberties and Commons for All* (Berkeley: University of California Press, 2009).

13. Barbara Klamon Kopytoff, 'Colonial Treaty as Sacred Charter of the Jamaican Maroons', *Ethnohistory* 21:1 (1979): 45–64, 52.

14. I can find no record of a formal survey of Trelawney Town before 1758, although it remains possible that one occurred. Later maps indicate the markers that had distinguished the traditional boundaries of Trelawney Town.

15. *The Journals of the Assembly of Jamaica* (St. Jago de la Vega, Jamaica: Alexander Aikman, 1758), 66.

16. St. James 184A, Cadastral Maps and Plans, National Library of Jamaica.

17. St Domingo is today know as Santo Domingo, Dominican Republic. These explanations appear variously in Edwards (*Proceedings*), Dallas, and *The Journals of the Assembly of Jamaica* for 1795 and 1796.

18. *Votes of the Honourable Assembly of Jamaica, 1791–92* (St. Jago de la Vega, Jamaica: Alexander Aikman, 1792), 7 March 1792.

19. P/240/XIII, National Library of Jamaica. A later copy of this image drawn by Edward Dayes and engraved by James Sargent Storer and simply entitled 'Trelawney Town, Chief Residence of the Maroons' appears as a fold-out in Bryan Edwards, *The History, Civil and Commercial, of the British Colonies in the West Indies*, vol 3., 3rd ed. (London: Stockdale, 1801).

20. Dallas provides an account of Col. Sandford's death in *The History of the Maroons*, I, 186–90.

21. Jamaican 'patwa' (patois) transfers uncomfortably to print. Shaw's comments could be stated in standard English as follows: 'All of Trelawney Town was a battlefield. We still find shot today. Trust me, I know history. I remember stories from when my grandfather would drink rum from Jimmy John bottles with old Maroons. Sometimes they saw the figure of a tall man standing over Sandford's grave wearing a red coat with gold buttons, so tall you could walk between his legs. Sandford – or his spirit.'

22. Lieutenant-Governor Balcarres's delighted words upon hearing of the impending Maroon surrender are revealing in this regard: 'the Maroons of Jamaica have got a blow nearly amounting to the extirpation of their principal nation' (qtd. in Alexander Crawford Lindsay, *Lives of the Lindsays; Or, a Memoir of the Houses of Crawford and Balcarres*, 3 vols. (London: John Murray, 1849), III, 17). For an eyewitness description of the Cuban bloodhounds deployed against the Maroons, see Marcus Rainsford, *An Historical Account of the Black Empire of Hayti* (London: James Cundee, 1805), 423–9.

23. On 1 May 1796, the Assembly of Jamaica passed 'An Act to Prevent the Return to this Island of the Rebellious Maroons of Trelawny Town, Sentenced to Transportation', which states that 'the said rebellious maroons shall, with all convenient speed, be transported off this island', concluding that, in the event of return, 'the said court shall find such maroon or maroons guilty of felony' for which they 'shall suffer death, without the benefit of clergy'. *Laws of Jamaica, 1792–1799* (St. Jago de la Vega, Jamaica: Alexander Aikman, 1799), 273.

24. On the role of the sacred in the process of indigenization among Jamaican Maroons, see Jean Besson, *Transformations of Freedom in the Land of the Maroons: Creolization in the Cockpits, Jamaica* (Kingston, Jamaica: Ian Randle, 2015).

25. *United Nations Declaration of the Rights of Indigenous Peoples* (New York: United Nations, 2008), 10.

26. Michael Hardt and Antonio Negri, *Declaration* (Argo Navis Author Services, 2012), 82.

27. Legal precedents for such prospects are mounting. See, for example, the 2014 Williams decision by the Supreme Court of Canada to recognize aboriginal title to land in British Columbia; or the 2015 decision by the Caribbean Court of Justice, recognizing the Maya system of customary land tenure as a source of property rights as defined by the Constitution of Belize.

28. On the former lands of Trelawney Town on 1 March 2015, the first annual Treaty Day celebration held to commemorate Kojo's agreement with the British in 1739 was inaugurated. Chief Michael Grizzle of the resurgent Flagstaff Maroons currently leads the effort both to reunite a people – latter-day Trelawney Maroons – scattered by forced exile and to recover their illegally expropriated land.

Bibliography

Introduction

Advertisement. *Urania's Mirror; or, A View of the Heavens*. London: Printed for Samuel Leigh, 1822. In *Monthly Critical Gazette* 7 (December 1824): 578.

Barrell, John. *The Idea of Landscape and the Sense of Place, 1730–1840*. Cambridge: Cambridge University Press, 1972.

Bodenhamer, David J. 'Making the Invisible Visible: Place, Spatial Stories and Deep Maps'. In *Literary Mapping in the Digital Age*, eds. David Cooper, Christopher Donaldson, and Patricia Murrieta-Flores, 207–20. Abingdon: Routledge, 2016.

Bodenhamer, David J., Trevor M. Harris, and John Corrigan. 'Deep Mapping and the Spatial Humanities'. *International Journal of Humanities and Arts Computing* 7 (2013): 170–5.

Bodenhamer, David J., Trevor M. Harris, and John Corrigan, eds. *Deep Maps and Spatial Narratives*. Bloomington: Indiana University Press, 2015.

Broglio, Ron. *Technologies of the Picturesque: British Art, Poetry, and Instruments, 1750–1830*. Lewisburg, PA: Bucknell University Press, 2008.

Brosseau, Marc. 'Geography's Literature'. *Progress in Human Geography* 18:3 (1994): 333–53.

Carlson, Julia S. 'The Map at the Limits of His Paper: A Cartographic Reading of *The Prelude*, Book 6: "Cambridge and the Alps"'. *Studies in Romanticism* 49:3 (2010): 375–404.

Carlson, Julia S. *Romantic Marks and Measures: Wordsworth's Poetry in Fields of Print*. Philadelphia, PA: Philadelphia University Press, 2016.

Cooper, David, Christopher Donaldson, and Patricia Murrieta-Flores, eds. *Literary Mapping in the Digital Age*. Abingdon: Routledge, 2016.

Cooper, David, and Ian Gregory. 'Mapping the English Lake District: A Literary GIS'. *Transactions of the Institute of British Geographers* 36:1 (2011): 89–109.

Cosgrove, Denis, and Stephen Daniels, eds. *The Iconography of Landscape: Essays on the Symbolic Representation, Design and Use of Past Environments*. Cambridge: Cambridge University Press, 1989.

Cumberland, George. *An Attempt to Describe Hafod, &c.* London: W. Wilson, 1796.

Curnow, Wystan. 'Mapping and the Expanded Field of Contemporary Art'. In *Mappings*, ed. Denis Cosgrove, 253–68. London: Reaktion Books, 1999.

Daniels, Stephen. *Fields of Vision: Landscape Imagery and National Identity in England and the United States*. Cambridge: Polity, 1993.

Dent, Borden D. *Cartography: Thematic Map Design*, 2nd ed. Atlanta: Georgia State University and Wm C. Brown Publishers, 1985.

Eaves, Morris, Robert N. Essick, and Joseph Viscomi, eds. 'Auguries of Innocence'. The Pickering Manuscript: Electronic Edition, *The William Blake Archive*, object 16. www.blakearchive.org/images/bb126.1.13.ms.100.jpg.

Kanas, Nick. *Star Maps: History, Artistry, Cartography*. Berlin, Heidelberg, New York, and Chichester: Springer Praxis, 2009.

Hewitt, Rachel. '"Eyes to the Blind": Telescopes, Theodolites and Failing Vision in William Wordsworth's Landscape Poetry'. *Journal of Literature and Science* 1:1 (2007): 5–23.

Hewitt, Rachel. *Map of a Nation: A Biography of the Ordnance Survey*. London: Granta, 2010.

Hewitt, Rachel. 'Mapping and Romanticism'. *Wordsworth Circle* 42:2 (2011): 157–65.

Hingley, P. D. 'Urania's Mirror – A 170-Year-Old Mystery Solved'. *Journal of the British Astronomical Association* 104:5 (1994): 238–40.

Hones, Sheila. 'Literary Geography: The Novel as Spatial Event'. In *Envisioning Landscape, Making Worlds: Geography and the Humanities*, eds. Stephen Daniels, Dydia DeLyser, J. Nicholas Entrikin, and Douglas Richardson, 247–55. Abingdon: Routledge, 2011.

Least Heat-Moon, William. *PrairyErth (A Deep Map)*. Boston, MA: Houghton Mifflin, 1991.

Malkin, Benjamin Heath. *A Father's Memoirs of his Child*. London: Longman, Hurst, Rees, and Orme, 1806.

Moretti, Franco. *Atlas of the European Novel, 1800–1900*. London: Verso, 1998.

Moretti, Franco. *Graphs, Maps, Trees: Abstract Models for a Literary Geography*. London: Verso, 2005.

'Qualitative Maps: An Introduction'. Historic Map Collection: Princeton University Library. http://libweb5.princeton.edu/visual_materials/maps/web sites/thematic-maps/introduction/introduction.html.

Ridpath, Ian. 'Alexander Jamieson, Celestial Mapmaker'. *Astronomy & Geophysics* 54:1 (February 2013): 1.22–1.23.

Roberts, Les, ed. Special Issue: Deep Mapping and Spatial Anthropology. 'Deep Mapping'. *Humanities* 5:5 (2016): 1–7.

Saunders, Angharad. 'Literary Geography: Re-forging the Connections'. *Progress in Human Geography* 34:4 (2019): 436–52.

Smith, D. K. *The Cartographic Imagination in Early Modern England*. Aldershot: Ashgate, 2008.

Tally, Robert T. Review of Franco Moretti. *Modern Language Quarterly* 68:1 (2007): 132–5.

Thacker, Andrew. 'The Idea of A Critical Literary Geography'. *New Formations: A Journal of Culture/Theory/Politics* 57 (2005–6): 56–72.

Urania's Mirror; or, A View of the Heavens. London: G. & W. B. Whittaker, 1824.

Walford Davies, Damian. *Cartographies of Culture: New Geographies of Welsh Writing in English.* Cardiff: University of Wales Press, 2012.

Wordsworth, William. *The Thirteen-Book Prelude*, ed. Mark L. Reed. Ithaca, NY: Cornell University Press, 1991.

Part I

Alexander, David. *Richard Newton and English Caricature in the 1790s.* Manchester: The Whitworth Art Gallery and Manchester University Press, 1998.

Alpers, Svetlana. *The Art of Describing: Dutch Art in the Seventeenth Century.* London: John Murray, 1983.

An Account of the Principal Pleasure Tours In Scotland. Edinburgh: John Thompson, 1821.

Anderson, George, and Peter Anderson. *Guide to the Highlands and Islands of Scotland.* London: John Murray, 1834.

Andrew, Graham. *A Plan of Part of Hudson's-bay, and Rivers, Communicating with York Fort and Severn. c.* 1774.

Anon. *A Plan of Fishguard Bay, Near Which the French Landed 1200 Men* (20 March 1797; published by Laurie and Whittle); Llyfrgell Genedlaethol Cymru/ National Library of Wales (Map 6466).

Anon. Review of *The British Atlas. Eclectic Review* 1 (1805): 868–9.

Anon. 'Welsh Battlefields Historical Research: Carregwastad Point, Fishguard (1797)'. http://battlefields.rcahmw.gov.uk/wp-content/uploads/2017/02/Carre gwastad-Point-Fishguard-1797-Border-Archaeology-2009.pdf.

ap Gwilym, H. L. (H. L. Williams). *An Authentic Account of the Invasion by the French Troops ... on Carrig Gwasted [sic] Point, Near Fishguard, 1797.* Haverfordwest: Joseph Potter, 1797.

Arrowsmith, Aaron. *Memoir Relative to the Construction of the Map of Scotland.* London: W. Savage, 1809.

Ayton, Richard, and William Daniell. *A Voyage Round Great Britain: Undertaken Between the Years 1813 and 1823 ... with a Series of Views*, 2 vols. London: Tate Gallery and the Scolar Press, 1978.

Baker, James. *A Brief Narrative of the French Invasion, Near Fishguard Bay.* Worcester: J. Tymbs, 1797.

Banks, Joseph. 'Observations on Mr Mudge's Application to Parliament for a Reward for his Time-Keepers'. Royal Society Archive MS: MM/7/100.

Barber, Peter, and Tom Harper. *Magnificent Maps: Power, Propaganda and Art.* London: The British Library, 2010.

Barrell, John. *English Literature in History 1730–80: An Equal, Wide Survey.* London: Hutchinson, 1983.

Beaglehole, J. C., *The Life of Captain James Cook.* Stanford, CA: Stanford University Press, 1974.

Beaglehole, J. C., ed. *The Journals of Captain James Cook on His Voyages of Discovery*, 4 vols. Cambridge: For the Hakluyt Society at the University Press, 1968–74.

Beeke, Henry. *Observations on the Produce of the Income Tax*. London: J. Wright, 1799.

Belyea, Barbara. 'Amerindian Maps: The Explorer as Translator'. *Journal of Historical Geography* 18:3 (1992): 267–77.

Belyea, Barbara. 'Mapping The Marias: The Interface of Native and Scientific Cartographies'. *Great Plains Quarterly* 17:3/4 (1997): 165–84.

Benedict, Barbara M. *Curiosity: A Cultural History of Early Modern Inquiry*. Chicago, IL: University of Chicago Press, 2001.

Bernstein, David. 'Negotiating Nation: Native Participation in the Cartographic Construction of the Trans-Mississippi West'. *Environment and Planning A: Economy and Space* 48:3 (2016): 626–47.

Bewell, Alan. *Natures in Translation: Romanticism and Colonial Natural History*. Baltimore, MD: Johns Hopkins University Press, 2017.

Bingley, William. *A Tour Round North Wales, During the Summer of 1798*, 2 vols. London: E. Williams, 1800.

Binnema, Theodore. 'How Does a Map Mean? Old Swan's Map of 1801 and the Blackfoot World'. In *From Rupert's Land to Canada: Essays in Honour of John E. Foster*, eds. Theodore Binnema, Gerhard Ens, and Roderick C. Macleod, 201–24. Edmonton: University of Alberta Press, 2001.

Bleichmar, Daniela. *Visible Empire: Botanical Expeditions and Visual Culture in the Hispanic Enlightenment*. Chicago, IL: University of Chicago Press, 2012.

Boswell, James. *The Life of Samuel Johnson*, 2 vols. London: Charles Dilly, 1791.

Bowles, William Lisle. *Sonnets, and Other Poems*, 7th ed. London: T. Cadell, 1800.

Brayley, E. W. *The Beauties of England and Wales; Or, Delineations Topographical, Historical, and Descriptive, of Each County: Volume 8*. London: Vernor, Hood & Sharpe, 1808.

Brayley, E. W. Letter to Mark Noble, 5 November 1816. Bodleian Library, MS. Eng. Misc. d.164, f.47.

Brayley, E. W. Letters to Mark Noble, 1 August 1806–27 December 1808. Bodleian Library, MS. Eng. Misc. d.159.

Brayley, E. W., ed. *The Works of the Late Edward Dayes*. London: Private publication (Mrs Dayes), 1805.

Brayley, E. W., and John Britton. *The Beauties of England and Wales; Or, Delineations Topographical, Historical, and Descriptive, of Each County: Volume 6*. London: Vernor & Hood, 1805.

Brewer, John. *The Beauties of England and Wales: Introduction to the Original Delineations, Topographical, Historical and Descriptive*. London: John Harris, 1818.

Britton, John. *The Autobiography of John Britton, FSA*. London: Charles Muskett, 1850.

Britton, John. *The Beauties of England and Wales; Or, Delineations Topographical, Historical, and Descriptive of Each County: Volume 9*. London: Vernor, Hood & Sharpe, 1807.

Britton, John. 'Edward Wedlake Brayley, Esq.'. *Gentleman's Magazine* 44 (1854): 582–6.

Britton, John. *An Essay on Topographical Literature*. London: Wiltshire Topographical Society, 1843.

Britton, John. *Fine Arts of the English School*. London: Longman, 1812.

[Britton, John]. 'The Late Samuel Prout'. *The Builder* 10 (1852): 339–40.

Broglio, Ron. 'Mapping British Earth and Sky'. *Wordsworth Circle* 33:2 (2002): 70–7.

Brown, John. *A Description of the Lake at Keswick*. Kendal: W. Pennington, 1771.

[Brydges, Samuel]. 'Preface'. *The Topographer* 1 (1789): i–viii.

Budgen, Thomas. 'Exeter', Ordnance Surveyors' Drawings. British Library, OSD 40 (1801).

Burney, Frances. *Cecilia; or, Memoirs of an Heiress*, 3 vols. London: T. Cadell, 1782.

Carlson, Julia S. *Romantic Marks and Measures: Wordsworth's Poetry in Fields of Print*. Philadelphia, PA: University of Philadelphia Press, 2016.

Carlson, Julia S. 'Topographical Measures: Wordsworth's and Crosthwaite's Lines on the Lake District'. *Romanticism* 16.1 (2010): 72–93.

Carradice, Phil. *The Last Invasion: The Story of the French Landing in Wales*. Griffithstown, Wales: Village Publishing, 1992.

Chubb, Thomas. *The Printed Maps in the Atlases of Great Britain and Ireland*. London: The Homeland Association, 1927.

Close, Charles. *The Early Years of the Ordnance Survey*. Newton Abbot: David & Charles, 1969 [1926].

Coleridge, Samuel Taylor. *Fears in Solitude ... To Which Are Added, France, An Ode; and Frost at Midnight*. London: J. Johnson, 1798.

Compton, Thomas. *The North Cambrian Mountains, or a Tour Through North Wales, Describing the Scenery and General Characters of that Romantic Country, and Embellished with a Series of Highly-Finished Coloured Views, Engraved from Original Drawings*. London: Thomas Compton, 1817.

Cookson, J. E. 'The English Volunteer Movement of the French Wars, 1793–1815: Some Contexts'. *Historical Journal* 32:4 (1989): 867–91.

Cradock, Joseph. *Letters from Snowdon, Descriptive of a Tour through the Northern Countries of Wales*. London: J. Ridley, 1770.

Daniels, Stephen. 'Mapping the Metropolis in an Age of Reform: John Britton's London Topography, 1820–1840'. *Journal of Historical Geography* 56 (2017): 61–82.

Daniels, Stephen, and Paul Elliott. '"Outline Maps of Knowledge": John Aikin's Geographical Imagination'. *Religious Dissent and the Aikin-Barbauld Circle, 1740–1860*, eds. Felicity James and Ian Inkster, 94–125. Cambridge: Cambridge University Press, 2010.

Darwin, Erasmus. *The Botanic Garden*. London: Joseph Johnson, 1799.

Daston, Lorraine, and Peter Galison. *Objectivity*. New York: Zone Books, 2010.

Daston, Lorraine, and Katharine Park. *Wonders and the Order of Nature*. New York: Zone Books, 1998.

Davidoff, Leonore, and Catherine Hall. *Family Fortunes: Men and Women of the English Middle Class, 1780–1850*. London: Hutchinson, 1987.

Davies, Hywel M. 'Terror, Treason and Tourism: The French in Pembrokeshire, 1797'. *'Footsteps of Liberty and Revolt': Essays on Wales and the French Revolution*, eds. Mary-Ann Constantine and Dafydd Johnston, 247–70. Cardiff: University of Wales Press, 2013.

Dawson, Joan. *The Mapmaker's Eye: Nova Scotia Through Early Maps*. Halifax: Nimbus Publishing and the Nova Scotia Museum, 1988.

Dearden, William, ed. *Poems by John Nicholson, the Airedale Poet*. London: W. H. Young, 1859.

Delano-Smith, Catherine, and Roger J. P. Kain. *English Maps: A History*. London: The British Museum, 1999.

Della Dora, Veronica. 'Performative Atlases: Memory, Materiality and (Co) authorship'. *Cartographica* 44:4 (2009): 241–56.

Dodsley, Robert. 'Agriculture: A Poem'. *Trifles*. London: J. Dodsley, 1777.

Donald, Diana. *The Age of Caricature: Satirical Prints in the Age of George III*. New Haven, CT: Yale University Press, 1996.

Douglas, Starr. 'Dr John Fothergill: Significant Donor'. *William Hunter's World: The Art and Science of Eighteenth-Century Collecting*, eds. E. Geoffrey Hancock, Nick Pearce, and Mungo Campbell, 165–75. Dorchester: Ashgate, 2015.

Dorrian, Mark. 'The Aerial View: Notes for a Cultural History'. *Strates* 13 (2007): 1–13.

Edgeworth, Maria. *Tales of Fashionable Life*, 3 vols. London: Joseph Johnson, 1809.

Edwards, George. *A Natural History of Uncommon Birds . . . Containing the Figures of Sixty Birds and two Quadrupeds*, 4 vols. London: Printed for the author, 1743–51.

Evans, John, and John Britton. *The Beauties of England and Wales; Or, Delineations Topographical, Historical, and Descriptive, of Each County: Volume II*. London: Vernor, Hood & Sharpe, 1810.

Faden, William. *Catalogue of Geographical Works Published by William Faden*. London: Faden, 1822.

Farmer, Jared. *On Zion's Mount: Mormons, Indians, and the American Landscape*. New York: Cambridge University Press, 2002.

Flint, Stamford Raffles. *Mudge Memoirs: Being a Record of Zachariah Mudge, and Some Members of his Family*. Truro: Netherton and Worth, 1883.

Franklin, Alexandra. 'John Bull in a Dream: Fear and Fantasy in the Visual Satires of 1803'. *Resisting Napoleon: The British Response to the Threat of Invasion, 1797–1815*, ed. Mark Philp, 125–39. Aldershot: Ashgate, 2006.

Franklin, Alexandra, and Mark Philp. *Napoleon and the Invasion of Britain*. Oxford: The Bodleian Library, 2003.

Friel, Brian. *Translations*. London: Faber, 1981.

Gascoigne, John. *Science in the Service of Empire: Joseph Banks, The British State and The Uses of Science in the Age of Revolution*. Cambridge: Cambridge University Press, 1998.

George, M. Dorothy. *Catalogue of Political and Personal Satires Preserved in the Department of Prints and Drawings in the British Museum, Vol VI, 1784–1792*. London: Oxford University Press, 1938.

George, M. Dorothy. *Catalogue of Political and Personal Satires Preserved in the Department of Prints and Drawings in the British Museum, Vol VII, 1793–1800.* London: Oxford University Press, 1942.

George, Wilma. *Animals and Maps.* Berkeley: University of California Press, 1969.

Gittings, Robert, ed. *Letters of John Keats: A New Selection.* Oxford: Oxford University Press, 1970.

Goffart, Walter. *Historical Atlases: The First Three Hundred Years, 1570–1870.* Chicago, IL: University of Chicago Press, 2003.

Goodwin, Gordon. 'Mark Noble (1754–1827)'. *Oxford Dictionary of National Biography.* www.oxforddnb.com/view/article/20221.

Graham, Andrew. 'Andrew Graham's Bird Observations Written at Severn, 1768'. Manuscript E.2/5, Hudson's Bay Company Archives, Provincial Archives of Manitoba, Supplementary Document #1 to *Eighteenth-Century Naturalists of Hudson Bay*, eds. C. Stuart Houston, Tim Ball, and Mary Houston. Montreal, QC: McGill-Queen's University Press, 2003.

Grainger, Margaret, ed. *The Natural History Prose Writings of John Clare.* Oxford: Clarendon Press, 1983.

Graves, Robert. *Collected Poems.* New York: Oxford University Press, 1975.

Green, William. *The Tourist's New Guide, Containing a Description of the Lakes*, 2 vols. Kendal: R. Lough, 1819.

Griggs, Earl Leslie, ed. *Collected Letters of Samuel Taylor Coleridge*, 6 vols. Oxford: Clarendon Press, 1957–71.

Hacking, Ian. *The Taming of Chance.* Cambridge: Cambridge University Press, 1990.

Hansen, Lars, ed. *The Linnaeus Apostles: Global Science and Adventure*, 8 vols. London: I. K. Foundation, 2010.

Harley, J. Brian. 'Deconstructing the Map'. *Writing Worlds: Discourse, Text and Metaphor*, eds. T. J. Barnes and J. J. Duncan, 231–47. London: Routledge, 1992.

Harley, J. Brian, *et al. The Old Series Ordnance Survey Maps of England and Wales, Vol 6: Wales.* Lympne Castle: Harry Margars, 1992.

Harley, J. Brian, and Yolande O'Donoghue, eds. *The Old Series Ordnance Survey Maps of England and Wales*, 8 vols. Lympne Castle, Kent: Harry Margary, 1975–92.

Harvey, P. D. A. *The History of Topographical Maps: Symbols, Pictures and Surveys.* London: Thames and Hudson, 1980.

Harrington, James. *The Common-Wealth of Oceana.* London: J. Streater, 1656.

Harris, Moses. *A Plan of the Harbour of Chebucto and Town of Halifax.* London: Edward Cave, 1750.

Haywood, Ian. '"The Dark Sketches of a Revolution": Gillray, the *Anti-Jacobin Review*, and the Aesthetics of Conspiracy in the 1790s'. *European Romantic Review* 22:4 (2011): 431–51.

Helgerson, Richard. 'The Land Speaks: Cartography, Chorography and Subversion in Renaissance England'. *Representations* 16 (1986): 50–85.

Hewitt, Rachel. *Map of a Nation: A Biography of the Ordnance Survey.* London: Granta, 2011.

Hewitt, Rachel. 'Mapping and Romanticism'. *Wordsworth Circle* 42:2 (2011): 157–65.

Hill, Arthur. *Plans for the Government and Liberal Instruction of Boys*. London: G. and W. B. Whittaker, 1822.

Hill, Draper. *Mr Gillray. The Caricaturist*. London: Phaidon, 1965.

Howse, Derek. *Nevil Maskelyne: The Seaman's Astronomer*. Cambridge: Cambridge University Press, 1989.

Hughes, John. *Poems on Several Occasions*, 2 vols. London: J. Tonson and J. Watts, 1735.

Hutchins, Thomas. 'Thomas Hutchins' Manuscript Accompanying Bird and Mammal Specimens Submitted to England from York Factory, 28 August 1772'. Property of the Royal Society of London, England, Supplementary Document #2 to *Eighteenth-Century Naturalists of Hudson Bay*, eds. C. Stuart Houston, Tim Ball, and Mary Houston. Montreal, QC: McGill-Queen's University Press, 2003.

Hutton, William. *Remarks Upon North Wales*. Birmingham: Knott and Lloyd, 1803.

Hyde, Ralph. 'Thomas Hornor: Pictural Land Surveyor'. *Imago Mundi* 29:1 (1977): 23–34.

Jefferys, Thomas. *A Map of the South Part of Nova Scotia and Its Fishing Banks*. London: T. Jefferys, 1750.

Jones, Ffion Mair. '"The Silly Expressions of French Revolution … ": The Experience of the Dissenting Community in South-West Wales, 1797'. In *Experiencing the French Revolution*, ed. David Andrews, 245–62. Oxford: Voltaire Foundation, 2013.

Jones, Ffion Mair, ed. *Welsh Ballads of the French Revolution, 1793–1815*. Cardiff: University of Wales Press, 2012.

Jones, T. E. *A Descriptive Account of the Literary Works of John Britton, FSA*. London: For Subscribers to the Testimonial, 1849.

Kennedy, A. J. 'British Topographical Print Series in Their Social and Economic Context, *c*.1720–*c*.1840'. Unpublished PhD thesis. Courtauld Institute, University of London, 1998.

King, William. *The Toast. An Heroick Poem*. London: 1747.

Knowles, John, ed. *The Life and Writings of Henry Fuseli*, 3 vols. London: Henry Colburn and Richard Bentley, 1831.

Knox, Thomas. *Some Account of the Proceedings that Took Place on the Landing of the French Near Fishguard, in Pembrokeshire … And of the Inquiry Afterwards Had Into Lieut. Col. Knox's Conduct*. London: A. Wilson, 1800.

'Legal Papers Regarding Case of Hugh Debbeig vs Lord Howe', National Archives, TS 11/944/3436, f. 1, 5 February 1782.

Lennox, Jeffers. *Homelands and Empires: Indigenous Spaces, Imperial Fictions, and Competition*. Toronto: University of Toronto Press, 2017.

Leslie, Charles Robert. *Life and Times of Sir Joshua Reynolds*, 2 vols. London: John Murray, 1865.

Lewis, Kathleen. *In the Steps of St Rhian: A History of the Church and Parish of Llanrhian* (1962). www.northdewislandchurches.org.uk/wp-content/uploads/2015/06/In-the-Steps-of-St-Rhian.pdf.

Linnaeus, Carl. *Linnaeus' Philosophia Botanica*, trans. Stephen Freer. Oxford: Oxford University Press, 2003.

Linnaeus, Carl. *Systema Naturae, 1735. Facsimile of the First Edition*, ed. and trans. M. S. J. Engel-Ledeboer and H. Engle. Nieuwkoop: B. de Graaf, 1964.

Löffler, Marion, ed., with Welsh-to-English translation by Bethan Mair Jenkins. *Political Pamphlets and Sermons from Wales, 1790–1806*. Cardiff: University of Wales Press, 2014.

Löffler, Marion, ed. *Welsh Responses to the French Revolution: Press and Public Discourse*. Cardiff: University of Cardiff Press, 2012.

Lord, Peter. *Words with Pictures: Welsh Images and Images of Wales in the Popular Press, 1640–1860*. Aberystwyth: Planet Books, 1995.

Lysaght, A. M. *Joseph Banks in Newfoundland and Labrador, 1766: His Diary, Manuscripts and Collections*. Berkeley: University of California Press, 1971.

MacDiarmid, Hugh. *Complete Poems: Volume I*, eds. M. Grieve and W. R. Aitken. Manchester: Carcanet, 1993.

MacDiarmid, Hugh. *Complete Poems: Volume II*, eds. M. Grieve and W. R. Aitken. Manchester: Carcanet, 1994.

Macnair, Andrew, and Tom Williamson. *William Faden and Eighteenth-Century Landscape*. Oxford: Wingatherer, 2010.

'Mam Tor and the Great Ridge'. www.walkingenglishman.com/peakdistrict04.htm.

Manley, K. A. 'Sir Samuel Egerton Brydges (1762–1837)'. *Oxford Dictionary of National Biography*. www.oxforddnb.com/view/article/3809.

Manners, John Henry (5th Duke of Rutland). *Journal of a Tour through North and South Wales, The Isle of Man, &c*. London: J. Triphook, 1805.

Mathias, Thomas James. *The Shade of Alexander Pope on the Banks of the Thames*. London: T. Becket, 1799.

Moll, Herman. *A New and Exact Map of the Dominions of the King of Great Britain on ye Continent of North America*. 1715.

Moritz, Charles P. *Travels, Chiefly on Foot, through Several Parts of England, in 1782*. London: G. G. and J. Robinson, 1795.

Morrison, Walter K. 'The Porcupine Map'. *ACML Bulletin* 62 (March 1987): 18.

Mudge, Thomas. *A Description with Plates, of the Time-Keeper Invented by the Late Mr Thomas Mudge*. London: Printed for the author, and sold by Mess. Payne, Cadell and Davies, Rivingtons, Dilly, and Richardson, 1799.

Mudge, Thomas. Documents. Royal Society, MM/7/91, MM/7/94, MM/7/100, MM/7/114, and MM/7/117–19.

Mudge, William. 'An Account of the Measurement of an Arc of the Meridian, Extending from Dunnose in the Isle of Wight … to Clifton in Yorkshire'. *Philosophical Transactions* 93 (1803): 383–508.

Mudge, William. 'An Account of the Trigonometrical Survey, Carried on in the Years 1797, 1798, and 1799'. *Philosophical Transactions* 90 (1800): 539–728.

Mudge, William, and Isaac Dalby. *An Account of the Operations Carried on for Accomplishing a Trigonometrical Survey of England and Wales; From the*

Commencement in the Year 1784, to the End of the Year 1796. London: Bulmer and Faden, 1799.

Mudge, William, Edward Williams, and Isaac Dalby. 'An Account of the Trigonometrical Survey, Carried on in the Years 1791, 1792, 1793, and 1794'. *Philosophical Transactions* 85 (1795): 414–591

Mudge, William, Edward Williams, and Isaac Dalby. 'An Account of the Trigonometrical Survey, Carried on in the Years 1795 and 1796'. *Philosophical Transactions* 87 (1797): 432–541.

Mudge, Zachariah. *A Sermon on Liberty*. London: F. Knight, 1790.

Nightingale, Joseph. *English Topography; Or, A Series of Historical and Statistical Descriptions of the Several Counties of England and Wales*. London: Baldwin, Cradock & Joy, 1816.

O'Brien, Sean. *Cousin Coat: Selected Poems, 1976–2001*. London: Picador, 2001.

Ordnance Survey. 'Old Series' map of Pembrokeshire (1819). Sheet 40.

Out-letters from Master-General, Board of Ordnance, and Commander in Chief, National Archives, WO 46/22, 1791–2.

Otto, Peter. *Multiplying Worlds: Romanticism, Modernity, and the Emergence of Virtual Reality*. Oxford: Oxford University Press, 2011.

Paterson, Daniel. *A New and Accurate Description of the Roads in England and Wales, and Part of the Roads of Scotland*. London: Longman, Rees, Faden, 1803.

Paulson, Ronald. *Representations of Revolution (1789–1820)*. New Haven, CT: Yale University Press, 1983.

Pennant, Thomas. *A Tour in Wales, MDCCLXXIII*, 2 vols. London: Henry Hughes, 1778 and 1781.

Philp, Mark. 'Introduction: The British Response to the Threat of Invasion, 1797–1815'. *Resisting Napoleon: The British Response to the Threat of Invasion, 1797–1815*, ed. Mark Philp, 1–17. Aldershot: Ashgate, 2006.

Pickles, John. 'Texts, Hermeneutics and Propaganda Maps'. *Writing Worlds: Discourse, Text and Metaphor*, eds. T. J. Barnes and J. J. Duncan, 193–230. London: Routledge, 1992.

Pindar, Peter [John Wolcot]. *Peter's Prophecy; Or, the President and Poet; Or, an Important Epistle to Sir J. Banks, On the Approaching Election of a President of the Royal Society*, 4th ed. London: G. Kearsley, 1788.

Portlock, Joseph. *Memoir of the Life of Major-General Colby*. London: Seeley, Jackson & Halliday, 1869.

Propert, Thomas. *A Plan of that Part of the County of Pembroke called Pen-Caer and the Sea Coast Adjacent, where between 1200 and 1400 French Troops under the Command of General Tate, made a Descent on a Point of Land called Garn or Cerrig Gwastad on the 22nd Day of Febry 1797* (11 February 1798). Llyfrgell Genedlaethol Cymru/National Library of Wales (Map 10823).

Quinault, Roland. 'The French Invasion of Pembrokeshire in 1797: A Bicentennial Assessment'. *Welsh History Review/Cylchgrawn Hanes Cymru* 19:4 (1999): 618–42.

Ramsey, Neil. 'Exhibiting Discipline: Military Science and the Naval Military Library and Museum'. *Tracing War in British Enlightenment and Romantic*

Culture, eds. Neil Ramsey and Gillian Russell. Basingstoke: Palgrave, 2015: 113–131.

Ramsey, Neil, and Gillian Russell. 'Introduction: Tracing War in Enlightenment and Romantic Culture'. In *Tracing War in British Enlightenment and Romantic Culture*, eds. Neil Ramsey and Gillian Russell, 1–16. Basingstoke: Palgrave, 2015.

Reynolds, Joshua. *The Works of Sir Joshua Reynolds*, 3 vols. London: Cadell & Davies, 1798.

Reynolds, Thomas Vincent. 'Queries Humbly Submitted to General the Duke of Richmond Relative to the Compilation of a Military Map of the Southern District'. National Archives, OS 3/5.

Richardson, John. *Fauna Boreali-Americana; Or, The Zoology of the Northern Parts of British America: Containing Descriptions of the Objects of Natural History Collected on the Late Northern Land Expeditions, under Command of Captain Sir John Franklin*, 4 vols. London: John Murray, 1829–37.

Roper, John, directed by E. W. Brayley. 'Index Map and Title Page'. In *The British Atlas: Comprising a Complete Set of County Maps, of England and Wales; With a General Map of Navigable Rivers and Canals; and Plans of Cities and Principal Towns*. London: Vernor, Hood & Sharpe, 1810.

Roper, John, after George Cole, directed by E. W. Brayley. 'Hereford'. In *The British Atlas: Comprising a Complete Set of County Maps, of England and Wales; With a General Map of Navigable Rivers and Canals; and Plans of Cities and Principal Towns*. London: Vernor, Hood & Sharpe, 1810.

Roper, John, after George Cole, directed by E. W. Brayley. 'Kent'. In *The British Atlas: Comprising a Complete Set of County Maps, of England and Wales; With a General Map of Navigable Rivers and Canals; and Plans of Cities and Principal Towns*. London: Vernor, Hood & Sharpe, 1810.

Roper, John, from a survey by Richard Thornton, directed by John Britton. 'Manchester and Salford'. In *The British Atlas: Comprising a Complete Set of County Maps, of England and Wales; With a General Map of Navigable Rivers and Canals; and Plans of Cities and Principal Towns*. London: Vernor, Hood & Sharpe, 1810.

Rose, Richard. 'The French at Fishguard: Fact, Fiction and Folklore'. *Transactions of the Honourable Society of Cymmrodorion* N.S. 9 (2003): 74–105.

Roy, William. 'An Account of the Trigonometrical Operation, Whereby the Distance Between the Meridians of the Royal Observatories of Greenwich and Paris has been Determined'. *Philosophical Transactions of the Royal Society* 80 (1790): 111–614.

Roy, William. *The Military Antiquities of the Romans in North Britain*. London: Society of Antiquaries, 1793.

Ruggles, Richard I. *A Country So Interesting: The Hudson's Bay Company and Two Centuries of Mapping, 1670–1870*. Montreal, QC: McGill-Queen's University Press, 1991.

Salmon, David. 'The French Invasion of Pembrokeshire in 1797: Official Documents, Contemporary Letters and Early Narratives'. *West Wales Historical Records* 14 (1929): 127–207.

Salmon, David. 'Histories of the French Invasion of Pembrokeshire'. *Cylchgrawn y Gymdeithas Lyfryddol Gymreig/Journal of the Welsh Bibliographical Society* 5:1 (1937): 41–8.

Salmon, David. 'A Sequel to the French Invasion of Pembrokeshire'. *Y Cymmrodor* 43 (1932): 62–92.

Scott, Walter. *Guy Mannering; or, the Astrologer*, 3 vols. Edinburgh: James Ballantyne, 1815.

Seccombe, Thomas, and David Penney. 'Thomas Mudge (1715/16–1794)'. *Oxford Dictionary of National Biography*. www.oxforddnb.com/view/article/19486.

Seward, Anna. *The Poetical Works of Anna Seward, With Extracts from Her Correspondence*, ed. Walter Scott. Edinburgh: J. Ballantyne and Co., 1810.

Sinclair, John. *The Statistical Account of Scotland. Drawn up from the Communications of the Ministers of Different Parishes*, 21 vols. Edinburgh: William Creech, 1791–9.

Smiles, Sam. *Eye Witness: Artists and Visual Documentation in Britain, 1770–1830*. Aldershot: Ashgate, 2000.

Smith, David. *Antique Maps of the British Isles*. London: Batsford, 1982.

Smith, D. K. *The Cartographic Imagination in Early Modern England: Re-writing the World in Marlowe, Spenser, Raleigh and Marvell*. Aldershot: Ashgate, 2008.

Smith, James Edward, ed. *A Selection of the Correspondence of Linnaeus, and Other Naturalists*, 2 vols. London: Longman, Hurst, Rees, Orme, and Brown, 1821.

Smyth, William J. *Map-Making, Landscapes and Memory: A Geography of Colonial and Early Modern Ireland*. Cork: Cork University Press, 2006.

Sobel, Dava. *Longitude: The True Story of a Lone Genius Who Solved the Greatest Scientific Problem of His Time*. London: Fourth Estate, 1996.

Sorrenson, Richard. 'The Ship as a Scientific Instrument in the Eighteenth Century'. *Osiris* 11 (1996): 221–36.

Stevenson, Anne. *Collected Poems of Anne Stevenson, 1955–95*. Oxford: Oxford University Press, 1996.

Stewart, Dugald. *Elements of the Philosophy of the Human Mind*, 3 vols. Edinburgh: Ramsay, 1792–1827.

Stuart Jones, E. H. *The Last Invasion of Britain*. Cardiff: University of Wales Press, 1950.

Surveyor-General's Minutes. National Archives, WO 47/118, 12 July 1791.

Tardieu, P. F., after J. Enouy. *Carte des Descentes Faites en Angleterre et en Irlande* (1798).

Thomas, J. E. *Britain's Last Invasion: Fishguard, 1797*. Stroud: Tempus, 2007.

Thomson, James. *The Works of James Thomson*, 4 vols. London: A. Millar, 1757.

Thornton, Thomas F. 'Anthropological Studies of Native American Place Naming'. *American Indian Quarterly* 21:2 (1997): 209–28.

Van Luijk, Ruben B. 'Maps of Battles, Battle of Maps: News Cartography of the Battle at Neerwinden, Flanders, 1693'. *Imago Mundi* 60:2 (2008): 211–20.

Vanek, Morgan. 'The Politics of the Weather: The Hudson's Bay Company and the Dobbs Affair'. *Journal for Eighteenth-Century Studies* 38:3 (2015): 395–411.

Verne, Jules. *Meridiana: The Adventures of Three Englishmen and Three Russians in South Africa*. New York: Scribner, Armstrong & Co., 1874.

Walker, Carol Kyros. *Walking North with Keats*. New Haven, CT: Yale University Press, 1992.

West, Shearer. 'Wilkes's Squint: Synecdochic Physiognomy and Political Identity in Eighteenth-Century Print Culture'. *Eighteenth-Century Studies* 33:1 (1999): 65–84.

West, Thomas. *A Guide to the Lakes*, 4th ed. London: Richardson, Robson and Pennington, 1789.

Widmalm, Sven. 'Accuracy, Rhetoric, and Technology: The Paris–Greenwich Triangulation, 1784–1788'. *The Quantifying Spirit in the Eighteenth Century*, eds. T. Frängsmyr, J. L. Heilbron, and Robin E. Rider, 179–206. Berkeley: University of California Press, 1990.

Whitaker, Katie. 'The Culture of Curiosity'. In *Cultures of Natural History*, eds. N. Jardine, J. A. Secord, and E. C. Spary, 75–90. Cambridge: Cambridge University Press, 1996.

Williams, Glyndwr, ed. *Andrew Graham's Observations on Hudson's Bay 1767–1791*. London: The Hudson's Bay Record Society, 1969.

Williams, Glyndwr. 'Andrew Graham and Thomas Hutchings: Collaboration and Plagiarism in 18th-Century Natural History'. *The Beaver* 308:4 (1978): 4–14.

Wilson, Kathleen. *The Island Race: Englishness, Empire and Gender in the Eighteenth Century*. London and New York: Routledge, 2003.

Withers, Charles W. J. 'Authorizing Landscape: "Authority", Naming and the Ordnance Survey's Mapping of the Scottish Highlands in the Nineteenth Century'. *Journal of Historical Geography* 26:4 (2000): 532–54.

Wordsworth, William. *Guide to the Lakes*, ed. Ernest de Selincourt. Oxford: Oxford University Press, 1977.

Part II

Abrams, M. H. *Natural Supernaturalism: Tradition and Revolution in Romantic Literature*. New York: Norton, 1973.

Alston, John. Letter to John Russell, 15 August 1839. National Archives, HO 102/47, MPI 1/63.

Alston, John. *Statements of the Education, Employments, and Internal Arrangements, Adopted at the Asylum for the Blind, Glasgow*. Glasgow: Printed by George Brookman, 1839.

Baugh, Daniel. *The Global Seven Years War, 1754–1763: Britain and France in a Great Power Contest*. Harlow: Longman, 2011.

Belzoni, Giovanni. *Narrative of the Operations and Recent Discoveries within the Pyramids, Temples, Tombs and Excavations of Egypt and Nubia*. London: John Murray, 1820.

Blacklock, Thomas. *Poems by the Late Reverend Dr. Thomas Blacklock; Together with An Essay on the Education of the Blind*. Edinburgh: Alexander Chapman and Company, 1793.

'Blind'. In *Encyclopaedia Britannica; Or, A Dictionary of Arts, Sciences, and Miscellaneous Literature*, vol. 3, 3rd edn., eds. Colin Macfarquhar and George Gleig, illus. Andrew Bell, 298. Edinburgh: Printed for A. Bell and C. Macfarquhar, 1797.

Branch, Jordan. *The Cartographic State: Maps, Territory and the Origins of Sovereignty*. Cambridge: Cambridge University Press, 2013.

Bowden, John E. *The Life and Letters of Frederick William Faber, D.d.* London: J. Murphy, 1869.

Bowdler, Henrietta Maria, ed. *Fragments in prose and verse: by Miss Elizabeth Smith. With Some Account of Her Life and Character*. Bath: Printed by Richard Cruttwell, 1809.

Bowles's Geographical Game of the World: In a New Complete and Elegant Tour Through Known Parts Thereof, Laid Down on Mercator's Projection. London: Printed for the proprietors Bowles & Carver, No. 69 St. Paul's Church Yard, 1797.

'British Isles'. Two duplicates of an embossed tactile map printed at the Asylum for the Blind, Glasgow. National Archives MPI 1/63.

'British Geographical Game', *The Literary Chronicle* (Dec. 1827): 824–5.

The British Tourist: A New Game. London: E. Wallis, 1820.

Broglio, Ron. *Technologies of the Picturesque: British Art, Poetry, and Instruments, 1750–1830*. Lewisburg, PA: Bucknell University Press, 2008.

Caeton, D. A. '"Veux-tu regarder, bourreau!": The Somanormative Dimensions of the Diderotian *Citoyen*'. *Journal of Literary & Cultural Disability Studies* 4.1 (2010): 73–88.

Caillois, Roger. *Man, Play, and Games*. New York: Free Press of Glencoe, 1961.

Carlson, Julia S. *Romantic Marks and Measures: Wordsworth's Poetry in Fields of Print*. Philadelphia: University of Pennsylvania Press, 2016.

Carlson, Julia S. 'Tangible Burns'. In *The Unfinished Book*, eds. Alexandra Gillespie and Deidre Lynch, 121–35. Oxford: Oxford University Press, 2020.

Carroll, Siobhan. *An Empire of Air and Water: Uncolonizable Space in the British Imagination, 1750–1850*. Philadelphia: University of Pennsylvania Press, 2015.

Clarke, Norma. '"The Cursed Barbauld Crew": Women Writers and Writing for Children in the Late Eighteenth Century'. In *Opening the Nursery Door: Reading, Writing and Childhood, 1600–1900*, eds. Mary Hilton, Morag Styles, and Victor Watson, 91–104. London and New York: Routledge, 1997.

Coleridge, Samuel Taylor. *Biographia Literaria*, ed. Adam Roberts. Edinburgh: Edinburgh University Press, 2015.

Coleridge, Sara. *Memoir and Letters of Sara Coleridge*, vol. 1, ed. Edith Coleridge. London: Henry S. King, 1873.

Cowper, William. *The Task. The Task and Selected Other Poems*, ed. James Sambrook. London, Longman, 1994.

Degenaar, Marjolein, and Gert-Jan Lokhorst. 'Molyneux's Problem'. *The Stanford Encyclopedia of Philosophy* (Winter 2017), ed. Edward N. Zalta. https://plato .stanford.edu/archives/win2017/entries/molyneux-problem/.

Diderot, Denis. *Diderot's Early Philosophical Works*, trans. and ed. Margaret Jourdain. Chicago and London: Open Court, 1916.

Diderot, Denis. *Letter on the Blind for the Use of Those Who Can See*, trans. Kate E. Tunstall. In Tunstall, *Blindness and Enlightenment: An Essay* (New York: Continuum, 2011).

Edinburgh Royal Blind School. www.royalblind.org/our-organisation/our-history.

Edney, Matthew. 'British Military Education, Mapmaking, and Military "Map-mindedness" in the Later Enlightenment'. *Cartographic Journal* 31.1 (1994): 14–20.

Edney, Matthew. *Mapping an Empire: The Geographical Construction of British India, 1765–1843*. Chicago, IL: University of Chicago Press, 1990.

Edney, Matthew. 'The Irony of Imperial Mapping'. In *The Imperial Map: Cartography and the Mastery of Empire*, ed. James R. Akermen, 11–46. Chicago, IL: University of Chicago Press, 2009.

Farrell, Gabriel. *The Story of Blindness*. Cambridge, MA: Harvard University Press, 1956.

Fleet, Christopher, and Charles W. J. Withers. 'A Scottish Paper Landscape'. *National Library of Scotland*. https://maps.nls.uk/os/6inch/os_info1.html.

Friel, Brian. *Translations*. London: Faber and Faber, 1981.

Galileo, Galilei. *Discoveries and Opinions of Galileo: Including the Starry Messenger (1610), Letter to the Grand Duchess Christina (1615), and Excerpts from Letters on Sunspots (1613), The Assayer (1623)*, trans. Drake Stillman. New York: Anchor Books, 1990.

Gall, James. *An Account of the Recent Discoveries Which Have Been Made for Facilitating the Education of the Blind, with Specimens of the Books, Maps, Pictures, &c. for their Use*. Edinburgh: James Gall, 1837.

Gall, James. *A Historical Sketch of the Origin and Progress of Literature for the Blind: And Practical Hints and Recommendations as to their Education*. Edinburgh: James Gall, 1834.

Gual, Jaume. 'Three-Dimensional Tactile Symbols Produced by 3D Printing: Improving the Process of Memorizing a Tactile Map Key'. *British Journal of Visual Impairment* 32.3 (2014): 263–78.

Guillié, Sébastien. *An Essay on the Instruction and Amusements of the Blind*. London: Printed for Richard Philips, 1819. Reprinted London: Sampson Low, Marston, and Company, 1894.

Hack, Maria. *Winter Evenings; or Tales of Travellers*. London: Darton, Harvey and Darton, 1818.

Haguet, Lucile. 'J-B d'Anville as Armchair Mapmaker'. *Imago Mundi* 62 (2011): 88–105.

Hannas, Linda. *The English Jigsaw Puzzle, 1760–1890: With a Descriptive Check-List of Puzzles in the Museums of Great Britain and the Author's Collection*. London: Wayland, 1972.

Harley, J. B. *The New Nature of Maps: Essays in the History of Cartography*, ed. Paul Laxton. Baltimore, MD: Johns Hopkins University Press, 2001.

Hartman, Geoffrey H. *Wordsworth's Poetry, 1787–1814*. New Haven, CT: Yale University Press, 1971.

Haüy, Valentin. 'Bienfaisance. Aux Auteurs du Journal'. *Journal de Paris* 274 (18 September 1784): 1158–9.

Hayhoe, Simon. *Blind Visitor Experiences at Art Museums*. Lanham, MD: Rowman & Littlefield, 2017.

Hewitt, Rachel. *Map of a Nation: A Biography of the Ordnance Survey*. London: Granta, 2010.

Jacob, Christian. *The Sovereign Map: Theoretical Approaches in Cartography Throughout History*, trans. Tom Conley, ed. Edward H. Dahl. Chicago, IL: University of Chicago Press, 2006.

Jacobus, Mary. *Romanticism, Writing and Sexual Difference: Essays on The Prelude*. Oxford and New York: Clarendon Press, 1989.

Jay, Martin. *Downcast Eyes: The Denigration of Vision in Twentieth-Century French Thought*. Berkeley: University of California Press, 1993.

Jefferys, Thomas. *The Conduct of the French, with Regard to Nova Scotia*. London: T. Jefferys, 1754.

Jefferys, Thomas. *The Royal Geographical Pastime: Exhibiting a Complete Tour Round the World, by T. Jefferys*. London: Thos. Jefferys at the Corner of St. Martins Lane, 1768.

Johnston, David. *The Uncomfortable Situation of the Blind, with the Means of Relief, Represented in a Sermon, Preached in the Tron Church, Edinburgh, on Tuesday May 15. 1793*. Edinburgh: Printed for the Society for the Relief of the Indigent Blind, 1793.

Johnston, Kenneth R. *The Hidden Wordsworth: Poet, Lover, Rebel, Spy*. New York: Norton, 1998.

Kaiser, Matthew. *The World in Play: Portraits of a Victorian Concept*. Stanford, CA: Stanford University Press, 2012.

Lacaille, Nicholas-Louis de. *Leçons élémentaires de Mathématiques* (1741).

Lajer-Burchrarth, Ewa. *The Painter's Touch: Boucher, Chardin, Fragonard*. Princeton, NJ: Princeton University Press, 2018.

Leslie, Camilo Arturo. 'Territoriality, Map-Mindedness, and the Politics of Place'. *Theory and Society* 45 (2016): 169–201.

Locke, John. *Some Thoughts Concerning Education*. London: Printed for a Society of Stationers, and sold by J. Baker at the Black Boy in Pater-Noster-Row, 1710.

Mandelbrot, Benoit B. *The Fractal Geometry of Nature*, updated and augmented ed. New York: W. H. Freeman, 1983.

Mandelbrot, Benoit B. *The Fractalist: Memoir of a Scientific Maverick*. New York: Pantheon Books, 2012.

Mandelbrot, Benoit B. 'Fractals and the Art of Roughness'. TED, 2010. www.ted.com/talks/benoit_mandelbrot_fractals_the_art_of_roughness.

Mandelbrot, Benoit B. 'How Long Is the Coast of Britain? Statistical Self-Similarity and Fractional Dimension'. *Science* 156.3775 (1967): 636–8.

Norcia, Megan. *X Marks the Spot: Women Writers Map the Empire for British Children, 1790–1895*. Athens: Ohio University Press, 2010.

Owen, Tim, and Elaine Pillbeam. *Ordnance Survey: Map Makers to Britain Since 1791*. Southampton: Ordnance Survey, 1992.

Packham, Catherine. 'Disability and Sympathetic Sociability in Enlightenment Scotland: The Case of Thomas Blacklock'. *British Journal for Eighteenth-Century Studies* 30 (2007): 423–38.

Panorama of Europe. A New Game. London and Sidmouth: J & E. Wallis, 1815.

Pasanek, Brian, and Chad Wellmon. 'The Enlightenment Index'. *Eighteenth-Century Theory and Interpretation* 56:3 (2015): 357–80.

Paterson, Mark. *The Senses of Touch: Haptics, Affects and Technologies.* London: Bloomsbury, 2007.

Paulson, William R. *Enlightenment, Romanticism, and the Blind in France.* Princeton, NJ: Princeton University Press, 1987.

Pedley, Mary. *The Commerce of Cartography: Making and Marketing Maps in Eighteenth-Century France and England.* Chicago, IL: University of Chicago Press, 2005.

Poincaré, Henri. *Science et Méthode.* Paris: Flammarion, 1947.

Poincaré, Henri, and George Bruce Halstead. *The Foundations of Science: Science and Hypothesis, The Value of Science, Science and Method.* Garrison, NY: The Science Press, 1913.

Pratt, Mary Louise. *Imperial Eyes: Travel and Transculturation.* London: Routledge, 1992.

'Proceedings of the Society for the Encouragement of the Useful Arts in Scotland'. *Edinburgh New Philosophical Journal* 20 (October 1835–April 1836).

Rankin, William. *After the Map: Cartography, Navigation, and the Transformation of Territory in the Twentieth Century.* Chicago, IL: University of Chicago Press, 2016.

Richardson, Lewis Fry. *Statistics of Deadly Quarrels.* Pittsburgh, PA: Boxwood Press, 1960.

Richardson, Lewis Fry. *Weather Prediction by Numerical Process.* Cambridge: Cambridge University Press, 1922.

Riskin, Jessica. *Science in the Age of Sensibility: The Sentimental Empiricists of the French Enlightenment.* Chicago, IL: University of Chicago Press, 2002.

Sala, George Augustus. *Under the Sun; Essays Written Mainly in Hot Countries.* London: Robson & Sons, 1872.

Scott, Walter. *Waverley,* ed. Claire Lamont. Oxford: Oxford University Press, 2008.

Seymour, W. A., ed. *A History of the Ordnance Survey.* Folkestone, Kent: Dawson, 1980.

Smith, Johanna M. 'Constructing the Nation: Eighteenth-Century Geographies for Children'. *Mosaic* 34:2 (2001): 133–48.

St Clair, William. *The Reading Nation in the Romantic Period.* Cambridge: Cambridge University Press, 2004.

Tilley, Heather. *Blindness and Writing: From Wordsworth to Gissing.* Cambridge: Cambridge University Press, 2017.

Tunstall, Kate E. *Blindness and Enlightenment: An Essay.* New York: Continuum, 2011.

Uttal, David H. 'Seeing the Big Picture: Map Use and the Development of Spatial Cognition'. *Developmental Science* 3:3 (2000): 247–86.

Uttal, David H. 'Spatial Symbols and Spatial Thought: Cross-Cultural, Developmental, and Historical Perspectives on the Relation between Map Use and Spatial Cognition'. In *Symbol Use and Symbolic Representation: Developmental and Comparative Perspectives*, ed. L. Namy, 3–23. Mahwah: Erlbaum, 2005.

'Variétés. Aux Auteurs du Journal'. *Journal de Paris* 115 (24 April 1784): 504.

'Variétés. Institut des Aveugles. Aux Rédacteurs du Journal'. *Journal de Paris* 338 (26 August 1805): 2376.

Wallis, John, with Archibald McIntyre (engraver). *Wallis's New Map of Europe Divided into Its Empires Kingdoms &c: From the Latest Astronomical Observations*. London: John Wallis, 1814.

Wallis's Locomotive Game of Railroad Adventure. London: Edward Wallis, 1835.

Wallis's New Geographical Game Exhibiting a Complete Tour through Scotland and the Western Isles. London: John Wallis and Elizabeth Newbery, 1792.

Wallis's Tour of Europe: A New Geographical Pastime. London: John Wallis, 16, Ludgate St, 1794.

Walker's New Geographical Game Exhibiting a Tour through Europe. London: W. & T. Darton, 1810.

Weimer, David. 'A Touch of the Sighted World: Tactile Maps in the Early Nineteenth Century'. *Winterthur Portfolio* 51 (Summer/Autumn 2017): 135–58.

Weygand, Zina. *The Blind in French Society, from the Middle Ages to the Century of Louis Braille*, trans. Emily-Jane Cohen. Stanford, CA: Stanford University Press, 2009.

Wilner, Joshua. '"Self-Displacing Vision": Snowdon and the Dialectic of the Senses'. *Wordsworth Circle* XXVIII:1 (2006): 27–33.

Wilson, E. F. *Missionary Works Among the Ojebway Indians*. London: SPCK, 1886.

Wilson, Sarah Atkins. *Botanical Rambles*. London: Baldwin, Cradock and Joy, 1822.

Wilson, Sarah Atkins. *An Evening in Autumn; or, The Useful Amusement*. London: Harvey and Darton, 1821.

Wilson, Sarah Atkins. *The Fruits of Enterprise Exhibited in the Travels of Belzoni*. London: John Harris, 1821.

Wilson, Sarah Atkins. *Grove Cottage*. London: Harris and Sons, 1823.

Wilson, Sarah Atkins. *The India Cabinet Opened*. London: Harris and Son, 1821.

Wilson, Sarah Atkins. *Real Stories, Taken from the Lives of Various Travellers*. London: Harvey and Darton, 1827.

Wordsworth, William. *The Excursion*, eds. Sally Bushell, James A. Butler, Michael C. Jaye, and David Garcia. Ithaca, NY: Cornell University Press, 2007.

Wordsworth, William. *The Five-Book Prelude*, ed. Duncan Wu. Oxford: Blackwell, 1997.

Wordsworth, William. *The Thirteen-Book Prelude*, ed. Mark L. Reed. Ithaca, NY: Cornell University Press, 1991.

Venn, H. *Sermons Preached on the Occasion of the Death of Mrs Wilson*. London: Seeley, 1863.

Part III

Adams, Richard. *The Plague Dogs*. London: Allen Lane, 1978.

Bakhtin, Mikhail. 'Forms of Time and Chronotope in the Novel'. In *The Dialogic Imagination: Four Essays by M. M. Bakhtin*, ed. Michael Holquist, trans. Caryl Emerson and Michael Holquist, 184–258. Austin: University of Texas Press, 1982.

Barfield, Steven, ed. 'Psychogeography: Will Self and Iain Sinclair in Conversation with Kevin Jackson'. *Literary London: Interdisciplinary Studies in the Representation of London* 6.1 (2008): 1–41.

Barrell, John. 'The Sense of Place in the Poetry of John Clare'. In *The Idea of Landscape and the Sense of Place, 1730–1840*, 98–187. Cambridge: Cambridge University Press, 1972.

Besson, Jean. *Transformations of Freedom in the Land of the Maroons: Creolization in the Cockpits, Jamaica*. Kingston, JA: Ian Randle, 2015.

Biggs, Iain. '"Deep Mapping": A Brief Introduction'. In *Mapping Spectral Traces*, ed. K. E. Till, 5–8. Blacksburg: Virginia Tech College, 2010.

Biggs, Iain. 'The Spaces of "Deep Mapping": A Partial Account'. *Journal of Arts and Communities* 2 (2011): 5–25.

Blythe, Ronald. 'Solvitur Ambulando: John Clare and Footpath Walking'. *John Clare Society Journal* 14 (1995): 17–27.

Bate, Jonathan. 'The Flitting'. In *John Clare: A Biography*, 387–401. London: Picador, 2003.

Borodale, Sean. 'Walking to Paradise', Maps 01–12. Grasmere, The Wordsworth Trust, 2011.R1.14.1–2011.R1.14.12.

Borodale, Sean. 'Walking to Paradise.' In *Walking to Paradise*, ed. Sean Borodale et al., 14–15. Grasmere: The Wordsworth Trust, 1999.

Campbell, Mavis. *The Maroons of Jamaica, 1655–1796: A History of Resistance, Collaboration, and Betrayal*. South Hadley, MA: Bergin & Garvey, 1988.

Campbell, Mavis. *Nova Scotia and the Fighting Maroons: A Documentary History*. Williamsburg, VA: Department of Anthropology, College of William and Mary, 1990.

Carey, Bev. *The Maroon Story: The Authentic and Original History of the Maroons in the History of Jamaica, 1490–1880*. Gordon Town, Jamaica: Agouti Press, 1997.

Carlson, Julia S. 'Topographical Measures: Wordsworth's and Crosthwaite's Lines on the Lake District'. *Romanticism* 16 (2010): 72–93.

Chopra, Ruma. *Almost Home: Maroons between Slavery and Freedom in Jamaica, Nova Scotia, and Sierra Leone*. New Haven: Yale University Press, 2018.

Clare, John. *John Clare By Himself*, eds. Eric Robinson and David Powell. Manchester: Carcanet, 1996.

Clare, John. *John Clare: Poems of the Middle Period 1822–1837. Vol. IV*, eds. Eric Robinson, David Powell and P. M. S. Dawson. Oxford: Clarendon Press, 1998.

Coleridge, Rev. Gerard Hartley Buchanan. 'Samuel Taylor Coleridge Discovers the Lake County'. In *Wordsworth and Coleridge: Studies in Honor of George*

McLean Harper, ed. Earl Leslie Griggs, 135–65. Princeton, NJ: Princeton University Press, 1939.

Coleridge, Samuel Taylor. *Collected Letters of Samuel Taylor Coleridge: Volume I 1785–1800*, ed. Earl Leslie Griggs. Oxford: Clarendon Press, 1956.

Coleridge, Samuel Taylor. *Collected Letters of Samuel Taylor Coleridge: Volume II 1801–1806*, ed. Earl Leslie Griggs. Oxford: Clarendon Press, 1956.

Coleridge, Samuel Taylor. *The Notebooks of Samuel Taylor Coleridge: Volume 1, 1794–1804*, ed. Kathleen Coburn. Abingdon: Routledge & Kegan Paul, 1957.

Cooper, David, and Les Roberts. 'Walking, Witnessing, Mapping: An Interview with Iain Sinclair'. *Mapping Cultures: Place Practice Performance*, ed. Les Roberts. London: Palgrave Macmillan, 2012: 85–100.

Corbin, Alan. *Village Bells: Sound and Meaning in the Nineteenth Century French Countryside*, trans. Martin Thom. London: Papermac, 1999.

Cosgrove, Denis. 'Cultural Cartography: Maps and Mapping in Cultural Geography'. *Annales de Géographie* 2 (2008): 159–78.

Dallas, R. C. *The History of the Maroons*, 2 vols. London: Longman and Rees, 1803.

Davies, Hunter. *Wainwright: The Biography*. London: Orion, 1998.

Denil, Mark. 'Cartographic Design: Rhetoric and Persuasion'. *Cartographic Perspectives* 45 (2003): 8–67.

Dodge, Martin, *et al.* 'Mapping Modes, Methods and Moments: A Manifesto for Map Studies'. *Rethinking Maps: New Frontiers in Cartographic Theory*. London: Routledge, 2009: 220–43.

Edensor. Tim. '*Walking in Rhythms: Place, Regulation, Style and the Flow of Experience*'. *Visual Studies* 25 (2010): 69–79.

Edney, Matthew H. *Mapping an Empire: The Geographical Construction of British India, 1765–1843*. Chicago, IL: University of Chicago Press, 1997.

Edwards, Bryan. *The History, Civil and Commercial, of the British Colonies in the West Indies*. London: Stockdale, 1801.

Edwards, Bryan. *The Proceedings of the Governor and Assembly of Jamaica in Regard to the Maroon Negroes*. London: Stockdale, 1796.

Edwards, Jess. 'Study, Marketplace and Labyrinth: Geometry as Rhetoric'. *New Formations* (2006): 126–144.

Fielding, Penny. *Scotland and the Fictions of Geography: North Britain 1760–1830*. Cambridge: Cambridge University Press, 2008.

Fulford, Tim. *The Late Poetry of the Lake Poets: Romanticism Revised*. Cambridge: Cambridge University Press, 2013.

Gambles, Robert. *Man in Lakeland: 2,000 Years of Human Settlement*. Clapham: Dalesman, 1975.

Grant, John N. *The Maroons in Nova Scotia*. Halifax: Formac, 2002.

Griffin, A. H. *A Lakeland Notebook*. London: Robert Hale, 1975.

Guyer, Sara. 'The Poetics of Homelessness'. In *Reading with John Clare: Biopoetics, Sovereignty, Romanticism*, 78–100. New York: Fordham University Press, 2015.

Haft, Adele J. 'Poems Shaped Like Maps: (Di)Versifying the Teaching of Geography, II.' *Cartographic Perspectives* 36 (2000): 66–91.

Harley, J. B. 'Deconstructing the Map'. *Cartographica* 26.2 (1989): 1–20.

Harley, J. B. 'Maps, Knowledge and Power'. *The Iconography of Landscape: Essays in the Symbolic Representation, Design and Use of Past Environments*, eds D. Cosgrove and S. Daniels, 277–312. Cambridge: Cambridge University Press, 1988.

Harley, J. B. 'Power and Legitimation in the English Geographical Atlases of the Eighteenth-Century'. In *The New Nature of Maps: Essays in the History of Cartography*, ed. Paul Laxton, intro. J. H. Andrews, 110–47. Baltimore, MD: Johns Hopkins University Press, 2001.

Harley, J. B. 'Texts and Contexts in the Interpretation of Early Maps'. In *The New Nature of Maps: Essays in the History of Cartography*, ed. Paul Laxton, intro. J. H. Andrews, 34–49. Baltimore, MD: Johns Hopkins University Press, 2001.

Hardt, Michael, and Antonio Negri. *Declaration*. Argo Navis Author Services, 2012.

Harris, T. M., J. Corrigan, and D. J. Bodenhamer. 'Conclusion: Engaging Deep Maps'. In *Deep Maps and Spatial Narratives*, eds. D. J. Bodenhamer, J. Corrigan, and T. M. Harris, 223–33. Bloomington: Indiana University Press, 2015.

Hart, Richard. *Blacks in Rebellion: Slaves who Abolished Slavery*. Kingston, Jamaica: University of the West Indies Press, 1980.

Heidegger, Martin. *Poetry, Language, Thought*, trans. Albert Hofstadter. New York: Harper & Row, 1971.

Hones, Sheila. 'Literary Geography: The Novel as a Spatial Event'. In *Envisioning Landscapes, Making Worlds: Geography and the Humanities*, eds. Stephen Daniels *et al.*, 247–55. London: Routledge, 2011.

Hudson, Martyn. 'Archive, Sound and Landscape in Richard Skelton's Landings Sequence'. *Landscapes* 16 (2015): 63–78.

Ingold, Tim. *The Perception of the Environment: Essays of Livelihood, Dwelling, and Skill*. London: Routledge, 2000.

Ingold, Tim. 'The Temporality of Landscape'. *World Archaeology* 25 (1993): 152–74.

Jeffrey, Francis. 'The Lay of the Last Minstrel: A Poem. By Walter Scott, Esquire'. *Edinburgh Review* 5 (1805): 1–20.

Kelly, Stuart. 'Show Me the Way to Tillietudlem'. *Five Imaginary Scottish Places*, BBC Radio 3 (1 June 2015). www.bbc.co.uk/programmes/b05xqtp0 (accessed 31 July 2017).

Kopytoff, Barbara Klamon. 'Colonial Treaty as Sacred Charter of the Jamaican Maroons'. *Ethnohistory* 21.1 (1979): 45–64.

Kövesi, Simon. *John Clare: Nature, Criticism and History*. London: Palgrave Macmillan, 2017.

Laws of Jamaica, 1792–1799. St. Jago de la Vega, Jamaica: Alexander Aikman, 1799.

Lindsay, Alexander Crawford. *Lives of the Lindsays; Or, a Memoir of the Houses of Crawford and Balcarres*, 3 vols. London: John Murray, 1849.

Linebaugh, Peter. *The Magna Carta Manifesto: On Liberties and Commons for All*. Berkeley: University of California Press, 2009.

Lockhart, J. G. *Memoirs of the Life of Sir Walter Scott*, 7 vols. Edinburgh: Robert Caddell, 1837.

'Lockhart's Life of Sir Walter Scott'. *Tait's Edinburgh Magazine* 4 (1837): 205–20.

Long, Edward. *The History of Jamaica*, 3 vols. London: T. Lowndes, 1774.

The Journals of the Assembly of Jamaica. St. Jago de la Vega, Jamaica: Alexander Aikman, 1758.

Macfarlane, Robert. 'Extreme Styles of Hunting'. *Guardian Review*, 21 May 2005: 35.

Macfarlane, Robert. 'Generation Anthropocene: How Humans Have Altered the Planet For Ever'. *Guardian*, 1 April 2016.

Macfarlane, Robert. *Landmarks*. London: Hamish Hamilton, 2015.

McEwan, Ian. *Amsterdam*. London: Jonathan Cape, 1998.

McKay, Carol. 'Richard Skelton'. In *Wordsworth and Bashō: Walking Poets*, 128. Sunderland: Art Editions North, 2014.

McRae, Lucy. 'Local Explanations: Editing a Sense of Place in Walter Scott's *Minstrelsy of the Scottish Border*'. *Forum* 3 (2014): 1–12.

McRae, Lucy. 'Walter Scott's *Minstrelsy of the Scottish Border* and the Dynamics of Cultural Memory'. Unpublished Ph.D. thesis. University of Edinburgh, 2014.

Marchitello, Howard. *Narrative and Meaning in Early Modern England: Browne's Skull and Other Histories*. Cambridge: Cambridge University Press, 1997.

'Maroon Town in the Parish of St. James Jamaica, with a representation of the attack in the Road leading to the Town in which Col Sanford & other respectable Gentlemen were unfortunately killed. Aug. 1795'. National Library of Jamaica. P/240/XIII.

Milton, John. *Paradise Lost*, eds. Stephen Orgel and Jonathan Goldberg. Oxford: Oxford University Press, 2008.

Modiano, Raimonda. 'Blood Sacrifice, Gift Economy and the Edenic World: Wordsworth's "Home at Grasmere"'. *Studies in Romanticism* 32 (1993): 481–521.

Monmonier, Mark. *Mapping It Out: Expository Cartography for the Humanities and Social Sciences*. Chicago, IL: University of Chicago Press, 1993.

Moretti, Franco. *Graphs, Maps, Trees: Abstract Models for a Literary History*. London: Verso, 2005.

Morley, E. J., ed. *Blake, Coleridge, Wordsworth, Lamb, etc. Being Selections from the Remains of Henry Crabb Robinson*. Manchester: Manchester University Press, 1922.

Morley, Simon. *Writing on the Wall: Word and Image in Modern Art*. London: Thames and Hudson, 2003.

Nichol, bp. *Man in Lakeland*. Toronto: Weed/Flower Press, 1978.

Nicholson, Norman. *Collected Poems*, ed. Neil Curry. London: Faber & Faber, 1994.

Nora, Pierre. 'Between Memory and History: Les Lieux de Memoire'. *Representations* 26 (Spring 1989): 7–24.

Nora, Pierre. 'General Introduction'. *Rethinking France: Les Lieux de Mémoire*, Vol. 1, *The State*, trans. Mary Trouille, 7–21. Chicago, IL: University of Chicago Press, 2010.

Nora, Pierre. 'Introduction'. *Rethinking France: Les Lieux de Mémoire*, Vol. 4, *Histories and Memories*, trans. David P. Jordan, 7–14. Chicago, IL: University of Chicago Press, 2010.

Palmer, Clare, and Brady, Emily. 'Landscape and Value in the Work of Alfred Wainwright (1907–1991)'. *Landscape Research* 32.4 (2007): 397–421.

Pearson, Mike, and Michael Shanks. *Theatre/Archaeology*. London: Routledge, 2001.

Rainsford, Marcus. *An Historical Account of the Black Empire of Hayti*. London: James Cundee, 1805.

Richardson, Autumn, and Richard Skelton. *Memorious Earth: A Longitudinal Study*. Cumbria: Corbel Stone Press, 2015.

Roberts, Les. 'Deep Mapping and Spatial Anthropology'. *Deep Mapping*, ed. Les Roberts, vii–xv. Basel: MDPI, 2016.

Rodaway, Paul. *Sensuous Geographies: Body, Sense and Place*. London: Routledge, 1994.

Rohl, Darrell. J. 'The Chorographical Tradition and Seventeenth- and Eighteenth-Century Scottish Antiquaries'. *Journal of Art Historiography* 5 (2011): 1–18.

Rylance, Rick. 'Three North Pennine Journeys in the 1930s: Auden, Trevelyan and Wainwright'. *Critical Survey* 10.3 (1998): 83–94.

St. James. 184A. National Library of Jamaica. Cadastral Maps and Plans.

St. James 184B. National Library of Jamaica. Cadastral Maps and Plans.

St. James 434. National Library of Jamaica. Cadastral Maps and Plans.

Scott, Walter. *The Border Antiquities of England and Scotland*, 2 vols. London: Longman & Co., 1814.

Scott, Walter. 'Essay on Romance'. In *The Miscellaneous Prose Works of Sir Walter Scott, Bart, 1834–1836: Vol. VI*, 127–216. Edinburgh: Robert Caddell, 1834–6.

Scott, Walter. *The Lay of the Last Minstrel: A Poem*. London: Longman & Co., 1805.

Scott, Walter. *The Letters of Sir Walter Scott*, 12 vols., ed. H. J. C. Grierson. London: Constable & Co., 1832–6.

Scott, Walter. *Minstrelsy of the Scottish Border*, 3 vols. Kelso: James Ballantyne, 1802–3.

Scott, Walter. *The Poetical Works of Sir Walter Scott, Baronet*, 11 vols. Edinburgh: Caddell & Co., 1830.

Shanks, Michael. *The Archaeological Imagination*. Abingdon: Routledge, 2016.

Shanks, Michael, and Christopher Witmore. 'Echoes of the Past: Chorography and Topography in Antiquarian Engagements with Place'. *Performance Research* 15 (2010): 97–106.

Sinclair, Iain. *Edge of the Orison: In the Traces of John Clare's 'Journey out of Essex'*. London: Hamish Hamilton, 2005.

Sinclair, Iain. *London Orbital*. London: Penguin, 2003.

Sinclair, Iain. *Lud Heat: A Book of the Dead Hamlets*. London: Albion Village Press, 1975.

Skelton, Richard. *Beyond the Fell Wall*. Fratrum Toller: Little Toller, 2015.

Skelton, Richard. *Landings*, 5th ed. Cumbria: Corbel Stone Press, 2015.

Skelton, Richard. *Limnology*. Cumbria: Corbel Stone Press, 2012.

Stafford, Fiona. *Local Attachments: The Province of Poetry*. Oxford: Oxford University Press, 2010.

Sutherland, John. *The Life of Sir Walter Scott: A Critical Biography*. Oxford: Blackwell Publishers, 1995.

Sweet, Rosemary. *Antiquaries: The Discovery of the Past in Eighteenth-Century Britain*. London: Hambledon and London, 2004.

United Nations. *United Nations Declaration of the Rights of Indigenous Peoples*. New York: United Nations, 2008.

Votes of the Honourable Assembly of Jamaica, 1791–92. St. Jago de la Vega, Jamaica: Alexander Aikman, 1792.

Votes of the House of the Honourable Assembly of Jamaica, 1841–42. St. Jago de la Vega, Jamaica: Alexander Aikman, 1842.

Wainwright. A. *Ex-Fellwanderer: A Thanksgiving*. Kendal: Westmorland Gazette, 1987.

Wainwright. A. *Fellwanderer: The Story behind the Guidebooks*. Kendal: Westmorland Gazette, 1966.

Wainwright. A. *Memoirs of a Fellwanderer*. London: Frances Lincoln, 2003.

Wainwright. A. *The Wainwright Letters*, ed. Hunter Davies. London: Frances Lincoln, 2011.

Walford Davies, Damian. *Cartographies of Culture: New Geographies of Welsh Writing in English*. Cardiff: University of Wales Press, 2012.

Wilson, Kathleen. 'The Performance of Freedom: Maroons and the Colonial Order in Eighteenth-Century Jamaica and the Atlantic Sound'. *William and Mary Quarterly* 66:1 (2009): 45–86.

Wood, Denis, John Fels, and John Krygier. *Rethinking the Power of Maps*. New York: Guilford, 2010.

Wordsworth, William. *The Prelude 1799, 1805, 1850*, eds. Jonathan Wordsworth, M. H. Abrams, and Stephen Gill. New York: Norton, 1979.

Wordsworth, William. *William Wordsworth*, ed. Stephen Gill. Oxford: Oxford University Press, 1984.

Wordsworth, William. *Wordsworth: Poetical Works*, ed. Thomas Hutchinson, rev. Ernest de Selincourt. Oxford: Oxford University Press, 1969.

Zips, Werner. *Black Rebels: African Freedom Fighters in Jamaica*, trans. Shelley L. Frisch. Kingston, Jamaica: Ian Randal, 1999.

Index

Abbot Hall Art Gallery, Kendal 264
Abbotsford 216
Aberdeen 171
Abo 159
Abrams, M. H. 200, 201
Accompong's Town 279
Ackland, James 105
Act of Abolition 91
Adams, Richard
    The Plague Dogs 267
Admiralty, the 35, 38, 39
    First Lord of the 31
Afghan Empire 156
Africa 61, 133, 139, 156, 157, 162, 271, 276
agriculture 2, 63, 82, 93, 174, 233, 284 *see also*
    Board of Agriculture
Aikin, John
    England Delineated 83
Airedale 62
Albany 45
Alberta 46
Algonquins 46
Alpers, Svetlana 34
Alps, the 2, 143
Alston, John 171, 174, 175, 176
    British Isles 174, 190
    'Maps for the Blind' 173
    Statement on the Education of the Blind 173
aluminium 287
Ambon Island 155
American War of Independence 57,
    104, 156
Americas, the 16
Anglezarke Moor 263
Anglican/Anglicans 132, 134
Anglo-Irish Union 62, 72
Anglo-Saxon/Anglo-Saxons 265
Anthropocene, the 264
anthropology 36, 227
anti-Cartesianism 177
anti-Jacobinism 94

antiquarianism 8, 21, 58, 85, 86, 87, 91, 94, 95, 132,
    211, 214, 215, 217, 223, 224, 226, 229
Apistiskeesh 46
Arabia/Arabs 139, 140
Arago, Dominique François Jean 61
Archithinue 42
armchair geographer/traveller 132, 161, 183
Arrowsmith, Aaron 211
Ascutimeg Lake 42
Asia 140
Assiniboine 42
Astronomer Royal 54, 55, 61
astronomy 10, 12, 35, 38, 39, 54, 55, 56, 67, 178, 180
Ateemouspecky or Dog-rib Indians 42
Athens 161, 162, 163
Athico Lake 42
Atlantic Ocean 41, 91, 158, 187
Atlas (mythology) 78
Atlas to *Walker's Elements of Geography* 160
atlases 12, 20, 72, 78
Aurelian 139
The Aurelian; Or, Natural History of English
    Insects, Namely, Moths and Butterflies 28
Aurelian Society 28
Australia 35, 40
Auteatewan Lake 42
Ayton, Richard 110
Azores, the 155

Baddeley, J. B.
    Thorough Guide to the English Lake District 255
Baker, George 87
Baker, James 105, 110
Balcarres, Alexander Lindsay 273
Baldwin, Cradock, and Joy (publishing house) 96
Balearic Islands, the 61
Bank of England 107
Banks, Joseph 35, 36, 37, 38, 39, 54, 61
Banner, Fiona 262
Bantry Bay 103, 115
Baptist/Baptists 108, 109

Milton Keynes UK
Ingram Content Group UK Ltd.
UKHW021931221023
431147UK00019B/107